"An important and fascinating story, elegantly told by Ellen Mickiewicz."
—Stephen Hess, author of *International News & Foreign Correspondents*

"From the days when Leonid Brezhnev clung to power through the tumult of Mikhail Gorbachev and the election victories of Boris Yeltsin, Russian leaders have struggled over the control of television. In this fine and penetrating book, Ellen Mickiewicz traces those struggles and examines the larger question still ahead: whether a free and independent television can emerge that will bolster prospects for a stable, democratic nation. No one else has better captured this important saga."
—David Gergen, Editor at Large, *U.S. News & World Report*

"A riveting look at the political struggle for control of television [in] the Soviet Union. . . . The policy debates detailed in *Changing Channels* have universal application to our digital communications future. They are explained with skill and competence by an author who is intimately acquainted both with the issues and the people involved."
—Bruce Christensen, former President and CEO of PBS

"For those who care about Russia's stormy evolution from dictatorship to democracy, here is an important story—the first extensive account of the crucially important revolution in Moscow television since 1985."
—Hedrick Smith, author of *The New Russians*

"[A] deep and detailed look at a long and occasionally fatal obsession with television's power on the part of Russia's political leaders."
—Ron Aldridge, Publisher and Editorial Director, *Electronic Media*

"This book will enthrall and enlighten its readers with its vivid revelations of political stratagems by politicians and journalists. . . . This is a definitive study, based on lengthy interviews with the movers and shakers in the world of politics and television by a brilliant participant/observer of the momentous changes in the making."
— ~~Doris A. Graber~~ iversity of Illinois at Chicago

CHANGING
CHANNELS

CHANGING CHANNELS

TELEVISION AND THE

STRUGGLE FOR POWER IN RUSSIA

REVISED AND EXPANDED EDITION

ELLEN MICKIEWICZ

DUKE UNIVERSITY PRESS   DURHAM & LONDON   1999

Printed in the United States of America on acid-free paper ∞

Originally published by Oxford University Press in 1997

Library of Congress Cataloging-in-Publication Data appear
on the last printed page of this book.

To Denis, Cyril, and Theresa

CONTENTS

PREFACE TO THE REVISED AND EXPANDED EDITION

Since the first edition of this book was published, Russia's economy collapsed, political extremism surged, Galina Starovoitova—one of the most famous champions of democracy—was murdered, and governmental power weakened. In the devastated economy, wages arrears grew, barter replaced money, children and old people suffered, malnutrition and illness mounted. A pair of critical elections for the parliament and presidency put pressure on the media. Television was right in the middle of all these events and the battle for control was waged on all fronts. The precipitous fall of the ruble made people poorer; newspapers went under, but broadcast television still cost viewers nothing. Dependence on the small screen, already high before the crash, was increasing. Communist Party and nationalist deputies in parliament again wanted control of the airwaves while the stations wanted to exclude them. Zero-sum television—a theme of this book—was still the tactic. Charges of Nazism and Goebbels-like tactics filled the air.

Economic collapse brought down many of the nascent institutions of post-Soviet Russia, including much of the new middle class. A good bit of the seemingly prosperous private sector had been a house of cards, built on corruption and illusion. However, the mass media were still standing and had given Russian citizens something of inestimable value: the opportunity to access and compare information. The face of news and the arena of speech had decisively changed from Soviet times. Thanks to television, this opportunity was no longer restricted to the well connected and well educated. But it was far from perfect, and much of this book and the new afterword examine the fragility of law and the unregulated media business.

In the afterword, I reflect on the implications of these developments and analyze the fundamental changes in television. Talking to television chiefs, attending a Yeltsin speech on the press, and learning how ordinary Russians navigate television news provided me with new insights, and they are included in the afterword. Galloping media concentration in the hands of a few powerful, so-called oligarchs collided with the wall of the '98 economic crash. After the crash, in straitened circumstances, they retrenched, merged, and shrank. Presidential hopefuls and their backers made alliances with media properties as they had done throughout the course of post-Soviet Russia's history.

A central theme of this book and of the new afterword is the weakness of institutions. Their vulnerable frames had had too little time to grow and were subjected to too much strain. The struggle for the upper hand to make public policy for a nation in crisis sharpened the institutional predicament. The legislature squared off against the executive, a spiraling replay of a contest that multiple elections could not solve. Control over television was always one of the prizes in this contest. The afterword discusses the declining capability of the government to control the news in a pluralized television system and the repeated attempts by outsiders to impose their will on the medium. Even though the financial crisis was eating away at the structure of the Russian television system, especially in the provinces, the national networks still offered essential news choice.

What exactly people got from that choice was never really explored. Although Moscow kingmakers and magnates routinely made assumptions and based strategies on a public they test-marketed for products and candidates, they never learned how viewers understood the news or how they responded to attempts to manipulate it. The afterword to this edition addresses this information gap and provides readers with unique material drawn from discussions about news programs among ordinary Russians and from observing them watch television news stories. Program ratings and audience attitudes are by no means the same, as America has learned during the Clinton impeachment trial. The long-running media fixation on this scandal led many to ponder the disconnect between the public and the pundits and to question the effects of nonstop spinning in view of the public's rejection of it. In Russia, Soviet-era habits of close reading and creative skepticism have proved remarkably durable and have given people striking analytical capabilities. Russian viewers are no fools. They can spot bias, they detest it, and they do not need a college education to do so. How these extraordinary strategies of ordinary people actually work is hitherto unexplored territory and has yielded rich information.

Perhaps because of Russia's vastness, its hugely uneven economic development, and the erosion of its national economy and paralysis of its government, the resources needed to join its parts dwindled. But television was one resource that remained. In the crisis of '98 and its aftermath, television suffered, as did other sectors of the economy, yet it continued to provide an important connective tissue to a crippled giant.

PREFACE

Television is sometimes mesmerizing, often trivial, occasionally gripping, but, except during wartime and natural disasters, rarely heroic. The story of television at the end of the Soviet Union and the transformation of Russia had moments of heroism and incompetence, tragedy and comic opera, war, but almost never peace. Prized by the powerful and invested with an almost magical impact, the medium became the battle ground, literally and figuratively, for those who would retain or gain political power. With institutions in disarray and a decentralizing impetus set in motion by weakness at the center, whose laws and edicts were only imperfectly and intermittently enforced, television at the end of the Soviet Union was just about the only institution left standing. In post-Soviet Russia, too, as the single most important information source in a country virtually totally penetrated by its signals, television was called upon to make extraordinary things happen.

In the United States, the impact of television is of particular interest during elections—and ballot issues, too, for that matter. Among scholars, public officials, and the press, it is a constant subject for reform, criticism, and, occasionally, praise. Less obvious, but no less important, the entertainment side of television is very much a part of the larger narratives, lessons, myths, and values that viewers, especially children, learn. That learning experience includes televised violence, and it is the debates about effects on children that have propelled the issue of violence in media to a prominent place in public policy discussions, especially during electoral campaigns. Although this study of television in Russia devotes a great deal of attention to news and public affairs on television, where the focus of public policy was, the rest of television, including entertainment programs and advertising, was also part of television's capacity to reach its viewers, especially when political advertising began.

When I first started studying media audiences in Russia, the Soviet system of information guidance and control was in force. Yet, even then—in the late 1970s—it was clear that this pervasive new medium was associated with some important changes in leisure time use and that the public was certainly not reacting in the uniform (and wholly positive) fashion their leaders expected. It seemed to me to be unwise to ignore television, even if it was centrally controlled for furtherance of state interests. Whatever the intentions of the state, the medium presented a field of information that significantly exceeded perfect control. Enhanced by a new system of communications satellites, the reach and penetration of television would increase exponentially and present to the leaders in the Kremlin what they believed to be a formidable new instrument.

Mikhail Gorbachev and his close advisors ordered television to implement an information revolution and render legitimate the practice of politics itself—a practice even the ordinary citizen could participate in through real, as opposed to theatrical, voting. What was surprising about that television revolution was that in the same institution (the same building, usually), at the same time, people who had come up in the same system, with the same rules of the game and the same vetting procedures, behaved very differently. Some kept as tight a ship as they could and punished the slightest deviation. Others took risks they knew would agitate the rulers, excite viewers, and push the limits of reform far beyond what was then permissible. Institutional boundaries limited individual behavior, to be sure, but the contest between leaders and the institutions they led was a bumpy ride over uncharted terrain. Waking the country to a new, more spontaneous, conversation, unearthing long-suppressed history, and, not least, exposing viewers to an entirely new electoral process in which the vote really did matter were the tasks the reformers at television sought to accomplish.

Under Boris Yeltsin—in his first term as president of (then-Soviet) Russia—acquiring television to challenge Mikhail Gorbachev made possible the country's first alternative, widely disseminated news coverage. Campaigning for his second term, he charged the medium with safeguarding the reform project from the challenge of the Communist Party. Television did much during an extremely short time to project a new and reformed version of the leader to a very divided country. But the Yeltsin administration, in its passionate attachment to television, often overlooked the fact—as had its predecessors—that television was no surrogate for the powerful reality of everyday life, whether in wartime or at election time.

Yeltsin and his advisors were also caught by surprise by how much the market had penetrated the media, both state and private, and by the de facto pluralization—or fragmentation—that was taking place. The market was hardly perfect; in television it began as entirely unregulated and, when the rules were made, the fortunes and interests were deeply rooted. Television was still the most desirable of political objects, and parliament and president alike attempted to take it, but the old monolith had already cracked before Gorbachev was out of office. It was not until the market supported a separate structure that some degree of autonomy was institutionalized.

The dilemma of the 1996 presidential election, framed by Yeltsin in very stark terms (as in the 1993 referendum) as either nullification of reform or retention and expansion of benefits, appealed to a new incentive structure. Individuals and their self-interest matter, including that less easily defined, longer-term interest of psychic gratification and "expressive need." Autonomy, especially of private television, became the jackpot in a wrenching bet: guarantee autonomy now by adopting a journalistically sound, critical stance toward all candidates and risk the end of autonomy in the future with a return to Communist leadership. Or, guarantee autonomy later by adopting a journalistically doubtful policy of supporting one candidate during the campaign. In the pages that follow, I discuss this dilemma and the television product that issued from the strategy.

During elections, television is thought to be particularly valuable and particularly effective. In 1996 in Russia—as in the United States that year—the largest proportion of campaign expenditures went into the television campaign. In Russia nine cataclysmic elections in eight years brought voters to the polls, always with a turnout exceeding that of recent quadrennial presidential elections in the United States. Time after time, Russian voters attempted by lawful means to overcome their profound divisions. It is an astonishing record, but not surprisingly, those divisions persisted and would continue to render politics dramatic and uncertain. It would be the task of future Russian administrations to heal those divisions, if they could, in large part by changing the structure of incentives and providing the benefits of reform to those who had been left out. The most challenging task would be to end zero-sum television, where the prize was the victor's and could not be shared when shared values were so few.

This is not a history of television in Russia. It concentrates on the Moscow-centered television networks that reached a huge national audience. They were the sources of information for most people, especially in times of crisis, such as the war in Chechnya. At the same time, local, privately owned television stations were growing vigorously, popping up in significant numbers and serving local constituencies. The rise of these local stations merits a separate study. This book seeks to illuminate the critical role television played at key times and with key political actors and institutions. In part, that role is related to the tension between reformers seeking autonomy and their opponents propping up political orthodoxy of the party in power. In part, the role is related to an entirely new political economy and market solutions. The viewing public is a central part of this equation, as the source of votes, the source of rating points guiding programming, and the source of beliefs about the permissibility of airing certain points of view.

This book covers several years, from 1985 to 1996. During this time, the basic mold of Soviet information policy was broken, but the deep social, economic, and political cleavages in Russia did not guarantee a protected, autonomous press. Indeed, perfect autonomy—from commerce and from the state—is granted to no press system anywhere, and the dilemmas and tensions are very much alive in Western democracies as well.

I have been privileged to work with an extraordinary group of media leaders, governmental officials, and academic experts in the Commission on Radio and Television Policy. Former president Jimmy Carter and Eduard Sagalayev, founder of the first private television station in Russia, cochaired this nineteen-nation nongovernmental organization, which began in 1990, and I served as director of the commission. In the course of our meetings on television policy in Russia, Kazakstan, Austria, and at The Carter Center in Atlanta, some of the most critical issues of television were considered; I have learned much from those policy deliberations. In addition, six working groups, conducted in association with the Aspen Institute, brought together more than one hundred experts and practitioners for an often contentious and always stimulating analysis of the issues at stake, the solutions attempted in a variety of contexts, and policy proposals for the future. The process of identifying a range of policy options and working out the trade-offs each one represented made very clear and compelling the central issues of electoral campaign coverage, coverage of minorities and ethnic conflict, privatization, and press autonomy. The policy guidebooks we wrote have been translated into over a dozen languages and have been distributed from Kazakstan to Romania, Hungary, and Bosnia, from Latvia and Lithuania to Morocco and the West Bank, and, of course, in Russia. They have become part of the process by which rules and practices evolved. Thus, I have had the chance not only to study the course of the development of television policy but also to hold discussions in a variety of settings about real options for policy choices that have to be made when a framework of rules and practices has not yet been established.

The research I report in this book is drawn from many sources, including many interviews. I have been able to talk to virtually all of the major decision makers in Russia about their involvement in television, and they are acknowledged in the notes. These interviews began during the Soviet period and continued through the 1996 presidential election in Russia. They were conducted while events were still fresh in the minds of the principals, almost all of whom were willing to speak at great length. Discussion of the most heavily charged episodes of intense political drama drew emotional responses and equally emotional rebuttal from other participants in the events at issue. No one I talked to, including Mikhail Gorbachev himself, was indifferent to questions about television. It was important to conduct the interviews when I did, for memories will soon erode, partly because of time and partly because political life has been so volatile. Earlier crises tend to shrink when dwarfed by new ones.

Individual interviews form only part of the background of this book. I have also been helped by access to a great deal of survey material and Russian television programs and the literatures of political science, both Western and Russian. As a longtime observer of Soviet, then Russian, media and politics, I found this period to be an extraordinary one to study. I should note that I have followed the system of transliteration based on pronunciation. Transliteration systems differ, and references will sometimes include other variants.

In such a large project, I owe thanks to many more than I can acknowledge here. I have benefited greatly from the intellectual environment of the Terry Sanford Institute of Public Policy at Duke University and of The Carter Center. I owe thanks to many individuals who have given me the benefit of their recollections and judgments; they are cited in the chapters that follow. I owe special thanks to Sergei Muratov, Alexander Oslon, Vsevolod Vilchek, Alexander Kopeyka, Leila Vasilyeva, Boris Grushin, Igor Klyamkin, Doris Graber, Barbara Ann Chotiner, Lidia Polskaya, Irina Petrovskaya, Masha Shakhova, David Dorsen, Andrei Richter, Marianna Orlinkova, Olga Oslon, Sarah Oates, Marc Berenson, Mark Whitehouse, Moshe Haspel, Phil Paolino, Damon Coletta, Jody Cornish, Scott Cooper, Edith Dulacki, Anne Hunt, Dee Reid, Jennifer Labach, Rita McGrath, Mimi Choi Whitehouse, and Julie Currier. I should also like to acknowledge Charles Firestone, director of the Aspen Institute's Communications and Society Program, for a rewarding collaboration over the years.

The John and Mary R. Markle Foundation supported the research on which this book is based. Neither the foundation nor any of the others mentioned here is responsible for the conclusions I reach.

CHANGING
CHANNELS

CHAPTER ONE

Television: The Prize

BOOKENDS: 1990 AND 1995

May Day 1990

The annual May Day parade had always been an opportunity for the power elite to be displayed, ranged along the balcony of Lenin's mausoleum to review the parade of Soviet citizens pledging loyalty to the Communist Party and its leader. Since the advent of television the Moscow parade had been relayed to all locales, with small windows in the coverage to bring in remote sites. State television hosts introduced their colleagues across the country, showing slices of look-alike parades from other major cities. Parades were public displays, a visual statement of massed political purpose and bonding, and, as in all Soviet rituals, public discourse was tightly controlled. In provincial towns, where the obligation to parade was accepted as a low-energy stroll in return for a day off, the exercise was lackluster and limp; but in Moscow, the country's camera lens, the procession was crisper and more muscular. It was expected that, although the form might change with the times, respectful fealty to the reviewing stand would remain unchanged.

On the hundredth anniversary of the May Day holiday, Soviet leader Mikhail Gorbachev was himself a captive of this myth. In his advocacy of change, Gorbachev underestimated the depth of his countrymen's disaffection and the explosive power of the dissatisfactions that his policies unleashed. Deprived of adequate sources of feedback, he expected support and gratitude for the changes he had initiated. He expected, too, that pressure for wider and more accelerated reforms would be tempered by a compliant understanding of the limits of compromise. May Day 1990 proved to Gorbachev that his assumptions about the effects of his reforms had been wrong. He lacked information to predict the real outcomes of his policies, and he found these outcomes repugnant. He would respond to unwelcome feedback by attempting to short-circuit it. In time, he would have fewer and fewer instruments for reining in his own initiatives. In television terms, he could only pull the plug.

The chain of events that was to shake the television bureaucracy and shock viewers began on April 20, 1990, when Gavriil Popov was elected mayor of Moscow. Popov, a combative economist from Moscow State University, was a flamboyant radical. From pushing for a market economy before it was widely accepted to speaking out on behalf of his Greek co-ethnics, Popov flouted the accepted boundaries of political discourse. Moreover, he was determined to make his city an island of reform. Within two days, Popov announced that Gorbachev's much touted but nonexistent safety net for the displaced and the elderly was overdue. He argued that free soup kitchens and free clothing stores had to be established as the city advanced toward an inevitably dislocating market system. As the city's chief executive, he now had the power that had been previously delegated to obedient subalterns in the Party apparatus. Structural arrangements and formal status would become significant in this instance, as in so many others during the transition away from the Soviet past; what had been merely for show now took on meaning.

Alarmed at the election of this maverick economist, Gorbachev issued a presidential decree the same day removing the right to control demonstrations and rallies in the center of the city from the Moscow city council. Party officials decided that the parade—up to a point—had to loosen with the times and should coopt those planning to demonstrate in competition with the national ceremony. Certain rules remained inviolable; the overall themes and slogans of the holiday had already been published, and the constitution had set certain limits. For the first time, the May Day festival organizing committee recommended that within this framework the slogans on the posters and banners show some diversity, and that each industry develop its own slogans to express its interests.

In arranging the parade, the committee had to reconcile the Gorbachev government's policy preferences with those of the mayor, who had just lost jurisdiction over public assembly in his city. First would come the official (though slightly unshackled) Party parade, and following it, under the mayor's auspices, would be the second parade of "voters' groups" (actually kernels of competitive political parties), public organizations, and other collections of public-spirited self-organized citizens (those not organized by official trade unions or any other Party-run "volunteer" organizations). Popov would join the Politburo rulers at the tribune. Characteristically, the veering stream of *glasnost* was unpredictable to its authors, both in the direction it took and in the force it directed at the objects it struck. Isolated at the top, Soviet leaders heard what they wished, as leaders often do. They expected the crowds to compare the present with the past and declare their gratitude. Instead, a rather different sentiment prevailed.

State television had always projected the unity of people and leaders to an average viewing public of some 150 million people across the country's eleven time zones. This May Day was to be another example of the public ritual television was so accomplished in presenting. As with all events involving the Party's Politburo and its leader, coverage was to be complete, lasting from beginning to end and preempting all other programming. The more politically central the event, the higher the tension, and the greater the responsibility of television people for controlling the output. Before 1990, they had not faced a public event with so many unknowns.

On duty that day was Pyotr Reshetov, operational head of state television. The Politburo could not have asked for a more faithful protector of its interests at Central Television. Reshetov had been brought in by television chief Mikhail Nenashev to be his "number two," and they were a strange duo. Nenashev, the television boss, commanded respect with his measured and thoughtful defense of reform initiatives while leaving the job of enforcer to his unpopular, abrasive, and thoroughly reactionary sidekick. The enforcer had real power. People who remember Pyotr Reshetov's time at state television—and I never met anyone who had forgotten it—independently applied the same epithets to him: he was "hysterical," a "chained dog." Television correspondent Vladimir Pozner said Reshetov reminded him of a prison guard.[1] Reshetov made a very specific impression on his co-workers.

On that day in May 1990, Mikhail Gorbachev, president of the Soviet Union and Communist Party General Secretary, mounted the tribune. With him were Nikolai Ryzhkov, chairman of the Council of Ministers, Anatoly Lukyanov, head of parliament, the speakers of both chambers of parliament, and Gennady Yanayev, representative for the trade unions. Yanayev's shaking hands would later be televised during his short-lived attempt to seize Gorbachev's place. Viewers heard Yanayev say: "Today, under the May Day banners those who preserve the solid faith in the strength of the working class, in the fighting traditions of its solidarity, unity, and brotherhood have come to historic Red Square."[2] Marchers moved past the reviewing stand, where Gorbachev and the other leaders stood, regarding the assembled labor force with benign approval. As usual, television cameras transmitted the ritual of the country's support of its leadership and new policies live to the entire country. All seemed to be going smoothly— until the newly permitted "unofficial" marchers came into view.

The country saw collective anger. The leaders atop Lenin's tomb were taken by surprise. Homemade banners and signs told Gorbachev: "The People no longer believe you—Resign!" They upheld Lithuania's right to independence and secession. They condemned the Communist Party and the KGB. Christian believers carried the image of Christ; the "cult of Lenin" was hooted down, and the end of the Red Empire was proclaimed. Workers shouted their fear of unemployment and high prices and the deprivation that was already becoming their lot.

After watching some of this counter-parade, the dismayed Gorbachev and his associates uneasily turned away from Red Square and disappeared into the mausoleum. Yegor Ligachev, the strongest traditional Party voice in the ruling Politburo, was standing close to Gorbachev when he saw the "crazies" come into Red Square. After three or four minutes, Gorbachev said to him that they probably ought to leave the reviewing stand. In 1993, recounting to me what he saw, Yegor Ligachev was still emotional and still angry. He called the people who yelled at Gorbachev in front of the mausoleum "hooligans, drunks, extremist forces"[3]

As the people in the news studio remembered it, the cameras were rolling, and they were transmitting the official march. Then came the counter-march, and the cameras kept on rolling. After all, the leaders were still up on the tribune reviewing this less-than-docile demonstration. Then, according to Oleg Dobrodeyev, a longtime news director who recalled this moment vividly, a call came in on the direct Kremlin line. Reshetov took the call, hung up, and ran at full tilt down the corridors to the newsroom. He took off "like a deer," said Dobrodeyev, and screamed at the newspeople in the studio to shut down the broadcast immediately: "When the deputy chairman says 'cut,' you cut." There were no questions. Only a few minutes of the unofficial parade had been shown. As the nation watched, the plug was pulled.[4]

Reshetov's story to me told of his struggle to maintain the status quo for national television in the face of unpredictable change. Extraordinarily careful control of key moments in symbolic politics, like the May Day parade, had long been assured, but this time Reshetov feared the unexpected for the broadcast. He knew what was going to happen, an hour before the tribune and the television audience did. All along the way, cameramen relayed what was coming back to television headquarters. Newsreaders told Reshetov what the banners were saying before they came into view.

In Reshetov's replay of the events, there was no need for the public embarrassment of political power. He had devised a procedure to prevent unauthorized views from reaching the audience. The day before, he met with the top leadership and proposed to cut the parade off if it became, as he put it, "dangerous." He believed he had come to an agreement with the Gorbachev group; he thought he had their promise to leave the tribune as soon as the official demonstration was over. If they had, television would not have been obliged to remain with the next parade—the one that could (and did) go beyond the bounds of ideological acceptability. In Reshetov's view, Gorbachev reneged—he and his colleagues remained on the stand as the angry marchers came by. As Reshetov put it, "there was nothing else on television on any station. That's why I had to cut it off." In return, Reshetov got an angry call from the tribune. He was told that "Mikhail Sergeyevich asks why you cut off the parade. He is not pleased." An obedient Reshetov turned it on again, but after a few minutes it went off again. Reshetov denied that anyone ordered him to pull the plug. He did it, he asserted, on his own; he called for coverage of the parade to be summarily closed down in front of tens of millions of viewers nationwide.

Mikhail Nenashev was also a major player in this incident of televised humiliation. In charge of television at the time, though not on duty at headquarters, he asserted that Gorbachev did not know that the counter-demonstration was on its way to hurl invectives at him. Nenashev also declared that Gorbachev gave no command; the decision was wholly Reshetov's. He added, disingenuously, that Reshetov had simply ended the broadcast when the events "were no longer interesting." This version of the story fails to explain the crisis reaction at state television and the summary order that quite obviously interrupted scheduled programming. There was no fallback plan, no smooth transition to planned alternative programming. The broadcasting giant was unprepared.

Isolated on the tribune, faced by a mass of angry demonstrators telling him that his plans and ideals were obsolete and dangerous, and that deeper structural change could not be contained, Gorbachev and his fellows in the Politburo quietly descended. Pyotr Reshetov performed his duty with alacrity. Lower down in the hierarchy, the newspeople were infuriated and humiliated by the ferocity of this political watchdog, who shattered their illusions of autonomy.

Afterward, Gorbachev denounced the unofficial protesters. Among the Politburo leaders, only *glasnost* advocate Alexander Yakovlev played down the event, allowing that although the slogans insulted the authorities, the incident itself "'should not be overestimated.'"[5] For Yegor Ligachev, this was another example of the lethally subversive role that his rival Yakovlev played. In fact, Ligachev remembered, Yakovlev charged the Communist Party with organizing the counter-demonstration to discredit Gorbachev. "That was a lie," said Ligachev, "and I said so to the Politburo!"

Two weeks later the Supreme Soviet, the USSR parliament, passed a law making it a crime to insult the president of the country. Hereafter, "the deliberate humiliation of his honor and dignity, expressed in improper form" by individuals was punishable by up to two years in a labor camp, up to three years in prison, or a three thousand-ruble fine. For media organizations disseminating insults, the fine rose to twenty-five thousand rubles or two years in a labor camp or six years in prison.[6] But like the earlier attempt to assert control over the unofficial demonstration, this law could not be enforced. About a month later, police swooped down on hawkers of nested dolls on Arbat Street, ordering them to remove the ones that caricatured the president, but nothing happened; the "insulting" dolls were soon back on the street.[7]

Chechnya, Winter 1994–1995

It was supposed to be a warm welcome. It was mid-December in the Znamenskoye district of the Chechen republic, one of the ethnic regions of the Russian Federation. Though Chechens predominated in the republic, Russians made up about a third of the population and as much as three-quarters of the population of Grozny, the capital. Both Russians and Muslim Chechens lived in this Caucasian region, which claimed sovereignty after the failed August 1991 coup and had successfully avoided taxes and other incursions of Russian authority for three years. Three years earlier, Chechen leader (former Soviet Air Force general) Dzhokar Dudayev had dismissed his parliament and crushed challenges to his power. This opposition, the most prominent members of which were in the pay of Moscow, survived and established a center in Znamenskoye, near the border of Chechnya and Russia. It was not surprising, then, that when the Pyatigorsk Division of the Ministry of Internal Affairs entered Znamenskoye, it had support from the population. People came out to greet the soldiers and, as welcoming custom dictated, the women scattered wheat in the tracks of the vehicles. In response, some drunken soldiers, possibly alarmed, fired on the crowd. Three died (a woman and two men); thirteen were wounded.

When Elena Masyuk, a twenty-nine-year-old field reporter for NTV, the largest private television station in Moscow, arrived to cover Chechnya, local Chechens told her about the incident. She found the division commander, who admitted on camera that the story was true and promised a court-martial.[8] NTV's audience—at the time not all of Russia by any means, but residents of Moscow and tens of millions in many cities beyond—was thus able to compare the story to official reports claiming smooth military operations.

In January 1995, official state television's largest station, Channel One (Ostankino), broadcast a news story about the inhumanity of the Chechen fighters. The station reported the castration of six Russian soldiers and relayed the testimony of the attending surgeon at the military hospital in Mozdok. Elena Masyuk had been covering Chechnya since September 1994, periodically returning to Moscow and then heading back to the Caucasus. She heard the report on Ostankino and went to the hospital to interview a Russian doctor on the staff. He confirmed the facts, but went on to tell her the whole story, the part that Channel One had left out. A young girl had been taking food to her brother, who was fighting on Dudayev's side. Russian soldiers stopped her and gang-raped her. Her brother and his friends then castrated the six who had performed the act. In Nazran, in neighboring Ingushetia, a representative of the Russian migration department confirmed the doctor's story. NTV then broadcast Masyuk's piece—on-the-spot coverage of a military conflict that the state-run television channel had portrayed differently.

In what looked like a replay of the Soviets' information management during the war in Afghanistan, the Yeltsin government's press center issued reports that Russian planes were only "pinpoint"-bombing in the Chechnya conflict. Official information stated that damage had been confined to military targets. Meanwhile, some seven kilometers from Grozny, Elena Masyuk filmed the remains of a bazaar, what was left of the kiosks lining the street. This had been a place where mainly women sold whatever they could to passersby. In the Russian raid, the vendors and their kiosks were destroyed. The women's bodies—or what could be found of them—were taken to the cemetery and laid on the ground so authorities could photograph them for identification by relatives and friends. Masyuk, who reached the area a few hours after the conclusion of the bombing, saw pieces of the kiosks, blood on the street, and women's corpses. In pictures that stunned the country, viewers of NTV saw vivid proof that the government's claim of "pinpoint"-bombing was false.

In mid-January 1995, in a rural settlement about eighteen kilometers from Grozny, Russian armor was destroyed by the Chechens and Russian soldiers were killed in their vehicles. Elena Masyuk saw dogs eating their corpses. She saw pieces of a skull of someone she thought was probably a young man because "the teeth were good." Women buried the corpses to keep children from playing with the bones and spreading disease. The women had no spades and had to bury the bodies in shallow graves, from which they feared the dogs would unearth them. In Grozny, some said the dogs would have to be killed: they had acquired a taste for human flesh and had begun stalking people. All of this went out on NTV's news programs. In Moscow, the Ministry of Defense continued to issue bulletins optimistically reporting military success and high morale. But viewers saw the contradictions with their own eyes.

Chechnya was the first war to be televised in Russia, and it was televised from several points of view, one of which—NTV—was institutionally and financially independent of the government. Of course, that independence was qualified: qualified by dependence on the government's control of signal transmission and its ability to tear up a legally granted broadcast-license agreement or to alter its conditions without effective opposition from the judicial system. As it turned out, the government did not shut NTV down. Evgeny Kiselyov, NTV's most notable on-screen news authority, said that all of the television stations—state-run and private—were in agreement on the government's obsolete policy. Igor Malashenko, NTV's president, reminded the government that Chechnya was not Afghanistan. Those news reports from the front catapulted NTV into the leading news position. With the tragic conflict in Chechnya, the world of Russian television had been transformed; Russia had broken, however imperfectly and incompletely, with the Soviet legacy of information control.

In the spring of 1996, as a momentous election drew near, the head of NTV voluntarily joined the presidential campaign team. It was not a reassertion of the old Soviet pattern of state control over the media, as chapter 8 details, but it removed much of that fragile wall of autonomy NTV had battled to achieve. Although the dismal failure in Chechnya was still covered in detail, Boris Yeltsin's campaign on the screen was upbeat and pervasive. The opposing Communist campaign was also covered on NTV; its leaders got airtime and the chance to convey their positions in their own words—a notable departure from the state-controlled stations and from past practices. The Communists got far less airtime than did the incumbent, and much non-news programming detailed the costly and cruel events of past Communist Party rule. Moreover, analysis (negative) of Communist positions was supplied, but not of Yeltsin's; nor was his health made a news issue during the period between the first and second rounds, when he disappeared from sight because of what was said to be a cold, but in fact was a serious heart attack.

It was a controversial call. Four days after Boris Yeltsin defeated the Communist challenge, a leading television anchor said that the "love affair" between Yeltsin and the media ended on election day. The drive to regain autonomy had begun.

1986   *"The TV image is everything."*—Alexander Yakovlev
1994   *"To 'take' the Kremlin, you must 'take' television."*—Alexander Yakovlev[9]

TELEVISION, POLITICS, AND SOCIETY

Glasnost, the reform that was to rock the Soviet political system and the countries it dominated, began on television. In May 1985, just two months after he came to power, Mikhail Gorbachev went to speak to Communist Party officials in Leningrad. At the airport he was given a videotape of his discussions, and when he came back to Moscow he showed it to his wife at their country *dacha.* Raisa Gorbachev reacted immediately, saying, "it is important that all the people hear and see these comments." After consultation with his ideology officials, the new General Secretary had the video-tape shown on national television. As he remembered the episode, "the population received hope that indeed something is going to change. Thus was the first step of *glasnost* made."[10]

In the mid-eighties, just back from political exile as ambassador to Canada, Alexander Yakovlev became Mikhail Gorbachev's closest collaborator in launching the media revolution. He, too, set his sights on television as the most powerful instrument of change. He spoke to me of using television to prepare people for policy changes and begin changing their views, of consciously using the medium to form opinion about the war in Afghanistan, and to accept pluralism in belief systems.[11] But it was still Mikhail Gorbachev who wielded the power of the General Secretary of the Party. Only he could make those initiatives happen, even though the power of his office had declined since Stalin's, or even Brezhnev's, days. Gorbachev also did not wield his power consistently, and he changed his tactics and allies over time; but in our conversation in the spring of 1995, there was no mistaking how profoundly he believed that when he came to power his mission was to make a dramatic change in Soviet society. He said that in the system he inherited people had been "made fools of," "stupefied" (*odurachivanie*); they had been denied information.[12]

Gorbachev and his colleagues in the Politburo, the Party's most powerful organ, were also deeply concerned about youth—the replacement generation that was increasingly remote from Party ideals and direction. Gorbachev was aware that youth were "losing interest" in the propaganda of Marxism as it was "so boringly conducted."[13] He came to power with a strong emotional conviction that this had to change. He also came to power with the notion that it was the "bureaucracy" that was faulty, recalcitrant, and in need of reform. It was "powerfully secret" and opposed democratically oriented reforms, and he believed the saying "bureaucracy fears light." "I read it in Lenin," he said, and then "found out it was from ancient Greek."

Glasnost was then—and still, in his mind—nothing less than the "reevaluation of values" (*pereotsenka tsennostei*),[14] and it was painful and wrenching. Mass media were the central component of this policy, and he said, as did others in his Politburo with whom I talked, that "every Politburo meeting started with the mass media." He himself watched television, and when we met, he energetically began talking about a television program he had watched the evening before.

Belief in the overwhelming power of television never changed across the years of Soviet power and those of post-Soviet Russia. Wars, elections, and vying bureaucracies (governmental or private) all made television a prize of inestimable value. Perhaps they exaggerated the effects of the medium, but from the time it began reaching the mass public, they had always done so.

Besides, attributing an enormous impact to television had become a world-wide preoccupation. Television did not create social and political realities, but it both reflected and helped to shape them.

The impact of the medium also overran borders and cultures. In rural Iran, even with government control of television, the images of sharp urban-rural differences sparked resentment of official policy and propaganda. The young longed to make a "pilgrimage" to the Los Angeles of the pirated videos; the old mourned traditional ways, saying, "'Television has ruined our lives.'"[15] Soon after protesting Chinese students were brutally removed from Tiananmen Square, Singapore's authoritarian leader Lee Kuan Yew said that their protest was all the fault of television. The catalyst for the mass demonstration was not the desire for freedom, but rather the students' misinterpretation of television coverage of earlier demonstrations in the Philippines and South Korea. They learned the wrong lesson, mistaking others' conditions for their own and assuming the media could and would wield decisive influence. "'I believe,' Lee stated, "it is this contextless television experience that led to the tragedy of Tiananmen.'"[16]

Ved Mehta, a keen observer of divisive Hindu revivalism in India, concluded that the country's rapidly developing television system, the only source of information for illiterate people in much of the country, had roused communal emotions. And not just the medium as such, but a particular program: the serialization of the Hindu epic of the *Ramayana,* which attracted the biggest audience in Indian history and kindled emotions of religious nationalism.[17]

The chain reaction that brought down the walls of Communist Eastern Europe has been linked to the effects of television and its sister technologies.[18] The election of Brazil's Fernando Collor de Mello in 1989 was attributed to favorable coverage by Globo Television's news programs.[19] In 1995, two Japanese television personalities with no party affiliation and little funding were elected to run the nation's two most important cities, Tokyo and Osaka, on the basis of viewer recognition (coupled with rejection of the traditional parties).[20] In the most clamorous and far-reaching connection of television power and political ambition, Silvio Berlusconi parlayed a private television empire into the leadership of Italy.

These, sometimes overblown, accounts can lead to the judgment that television affects all in the viewing public directly and equally. This is certainly untrue. Some viewers are affected very differently than others, depending on their past exposure and education, and on how political information is mediated or "cued" by elites through the broadcast system. Undeniably, television plays a major role in structuring public opinion in the West, as Richard Brody points out: "Since the public is not always certain what news implies about the success or failure of policy, it often takes its guidelines on the meaning of the news from political opinion leaders. . . . The news carries these interpretations to the public along with the details of the events themselves."[21]

The viewing public is by no means, though, a passive recipient to be stamped by the messages from the small screen.[22] Viewers bring much to the experience in the way of psychological predispositions and experiences; they participate in the construction of the meanings they receive.[23] Research in the United States suggests that the effect of television news on political attitudes is probably massive, but it is indirect, and it shifts with amounts of exposure.[24] The relationship between television and the formation of public opinion is most important in those nations where the public determines the futures of the politically ambitious, and thus the direction of the country, with its vote.

In Russia, on the basis of political parties, this role for the public began only in 1993. The importance of television in that election made it a major player in the campaign process because the campaign was so short, the parties so new (and therefore party loyalties so unformed, with only the Communist Party exploiting strong holdover effects), and the nation of Russia so vast. Future elections featured different candidates, different parties, different themes, and different rules, but the basic outline had been set in 1993: television, in Russia as in the West, would constitute the most strategic asset.

Whether the end of the Soviet Union was a result of revolution or of evolutionary state-guided change (albeit with extreme political and economic changes occurring simultaneously) is a matter of question.[25] But it is clear that what happened in and to television was indeed revolutionary. The television revolution that Mikhail Gorbachev set off—and that helped to bring down a political system—was fundamentally completed in an important and vivid way by Boris Yeltsin's war in Chechnya. That coverage gained widespread legitimacy for private television news and, in the process, marked the end of the Soviet information system. With Chechnya, pluralistic television was institutionalized and broke through the shell of an obsolete, monopolist hold on information. It had taken ten years; it had not played out the way the leaders had intended; and many changes, dangers, and uncertainties still lay ahead, but the arena had changed in a way it could not have done at any time before.

Television is important to people in power everywhere, but in the Soviet Union it was virtually an obsession. When Mikhail Gorbachev launched his media revolution, Party officials made a distinction between "large-caliber" and "small-caliber" media. Scale of audience was all; television was unmatched. Newspapers, with their comparatively well-educated readership and much smaller audience, could print what television could not say. Even so, under Gorbachev the previously standardized, ritualized presentations of television began to look and sound different in a puzzlingly incoherent way. *Within* the huge mammoth of state television, political cleavages appeared and directly affected the content of broadcasts, and this could not have happened had there not been deep cleavages within the ruling body of the Soviet Union. Those splits enabled television to follow suit.

Thus we have a fascinating and dramatic record of an institution in which all the officials rose through the same system of training and vetting, yet behaved in very different ways, and often at great personal risk. They were members of the elite, but they were also the products of the same changing society with whom they had a responsibility to communicate. The role of the individuals controlling television and interpreting the news for Russians in critical times of change and uncertainty was of vital importance in a country increasingly dependent on this medium. This was what Mikhail Gorbachev and Alexander Yakovlev thought, and this is what Boris Yeltsin thought as he sent troops to defend the television center.

Increasingly fragmented by ethnic tugs-of-war, regional pushes for autonomy, highly personalized political movements, and deep economic divisions, the shards of the shattered Soviet monolith bear little resemblance to the system Mikhail Gorbachev inherited in 1985 or the one Boris Yeltsin took over in 1991. But over this span of time and enormous distance, one institution functioned with astonishing effect; it gained more and more adherents and became the key political asset sought by all contenders for power.

Television emerged during the time of Leonid Brezhnev. It was then that resources were poured into communications satellites and the production of television sets. Affordable and widely available, television sets soon became necessities of household life. By the time Mikhail Gorbachev came into office, 93 percent of the population were viewers—virtually all urban households and 90 percent of rural households.[26] In 1992, just under half the people in St. Petersburg and Moscow had more than one television set.[27]

The struggle for control of television mirrors and explains the larger fate of the Soviet Union and post-Soviet Russia. As competing sources of information and persuasion declined due to rising costs and plunging household incomes, television was just about the most notable institution left standing, and, as before, all those who coveted power sought television's most valuable product—airtime. The intrinsic properties of this medium were simply thought to produce an effect like no other. Then, as now, it was the coveted prize for power-holders and power-seekers alike. The poet Andrei Voznesensky said that the Moscow television spire was a "syringe for ideological injections."[28]

To make the media revolution work, the Gorbachev leadership introduced measures to enhance credibility and engage an alienated audience. Its first task was to reduce censorship. Establishing the credibility of the media, in turn, required airing subjects previously off limits, packaging messages in new and attractive forms, and—not least—determining audience demand through previously outlawed public-opinion surveys. The media were sharply critical of the armed forces, the KGB, and previous Soviet regimes, and they re-introduced to the Soviet population such figures from the concealed past as Leon Trotsky, Nikolai Bukharin, and Tsar Nicholas II and his family.

Did Gorbachev, then, intend the changes that brought an end to the Soviet Union? In doing the research for this book, I utilized a number of research sources, including television programs and public-opinion surveys, and I interviewed people who had made the key decisions in television policy from the beginning to the end of the decade-long television revolution. All of the interviews and testimony recounted here were collected explicitly for this project or are part of the public record. They do not derive from conversations with television officials in the course of other meetings. Naturally, there are problems with recollections; memory can erode. But I did not find memory a problem for the short, highly-compressed period covered here; and since a number of people were interviewed (or re-interviewed) about the same events, it was possible to triangulate.

Another issue is deliberate distortion. Given the volatility of political change in Russia, it may be professionally (or legally) useful to claim rather different views after the fact, to have been a convinced democrat from the beginning instead of one of the Party faithful, or if a different wind is blowing, a Russian populist instead of a Westernizer. Without doubt, one expects to hear some significant degree of self-serving testimony, but the multiplicity of sources tends to offset the effects of embellishment. Perhaps a greater problem for the analyst is related to the way the policy changes have played out: change in Russia has been so rapid, and so devastating for some, that many of the key officials who *began* a process were blamed for its *outcome,* whatever their true intentions or influence over later events might have been. And therefore their motivations were rescripted as time went on and as consequences became clearer. This connection between intention and responsibility is an eternally vexing one.

I contend that there never was an overarching policy of information or media reform, the components of which were neatly charted on a drawing board. Neither Gorbachev, nor his chief policy architect Alexander Yakovlev, nor his comrade-in-arms Eduard Shevardnadze, nor his early supporter and leading challenger Yegor Ligachev had anything like a precise view of the policy that would turn out to launch a revolution. There was some common ground that all could agree on as components of "reform," but each retained his own vision of the endpoint of that reform. Their ambitions and dreams then diverged markedly, and all used television in their battles. Each had a hand in individual programs, both in creating them and in shutting them down. The recollections of the participants are particularly valuable, since the Party leadership was always careful not to leave a paper trail. It all worked by "telephone law": direct, untraceable conversations on the phone with the bronze seal.

"'Children resemble the times more than they do their fathers,'" says an Arab proverb.[29] Mikhail Gorbachev never understood that current demands outrun past gratitude. The salient referent was not the increment of his reform compared to the Stalinist past, but the reforms *not* implemented compared to the hopes the Khrushchev generation had bitterly seen collapse and the far more radical sights their juniors set on standards outside the Soviet Union. Gorbachev still thought in 1995 that his policies, in their extreme democratic thrust, far outdistanced even the most "enraged" *(yarostnaya)* radical reform opposition. He did not underestimate the tremendous difficulty that his media revolution and its "reevaluation of values" produced, especially for some segments of the population. He admitted that what he had introduced had created "suffering" *(perezhivanie),* especially among the older generation. He told me that "we had collectivization," and "Stalin." During the exposés of *glasnost,* old people who lived through those times thought, "What did we live for? For filth *[gryazi]*?"[30]

When he returned from his Crimean captivity in the summer home at Foros, Gorbachev was still convinced that the Communist Party could and should be reformed and that its great mission was still unfulfilled.[31] The Party was reshaped, but not the way Gorbachev had predicted. Just four years later, Russia's Communist Party, champion of the victims of the "misery index," became a dominant force in parliament, and its leader, Gennady Zyuganov, a far more popular presidential candidate than Gorbachev, who warned of turning the clock back with these die-hards. They were foes of his reforms, he charged, as he and his wife campaigned across the country in his hopeless contest for Russia's highest office.

Gorbachev was confident that he could initiate *contained change;* presumably it could be carefully calibrated and match desired outcomes. But he did not sufficiently appreciate the internal coherence of the system.[32] Soviet rule had left a flattened landscape and had extirpated secondary associations—the network of grass-roots, local interactions that have such a strong connection to the potential success of democracy.[33] The media revolution that spun out of control began with mild and limited challenges to the Soviet past. It swept across the barren plain of desiccated doctrine. The Gorbachev reforms, as carried on television, played to an entire country at once. The television system had been designed just for this: to carry the

Kremlin's campaign uniformly and speedily to every corner of the land-mass. This, too, heightened the probability that once set in motion, the changes would not be attenuated by distance. Television helped to bring these changes into focus as a *national* phenomenon.[34]

At the same time, contrary movements began—groups began to pull away from the mainstream by demanding greater attention to their specific attributes. Everywhere new demands for maintenance of language or rhetoric, religious practices, and cultural norms tend to greet the incorpo-ration of groups into the single national site that television creates.[35] As television selectively presents some groups—along with their values and their political goals—as mainstream, those who are denied coverage protest. After all, portrayal on television is the measure of importance and legitimacy, and these countervailing vectors were very strong when the Baltic states asserted their sovereignty and effectively captured their own branch of the national system.

What neither leaders Mikhail Gorbachev nor Boris Yeltsin understood was the downside of a television monopoly: by dominating the television screen, the political leadership may make itself a magnet for popular dissat-isfaction and blame. By presenting events in a state-dominated frame, in-stead of as personal or individual-centered stories, television can invite the public to attribute responsibility to the government, particularly in a col-lectivistic, rather than individualistic, culture.[36]

Monopoly posed other problems for the state. Coverage of ethnic con-flict, where at least one party always became aggrieved and blamed the government for television "bias," was particularly sensitive. The only solu-tion was silence—the old pre-Gorbachev way—but that only left the field open to foreign media and vigorous rumor and destroyed the credibility of state television. In short, television as state monopoly, far from being an un-alloyed asset, could have a boomerang effect.

The very rigidities of the Soviet system presented opportunities for the proponents of change to subvert the system.[37] The Soviet constitutional structure divided the Soviet Union into "republics" that enjoyed little true autonomy, but whose formal distinction and titular status created the basis for the Baltic republics' taking over "their" television, and later the "inde-pendence" of the Chechen republic. This was the same basis on which Boris Yeltsin laid claim to television time on behalf of the Soviet Russian republic and presented the first alternative political news.

How did this giant television industry develop a split personality virtu-ally from the beginning of the Gorbachev era?[38] How did the individual players in this drama take sides and risks deciding what the millions in the audience would see? The rules of the game had been changed, and, as with all massive institutional change, the outcome could not be predicted.[39] Within the single institution of television, different people took different actions and were motivated by different values. Their capacity to affect the outcome was by no means unconstrained and at various points was subjected to bounded institutions, but they could and did push those boundaries—push the envelope. We should not underestimate the role of the human actor. Throughout the pages that follow, there is a tension between the inherited institutions that created the environment and the preferences of individuals in positions of power. "Structuralism and individualism are not, therefore, rival and mutually incompatible approaches to the study of social change. They are essential components of a single theory."[40]

In both Soviet and post-Soviet Russia, the clashes of opposing leaders over control of television set up a "zero-sum" environment. It was all or nothing: no compromises, no middle ground. That was the Soviet way: one side's victory was a loss for the other. Power was not to be shared where shared values were so few. There was no legal order to regulate the operation of the game, and checks and balances, if any, were generated by the relative power positions of the players rather than a constitutional structure.

Zero-sum television successfully applied itself to the destruction of the old order. Television had a special role in rousing the public to make end-runs around the calcified bureaucracy about which Mikhail Gorbachev complained. But zero-sum television was ill suited to the construction of a new order in which multiple points of view were not only legitimate but essential to the success of the democratic enterprise.

Russia's transition from Soviet rule had not been "pacted"; it was not based on the agreement of power claimants.[41] It took the Chechen war and the transformation of the television market to break up the previously two-person game: state power versus journalistic autonomy, battling within a single state structure. Private television enlarged the system and presented an institutionally-grounded and (financially) protected alternative to state-controlled information. Even though the state-owned television system continued to be buffeted by rapidly cycling administrative and organizational changes, the coming of age of privately-based competitors in the fire of that Caucasian conflict marked a major turn in the game. From this point on, the system would reflect the tension between the state and the market on the one hand, and between managers and journalists on the other. What constituted the public interest was always more elusive. In states with much longer traditions of democratic politics, the definition of public interest as dependent either on the workings of the market or on the oversight of government left much room for dissatisfaction. The public—and its interest—was still emerging in Russia; the solutions were still over the horizon.

The television revolution began with a profound change in the rules: legitimizing pluralism, which legitimizes opposition, does not create democracy, but it is a necessary precondition to and companion of democracy. For pluralism to work, it has been argued, certain preconditions are necessary: consensus on procedures; overlapping membership in several groups (thus minimizing all-or-nothing challenges to the very existence of the groups); open access to the political arena; and a sufficiently large number of competing groups, so that no single group can tyrannize. At the end of the Soviet Union and in post-Soviet Russia the formation of competing new groups produced an incipient pluralism. Perhaps most problematic were two fundamental issues: the concentration of wealth and power in a relatively small number of groups dominating the political system, and the challengers' readiness to destroy the rules, fluid though they were.[42]

Television plays a central role in the way party systems develop and in how they reach the citizenry and activate their support. For challengers outside the system, even in the United States, the way into the system is difficult. William Gamson wrote that the "pluralistic image, then, is a half-truth. It misleads us when applied to the relations between political challengers and members of the polity. The appropriate image for this political interaction is more of a fight with few holds barred than it is a contest under well-defined rules."[43] The difficulties challengers outside the system have in vying for attention and support include entrée into broadcast television news, which tends to portray an accepted and relatively narrow range of views.[44]

In the Soviet Union and Russia, the central story of the television revolution takes the powerful medium from "frontier pluralism," where only wars among the elites made it possible, to "institutional pluralism," where the operation of a television market created the possibility of a more legitimate pluralism, and where the war in Chechnya vividly demonstrated its importance to viewers and public officials. Whether this pluralism provides the necessary access for competing political groups or, on the contrary, enhances the restraining power of oligopolists is critical. Equally important is the tenor of the pluralism that television disseminates: Does the clash of uncompromisingly hostile, uncivil positions of enemies ("hate" radio and confrontational talk shows in the United States and Vladimir Zhirinovsky's appearances on Russian television) predominate? Or is the norm a conversation proceeding from a larger base of agreement, at the very least regarding the mode and limits of discord? The legacy the Soviet Union left to Russia was notoriously poor in the culture of law. The necessary buffers—independent regulatory agencies and effective recourse to legal remedies—were not in place and would require that institutions be designed and civic habits developed.

For most of the Soviet period, domestic news was unwaveringly upbeat and the Politburo—especially its General Secretary—dominated the news. The Soviet leadership did not suspect that viewers were busily deconstructing what they saw. But as one television viewer put it, "The experienced viewer, comparing the paradise on the screen with what he saw himself, drew his own conclusions, but preferred to keep quiet about them."[45]

The Soviet leaders were woefully out of touch with their own appearances and unaware of the inexpert, virtually haphazard way they created their own images. It is remarkable that, for a group of leaders consumed by the power of television and scrambling to present themselves as much as possible on the small screen, they were so unconcerned with how their images were received. After the end of the Soviet Union, Russian leaders were often unable to create an image of political leadership that would connect with the long ignored public, now undergoing unpredictable and unexplained change.

Mikhail Gorbachev started a revolution in political discourse; television magnified and spread it; Vladimir Zhirinovsky understood it. For over seven decades of Soviet history, the stuff of politics was forbidden. It was out of bounds for ordinary people, the domain of self-selected leaders. Accordingly, speech was transformed into an abstract ritual that only the political priesthood could modify. Nothing important was called by its true name; incantation replaced passion; few actually understood many of the most frequently invoked terms. The war in Afghanistan was termed "internationalist duty of a limited contingent." The division between public and private life was extreme, and there was no common discourse, a fully appropriate state of affairs for a nation in which the public was not to engage in politically relevant behavior of its own devising.[46]

Mikhail Gorbachev began to close this gap in his long perorations on television. He extended a rhetorical invitation to bring in the public and attract the energies of an alienated, passive subject population to his notion of citizenship. No matter how problematic those presentations were, as I will discuss later, the public found it a stunning change to hear ordinary speech issue from the leader. It took Zhirinovsky to complete the revolution by merging the public and the private, and he did so by liberating the previously unuttered dark thoughts of the heart.

In times of crisis, it is difficult to hold to the moderate middle. As Thucydides observed when Athens and Sparta clashed, the polarization of wartime crowds out intermediate positions. Throughout its lifetime, the Soviet Union emphasized the reality and symbol of threat; in crisis there could be only loyalists and traitors.[47] In post-Soviet Russia, the crises were palpable: loss of great-power status, ethnic conflict, severe economic decline, health and welfare emergencies, and profound disagreement on the very legitimacy of the government. A closely spaced series of critical national elections and referenda—*nine* in *eight* years, from 1989 to 1996—put great pressure on the growing, but still fragile autonomy of the television system. Alternation in power, the democratic way, might have nullified the post-Soviet reform project. Perhaps it was understandable that Boris Yeltsin's government believed that it could not relax its lock on television. What else could keep democratization on track? And during the Chechnya conflict, so the official rationale went, what else would avert civil war and prevent the domino effect of separatist claims from other republics? For a democratically reforming government to deprive itself of its principal instrument of success in the stress of nation-threatening crisis was simply unthinkable for Russia's leaders.

Running through the story of television and its impact on the dismantling of the Soviet Union and the construction of a new Russia is also the theme of America. The United States was a leading actor on Soviet television long before Mikhail Gorbachev came to power. As chief threat and puppetmaster of proxy enemies during the cold war, the United States was attacked in emotional television coverage. The Gorbachev information revolution changed that, and, as editorial bias declined, the positive sides of America, particularly at the microeconomic level (local success stories) replaced demonization.[48] McDonald's was a marvel of food delivery and inducting the young into the world of work; family farms showed how small-scale units could show large-scale initiative.

The "American effect" was far deeper than coverage, however. The entire media revolution arrived in American wrapping: the new television shows looked more like U.S. shows than European shows. The heavy emphasis on appealing to a disengaged young Soviet generation meant that rock, with its subversive beat and shocking images, roared onto home screens. Violence in imported movies and series roused the ire of older viewers and of 1996 Communist Party presidential candidate, Gennady Zyuganov, who promised to remove it all and institute content monitoring boards. Product advertising invaded television, making up for much of the loss of state subsidies as the Gorbachev—and then, with greater speed, the Yeltsin—administration lost control of the industry's finances. Advertising created demand not only for unaffordable Western products, but for the distinctly American look of the ads.

Advertising also entered politics; but whether or not political advertising was a part of election campaigns, elections were in no small measure "Americanized."[49] The overlay of America on the Soviet legacy and a tentative Russian identity became a significant factor in Russian politics (the Snickers candy bar came to stand for an entire political and economic revolution), and that factor reached mass audiences principally through television.

Though they were unaware of the full import of the changes they promoted, leading television figures did self-consciously and deliberately use the medium to effect change. They had a better bully pulpit than Gorbachev or Yeltsin did, because they, unlike their masters, were adepts of the medium, and several of the most influential used it to advance into parliament. The television stars could then directly shape the course of the country and, in the process, acquire another key political commodity; legal immunity. A little over two years before he was murdered, Vlad Listyev, a hugely popular public-affairs program anchor and game-show host, when he considered governmental actions too precipitate, reminded Boris Yeltsin that "the current power got into the Kremlin largely thanks to certain people in the press and on television."[50]

In October 1993, when the main studio building of state television was in flames, a famous actress made an appeal from a distant studio: with gunshots in the background, she begged the viewers to abort a replay of the Revolution of 1917. Boris Yeltsin said he would never forget that moving plea in the early hours of the morning; it was television, he concluded, that enabled his government and his reform to survive. Whatever the actual path and full magnitude of television's effects, the political significance of the medium to the contenders for power has not diminished. The notion of television as preternaturally persuasive has endured, even as power has leached out of other structures and institutions. And in struggles for power, television is still the prize.

CHAPTER TWO

Soviet Television Rulers and Their Empire

Monday, June 12, 1995, was Russian Independence Day, a day at the *dacha* or for tending to personal chores or watching television. There were no big parades or pageants; those had been done the month before when Russia celebrated the fiftieth anniversary of the end of the war with Germany. On state television's Channel One that evening a television program hosted by the bicontinental, bilingual Vladimir Pozner came on. Like the old shows he used to do in the Soviet Union and with Phil Donahue in the United States, Pozner chatted with people in the studio. On this occasion, when the conflict in Chechnya was still engaging Russians and their president was more than usually remote, a middle-aged woman in the audience was visibly disturbed that the press was on the attack: Why don't they curb (*obuzdat*) the press?

Pozner set about unpacking the notion. Did she mean censorship? No, the woman said, but it's necessary to "work with the press." She was, of course, using the terminology of the Soviet way of keeping the media in line through a system of organized oversight. With the help of that day's guest, Georgy Satarov, Boris Yeltsin's political advisor, Pozner concluded that although the country was experiencing growing pains in adjusting to the new freedoms, they were constructive, and he noted that Mikhail Gorbachev had had much more contact with the press than the current president, and warned that a political leader cannot ignore the press.

The next day, a gladdened Mikhail Gorbachev brought up the program in conversation. He was pleased that Pozner had approvingly noted the frequency with which he had met with the press and he agreed: it was necessary to work with the press. "Work with the press" had a long history, and Mikhail Gorbachev made it deeply ambivalent.

By June 1995, television had become, without any doubt, the most important and influential component of the media system. It was not until the first communications satellites were launched, in the late 1960s, that it became possible to reach the huge country. By turning significant resources to building broadcasting facilities and producing television sets for individual ownership, the government had rapidly achieved near total penetration. In 1960, only 5 percent of the Soviet population could watch television, but by 1986, the second year of Gorbachev's administration, only remote settlements were left out, and the average prime-time audience for the nightly news was estimated at about 150 million people.

Soviet television, like newspapers, was organized at the national level, and at the republic, regional, and city levels. Two Moscow-based channels (Channel One and Channel Two) broadcast programs in Russian to all of the fifteen Soviet republics, but Channel One had greater penetration. Non-Russian republics had their own stations, accountable to Moscow and broadcasting both in Russian and in the language of the titular nationality. City or county broadcasting was minimal, consisting of "windows" of programming inserted into the broadcast day of the second channel. From the standpoint of the Soviet leaders, no program was more crucial than the evening news, *Vremya* (Time), and no station anywhere was permitted to broadcast competing material during that time slot.

In Leonid Brezhnev's time, when live broadcasting was curtailed to increase central Party control over content, one program remained live: the news. Because of the huge size of the country, television broadcasts were aimed individually at each region, or "orbit," as the day advanced, with Moscow the last. The news went out live, not tape-delayed, so it was a long production, repeated five times with changes as new stories were inserted. An anchor duo, male and female, hosted the program in the manner of genial, if somewhat formal, newsreaders. Altogether, seven pairs of newsreaders worked on the news; some were confined to the orbits and never made it to the height of prestige and importance of the 9:00 P.M. Moscow edition.[1]

The Moscow edition was the one the Kremlin saw and was therefore most politically sensitive. Even though this one "live" program was minimally live (the taped news stories were seen in advance) censorship could still be applied by requiring written projects and scripts to be approved in advance (the *mikrofonaya papka,* the text of the upcoming news show, was always subjected to scrutiny), and programs that went out to the Far East orbit were watched to catch any offending stories before they could reach the capital. With their Moscow-centric vision, television's leaders had little concern about the political health of Far Eastern viewers.

Eduard Sagalayev, a prominent figure in Soviet state, and later Russian private, television remarked wryly that "those who live in other time zones are the most informed part of society."[2] The Kremlin leadership then, as later, was encapsulated in Moscow; an inside-the-beltway mentality was at home inside the Garden Ring road. The news reflected this preoccupation while it slighted the rest of the country, a practice that was to be remarkably resistant to change and survive the Soviet period virtually intact.

The electronic media were inordinately appreciated by a Soviet leadership that, from the beginning, promulgated a doctrine infatuated with the new science of the twentieth century. Radio, and then television, were mighty wonders to be exploited. Soon after the Bolsheviks won the Revolution, Lenin, recognizing that a revolution required a campaign for massive change in attitudes—and understanding the twin problems of illiteracy and the dispersion of a population across a large territory—decreed the rapid development of the new technology of radio. Radio, like electrification, would be a prime instrument in Lenin's program of revolutionary transformation, reaching the entire population, even the illiterate majority. The new electronic medium was reinforced by a Leninist invention: personal agitation, the enhancement of standardized remote messages with face-to-face follow-up by members of the Communist Party and their allies. Together, the electronic medium and the armies of agitators would carry the message of Moscow's new leadership to a largely rural and ethnically heterogeneous country.

Stalin later centralized the media system and sharply curbed the profusion of modernist experimental styles, which had mushroomed in the volatile revolutionary period. The modernists were eliminated in favor of a standard of expression that would be widely intelligible in a traditional, rather Victorian, fashion. Nineteenth-century classics, twentieth-century realist epigones, and large dollops of purely decorative folk art (but not the subversive energies of assertive and authentic ethnic culture) defined the acceptable in a strict hierarchy of official values.

The Stalinist pattern was maintained until Mikhail Gorbachev loosened its strictures. The most important features of the old model were **centralization** of media organs and personnel, **Communist Party control** of information, and **saturation.**

Centralization was effected by several mechanisms. First was the dual authority to which all media were subject: the new electronic media operated under a ministrylike state committee (the State Committee for Television and Radio Broadcasting—Gosteleradio—sometimes called Ostankino after the suburban Moscow district where the television center was located), but the media were also subordinated to the Ideological Department of the Central Committee of the Communist Party and to the "second secretary"—the second most powerful individual in the ruling Politburo. The final arbiter was the General Secretary, the Party's leader.

For the most part, the exercise of control was effected through "telephone law"—direct voice communication from Party headquarters. This procedure received immediate response and had the added advantage of eliminating documentation and accountability. The government provided substantial, even generous, allocations to the media as "budgetary organizations," without any viable system of cost accounting or incentives to contain costs or meet audience demand. Another agency, the security police (KGB), had a particularly strong interest in media organizations with foreign connections.

The system of oversight and control prevented electronic media from using messages that might conflict with one another or display something less than a uniform stance on events or policies. Some subtle signs of cleavage could occasionally be divined by close scrutiny of codes, like the placement of officials on reviewing stands or signatures out of order on an obituary.[3] It was not until Mikhail Gorbachev was in power that individual members of the Politburo openly used the media to advance their contending political interests and views.

The leadership also controlled television through the *nomenklatura* system, which required that leading positions in prominent media organizations be filled by Party members agreed upon by the Politburo.[4] In addition, the system of "creative unions" brought most professionals in culture and media into Party-controlled organizations and provided authorized outlets for their work while denying them alternatives. In 1987, the Journalists Union boasted a membership of 85,182 out of a total of about 100,000 journalists working in the country.[5]

Attempted government control of information relayed to the public was the second feature of the pre-Gorbachev pattern of media organization. To keep out signals generated by foreign broadcasters (the most popular of which were the BBC, The Voice of America, Radio Liberty, and West Germany's Deutsche Welle), jamming stations were widely deployed. The flow of people into and out of the Soviet Union was subjected to scrutiny by internal security organs; foreign periodicals and books were reserved for those with special permits; and movie imports (both for theatrical and television viewing) were restricted to products reinforcing the main messages of the media. For censorship of domestically generated messages, Glavlit (Chief Administration for the Affairs of Literature and Publishing Houses) was founded in 1922.

In the early days of television, before the introduction of film and later videotape, programs went out live. When it became possible to tape programs for prior censorship, the number of live television programs declined rapidly until only the news was broadcast live. Regional television stations, which had acquired some flexibility simply because central television in Moscow lacked the technical capacity to penetrate their areas, were then sharply brought in line. Sergei Lapin, Leonid Brezhnev's television boss, tightened Party control and vigorously shut down local television broadcasting to enforce his centralizing policies. TASS (Television Agency of the

Soviet Union), the official wire service, was the uniquely valid source for breaking news.

No system of information blocking can be fully effective, however, and the increasing information interdependence of the modern world did not exclude the Soviet Union. Border areas were porous and difficult to isolate. Estonians, for example, regularly watched Finnish television. Foreign radios had a substantial audience, especially among urban men.[6] Later, even though "video contraband" was criminalized, the government found it practically impossible to halt the flow of pirated cassettes, and local entrepreneurs were undeterred by a string of highly publicized trials and sentences of two years in labor camps or prison. Finally, though retarded by official policy, the development of computer-based communications was proceeding. This form of communication, as well as other types of information dissemination, such as photocopying, were embedded in a tangle of regulations and restrictions which eventually proved obsolete, largely unenforceable, and increasingly deleterious to economic development.

The third principal feature of the Soviet media system before Gorbachev was saturation. I mean this in two senses: first, the political leadership sought total penetration of the potential audience; second, the approved message pattern and content was to thoroughly infuse the output of the media, purveying a single "line" and eliminating the possibility of counter-system messages. However, by attempting to mobilize the population on a hitherto unknown scale, Soviet media policy was also linking individual existences, with all of their dissatisfactions, to a political center with insufficiently responsive institutions. As Karl Marx might have observed, mobilization was carried out, but not just as the center intended, and the government undoubtedly set itself up as the target of dissatisfaction.[7]

Western research on "framing" suggests that the *way* a news story is presented can affect the viewing public's attribution of responsibility. In a political culture more individualist than collective, such as the United States, people tend not to blame the government for personal misfortunes, and this is reinforced by the presentation of news as a personal story rather than as the outcome of the government's policy.[8] In the Soviet system, television news focused overwhelmingly on government and leaders, and the political culture also focused on attributing responsibility for individual well-being to the authorities. With the intention of generating gratitude and pride, the leaders also positioned themselves to be held responsible for mounting dissatisfaction. And post-Soviet Russian politicians did not learn the lesson.

Given the constraints of the Soviet period, the question might be asked whether journalists were journalists at all. In the Soviet Union, propaganda was an explicit mission of both entertainment and the news media. Television news programs were not only heavily censored, but also guided by strict ritual regarding the power structure, with unvarying requirements of time allotments by rank. State security officers were active in the media, particularly in foreign news bureaus, adopting the protective coloration of correspondents. Nonetheless, at the level of allowable critical newsgathering—such as investigative reporting of petty malfeasance or social ills that did not implicate the system, as such, or its leadership—some professional work could be done.

In consequence, responsiveness was an attribute the public attached to the media more than to the institutions of government and Party power, and readers were more likely to address newspapers for redress of grievances than trade unions, the Party, local government, or any other public institution.[9] Even within the pattern of constraining oversight and restrictions, newspaper editors enjoyed considerably more discretion in crafting messages and an individual identity than did television officials. The newspaper *Literary Gazette* regularly featured a page of veiled satirical notes that its highly-educated readers understood as politically provocative. But television was considered too powerful to permit experimentation or intellectual games.

Since the purpose of the media was very clearly stated as the socialization of the audience in the values and rules of the regime, it was considered inappropriate to assess audience demands, much less be driven by them. Nor was it necessary, since the KGB considered itself the prime information-gathering resource for the Party elite.[10] In addition, Party meetings and Party agitation were sources of (very flawed) feedback. The innovative public opinion survey research that flourished shortly after the 1917 revolution was prohibited by Stalin and only partially restored by Nikita Khrushchev and Leonid Brezhnev.[11] Those limited, officially sanctioned surveys (such as large-scale surveys of attitudes of newspaper readers and television viewers, of labor turnover, family planning, divorce, and alcoholism), initiated to improve planning in Brezhnev's time, did reveal some startling results.[12]

Two myths were cherished by the Soviet leaders: one held that legitimacy was essentially a matter of cognition. The "scientific" grounding of Party rule, based on Communist doctrine, provided the source of its legitimacy. It stood to reason, then, that persuasion was only a matter of enabling people to understand the Party's message. As educational levels rose and benighted older folk were replaced by those who grew up free of the "superstition" of religion and bourgeois values, attachment to the Party's cause was expected to grow.

The other myth concerned media's effects. The theory here was simple: stimulus and response.[13] Messages that went out from Moscow on the mass media would be assimilated as sent—Voznesensky's television tower as ideological syringe. But, in fact, the early surveys of the 1970s showed the opposite. College graduates were *most* critical of books by contemporary Soviet writers; the better educated were *most* dissatisfied with television programs in general; the well-educated were most interested in and *least* satisfied with political and news analysis programs on television. They were also the most avid consumers of newspapers, but most frequently disagreed with the editorial position. Political information lectures were received *more* critically by people with higher levels of education.[14] Similarly, a large-scale survey of Soviet citizens who emigrated to the United States in the late 1970s found that "the long-term growth of educational attainments works to undermine support for established institutional practices."[15] Media officials and larger numbers of their colleagues in the Party were also part of this social phenomenon.

One other important factor was woefully underappreciated by the Soviet leadership: a generational change was taking place, as the young increasingly turned away from the old symbols and values.[16] When Mikhail Gorbachev launched his reforms in 1985, it was apparent to the Politburo that something quite different had to be done to recapture the youth and prevent the generational shift it feared. This was to be one of the prime motivations for the television revolution that spun out of control when Mikhail Gorbachev took power with Alexander Yakovlev at his side.

PARTIAL REMEDIES AND CONSTRICTED LIBERALISM

Sociologist Tatyana Zaslavskaya and others present at the creation of Mikhail Gorbachev's policy of *perestroika* trace the roots of that liberalization to an earlier one, in the 1960s under Nikita Khrushchev, when the intelligentsia experienced, as she put it, "a swallow of freedom."[17] The Khrushchev "thaw" did indeed extend the range of permissible subjects of discussion, including the delegitimation of the Stalin cult, but not the basic Stalinist power structure or constitution. Nor did the "thaw" introduce a dynamic for its continual expansion and permanence.[18] Still, the liberalization of the Khrushchev period was palpable at the time. With the Soviet leader's son-in-law at the helm, the newspaper *Komsomol Pravda* boldly pushed for a livelier provision of information, especially to the young; Alexander Solzhenitsyn published his pathbreaking *Day in the Life of Ivan Denisovich;* Grigory Chukhrai directed a new genre of humane, nuanced films.

This top-down liberalization was certainly not intended for all spheres: religion was severely constrained; volunteer "people's militias" and auxiliary courts unconcerned with legal procedure came into being; "parasites" (those who were living on unearned income, including "unofficial" creative artists) were subject to summary sanctions. The subsequent Brezhnev chill (including trials of dissidents, use of psychiatric hospitals for political deviants, broad application of libel and slander laws) instilled in many of the generation of the 1960s the commitment to irreversible reform at the next opportunity—though their goals would later appear too limited for younger activists. The generation of the 1960s would begin *perestroika* with Gorbachev and then find themselves marginalized by a more radicalized younger generation.

With respect to the media, changes were taking place in the way the leadership thought about means and goals. Late in the 1970s, theoretical discussions surfaced within the Party regarding the conceptualization of the communications process. Party theoreticians began to write about political communication as an enterprise considerably less mechanistic than stimulus-response reasoning would suggest. They began to see communication as interactive and probabilistic (dependent on a variety of attributes of both message and recipient), a process in which the recipient of the message must be at the center of attention.[19]

It was also increasingly understood that a powerful psychological advantage belongs to the source breaking the story. Those who attempt to respond to correct what they see as inaccuracy or distortion face a much greater persuasive challenge. The usual policy forbidding timely and accurate coverage of locally relevant news inevitably ceded salience and authority to unofficial sources: gossip and rumor, or foreign radios. By the time Yegor Ligachev, ideology chief under Gorbachev, came to join the central leadership in Moscow he had learned from experience that "there exists an unwritten psychological law of primacy: the first impression of a fact or event is the fullest, while subsequent ones, if they contradict the first, merely seem to be in conflict with it."[20]

The importance of assessing the media's impact was heightened—but I do not think fundamentally caused—by an international political shift. The Reagan administration adopted an aggressive communications policy to penetrate the "evil empire" and augment transborder communications facilities. Konstantin Chernenko and Mikhail Gorbachev both viewed this effort as imperialism and intervention, and were pressed to consider the effects of their own media more urgently (though at the time they had insufficiently rigorous methods for doing so).[21]

Since jamming was known to be imperfect, and national boundaries increasingly permeable, the Soviet elite was compelled to fashion a more pragmatic counter-communication agenda. They acknowledged that saturation of official messages did not automatically spell assimilation, and that underreporting did not quell curiosity.

Official concern with the media's effects and the growing sense that the Soviet public was alienated from its own communications sources, especially the well-educated and the youth (the present and future elites) was part of a more generalized understanding of citizens' alienation and the

country's economic decline. The widely-leaked secret memorandum prepared by sociologist Tatyana Zaslavskaya for Yury Andropov detailed the
deep divisions and dissatisfactions in Soviet society for the Party leadership.
Western observers have written extensively about the secular decline of the
Soviet system and the failure of institutions: the effects of modernization
and the inability of the system of elite mobility and circulation to incorporate the values and priorities of increasingly well-educated, professional,
urbanized people. This political stultification, linked to economic decay
and a progressively more serious problem of growth, in spite of massive investment and a skilled labor force, set critical brakes on the economy.[22] Ad-
ditionally, the war in Afghanistan and the capacity (largely unchecked by
the Brezhnev regime) of the military to siphon resources further constrained investment available to reform the deteriorating system.

Under these conditions of system-wide erosion, it was nonetheless the
decisions taken by the Gorbachev leadership that launched the process of
change and selected, at least initially, the sectors and sequences of liberalization. First among them were the mass media.

FISSURES AT THE TOP

In 1985, when Mikhail Gorbachev became General Secretary of the Communist Party and thereby leader of the Soviet Union, he and the Politburo
initiated a drive for radical reform, the outcome of which the authors neither foresaw nor desired. They were determined to effect a change more
profound than the numerous abortive policies of past leaders. After all, they
had experienced the Khrushchev "thaw," seen the window close, and a chill
return.

Mikhail Gorbachev reflected on the failure of so many aborted reforms
in the past and noted that the "decisive mistake was . . . that one didn't engage the population itself in the process."[23] Among the members of the
Politburo in March 1985, there were substantial differences in the scope of
liberalization they envisioned, and it would take time for Gorbachev to refashion the power structure.[24]

The leading players in the Gorbachev Politburo reshaping the stagnant
society were: Alexander Yakovlev, the architect of *glasnost,* who imagined
democratic elections with a limited number of competing parties; fellow
liberalizer Eduard Shevardnadze, the Georgian Party leader who later became Soviet foreign minister (and then president of independent Georgia),
who did not share this radical a view; and Yegor Ligachev, Gorbachev's
second in command—the restorer—who advocated reform of the Communist Party and "did not see any other force in the country that could sufficiently reform society."[25]

From the perspective of 1995, a decade after he came to power, Mikhail Gorbachev was convinced that his policies had been more democratic and more reforming than those of Boris Yeltsin's government. Gorbachev said his press law "removed all prohibitions," and that there was no more "professional press law than ours." Certainly, the press freedoms he initiated and which were codified in a long-deliberated law on the press were path-breaking, but he also veered into quite contradictory paths, asking for the suspension of that very law and supporting one to forbid insults to the president, and bringing state television to heel in the fall of 1990.

The course of Gorbachev's policies with respect to the information revolution he launched was not direct or consistent. His vacillation was in part a tactical response to turbulent political opposition and unexpected social consequences, and in part to a genuine devotion to and respect for values he perceived to be at risk. At times he upheld the more liberal policy direction associated with Alexander Yakovlev, and at times he countenanced the opposite. It depended on the political strategy of the moment and on an enduring conviction of the rightness of socialism as he understood it.

In 1995, Mikhail Gorbachev expressed pride in his achievements in economic reform and talked about the Nineteenth Party Conference (in the summer of 1988) as a boundary (*rubezh*), after which there was reform, pluralism—"true freedom." At the time he said that his vociferous critics on the left only wanted to *transform* socialism into "socialism with a human face." "Not one," he emphatically recalled, "said we had to move to the market. . . . I did more. We were ready to go much further than they were."[26]

He saw his political and economic reforms as interconnected, but history records rather different degrees of attainment. On the political side, the Nineteenth Party Conference was indeed a watershed: it was this meeting that laid the groundwork for deep changes in the Soviet system. Under Gorbachev's driving leadership, it was decided to form a new kind of legislature, institute competitive elections, limit the terms of Party leaders, trim the Party bureaucracy, and, by fusing Party and government-elected posts, force the Party to submit to popular elections.[27]

For a Western economist like Anders Aslund there was no parallel achievement in economic reform. Aslund agrees that the Nineteenth Party Conference deprived the Communist Party of much of its oversight over the economy, a process in which it had always interfered. But, in his view, Gorbachev's own *apparat* was too weak to wield effective control, and too cautious. Piecemeal tinkering with the socialist system had resulted in hoarding, rising inflation, unbalanced food distribution, and rationing. From Siberia to Ukraine, in the Kuznetsk and Donets Basins, miners struck for political as well as economic demands. The antialcohol campaign, with which Gorbachev inaugurated his administration, backfired, reducing not the evils of alcohol but much-needed revenue for the state budget. On the international scene, the oil glut meant plummeting prices for the Soviet Union's lucrative export and hitherto assured East European markets were moving out of the Soviet orbit: since Gorbachev's bold assertion that the Brezhnev doctrine was dead, the Soviet Union would no longer intervene. Aslund's judgment was unsparing: Gorbachev, as economic reformer, "was just a reform communist, not prepared to launch full-fledged systemic changes."[28]

The Nineteenth Party Conference moved the country sharply ahead in political reform, but, as a consequence of genuinely competitive elections at the national and republic levels, it also released pent-up demands for autonomy, then sovereignty, and then independence. Newly legitimized and institutionalized by competitive elections, local bases of power and authority vied with the increasingly hamstrung central ones, and it was this tendency, especially in the Baltic countries, that most alarmed Gorbachev. Throughout the country, there were new incentives for Party leaders to distance themselves from the central Party organization.[29] And Boris Yeltsin, cast down from the Party's heights, was moving up on the flank. As these forces coalesced, Mikhail Gorbachev sought hard-line allies to save the union.[30]

How much was the media revolution that Gorbachev began a democratic one? At the time, he insisted that *glasnost* would renew socialism. When he came back from his Crimean captivity in the summer of 1991, he proclaimed his devotion to communism. Later, too, he declared he had continued, not diverted, the socialist tradition. *Glasnost* may have been protean, ill-defined, and unplanned, but some bold move had to wake the passive, outwardly conforming, alienated citizens of his country. In 1995, Mikhail Gorbachev strongly disapproved of the contemporary attitude toward socialism, how people now "anathematize socialism." He claimed credit for beginning a multi-party system. He called it a "different reading of socialism," one that did not "contort the ideas of socialism."

The true basis of pluralism for which Gorbachev had only wavering support required institutions with genuine autonomy from the state,[31] and he was not consistently the reformer of his backward glance. There was a profound ambiguity in his own "socialism": how much it supported the centrifugal movements of peoples and parties and how much of the past he wanted effaced. When Gorbachev's media reform began and the Politburo discussed it in its weekly meetings, there were reservations, he recalled. He was told that it was not right to open for discussion the notion that "Party life was in vain." Many sacrifices had been made, he said, "one cannot disclaim them."[32]

Official Party pronouncements issuing from authoritative sources had always set Soviet policy, and they did so with respect to this new policy of media reform as well. The difference now was that instead of the usual gray uniformity, these august dicta were confusing and internally contradictory, for a deep rupture had taken place within the leadership. The breach had immediate consequences because of an organizational irrationality: the two most profoundly opposed competitors were simultaneously charged with the almost identical political jurisdiction. Mikhail Gorbachev was the arbiter, but he had deliberately undermined the expected pattern of ideological leadership. Instead of maintaining the strict senior-junior pattern of authority, Gorbachev introduced Alexander Yakovlev as a political and doctrinal counterweight to Yegor Ligachev. Though Ligachev was still senior, Yakovlev had proximity to the General Secretary. As Gorbachev recalled, "I had in mind not to leave the ideological sector for the foreseeable future to Ligachev alone," who was too "conservative."[33] In conversation, Gorbachev put it simply: Yegor Ligachev wanted to keep tight control over the press.[34]

Mikhail Gorbachev rose in the *apparat* of the Communist Party to its apex. He knew the standard operating procedures. The organizational irrationality he introduced affected the entire institution. In Leonid Brezhnev's day and before, when Mikhail Suslov ruled ideology as the "second secretary," there was no doubt at all about who ruled ideology.[35] Later Party Central Committee functionaries contemptuously derided the reduced status of Vadim Medvedev, a Suslov successor, by calling him *suslik* (a pun meaning both little Suslov and gopher).[36] Suslov was the *eminence grise,* the kingmaker, whose gaunt figure dominated propaganda and ideology until his death in January 1982, just nine months before Leonid Brezhnev's. When he died, the powerful Suslov had served in the Party elite for over thirty years. Suslov's last protegé, the ineffectual holdover Mikhail Zimyanin, was pensioned off at seventy-two at the beginning of 1987. In the words of Ronald Hill and Alexander Rahr, he was "the last secretary to have been born before the revolution, the last to have served on a Central Committee under Stalin. . . . His departure may thus be seen as symbolic of a change in a political era."[37]

After the brief interregna of Andropov and Chernenko, the pattern of media oversight appeared to have endured: a senior official as the Party's "number two" and a deputy of much less stature. Mikhail Gorbachev promoted Yegor Ligachev (originally in a Central Committee secretary's spot as an appointee of Yury Andropov) to the top Politburo ideology position.

Alexander Yakovlev's extraordinarily rapid rise in the party elite destroyed the senior-junior lines that had, in Mikhail Suslov's seemingly endless tenure, so clearly differentiated the ideology boss from his own chosen propaganda lieutenant. Further obscuring the lines of authority, the distinctions between the arenas of ideology as opposed to propaganda were easily blurred. The "senior secretary" commanded ideology; the "junior," propaganda. The job description might seem to work on paper, with ideology referring to the large-scale contours of the belief system inculcated not only by the media, but also by science, education, the family, the legal system, and many other institutions. On the other hand, the propaganda subordinate dealt with such matters as media personnel, day-to-day supervision of the media, and other activities designed to implement the overall concept of the senior secretary and his superior, the General Secretary.

Exiled to Canada as ambassador by Leonid Brezhnev, then brought back to Moscow by Yury Andropov, Alexander Yakovlev rose quickly in Gorbachev's administration. His last Party position before leaving for Ottawa was chief of the radio and television section of the Central Committee's Propaganda Department. By July 1985, he had become head of the huge Ideology Department of the Central Committee, and then Central Committee secretary in charge of ideology. In January 1987, Yakovlev became a nonvoting member of the Politburo, and only a few months later was promoted to full membership. Yakovlev took advantage of his personnel responsibility by putting in place a pack of new (but vetted and presumably acceptable) newspaper and magazine editors who would push the reformist agenda.[38] Faced with a two-headed media policy, television industry players could follow one or the other. It all depended on their values and their propensity for risk. As a television official told an American correspondent, in the Politburo it was often only Alexander Yakovlev who defended the bold new shows.[39]

This was to be an enormously disruptive change. Elites provide cues and mediate television messages for the mass viewing public, and even in democracies pluralism is not without limits in the range of contending positions given access.[40] In the United States during the Vietnam war, the conflict between political elites spilled over into more aggressive and sharply contentious television coverage of the war.[41] I raise this example to show that in a media system where the First Amendment vigorously protects broadcasters' autonomy, leaks by disgruntled political decision-makers and the public airing of policy differences provided a powerful incentive for a much more tenacious and independent stance by the press. For the Soviet system, the effect of elite division on the media was nothing short of revolutionary. Controlled strictly by the center, television had always presented a unified presence, even when internal power struggles, unregulated by constitutional procedures, changed the direction and composition of the leadership. Virtually from the beginning of Gorbachev's administration, the shell of unity cracked and the principals went to television to make their opposing cases.

Gorbachev had the Politburo's support for *glasnost* as a means to reform the Soviet system. All agreed that reform was needed. However, within the Politburo divisions arose over the instrumental use of *glasnost* to both reform and retain the fundamental system and the more far-reaching aim of (still-limited) democratization. *Glasnost* and *perestroika* may have sounded like defined policies, but to those in Soviet television who had to produce concrete and timely implementation, the words had little operational specificity.

From Politburo members the cues were too many, not too few, and they did not add up to a coherent policy. Indeed, it was unclear to many in the power elite themselves just what Mikhail Gorbachev had in mind. He certainly focused on the media, saying that "the mass media are playing and will continue to play a tremendous role in this . . . they are the most representative and massive rostrum of *glasnost*"[42] Gorbachev himself recalled afterward that *glasnost* could not be "contained within the boundaries we tried to draw in this process at the beginning, and it took on a character which was independent of the directives." This had both advantages and shortcomings, and among the latter he noted that the mass media sowed hatred and enmity in society.[43] The process had gone too far.

Yegor Ligachev was a man of strongly held opinions. In his retirement, his clear blue eyes were still alive with energized conviction, and he still loudly orated, even over tea. He was a Bolshevik to the end, and in his speech the Marxist–Leninist categories flowed naturally. He prided himself on his Siberian toughness and puritanical probity. Not only was he abstemious himself, he saw alcohol as the plague of the nation, breaking up families, reducing labor productivity, increasing labor turnover, and contributing to crime and drug use. The human wastage distressed him and deeply compromised the possibility that a strong, healthy, productive working class would attain the Marxist goals he advocated so passionately. He was the leading force behind the disastrous antialcohol campaign and, according to Gorbachev, "with unbridled eagerness" he drove it "ad absurdum."[44]

About what was to be a momentously important conflict, Alexander Yakovlev remarked that he did not have "direct confrontations" with Yegor Ligachev, though he acknowledged that they were profound opponents.[45] A serious, controlled figure, Yakovlev spoke softly and deliberately, sometimes smiling mysteriously in tacit acknowledgment of a point, sometimes criticizing his former Party colleagues forthrightly, but seemingly without emotion. Yakovlev, the more subtle strategist, could conceal his purposes, while his blunt opponent played by the old and rapidly obsolescing rules. Ligachev, when, in 1987, he had his first open clash with Alexander Yakovlev over the content of a resolution summarizing the deliberations of the Politburo on the course of *perestroika,* saw an apparent consensus unravel. His draft included criticism of the mass media and individuals who "blackened our history." According to Ligachev, Yakovlev deleted it.[46]

Thus it was, that on the policy issue of the mass media the split in the leadership broke into the open. It was this split, with its opposing sets of instructions, that enabled media officials to take sides in the policy battles.

There was no assurance that either side would enjoy sufficient political protection and certainly no guarantees that the losers would emerge unscathed. The complete loyalty of *all* the media people had been assured by the usual process: they had risen with prudence and circumspection through the ranks of the Soviet system, and if they had displayed boldness it had not exceeded the acceptable level of compliance.[47] That the pool then yielded both curmudgeonly conformists and radical experimenters suggests that the hold of the central Party leadership over the attitudes of its many millions of members had been attenuating over the years.[48]

Television officials were all members of the Party, vetted by the system they understood and could, to a certain extent, manipulate. Eduard Sagalayev was an official of the Communist Youth League before going to television; Igor Malashenko had experience in the Central Committee and presidential apparat; and Alexander Lyubimov, son of a KGB colonel, was in the foreign department of Radio Moscow. That they behaved differently in the same organization attests to the role that individuals could and did play at this pivotal time. To be sure, the resistance of these insiders could not be compared to that of dissidents, like Andrei Sakharov and so many others, who were sent to exile or camps and emerged, if they did at all, broken in health if not in spirit. Those rebels, especially Sakharov, were often the conscience of the ones who made the changes—from *within* the system. Ligachev later complained, "How could I have suspected that Yakovlev was forming a radical media team that would have a very special role in the coming events?"[49]

Yegor Ligachev thought he and the others in the Party leadership had signed off on a purifying reform to liberate the minds and energies of a passive and alienated population. It was a reform to advance social justice and the collective goals of a populist socialism that would, finally, reengage a huge population whose failure to contribute was threatening the future of the economy. The structures of the political system would be shorn of the adventitious roots of privilege, corruption, arbitrary punishment, and careerism. As Ligachev remarked to me: "reform does not change the foundations; reforms improve the structure. We were *all* for reform. There were no dissidents on the Politburo on this issue. There were discussions on *methods,* but *within* the socialist system, about their depth, tempo, and scope."

Mikhail Gorbachev later recalled Ligachev's sudden "didactic" objection at a Politburo meeting when the powerful second secretary maintained that democratization was only a "lever" for *perestroika,* and the purpose of both was the "strengthening of socialism."[50] Ligachev attributed enormous power to the media and the cost of unbridling it was too great. After the 1989 election that effectively created a new and contending power base for Baltic separatists, Gorbachev recalled Ligachev's saying at a Politburo meeting that the media caused the public to turn away from the Party and the military: "'Also, in Hungary and in Czechoslovakia everything began with the media.'"[51]

Did Ligachev think Alexander Yakovlev merely appeared to acquiesce, while advancing a radically different strategy? Absolutely not. Ligachev insisted he knew Yakovlev too well for that; their friendship went back to the 1960s, when they served together on the Central Committee. When Yakovlev went to Canada and Ligachev to a Party post in Siberia, they exchanged letters, telegrams, and souvenirs. When they both returned to Moscow, they had "normal and good relations." There was no possibility, Ligachev insisted forcefully, that as they launched the reforms an unseen cleft lay under the surface.

Perhaps he should have paid more attention to a deep philosophical difference he had always had with Yakovlev and about which he talked to me after the 1993 October revolt in Moscow. With the Russian White House still blackened by fire, Ligachev bitterly referred to the campaign of "the bourgeoisie" to set Russia back on the capitalist path. Here, he said, he always differed from both Mikhail Gorbachev and Alexander Yakovlev. They denied the power of social class and grounded their policies in "common human values." Ligachev could not agree and said he used the power of television to reinforce the orthodox Marxist-Leninist view whenever he could. As 1993 drew to a close, Ligachev affirmed the rightness of his views and confidently asserted that the Communist structure still survived in Russia and the struggle was continuing. Two years later, he saw the Communists re-emerge as the leading parliamentary party and second in the race for the presidency. The Communists lost the second round of that election, but Ligachev had correctly estimated the durability of old structures and the depth of alienation and anger among people who perceived no present or future benefit. He had overestimated their numbers.

Yegor Ligachev forcefully denied that he ever interfered with television, calling it a "falsification" of the West. "Sometimes I went to television, three or four times. I talked with the heads of departments. I gave my point of view; they gave theirs. I gave my recommendations."

His views were also carried by his subordinates. He loftily proclaimed that "we" on the Politburo did not interfere with individual programs, but, on the other hand, "we sent communists to television with our opinions." Ligachev despised rock music, that subversive import of the West, along with other values of the glitzy consumer society he hoped the Soviet Union would never become. His own taste ran to Tchaikovsky, Rachmaninov, Glinka, and Rimsky-Korsakov or folk music and Soviet music, both "optimistic and sad." He found rock repellent and cacophonous, and told the head of television to feature Russian folk music instead. "I do not understand metal rock or loud music." Then, sardonically: "I haven't advanced to that." But the head of television knew he needed rock to attract the youth audience, and he had to figure out the right proportion of each kind of music so as not to tip the balance and bring down Ligachev's censure. Still, Ligachev met three times with television officials to complain about rock music on television.[52]

Listening to a description of Ligachev's version of his methods, Oleg Dobrodeyev, who at the time had been in the news department at state television, was outraged. From his experience as a longtime news executive, Dobrodeyev stated, in no uncertain terms, that it was a fact that Ligachev was responsible for the termination of programs. Ligachev did come to television to display his views and to tell them how to do the news: "how to act and how not to act." True, he was not as crude or openly threatening as the Politburo's man in agriculture, Viktor Nikonov, who stomped into television and told them that there were not enough programs on agriculture and things better change—"or else." Ligachev did not do that, but he hardly needed to. When a member of the Politburo gave his views, it was not academic or up for discussion. The sessions with television people and the instructions from Ligachev's underlings were taken as orders. Ligachev may be literally correct that he did not give *direct* orders, but to the people at television, Politburo members never idly pondered issues or dealt with vague hypotheticals. Ligachev knew full well the effects his "recommendations" would produce. He was the "darkest figure of them all," in Dobrodeyev's recollection.

At times, the Ligachev-Yakovlev differences broke directly into the august national news programs. In August 1988, in one extreme verbal skirmish, Ligachev took the opportunity of Gorbachev's absence from Moscow to acquire a large slice of newstime for a speech he gave in the city of Gorky. Formatted as a leader's message, it provided a *tour d'horizon* of both domestic and foreign policy. The remarks directly and specifically challenged the Gorbachev program of reform, even pressing for a return to a class-based reading of international affairs, instead of Gorbachev's "common human values." Mikhail Gorbachev recalled that Ligachev's conduct "worried me." It was "dogmatism of the old kind."[53] Alexander Yakovlev was soon on the news, contradicting every major point Ligachev made. A year later, Gorbachev sealed his reforming commitment with a declaration that the Soviet Union had no moral or political right to intervene in the affairs of Eastern Europe and that the Brezhnev Doctrine was dead.[54]

Television had a choice: two authoritative sources pointed in different directions. For the first time, ambivalence at the top became a policy issue for television, or more precisely, for the different parts of television. At times the positions conveyed by the Party's Central Committee to television reversed themselves with dizzying speed and sometimes flatly contradicted each other. Alexander Tikhomirov, the pioneering investigative reporter whose shows had been closed down more than once, asked: "how can we strike a balance, when from there [the Central Committee] we hear simultaneous calls to do away with the cooperative movement [by returning to state management] and to force the transition to market relations in the economy? For a broad intra-Party debate and at the same time for purging [Party] ranks of those who failed to swear allegiance to the platform . . . ? [What should we do:] Today support one point of view, and the next day the opposite? Or both at the same time?"[55]

Each department could choose under which leader's umbrella to seek shelter, knowing that the disarray might be only temporary, and the ability of the patron to shelter the client limited. For many of the fiefdoms at the huge state television headquarters in Moscow, the choice was simple: remain as conservative as possible and follow the ranking Party leader, Ligachev. But for some, Yakovlev's counter-ideological authority might be enough justification to push the envelope.

A year after the 1991 coup attempt, Alexander Yakovlev ruminated about the battle for television. "Television was the state—it had to serve the government." And serving the government meant initiating reform from the top. Looking back at 1985, he commented that the Soviet people had to climb out of the deep "pit" in which they were mired. We needed, he told me, to construct a democratic society. To do so, he said, "we wanted to accustom people to accept several points of view." The old battle cries invoking opposing points of view as betrayal and treason had to end. He said people had to be led to dialogue, out of the "monologue" of political discourse and values. To do this, at first he intended to propose to the Politburo the importance of showing contending points of view that took issue with basic policy. But knowing that such a radical departure would never be permitted, he began by advocating multiple points of view, all of which would be useful to the government.

The Politburo approved the policy and, as a consequence, television began a series of live programs, discussions, and for the first time commentators and guests gave their personal views. It was a break from the past and not always appreciated by the public. The leading journalism magazine reported that letters were coming in that said, "On the screen [I saw] expressed three completely opposed points of view, but I simply cannot understand which of them is the correct one."[56]

Yakovlev's concern about the absence of political culture or discourse necessary to support democratic society proved far from idle. The ability of post-Soviet society to engage in and tolerate contending points of view—to champion simple and direct speech in which the rules favored the creation of a compromising, moderate middle prepared to tolerate controversial views, not the Leninist annihilation of one side by the other—was at the root of the installation and survival of democracy. Yakovlev's comprehension of the importance of political life in which democratic controversy would be possible around a legitimate center with fundamentally consensual wings proved to be just as serious in post-Soviet Russia.

MIKHAIL GORBACHEV ON TELEVISION

Gorbachev's "walkabouts" on his travels, his spontaneous discussions with crowds at home and abroad, were remarkable. His accessibility and his plain speech were entirely new for a Soviet leader. Perhaps he had learned from his dilatory performance at the time of Chernobyl.[57]

With information policy not yet set, it was put to the test by the explosion of that nuclear power plant early in the morning of April 26, 1986. On April 28 the evening news carried a short piece, without pictures or reference to radiation, placed sixth in the program. The long period of silence from the Kremlin was attacked by the West, and Soviet leaders responded by taking the offensive.[58] Boris Yeltsin, while visiting West Germany, said the West and their "bourgeois propaganda media' are concocting many hoaxes around the accident at the Chernobyl atomic power plant."[59]

The measures taken by the Soviet government were cruelly deficient. On May Day, just days after the release of radioactive material from Chernobyl, citizens of Kiev were pressured to come out for the May Day parade. It was a sunny day in the Ukrainian capital, and *Vremya* showed young mothers and children strolling in the center. Evacuation was delayed, officials said, to avoid panic; sufficient care was not taken to remove contaminated soil and food products;[60] health officials were slow to distribute thyroid medicine to children exposed to radiation. While ordinary citizens were kept in the dark, families of Party officials were better informed. *New York Times* correspondent Philip Taubman recalled seeing trainloads of them arriving in Moscow.[61] Eighteen days after the accident Mikhail Gorbachev addressed his country on television for the first time.

The Politburo first met at dawn on April 26, several hours after the blast. Gorbachev recalled that the report on the accident was general and they did not have an idea of the scope of the disaster. A team was sent to investigate and the report they sent back was not helpful. Gorbachev characterized it as "distinctly incomplete" with "no conclusions whatever."[62] On April 28, the Politburo convened again, and apparently there were contradictory voices, if not dissension, within that high body. Alexander Yakovlev was there but not voting. He remembered the meeting well. "I had the impression," he said, "that the Politburo didn't know" what had happened. The leading scientists were there: Valery Legasov (who committed suicide two years later), Evgeny Velikhov (the president's science advisor), and "they didn't know." The experts said "different things."[63]

About a month later, Legasov remarked that although information from Chernobyl arrived in Moscow immediately, it was "contradictory and strange." He himself was totally unprepared for the scope of the accident he went to study. He said, "It was only on driving toward Pripyat and seeing the glow that I began to guess the nature of what had happened."[64] Yakovlev said everyone was at a loss. They lacked experience, but also there was a distinct "absence of responsibility."[65] There had been nuclear accidents before, but for thirty-five years they had been covered up.[66] Nikolai Fomin, the chief engineer at Chernobyl, had said that the plant was equipped with so many safety features that the odds of a major accident were one in ten thousand years.[67]

On May 3, a Politburo team of Nikolai Ryzhkov, the prime minister, Yegor Ligachev, and Ukrainian leader Vladimir Shcherbitsky inspected the plant. When they returned, the Politburo was again convened. On May 3 and 4, newspapers reported their observations, and television did so on May 4. Ligachev justified the schedule, saying that they needed to determine the extent and seriousness of the event before telling the country. He told me they had to give reliable information, or "thousands would have perished." While in Chernobyl, the team wore special protective suits, but both he and Ryzhkov still suffered from a thyroid condition he said the radiation caused. Looking back on those days, he recalled with keen disapproval that Gorbachev did not go to Chernobyl then and went there only two years later. Before leaving on his mission, Ligachev said, he told Gorbachev he should join them. Gorbachev responded that he supported their trip and hoped he could go.[68] To Ligachev's disapproval, the president did not travel to the stricken town.

Chernobyl was an information failure from which Gorbachev learned. He learned to dominate the television screen in entirely new ways. Gorbachev had a directness and an openness to match his policy of radical change. He was not another frozen, incomprehensible Communist oracle, but a motor of energy. Gorbachev is credited in the West with a masterful understanding of television and brilliant manipulation of the medium.[69] In one extraordinarily important respect, Gorbachev was indeed a master: his drastic turn away from the Marxist-Leninist rhetoric of high-flown abstractions with no concrete referents broke with the past. He re-introduced plain speech to talk about matters that had been reserved for the language of ideological ritual. That meant that for the first time in decades the stuff of politics could be addressed by those who were not its high priests, so political life was reborn in speech and rescued from its frozen wasteland. Television provided the most effective and rapid channel for this new way of communicating, and Gorbachev was its most fervent apostle.

In other ways, Gorbachev was a less successful television personality. On news programs in the United States, his comments were squeezed into sound bites. They came across as pithy, energetic, active, and enthusiastic—the words of a young and vigorous leader out to remake his country. But Soviet television was not about to reduce its country's leader to sound bites. The evening news stretched sixty, seventy, or ninety minutes to accommodate his uncut remarks. These addresses were marked by expansive talk and verbal bullying. His opponent and eventual successor, Boris Yeltsin, complained that "people were sick of Gorbachev's failed reforms and his long rambling speeches."[70] Gorbachev employed these techniques when he chaired parliamentary sessions as well. When the Soviet leader spoke at very great length, his command of Russian tended to falter, and satirical anecdotes about his confusion of words and accents spread quickly through Moscow. Playwright Ludmilla Petrushevskaya had her characters mocking Gorbachev's errant pronunciation in the hit Moscow play *Cinzano*.[71] Leonid Parfyonov, an experienced television professional, was always surprised that the attention the Soviet leadership lavished on television was totally unrelated to how the viewers were receiving it.

Politburo members anxiously watched their own coverage, as well as that of their supposed comrades. Fyodor Burlatsky, a journalist close to the Brezhnev leadership, remarked that the power elite was riven by jealousy, perhaps especially because, in theory, they were supposed to be equals. "Therefore, each appearance of a peer at work agitates them horribly, especially in the press and on television, before a wide Party and popular audience."[72]

It is to some degree paradoxical that the political leadership paid little attention to *how* viewers saw them and were indifferent to any but the most obvious camera techniques (shooting up from the ground to make the leaders appear taller). One need only remember slurring, nearly immobile Leonid Brezhnev, or wheezing, barely audible Konstantin Chernenko grasping the edge of his desk to stay on his feet while awarding medals to cosmonauts at a Kremlin ceremony, or the hospitalized Yury Andropov, dominating the airways in the dry, longwinded statements read by colorless newsreaders. These leaders were adamant about being covered as much as possible.

In part, this attention was generated by the simple notion that being on television was all that mattered and that the intended message was sure to be the one received.[73] Television coverage accompanied power and conferred it; it reflected the standing of the politician in the high-stakes struggle for status and authority. In vain the leadership was told, by those who dared, that their image on television may not have accorded with their intentions.

Yegor Ligachev remembered the excruciating displays of moribund Konstantin Chernenko: "For me, and I think for millions of television viewers as well, it was painful and embarrassing to watch a severely ill man being wheeled out almost forcibly to read torturously a short prepared text."[74] Mikhail Gorbachev remembered that Chernenko was taken from his deathbed, dressed, and taken to a room in the hospital (outfitted as a voting site) to cast his ballot (as General Secretaries always did) for the television cameras in the 1985 parliamentary elections. Chernenko had resisted the advice of his doctor and collapsed. That part was not shown on the evening news.[75]

Later, Leonid Parfyonov remembered that the day before Prime Minister Nikolai Ryzhkov was expected to order an increase in the price of basic foodstuffs, television news showed long lines trying to buy macaroni. The same newscast showed Raisa Gorbachev, in the United States with her husband, being feted at a San Francisco "friends of Raisa Gorbachev" party. Parfyonov's warning to state television that "whoever is defining the system of showing the couple Mikhail and Raisa Gorbachev doesn't understand anything about the psychology of perception," fell not so much on deaf, as on powerless ears. Every person in the breadline at home, Parfyonov feared, was now an "unfriend" of Raisa.[76]

The issue of Raisa was a constant problem. She was a novelty in Soviet society: a woman who was politically active at the most visible public level; a leader's wife with a mind of her own; a youngish and fashion-conscious female. But Raisa was also pedantic. In short, Raisa's record was mixed and she had an uphill battle trying to break new ground. She saw the negative reactions directed at her as society's resistance to a changed role for women—even in a Soviet society that rhetorically supported women's equality.[77]

According to her husband, Raisa Gorbachev made a strong contribution to the policy process. He recounted that at a planning meeting of his closest advisors, Raisa directly participated. "Her knowledge of social research, her yearlong collaboration with young students, but also her plain knowledge of everyday life and her female intuition proved useful. She pointed out to us that in the planning report the position of the family and women in society were too sparingly presented," and she told the group how to develop it more comprehensively.[78] This was unprecedented.

Yegor Ligachev said that Gorbachev once asked him about television coverage of Raisa. In recounting this incident, Ligachev noted that he refused to comment on a private matter, saying that it was Gorbachev's business, not his. But he did warn the Soviet leader to "take account of the traditions and habits of our people."[79] Leonid Kravchenko, the last Gorbachev appointee to head television, remembered that he told Gorbachev straight out that in his opinion, the shorter the story with her the better. Gorbachev reacted in a pained way, citing foreign leaders who always traveled with their wives. "I answered: yes, they travel, but their wives as a rule don't make any declarations on TV."[80]

Mikhail Nenashev, the head of television from 1989 through the fall of 1990, shook his head when asked about Raisa Maximovna. She was a problem: "she spoiled the mood of everyone at television." Whenever Gorbachev traveled an additional camera crew went with her. Nenashev objected to her coverage in principle, but even more, he reacted negatively to her penchant for giving speeches filled with empty banalities. In uncharacteristically sharp epithets, he called her "ambitious, unhealthily ambitious." After the crew filmed her visits to museums and children's homes, Nenashev applied the scissors, attempting to take out the pseudo-official speeches: "I was sharp and cruel." And a scandal usually erupted, but not involving Gorbachev directly. "Gorbachev never talked to me about it."[81] But his aides constantly pressed Raisa's interests at television. Even though Politburo ideology chiefs Vadim Medvedev and then Alexander Dzasokhov agreed with Nenashev, they could not budge their leader.

Sergei Lomakin was the handsome television correspondent who became Gorbachev's favorite after his reports on Raisa Maximovna. Looking back, he was far more charitable than the people who ran television. He thought it natural that on their trips Raisa have a "humanitarian" program, while her husband had a political one. Kravchenko recalled that separate television coverage had to be put together about the various events on his wife's schedule. But the country was not prepared to accept this new role. Lomakin observed that later, on official trips, Boris Yeltsin's wife also had a separate program, but television "refused to cover it." Gorbachev intended to show the Soviet people "world standards," and they did not accept them. Actually, Lomakin thought Raisa accomplished a great deal. In London, she met with Yehudi Menuhin and extended to him his first invitation to play in the Soviet Union. She went to a children's hospital and reached an agreement with physicians to provide assistance and medicine to Russian hospitals.

It may be too much to say that Raisa was a tragic figure in the politics of Soviet television. Perhaps she was not quite the right person to challenge the system on behalf of a new generation and a burdened gender. Her attempts to transform codified Soviet practice were thwarted by her own well-advertised achievement in that system. Holder of an advanced degree, author of a thesis on rural sociology, she assumed the domineering role of the privileged political class. But she had lost her credentials when she became the leader's spouse and, less gifted than he, sought equality before an audience kept in ignorance of the private lives of their leaders.

TRIO OF TELEVISION CHIEFS

There were three "ages of television" under Gorbachev—and three chairmen of state television: Alexander Aksyonov, Mikhail Nenashev, and Leonid

Kravchenko.[82] The head of state television was accountable to the propaganda department (and its television section) of the Central Committee of the Party, the huge bureaucratic apparatus that staffed and implemented Communist Party rule. Propaganda department officials and their section chiefs regularly met with the television heads to critique television policy and individual programs and to provide instructions about upcoming speeches by Gorbachev and other assignments. Central Committee officials daily collected the requests of Party secretaries in Moscow, the republics, and the regions, and constantly bombarded Ostankino. And when television was on the agenda, the chairman of state television was asked to attend meetings of the highest ruling group, the Politburo. But that was only a part of the responsibility. The head of television also received individual calls from aides and advisors of Politburo members and from the Party's chief, the General Secretary. As a minister in the government, the head of television reported to parliament. He had to run a huge operation, employing about one hundred thousand people, while answering without fail to the Party chief.

Mikhail Gorbachev's removal of septuagenarian Sergei Lapin, the Brezhnev-era television boss for fifteen years, was a visible step to end the era of stagnation, as it was officially called. Alexander Aksyonov understood very little of the revolution that *glasnost* was unleashing and the divided forces stirring within Ostankino. With each new development, each new challenge to the grey uniformity of the past, Aksyonov would intone with anxiety, "They'll take our Party card away."

But Aksyonov had little to do with what Leonid Kravchenko, his chief deputy at the time, called "the creative process," that is, he was a caretaker, a figurehead, and a not-too-expert spokesman. To keep his distance from the television professionals, he moved his office out of the Ostankino headquarters and into the center of the city.

The weakness of Aksyonov's leadership coupled with the Yakovlev-Ligachev policy cleavage in the Politburo and reverberated in Ostankino, where the different departments grabbed at more active policy roles. The final push that ousted the ineffectual Aksyonov was Moscow playwright Mark Zakharov's incendiary conversation on the late-night program *Vzglyad* (Viewpoint). In that broadcast, Zakharov saved for the Moscow time-zone edition what had never before been said on television: that Lenin's body should be removed from the mausoleum and buried. Aksyonov had to face an enraged plenum of the Party's Central Committee to take full blame and to say helplessly that with live broadcasts, censoring things of this sort had become extremely difficult, if not impossible.

Later, the best that Aksyonov's successor, Mikhail Nenashev, could say was that he "felt sorry for Aksyonov."[83] Why? Because Aksyonov had not figured out that the old way of running state television was obsolete and hopeless. In Nenashev's view, Aksyonov was the "last representative" of the traditional method of Party monopoly of television.[84] For Nenashev, Aksyonov was an anachronism who failed to see how much had changed since 1985: how riven state television—and the country—had become, and how mobilized the viewers. Vadim Medvedev, one of the last Politburo ideology chiefs, summed it up: "Aksyonov had old views."[85]

Mikhail Nenashev was determined to recognize the changed state of affairs when he took over in May 1989. He was a reluctant candidate who did not particularly care for television and had to be persuaded by Gorbachev personally. A wry, subtle figure, Nenashev gave the impression of an ascetic and contemplative observer. He had originally come to Moscow at the behest of Alexander Yakovlev in the late 1960s,[86] and now came to television with certain goals: he wanted to convert the institution from reliance on unpredictable, personal power relationships to a structure of decentralized, autonomous, competitive units. For this he needed new people, new sources of revenue, and, most of all, patience and time from those who appointed him. Nenashev also believed that television functioned inevitably as a mirror of life outside the Kremlin walls, and that to sever the medium from the world it reflected was fruitless.

Assessing Nenashev's administration of television is complicated by the arrangement he had with his deputy, Pyotr Reshetov. At that time and well after, in spite of floods of complaints, Nenashev always defended his faithful and abrasive deputy, whose rages and unrestrained interference provoked contempt and indignation. In 1993, Nenashev asserted that what he valued in Reshetov was his total altruism, his commitment to the "fate of the people and his pain for his insulted fatherland." Few people, Nenashev remarked, could understand how Reshetov suffered for his candor in defending Nenashev before the Party. Unlike others, Reshetov never concealed his devotion to Party principles.[87] Unquestionably, he preserved Nenashev's image with subordinates at Ostankino and with assessors at Party headquarters. Eduard Sagalayev, who led his departments at state television to the forefront of reform, commented thoughtfully some years later that "Reshetov was part of Nenashev." Nenashev, he remarked, did not advocate thoroughgoing, deep-seated change, though he had been a bold editor of the newspaper *Soviet Russia*. Both Nenashev and Reshetov would have given their lives for socialism, but to different degrees. Nenashev was the "good socialist"; Reshetov, "the bad."[88]

Oleg Dobrodeyev thought Mikhail Nenashev was one of the most professional, knowledgeable, and bold leaders of state television who tried without success to save programs. When he was first appointed, Nenashev told Gorbachev that it was no longer possible to restrict pluralism of viewpoints because the country itself had become differentiated and pluralized. From that early talk it was apparent to Nenashev that Gorbachev and his allies intended to keep the main source of information and news firmly in their hands and to limit access by the opposition. According to Nenashev, the Kremlin overseers of television simply were unaware of what was happening in the country. He repeatedly had to defend the content of television programs and found an "astonishing lack of understanding." He recalled that government and Party leaders alike, and especially Gorbachev's advisors, still preserved the outmoded idea that "everything depends on to whom and how access to the microphone is given."[89] This extraordinary devotion to the stimulus-response model of communication, the total lack of interest in the way the message was received or assimilated, and the notion that power flows unimpeded from the airwaves was deluded and static. Experts and specialists knew that, but the country's political leaders were not open to those arguments.

In the spring of 1990, Gorbachev came to the studios and gathered the television people to advocate more pluses in addition to the minuses. The problems of reform, especially the calls for sovereignty from the Baltics, deeply disturbed the Soviet leader. In this atmosphere, Nenashev recalled, "it was a rare day when he [Gorbachev] did not express his demands to state television and to individual programs." He also remarked that at a minimum, he talked daily with Gorbachev.[90] At the same time, to the editors of the reform newspaper *Moscow News* and the magazine *Ogonyok,* Gorbachev expressed his support for openness and democratic values. Nenashev thought this behavior hypocritical, but it was a consistent application of the rules of contained change: let the relatively small-circulation elite intellectual print media push the frontiers of free speech, but do not lightly unleash the firepower of mass-audience television.

In November 1990, Gorbachev fired Nenashev and appointed Leonid Kravchenko to head state television. Unlike his successor, for whom he had considerable contempt, Nenashev remarked that he preferred not to ask Gorbachev's permission for his initiatives—he had decided to be independent.[91] But without structural, economically viable independence, there was no guaranteed autonomy. The Law on the Press, the subject of protracted political battles until it was finally passed in 1990, had its weaknesses—it did not deal with the state monopoly over newsprint or the high costs of distribution. It also required registration of all media, removed rather broadly defined areas of hate speech from protected speech, and favored the licensing of journalists. But it did shatter the state monopoly over the print media by allowing individuals and groups to establish their own newspapers and magazines.[92] The appropriation of state-owned property by the newly independent publisher-editors was not to go unchallenged, and the battle for control of freedom of speech in print media would shift into the murky region of property rights.

Though generally greeted (incorrectly), in the Western press as a move toward democratization and expansion of free speech, the decree on television and radio prohibited "changing the legal and property position of the functioning subdivisions of the USSR State Committee for Television and Radio Broadcasting." There was to be no privatization by seizure or conversion, as had happened at newspaper offices, either by regional affiliates or organized groups. Greater initiative was to devolve on the locales, and new stations could be founded by public institutions, not by individuals. And in a portentous paragraph, the decree banned "monopolization of airtime" by a party, political movement or group, and forbade television journalists from broadcasting their "private political views," a provision that would be used by Nenashev's successor to shut down programs that disseminated politically objectionable views. On the positive side, the decree supported contractual arrangements between production companies and the television administration, thus launching a system of competitive awards of contracts.[94]

Nenashev thought he had been appointed to effect structural change and to create genuine competition among the state television channels, to launch what he called "genuine alternative television."[95] He was wrong. The president's intentions had either changed under the pressure of demands or had never countenanced this degree of change. Nenashev recalled: "Gorbachev's reserve of patience toward me was exhausted and he began to look for another director of USSR state television who could execute and obey and also someone who would not ask questions."

In September 1990, Nenashev learned that Gorbachev was actively seeking a replacement. Soon Gorbachev would no longer see Nenashev, instead sending his orders through his advisors. At their last meeting, Gorbachev told Nenashev that "he was hoping for the decisiveness of L. Kravchenko."

Mikhail Gorbachev's reaction to my mention of Nenashev's criticism was instant and negative. One can only "mildly trust" (*slabo doveryat*) Nenashev, and he was not good at television. Gorbachev said he had been in favor of Nenashev's appointment at the time and now had little patience with Nenashev's argument that the "roots of the present" were all in place back then; all was clear, and if only Nenashev had stayed "all would be well." These are "pathetic people" (*zhalkie liudi*), Gorbachev added contemptuously.[96]

In retrospect, Eduard Sagalayev said that Gorbachev lacked "big ideas." He did not have them while he was in power, or later. His great gift was a sense of political opportunity: he was at his best at the given time of a decision. But that very strength of mastering the moment resulted in frequent changes of direction. From the beginning, Gorbachev saw television as an ideological weapon, useful for propaganda and for pressure. In dealing with television he followed what he perceived as a balance-of-power strategy: he backed Ligachev when he thought the Politburo favored one course; when he believed the intelligentsia, to whom so much of his reform package was directed, were unhappy, he took the position of Yakovlev. Looking back from 1993 in disillusionment, Sagalayev regarded Gorbachev's approach as Leninist: betraying some allies today, and others tomorrow. Gorbachev once said to Sagalayev that the Party was a dying tiger, but they had to take out its teeth. Sagalayev concluded that Gorbachev was part of the tiger himself.[97]

In the fall of 1990, Leonid Kravchenko came back to the state television system, where he had been deputy chairman only a short time before to carry out the will of President Gorbachev. Nenashev thought the project doomed from the start, and concluded that in Kravchenko's short stay as head of television, he "only accelerated the processes of deformation and contradiction in central television."

Kravchenko's brief to restore unified central control over television and turn the clock back on nascent pluralism was given the force of law by another important presidential decree. On February 8, 1991, state television was converted into the All-Union State Television and Radio Company, retaining all of the assets, appropriations, staff, functions, rights, and duties of its predecessor.[98] Kravchenko put simply and forcefully what this legal sleight-of-hand meant: "'I can be removed only by the president of the USSR, who appointed me to this position with his decree.'"[99] The appointment also involved absolute fidelity to the wishes of the president: now television would be the "president's channel." A desperate Soviet leadership increasingly sought the quasi-magical effect of television to alter the downward course of its prospects.

Leonid Kravchenko was the last of the Gorbachev appointees. He ruled television as the president's man and worked under the occupation of Ostankino during the August 1991 coup attempt. After the dust settled, he took up writing under a pseudonym as a political observer of a newspaper specializing in legal issues. He did not give his real name, he said, so that his articles would be read without prejudice.

A year after the 1991 coup attempt he was still going over the roads not taken that would have removed him from Moscow that fateful August day.[100] "I was on Gorbachev's team and I played to the end. Other people left Gorbachev; I was with him the whole time. I was in contact with him three times a day, in meetings and on the telephone." They talked about television; they talked about what programs were planned, and Gorbachev would steer him in the political direction he wanted, saying what he "supports and doesn't support," and one figure to be kept off television was Lithuanian nationalist leader Vytautas Landsbergis, whom Gorbachev thought an "ominous figure." On August 21, said Kravchenko, he was supposed to fly to Edinburgh, but "Gorbachev would not let me go" because of a scheduled five-hour television program on the signing of the union treaty, a new regime for the restive republics. Had Kravchenko gone to Scotland that day he would not have been summoned by the KGB to follow the orders of the committee that deposed Mikhail Gorbachev. Thinking back, he saw that quirk of circumstance as fateful. Others who worked in state television remembered many months of a faithful lieutenant energetically making television "presidential."

CHAPTER THREE

Closely Watched Targets: The Nightly News, the Military, and Lenin

STATUS AND PROTOCOL IN THE NEWS

Television reflected and conferred status. That applied not only to the top leadership, scrambling to be on the small screen, but also to the portrayal of state interests. Television was an instrument of international diplomacy expressing the priority accorded by the Soviet state to other states and foreign dignitaries. Failure to include their visits and activities on state television bespoke a decision to downgrade the entire political and economic relationship.

In December 1987, Grigory Shevelyov, then head of news at state television, said that ceremonial receptions and visits of foreign dignitaries always required news coverage; a lapse would be insulting to the visitor. During his long career at state television, Shevelyov could not recall any exception to this practice. As he put it: "State television is part of protocol; the presence of the television camera is an element of protocol."

That is why Soviet television viewers saw, on all channels, the same pictures of the arriving foreign leader's plane, the review of the honor guard, the performance of both anthems, and the limousines driving off to the Kremlin. Sometimes the tarmac was rainy or windswept, sometimes snow fell on the unflinching soldiers, but the symbolism was unvarying. State protocol also required that every country accredited to the Soviet Union address the Soviet people on the occasion of its national holiday. At least weekly, sometimes more often, an ambassador stiffly seated at a table with his (female ambassadors being scarce) flag behind him, read from a prepared text about the great achievements of his people and their growing friendship and cooperation with the people of the Soviet Union. These boring talking heads were of little interest to viewers, but what did that matter? It was television's duty to further state policy.

As I observed in 1988, televised official ritual was carefully crafted. On July 8, a monument to Mahatma Gandhi was dedicated in Moscow. The ceremony brought together the president of the Soviet Union, Andrei Gromyko (the foreign minister for decades before); the president of India, Ramaswamy Venkataraman, and Moscow city boss Lev Zaikov (Boris Yeltsin had been removed from this post the previous year). The minister of culture was also there, as was the Central Committee's culture chief, and a deputy chairman of the executive body of the parliament. It was a high-profile event, given the centrality of India to Soviet foreign policy, and the unveiling of the statue, with the attendant speeches by the three officials, received ample coverage on prime-time television news and in newspapers as well.

The stories reported that thousands demonstrated on behalf of Soviet-Indian relations.[1] The crowd I observed was actually about five hundred, and the real event was neither spontaneous nor entirely smooth, even though carefully prepared.[2] The day before the ceremony Ostankino personnel put up three large cameras around the statue and tribunal. Bolted onto platforms, the cameras were then swathed in protective plastic and left all night, while uniformed patrols kept watch. The next morning, traffic was rerouted and thirteen long, black limousines, two yellow cars, and a dozen black cars lined up. A wall of police and metal barriers was put up and those who strayed into the restricted area were shouldered aside. Chartered buses brought in many of the specially invited crowd, while their leaders, looking like union organizers in old Hollywood movies, wore red armbands and carried identical black fold-up umbrellas. Each had a large, square, newspaper-wrapped package containing paper flags (Soviet and Indian), a pair of which was given to each demonstrator. Most of the participants had received invitations from the Ministry of Culture, and local party, trade union, and youth organizations. Demonstrators with jobs were given time off. Indian students were brought out in force.

Lev Zaikov was a tank of a man and it was his event. He gave a short welcoming speech and introduced Gromyko and the Indian president, whose name he mangled even though he carefully read it from a card. The demonstrators had their instructions down pat: they waved their flags when the dignitaries came onto the tribunal, when each official was introduced, at the beginning of a speech, at the end of a speech, at any mention of Soviet-Indian friendship, and upon the unveiling of the statue. Gromyko was listened to attentively, though he said nothing new. He was, after all, a legendary figure now weakened by a stroke, slurring his words and soon to die. When Zaikov introduced the Indian president a second time, he had even more difficulty, stopping and starting as he made his way across the letters on an index card. At the end of the ceremony, exactly one-half hour after it had begun, the officials entered their limousines to drive to the center of Moscow now decorated with banners heralding Soviet-Indian friendship.

No ritual was more important than the news program itself. *Vremya* was a closely watched target. Unbridled competition for coverage of Politburo members was held in check by rules relating to status. Members of the ruling Politburo were to be covered in full; candidate members and Central Committee secretaries could be edited. A member of the Politburo *always* had to be placed at the top of the nightly news program. Oleg Dobrodeyev, news head before and just after the 1991 putsch, recalled one day when *Vremya* was about to go on the air. To the horror of the producers, there was a story toward the end, a piece of little consequence, in which a non-voting member of the Politburo could be seen. Just minutes before news-time the script and visuals had to be redone and the order changed.

It was also a strict rule that when the Politburo was shown *all* full and candidate members had to be named. With well over a dozen normally in that powerful body, a great deal of airtime could be consumed, especially when the Politburo figured five or six times in the program, as frequently happened.

One of the earliest attempts to assert the independence of television news was the decision by Eduard Sagalayev in 1989, when he came in as chief producer of the nightly news, to discontinue this practice. One night he did not invoke the entire list of Politburo members and the next day received a disciplinary call from the Kremlin. Sagalayev kept pushing, recalled his deputy Oleg Dobrodeyev, and the next time, instead of listing the entire Politburo four times, he reduced it to two. Each of these attempts took a great deal of courage, remarked Dobrodeyev.

Though the droning list of a couple of dozen names might seem a trivial matter, it was extremely significant to the contending leaders in their fanatical devotion to symbolic politics. Public opinion expert Tatyana Zaslavskaya thought that televising these rituals, rather than confirming the symbolic politics of leadership, deconstructed their meaning. "The pompous festive meetings, public award ceremonies, and the numerous speeches that went on for several hours and were televised throughout the seventies when television became a real mass medium in our country could all be watched by millions of people . . . nothing contributed more to the decline of the authority of the 'stagnation leaders' than television."

Scrutiny of the broadcast news operation was exceptionally careful, as well it might be, given the leaders' obsession with it. At the time of Gor-

bachev's information reforms, the principal home of state television was located in two buildings facing each other across a wide boulevard in what
was once the Moscow suburb of Ostankino. Next to them rose the tallest
structure in the city, the Ostankino television tower. The massive win-
dowed concrete boxes housed administrative offices and studios, and entrance to the buildings was strictly controlled. Armed guards stood at the
entrance to review the special passes even the well-known stars had to present. Within the building, the door of the news studio itself was guarded by
uniformed policemen with machine guns. What would go out on the news
was a matter of highest importance.

The news operation was always a tense affair. A mistake in reading a
Politburo directive or a leader's statement could have serious consequences.
Each evening the script for the news was prepared on a number of thin
typewritten pages. As preparations for the first newscast to go out to the
earliest time zone in the east were made, the anchors sat in a holding room,
going over the scripts. They underlined words to emphasize, marked special
accents on easily confused words, and noted the rise and fall of the rhythm
of speech. The newsreaders, a male/female pair, would also go over the
order of the assignments, sometimes swapping stories, tossing them to each
other across the polished table and hastily incorporating them in the folder.
In the end, as the minutes to newstime ticked away, each of the newsreaders had a sheaf of papers, some dog-eared from their travels. At times this
process was interrupted by orders from above, and one of the most notable
intruders was Pyotr Reshetov.

In February 1989, Pyotr Reshetov came to Central Television; he left in
the spring of 1991. He was Mikhail Nenashev's chief "enforcer" for all of
Nenashev's term and much of Leonid Kravchenko's. Reshetov began his
Party career in information, working in the Central Committee's International Information Department, and for two decades before entering the
television industry he had served as head of the department of ideological
work at the Party's Academy of Social Sciences. Reshetov saw rather little
difference between his two bosses. Kravchenko was harsher and more obedient to Gorbachev, but Nenashev appeared more conciliatory only because of an agreement with Reshetov, who had told Nenashev, during
those early days together at television, "I will take things out and you can
put things in."

Reshetov did not mind his role of bad cop in the least; he reveled in it.
He seemed to take particular satisfaction in the congruence of his actions
and convictions. Hypocrisy was quite foreign to him. Reshetov was proud
of being the first at state television to actually sign orders instead of relying
on the elusive "telephone law" that concealed all traces of responsibility.
Even his most bitter enemies agreed that Reshetov was unusual in his will-

ingness to sign his orders. When I asked him about censorship on television, he looked puzzled for a moment at the question, and then beating his chest, affirmed, "*I* was the censor!"[3]

For Oleg Dobrodeyev, Reshetov was "ideologically illiterate," but that did not stop him from writing news copy, especially at critical times. In fact, his habit of replacing news copy, virtually at will, almost caused a brawl in the studio. Olvar Kakuchaya, a thirteen-year veteran in the Ostankino newsroom, found it "very difficult" to work with Reshetov. According to Kakuchaya, Reshetov would write whatever he wanted to go into the news and order the readers to include it. Kakuchaya was infuriated at the constant incursions on his territory and at the level of the writing. "I often wrote news scripts," Reshetov said. He received information from top government officials, wrote it up, and handed it to the newsreader. He saw no problem whatever in handling the news this way.

The confrontations between Kakuchaya and Reshetov rapidly escalated, and when Reshetov insisted on inserting material he had just produced they very nearly came to blows in the office. In January 1991, when the Vilnius television tower was taken over by Soviet troops, Sergei Lomakin, Gorbachev's favorite anchor, said that Reshetov gave him a handwritten page of script with orders to read it that evening on *Vremya*. Lomakin returned it, saying it was not the job of the anchor and that Reshetov could give his text to a newsreader but not to an anchor, and then Lomakin walked out. He went to Kravchenko and handed him the news script Reshetov had just written for that night's program and said, "Look what Reshetov is telling me to say." Kravchenko took it, read it, and called it gibberish.[4] Kravchenko ruled the newsroom off limits to his deputy and told him to take ten days off, beginning immediately.

THE MILITARY AND TELEVISION

Foreign affairs and the status of the Politburo leaders were closely watched topics on television. The military was another. Gorbachev's media revolution loosened the supports holding up the Soviet military as an institution of selfless dedication, and to many the myth of the armed forces was more meaningful and more affecting than the Party's dry Marxist-Leninist texts. Here was the true national soul; here, the ties to the glory and sacrifice that had created the nation, which, depending on the threat, was either the Russian nation or the Soviet state. The military had been absolutely off limits to any kind of public discussion. That the monolith was imperfect, everyone knew. The brutal hazing, the ethnic tensions, the lack of concern with the safety and well-being of the troops—these, of course, could not possibly be hidden by such a huge organization that drafted nearly all eligible men. In the Soviet Union, the public face of the armed forces had to be unseamed and unscarred. In an officially atheist country, the word "sacred" was applied to the obligation of military service.

Glasnost changed all that. As soon as the searchlight was turned on the military, its resistance began. The battle over the media was both a cause and symptom of the threat that the generals were ultimately powerless to confront. The military's inability to adapt to change was mirrored in its showcase, the Sunday-morning television program *I Serve the Soviet Union*. The program extolled military life, especially targeting future inductees, but its demographics were quite unfavorable; the audience was far older and less educated than the country's average.[5]

The Soviet military began to lose its grip on media communications about military activities virtually from the beginning of Gorbachev's rule. In 1985, when Mikhail Gorbachev came to power, he began a reassessment of the war in Afghanistan, following more boldly the review that former Soviet leader Yury Andropov had initiated.[6] Well before the official announcement in February 1988 that the Soviet Union would consider withdrawal, television news coverage changed to prepare public opinion and disarm the political elites who opposed the policy. Stories about the war in no way denigrated the army, but they did move from sugarcoated advocacy of social reform in Afghanistan to grainier coverage of fighting. Alexander Yakovlev believed that covering the war as conflict would lead to public distaste for fighting (and not to rallying around the flag to pursue the war to a victorious end).[7]

The military opposed withdrawal from Afghanistan, as did the KGB, and opposition did not cease when the policy change was announced. It continued well into the winter of 1989. According to war correspondent Mikhail Leshchinsky, the army was divided on the issue, with General Boris Gromov, head of the ground troops in the war zone supporting withdrawal, and General Dmitry Yazov, chief of staff in Moscow, opposing it. Under the new Gorbachev-Yakovlev policy, news stories began to cover the war as conflict for the first time. Fighting was shown, in contrast to earlier coverage of social revolution and peaceful collaboration between helpful Soviet experts and fraternal Afghan leaders. But the military still exercised control over the television reports from Afghanistan, approving pictures sent by satellite and texts telephoned back to Moscow.

In Afghanistan television correspondents were dependent on and shared the values of the Soviet armed forces, and together they faced the unrelieved tension of guerrilla warfare against an occupying army. The military supplied transport and information for correspondents and the television/military symbiosis resulted in close friendships between the correspondents and the generals: Mikhail Leshchinsky and General Gromov, and between Alexander Tikhomirov and General Alexander Rutskoy, later

Boris Yeltsin's vice president and opponent in the October 1993 revolt. (Tikhomirov eventually became the rebel general's chief advisor.) In fact, Leshchinsky implied that he had more in common with the military in Kabul than with television officials in Moscow. Though state television's opinion of Leshchinsky was mixed at best (on personal as well as professional grounds), he remained until the last soldier left.

As the soldiers were returning home, there was little television attention to the aftermath of a failed war and its human wreckage. Alexander Yakovlev remarked that the Soviet leadership determined not to focus on the failure of the Afghan war. He believed that criticizing the soldiers was out of order, but criticizing government policy was not.[8]

On April 29, 1989, the military attempted to strike a blow directly at the media. It was twenty days after armed troops used poison gas to put down a peaceful demonstration in Tbilisi, the capital of Soviet Georgia. In a resolution of the secretariat of the Communist Party's Central Committee, several media organs came under attack for criticism of the military and a plan was devised to muzzle them. The resolution ordered Communist Party organizations within the media to block excessive criticism. In a blistering attack on a number of magazines and newspapers, the resolution denounced articles that show the army as "isolated in our society . . . a source of everything that is dogmatic and antidemocratic." It complained that "a censuring and satirical tone is used in explaining such principles of combat readiness as strict adherence to military discipline" and objected that army life was compared to a prison community. The resolution bewailed the disappearance from the media of calls to "duty, honor, integrity . . . loyalty . . . heroism, romanticism, . . . the lofty calling of military service," but it feared the impact on the young most.[9] The possibility that the next generation and the new draftees would avoid service altogether struck at the core of the military's being and its survival, and the Party suspected the traditional role of the media in preparing youth for their inevitable service in the military was becoming seriously compromised. They were right to worry.

The resolution concluded that the Communist Party, together with the political administration of the armed forces, "jointly with the managers of the central press organs, radio, and television" were to take measures to achieve the kind of positive coverage they preferred. Specifically, "qualified military journalists" on duty in the Soviet army and navy would be assigned to the editorial offices of the major media organs.

The blustering resolution produced an empty formality. True, military men were assigned to the media—print and television—and true, their job was to produce stories showing the military in a favorable light. This new presence presumably would turn the tide of criticism and reinvigorate a population that had seriously begun to doubt the high-flown myths the army put out about itself.

In the television industry, the new restorers of the military myth turned out to be marginalized figures in the highly competitive game of getting material on the air. According to Boris Nepomnyashchy, at state radio at the time, the military consultants came to Ostankino as the resolution had decreed. Though they wanted to get on the air with their material for the extra honorarium, they were not often successful. As Nepomnyashchy recalled, "they sat around and didn't do anything."[10] This was a decree supposedly of the highest political import that went nowhere and did nothing to stem the tide of criticism of the military. It was carried out to the letter, but hardly in the spirit of the resolution.

Yegor Ligachev certainly agreed with the intent of the resolution defending the status and image of the armed forces. He told me that the army had suffered "slanderous" actions and that it was a "respected institution of the state." He thought the initiative came from armed forces chief Dmitry Yazov. Notwithstanding his sympathy for the action, Ligachev acknowledged that the resolution and the actions flowing from it were of "insignificant effectiveness."[11]

The military also attempted to work through the newly elected parliament, but with no real knowledge of or interest in the politics of negotiation and persuasion. Mikhail Poltoranin, then a leader in the parliamentary committee on freedom of speech, recalled a visit by marshals and generals, with all their medals and ribbons, ordering the committee to take action against *Ogonyok*. They were particularly agitated by articles on generals who bought summer homes at government expense, but Poltoranin thought they were also smarting from Gorbachev's continued reallocation of resources away from the military. As Poltoranin wryly recalled, the complaint came from the architects of the "idiotic action" in Afghanistan. The parliamentary committee looked at the army's complaint and decided that it displayed their ignorance of the new policy of *glasnost;* it was disallowed.[12]

Three years after the military decree, Oleg Dobrodeyev and Boris Nepomnyashchy sat in the office of the news chief at Ostankino and recalled their service in the battle for television. But of all the episodes they recalled, this was probably the least memorable—something of a very small-scale Potemkin Village: the military and the Party standing at the shore futilely inveighing against the information tide, while the military journalists collected their pay and sat idly by.

The military continued to find itself beleaguered and puzzled by its rapid descent from near-sacred status,[13] and particularly distressed by a growing problem with the youth and the adequacy of recruits. Defense Minister Yazov warned in the spring of 1990 that young men across the Soviet Union were evading the draft. Credit for this, he said, was partly the fault of "many mass media that, with a zeal worthy of a better cause, are 'debunking' the armed forces past and present," and disseminating the view that there was no external threat and military service was no longer necessary.[14]

When Leonid Kravchenko came to crack down on television the military was pleased. In January 1991, a few months after the Kravchenko regime had been installed at state television, A. V. Terentiev, chief of staff of the Transbaikal Military District sent messages to all units saying that with Kravchenko's arrival, a "change in the coverage of the activity of the USSR armed forces has taken place." It has become more "objective, truthful, and conducive to normal relations between the army and the people, and shows a true picture of the role and significance of the USSR armed forces in society." The unit commanders were told to send telegrams of support to Kravchenko.[15]

After the Soviet Union dissolved, the military still had not learned how to operate in a competitive media market in which private ownership protected press autonomy. As chapter 11 details, they misjudged the importance of a coherent and responsive information policy in the disastrously ill-prepared campaign in Chechnya. By withholding accreditation to true investigative journalists and issuing sporadic bulletins in Moscow, the ministries of defense and internal affairs believed they could control the media. At the end of 1994 and on into the winter of 1995, the decline of the Russian military was all too clear from the pictures transmitted from the battlefield of Chechnya by NTV, private television, and then Russian Television (Channel Two). There, the images of rosy-faced teenagers with all of six months' training gunned down or incinerated in that wintry hostile land exposed more than any television coverage or any newspaper articles had done before.

The disconnection of the high military leadership from this reality was stunning. Amid the carnage Defense Minister Pavel Grachev told television reporters that these young boys died "with a smile on their face" at the thought of giving up their lives for Russia, and that Sergei Kovalyov, the respected human rights champion was, in Stalin's much-used phrase, "an enemy of the people." The military had been quite right to see, in the liberalization of television, a direct threat to their hold on the myths and values of society. From the identity of the armed forces had come, for all those decades, the very definition of the nation. The graphic and horrifying pictures now told another story.

ICON TAMPERING: CULTURE AS FARCE

Perhaps the most closely watched target of all was Vladimir Lenin, the founder of the Soviet system and the bedrock of its legitimacy. Eldar Ryazanov was a burly outspoken film director who invoked Lenin in an affectionate but ambiguous fashion. In 1988 the outspoken Ryazanov collided with Sergei Kononykhin, and their encounter tells much about the minute details of oversight the Party exercised, and how difficult programming decisions could be.

Kononykhin was once a champion figure skater in the Soviet Union. He had a small, almost delicate frame, prim bearing, and disciplined speech. For his contributions to sport, Kononykhin was made head of the film department of state television, dictating what was shown and when.[16] In 1988 the program at issue was a four-part series on the popular "bard" Vladimir Vysotsky, whose death in 1980 was mourned by thousands streaming to his graveside, still a pilgrimage for young people. Frank and unafraid, Vysotsky's ballads were a virile appeal to youth when only poetry could communicate through the veils of censorship and control.

Nothing happened until the fourth program in the series, and then the order was given to cut seven and one-half minutes without telling Ryazanov. Normally he would have learned about the cuts from the early broadcasts on the "orbit" before it played in Moscow; Ryazanov and his production crew were at the Ostankino studio to preview the first orbit airing of the last Vysotsky segment, but that night the monitors were down. They were told it was routine maintenance, but somehow the downtime exactly coincided with the Vysotsky program. Some two hours before the program was to go on, Moscow time, one of the men in the production crew heard from an employee in the film department that cuts had been ordered. Enraged, Ryazanov called Kononykhin to find out what had happened. Kononykhin, assuming the most bureaucratic posture, told the director he had ordered the cuts; they were done most professionally and did not require either the services or knowledge of Ryazanov, and that it was a "technical thing." Ryazanov cursed and swore, while the former skater huffily retorted that he was not obliged to speak to someone who used such low language.

According to Ryazanov, what they cut was the "intellectual core" of the program: a discussion of the fates of Russia's greatest twentieth-century poets who had suffered under Communism. According to Ryazanov, to make matters worse, when the repeat was set to be aired, the overseer on duty the next morning had heard that seven and one-half minutes needed to be cut and, without checking whether or not the cuts had been made, cut still more. The bureaucrats kept telling Ryazanov that they had made only small cuts and really nothing had been lost. Ryazanov retorted bitterly: "By the way, when they make a man into a eunuch, they also cut very little." With these parting shots, Ryazanov quit his popular television show on new cinema and called for an end to censorship.[17]

That editing had occurred was undeniable, and that it was more than a "technical" time-saving device was also admitted by both sides. What exactly the censor's cuts were about tells us a good deal about what the apparatchiks thought they were mandated to regulate. One view came from

Marina Tarasova, then head of the Press Center of state television. She maintained that Ryazanov, though talented, was also extremely ambitious and overvalued his gifts. She thought it remarkable that the editors left in the ending where Ryazanov recited his own poems and attempted to establish himself in the company of the great twentieth-century poets, Osip Mandelstam and Boris Pasternak. Tarasova said the excellent film director was a very mediocre poet and "disappointed many viewers." It was proof of television's good will that they acceded to the director's wishes and neither cut the material nor "persuaded him to do something else." Unfortunately, she remarked bitterly, the press didn't cover this example of generosity.

I spoke to Sergei Kononykhin while the charges were being traded publicly and intellectuals in Moscow were talking about the scandal. Seated at a long table, his small, precise hands folded before him, the former skater provided a glimpse at the psychology of the television censor intent on keeping cultural icons properly preserved. First, though he took credit for the four Vysotsky programs, Ryazanov was not the only person involved. After all, Kononykhin said, "our department provided technical assistance, studio, honoraria, our editor, our director," and "naturally, there is a point of view we have a right to express." He recounted what went on in that long conversation when Ryazanov was asked to shorten the episodes. He told the movie director that some parts of the series hadn't been thought out; some were ambiguous and banal; some were not very interesting. Ryazanov was a "maximalist—for all or nothing, and state television did not go in for ultimatums."

It was clearly the content that bothered Kononykhin.[18] First was Ryazanov's approach to military service—negative and "antipatriotic." The cuts were not inappropriate, the official said, because they had nothing to do with Vysotsky's creative output—the subject of the piece. The armed forces were still irritated. Mikhail Gorbachev recalled that Defense Minister Dmitry Yazov complained in a Politburo meeting that "For four days television talks exclusively about Vysotsky and his sketches. And what has Vysotsky done? What has he actually done? Whenever I visit army units I am asked with surprise, what heroic deed has Vysotsky actually performed? My opinion, Mikhail Sergeyevich, is that we should guide and lead the press."[19]

The really flagrant and even more serious mistake was a joke about Lenin—one that actually cast Lenin in a favorable light. Kononykhin was too cautious and too doctrinaire to see that; he only perceived that Lenin seemed to be taken lightly, and the reference to the name that could still be uttered only reverentially was somehow in the wrong key.

The anecdote told of Lenin and his culture minister A. V. Lunacharsky looking at a display of modern art. They saw some circles and squares, something very strange, some completely white canvases, and Lenin turned to Lunacharsky and said, "'Anatoly Vasilievich, do you understand anything?' Lunacharsky answered, 'Vladimir Ilych, honestly I don't understand a thing.'"[20] And they both tiptoed out of the hall. "That was the last Soviet government that didn't understand art."

Ryazanov was praising Lenin for what he considered a tolerance and modesty that no subsequent "omniscient" government would ever display. Kononykhin, on the other hand, kept saying to me that Lenin *did* know a great deal about art and so did many people in his government, that Ryazanov was not an expert in literary or cultural history: he had spoken without respect and without sufficient knowledge, and his words were superfluous, insulting, and antihistorical. Furthermore, the tortured logic continued, since this was a documentary, viewers would expect truth, not some kind of artistic fantasy. Thus, it was even more reason to impart only what was fact and not conjecture. The scissors were applied.

In state television's press center, Marina Tarasova said that if Ryazanov had added the word "claim," the piece would not have been cut; if the anecdote said: "This was the last Soviet government that did not *claim* to understand art," all would have been solved. Standards of accuracy would have been upheld, and, as she put it, the editor was interested in "improving product quality, not in censorship." It is hardly likely that at the time Ryazanov could have taken on Lenin with anything other than worshipful simplicity. "Claim" would not have ended the standoff.

As for the "intellectual core"—the conversation about the smothered poets whose works were coming out only generations after their deaths— that was an easy call for Kononykhin. In the program, Ryazanov had said that "as a rule, generally our poets for some reason do not live long," and named Alexander Blok, Sergei Esenin, Vladimir Mayakovsky, Osip Mandelstam, Anna Akhmatova, Nikolai Gumilev, Marina Tsvetayeva, and Boris Pasternak. There was a "fatal inevitability" about their deaths under communism.

Once again, Ryazanov—in a documentary—had got his facts jumbled by saying that a whole pleiad of poets had died young. No, Kononykhin fastidiously pointed out, Pasternak and Akhmatova did not die at an early age, while Gumilev, Blok, Tsvetayeva, and Mandelstam did. The film department had to be exacting in its standards for accuracy, and besides, the slight bureaucrat continued, all of this was tangential to the subject, anyway. No great need to keep it—out came the scissors.

It was better to be safe when one was on slippery ground and *glasnost* was not yet codified. This was a department at state television that chose the path of defensive resistance to reform. At virtually the same time in another department, under a quite different leadership, the same political overseers were kept at bay—not permanently, to be sure, but long enough for the viewing public to have witnessed something entirely new.

A curious element of this whole episode bears notice: all that Ryazanov had to say, and for which he was censored and had his work cut without his approval or even knowledge, was published in the pages of *Ogonyok* and the newspaper *Soviet Culture*. What was absolutely off limits for television was perfectly acceptable for print media.[21] The impact of print was judged to be much slighter and much more narrowly targeted to intellectuals.

In a cynical appreciation of the process, it was clear to the Kremlin that this group was already aware of the profound problems of Soviet power and that it could be appeased by "its" media. The larger public, the public that could be mobilized, possibly beyond containment, was the audience for television, and levees had to be set up on the information banks. The very popular *Ogonyok* could count about two million readers, while the audience for television could reach 180 to 200 million.

Sergei Kononykhin ruled over his department until Yegor Yakovlev came to head state television after the 1991 putsch. Yakovlev defended his removal of the skater as simply common sense: "Let's say a sports announcer Kononykhin headed a film program studio. Is that rational? So, I honestly said to him: with all my respect, you are less valuable than those film masters who, because of you, do not want to work with us. To me, Ryazanov's participation in the work of the company is more important because the author is always more important than those who serve him."[22]

In Soviet times, the guards at the checkpoints of television liberalization were indeed numerous, and, to varying degrees, effective. That effectiveness, in turn, depended on a number of factors, not the least of which was the way people in charge of departments chose to act. In the youth department, unlike the film department, individuals encountered limits in the institutions they sought to change, but took risks and persistently worked at reforms that would startle viewers and set a model for the medium after Soviet power ended.

CHAPTER FOUR

Pushing the Envelope: Reforming from Within

The rules of the game had changed relatively little for state television's film department and its doctrinaire head, but another department and its leader behaved in an altogether different fashion. In part, it was a question of exceptional leadership groups; in part the difference was structural: the target of their programming was youth. The Kremlin was deeply agitated by the possible loss of the replacement generation to the styles and worldview of the West. Young people were effectively opting out of the Soviet future, and the Gorbachev administration was determined to utilize its most powerful asset, television.

In his speeches about the new information policy, Mikhail Gorbachev sought to maintain his power coalition by speaking to both sides of the issue of the foreign information assault: a more professional, more responsive media system could compete more effectively with the more vigorous and intrusive West—a West that was stepping up transmissions aimed at urban Soviet youth. But he also struck the antireform note: the Soviet Union's media must remain vigilant to unmask bourgeois propaganda and counter its effects.[1]

Cloaking the reform process in a security rationale was one method of justifying the changes before the more conservative reformers in the Politburo. Accordingly, in 1986, a group from a wide range of Academy of Sciences institutes, Communist Party Central Committee experts, specialists in counter-propaganda from the Novosti Press Agency, TASS, and several news publications, and officials from the Central Committees of the Communist Parties of Armenia, Georgia, and Estonia rated television fare in terms of its contribution to counteracting Western propaganda. (Estonia received Western television via linguistically-related Finland.) They agreed

that the struggle for the minds of Soviet youth was one of the most important fronts in the battle of ideologies. "Soviet young men and women have
become the object of massive propaganda by Western radio stations: specialists calculate that programs for youth occupy first place among the
broadcasts addressed to various social groups of our society," observed the
report. "Bourgeois propaganda attempts to implant standards of its image of
life, dull the class consciousness of Soviet youth, and lead them to skepticism, political apathy, and permissiveness."[2]

Clearly, here were hard-line sentiments with which Yegor Ligachev could
heartily agree, but the solution to the problem was something Alexander
Yakovlev, not Yegor Ligachev, would support. Under the umbrella of a national security need which was defined, class based, and adversarial, reform
could be justified. National television should be the chosen instrument, because it was the most effective instrument for counter-propaganda, 97 percent of the group concluded. Eighty-six percent thought newspapers most
important. In contrast, only 15 percent thought republic-level television and
19 percent thought republic-level newspapers were effective. The counter-
propaganda experts determined that a show called *12th Floor* exemplified
"innovation in Soviet television," "truthfulness," "political sharpness," "boldness in presentation of problems," and "attention to real life."[3]

12TH FLOOR

In 1986, when the Kremlin turned to television to stem the tide of youthful defections from its version of the Soviet future, Eduard Sagalayev was in
charge of the youth department of Ostankino. His early work had been in
Uzbekistan, where he was born in 1946. He started in newspaper work
there and then went to the Moscow headquarters of the Communist Youth
League (in "agitation and propaganda"), and then to state television in
Moscow. In many ways, this story of reforms tried and failed, of innovations born and choked, is the story of Sagalayev's leadership and the
boundaries of bureaucratic norms and powers. As he mused in 1992, "I was
not on Gorbachev's team, but I also wasn't on Yeltsin's. I'm an outsider for
them, not least because I was not born in Russia. I was told that in very
high offices they would discuss [me]: how come this half-Uzbek, half-Jew,
born in Samarkand, is in charge of Russian television?"[4] Early in 1996,
Sagalayev's department ran a remarkable television show. Correspondent
Vladimir Pozner sat down with wonderfully articulate British schoolchildren to argue politics. Later in the program, Pozner took on Serge Schmemann, then *New York Times* bureau chief in Moscow. This debate was more
nearly equal, and two thoroughly opposing points of view emerged with
great clarity. A real debate with real opposition of political positions was

new for Soviet viewers and could not have been achieved without a prior breakthrough.

During the first winter of the Gorbachev administration, Pozner and Phil Donahue, the popular U.S. talk show host, taped a live, interactive discussion via satellite hookup (called a "space bridge") between a studio audience in Seattle and one in Moscow. The "Citizens' Summit" was contentious and candid. Pozner pitched the program to his bosses at a meeting in January 1986. Alexander Aksyonov, head of state television, presided, with his deputies and a representative of the Party's Central Committee present. They previewed the tape in total silence, Pozner recalled. Aksyonov first queried his deputy Alexander Yevstavyev, who thought it "needed work." In any case, it should not be shown before the approaching twenty-seventh Congress of the Communist Party, and even then, it should be shunted off to the St. Petersburg channel. The Central Committee emissary disagreed; he pronounced the program "real television," what television should be. Aksyonov took his cue and ordered the program to be shown as a "gift to the Party Congress." Pozner learned later that Gorbachev (and Alexander Yakovlev) had seen it and authorized the broadcast, as the Party *apparat*'s man at that "decision-making" meeting knew full well. Back in 1979, when Yakovlev was ambassador to Canada, Pozner had been a guest on five television shows in Toronto. According to Pozner, Yakovlev invited him to Ottawa, where they talked at length. Yakovlev's approval of the space bridge resulted in Pozner's promotion and permission to take the trip to Scotland to talk to children on the BBC's *Open Question* show.[5]

Eduard Sagalayev, with a sense of the new generation, its dissatisfactions, and its alienation, launched the politically boldest television show yet, *12th Floor* (where youth department offices were located). What made the show unusual was its inclusion, for the first time on Soviet television, of the genuine voice of young people secure *on their own turf*, and they challenged the old verities and the officials in the studio. *12th Floor* was an unruly innovation. Nearly nine years later, Sagalayev looked back on his career and said that at the time he was clearly conscious that the experiment he was planning would be a "big breakthrough in public opinion."

Sagalayev maintained that none of his superiors knew in advance what he planned. Since his appointment to head the youth division required approval by the Central Committee of the Communist Party (the job was on their *nomenklatura* list) and since he had served as ideology official in the Central Committee of the Communist Youth League, he had automatically acquired the right to substitute his approval for that of higher authorities. Sagalayev could sign on two lines authorizing broadcast of programs—one for approval as chief editor and one for approval as censor. He asserted that he gained the prior consent of neither Mikhail Gorbachev nor Alexander Yakovlev, nor anyone in charge of television.[6]

Sagalayev also avoided advance scrutiny by providing his superiors with only the blandest of summaries of planned broadcasts. He would write, for example, that the next show would look at "youth and ecology," while manipulating the system and subverting the formalized, rigid structure of authority and control through which he himself had so rapidly advanced. But Sagalayev knew very well he could produce sensational new experiments only a certain number of times. The institutionalized hierarchy that permitted him to seize the day a first time would also, after "once or twice or ten times," eventually react.

Seated in the television studio were Sagalayev and officials from the government bureaucracies that most affected the lives of young people. Teenagers talked back from the safety of their stairwells and streets. Quite deliberately, Sagalayev wanted to give them the freedom of expression and ease he knew would be lost if they were shepherded into the daunting television studio. Picked up by remote cameras, the young people challenged officials; they told education officials that "very little happens in school"; that "they talk about duties, but you don't hear anything about rights." They argued for the restoration of proscribed writers and wanted to know more about the West. They challenged the deputy minister of education to confess that he knew nothing about new methods of teaching, and complained that their textbooks were hopelessly out of date. In every show, the plaint of the youth was repeated: "Why are things decided on top and not here?"[7] And, most important, the censors were hamstrung because it was all broadcast *live*.

Inside the power structure, the response to *12th Floor* was immediate. The head of television called Sagalayev in alarm after the program was shown the first time. According to Sagalayev, Alexander Aksyonov asked him who had authorized the show and Sagalayev responded that "as a Communist" he understood what Party policy required. In turn, Aksyonov warned him that "they will have our heads for this." Sagalayev then sat down to wait for the inevitable calls from the Central Committee, but no one called. His conclusion was that each official thought another had approved the program.

The press praised Gorbachev for launching *12th Floor*. After the second episode, the poet Andrei Voznesensky wrote that it was a beacon to young people against the bureaucracy. The program engaged in confrontations, attacking first the education establishment and then the Party youth organization leadership while encouraging grass roots efforts to outflank the bureaucrats—a goal quite consistent with the Gorbachev agenda.

Sagalayev directly opposed institutions controlling youth socialization and mobility, including the Academy of Pedagogical Science, the Committee on Trade Education, and the Ministry of Education. He claimed that Education Minister Shcherbakov was removed because of the program. In the fall of 1987, *12th Floor* was suspended. It came back on the air in May 1988, but as a weak copy with a changed format and it was canceled again.

Sagalayev later explained that after the first editions aired, the deputy heads of state television began to require it to be taped in advance, and in Sagalayev's words, "the sharpest parts were cut." Yegor Ligachev came to Ostankino and complained about the program. Incredulously, he asked Sagalayev where he found those young people. Had he got them out of jails? Ligachev said that there simply were no such young people in the Soviet Union and advised Sagalayev to do some programs about the Komsomol. With such clear pressure from the Party's ideology chief and the new requirement that the program be vetted and cut, Sagalayev understood that he had to end the program. He was the one who closed down *12th Floor.*

Very shortly, with appreciation from the Party leadership for his compromising and flexible stance, Eduard Sagalayev was named head of the television news department, the country's official information nerve center. While *12th Floor* was off the air and before he went off to the news department, Sagalayev and his youth programming team were exploring a new program, *Vzglyad* (Viewpoint), which was to become the most successful and controversial of the era.

VZGLYAD: NEW MODELS AND THE NEW PROFESSIONALS

In October 1987, the youth department started a late-night weekend show that had been in the works since 1985.[8] It looked radically different from any show on television and it was to become the single most popular program of the Gorbachev era. It launched the careers of its stars, who remained at the top of the ratings charts in post-Soviet Russia, and pushed the bounds of freedom of speech well beyond the Party's toleration. The show careered wildly between popular acclaim and censored blackout. The team of young people who ran it never knew what lay ahead, and their brash confidence and the support of their department kept them going.

According to Anatoly Lysenko, television journalist in the youth programming division of state television and later the deputy head of Channel Two, he had waited ten years to develop a show that would be casual and inviting to viewers. It would have the easy conversation of a chat around a kitchen table; the moderators would talk about political issues, interspersing conversation with music; and the mode of discourse would be altogether new: unaffected and natural.[9] At the same time, Alexander Yakovlev informed television officials that jamming was to be stopped, and he warned them that to compete successfully with the West there would have to be good programs for young people, morning and evening. Two new, live shows were developed: an early morning news and music program called "60 Minutes" (later expanded to two hours and called *Utro* [Morning]) and the late-night *Vzglyad*.

Four new faces were brought in from the foreign division of Radio Moscow to host the late-night program. Alexander Lyubimov was one, and he quickly became a major star in Soviet and then post-Soviet Russian television. Another, Vlad Listyev, made his later career in game shows, talk shows, and briefly (until he was murdered) as head of Ostankino state television. Precisely because the foreign division's broadcasts were not heard at home, there was relatively greater freedom of expression.[10] Moreover, the foreign division broadcast to listeners who had a variety of choices in a competitive environment.

Later, in the fall of 1991, Listyev went on to start a quiz show that looked like the American show *Wheel of Fortune* and a talk show that looked like *Larry King Live*. Listyev said at the time that although he looked at various foreign models, the underlying concept was purely Russian.[11] Mikhail Nenashev did not think the team was inspired by Russian models. He believed that having spent many years abroad, "often they tried to measure many domestic problems with a Western yardstick, strenuously thrusting on our fatherland opinions born on alien soil."[12] The meaning of America had become an essential part of the country's understanding of television and of itself.

Reviewing the birth of *Vzglyad,* Eduard Sagalayev said that it was entirely coincidental that the team of young hosts was drawn from foreign radio. His idea was to present young viewers with people with whom they could identify—a Soviet version of the Beatles. He wanted to find four friends who would look more like the young people they would address and be able to talk the same new slang. He wanted "thinking boys," not those perfectly groomed Komsomol figureheads made of concrete. He wanted "rebels," a "new mentality." He dismissed the fact that they were all drawn from Western radio as having no importance. After all, these kids "were against the West; they did counter-propaganda on the radio."[13] Whatever the intentions, whatever the justification at the time and later, the fact remains that a quartet of young men, each with a thorough knowledge of a foreign Western language and some knowledge of Western audiences, produced a revolutionary new television message and the Soviet public responded.

Sasha Lyubimov recalled that in 1987 he was invited by Eduard Sagalayev and Anatoly Lysenko to take charge of a new program with a new concept.[14] They had the right man. Lyubimov and his copresenters were young, attractive, brash, deeply engaged in the political scene, but—addressing it with sharp-witted observations—mostly ironic or sarcastic, quite a change from wheezing agitprop discourse. In November 1987 the team decided to call the show *Vzglyad* (Viewpoint—the Russian word also means a glance, and both meanings were intended to signal a rapid-fire, glancing contact with many controversial positions).

With irreverent young hosts in sweatshirts, the excitement of live television that appeared uncensored, and the rapid-fire cutting from interviews and information to rock music, the show took off and soon rose to the top of the poll rankings. Relations among the young stars were often tense, as ambitions clashed and they jockeyed for prominence. The new television bred colossal egos.

Vzglyad became popular. The demographics told the story: *Vzglyad*'s viewers were the movers and shakers of the new future, better educated, younger, and more urban than average viewers, while *Vremya*'s audience was older, less well educated, and more rural than average.[15] This was a warning to the Kremlin. Though there was still no competition for the official news program in its time slot, the public had begun to heed a very different, competing messenger. The public, whose preferences had been of so little interest to officials, was clearly becoming differentiated and not only by the usual demographic measures but also politically, and the large audiences made *Vzglyad* more vulnerable. Lyubimov said that for three months in 1988 he did absolutely nothing, while the show was suspended. In February 1989, *Vzglyad* startled the audience by showing an interview with an Afghan student who told viewers that the Soviet-supported regime of Najibullah was in a miserable position. Within days, the last of the Soviet troops would be home from that unpopular war.

When youth department head Eduard Sagalayev moved up to run the news programs in January 1989, the fortunes of *Vzglyad* rapidly declined. A week later, another Afghan student made an appearance on *Vzglyad,* this time reading a prepared text contradicting the points made by the dissident student interviewed earlier.[16] For the conservative camp, contained change was essential; openness was justified only to the degree that the system itself was not culpable and workable solutions could be implemented. *Vzglyad* was off the air the next week.

It returned the first week in March. In mid-March, the show was again explosive. Journalist Mikhail Poltoranin, one of Boris Yeltsin's closest associates and later a key member of his government, accused state television of fabricating viewers' questions to embarrass Yeltsin in his parliamentary campaign debate with opponent Evgeny Brakov, a factory director.[17] The program was in trouble again the next month, when it was prevented from showing a videotape of troops attacking unarmed citizens in Tbilisi, the capital of Soviet Georgia.

On April 21, 1989, Mark Zakharov, a well-known theater and movie director and head of the first theater company to renounce state subsidies (and thereby, he hoped, state censorship), appeared on the program. Host Vladimir Mukusev remarked that cosmonauts come to see Lenin before a flight into space, and he wondered if Lenin would have approved of the icon into which Soviet rule had transformed him. How could the historical Lenin be fitted to this legacy congealed in portraits and pins and songs and mental genuflection before the bier on Red Square? The discussion was apt, for that day was the 119th anniversary of Lenin's birth.

Zakharov, after ticking off Lenin's contributions, including his "boldness in changing course," offered this view: "You can hate a person as much as you like, or love him as much as you like, to the point of distraction, but we do not have the right to deprive a human body of burial, imitating the ancient pagans. . . . Even the pagans, the barbarians, bade farewell to a person just once."[18] This remarkable celebration of the Lenin holiday and challenge to the most potent of political symbols slipped by the censors because Vladimir Mukusev instructed Zakharov not to speak about Lenin on the first orbit beamed to the Soviet Far East. Seeing nothing unusual in the program, the censors let the Moscow orbit proceed live.

The Kremlin was caught by surprise and incensed by Zakharov's addition to the Moscow orbit. Politburo ideology chief Vadim Medvedev came to state television to meet for more than two hours with the *Vzglyad* group, and on May 16 Alexander Aksyonov was removed from his job as head of state television, ostensibly to retire. Just before, on April 27, Aksyonov had been summoned to the Central Committee plenum, where the scandalized *apparat* was after his head for permitting the most egregious sacrilege. The humiliated television chief took responsibility, though he had been a largely absentee and weak leader, content to have more aggressive deputies run his shop. He told Party leaders that the main problem was with anchors and hosts of public affairs programs, those who take "*glasnost,* openness and democracy in their own way and under their flag" push their extremist positions on behalf of reform. Most troubling of all, since the program went on live, Aksyonov had been unable to interdict the offending passage.[19] Mukusev became the target of virulent letters that purported to be from all over the country, but some contained information that was known only to his superiors at state television. A particularly nasty one said: "How dare you, you son of a bitch, snot, on the birthday of the greatest of great people—Lenin—invite two scrofulous Yids . . . functionary, double-crosser, jerk."[20]

The Zakharov-Lenin affair stunned the Kremlin as well as the viewers, to whom Lenin's name was off-limits to criticism of any kind. (As we shall see in chapter 9, what can be tolerated in discussing the founder of the Soviet state is a kind of marker, telling us much about the limits of free speech and people's views, both those of media elites and ordinary viewers.)

In the fall of 1989, *Vzglyad,* always testing the waters and pushing for greater press freedoms, had arranged for a live interview with Andrei Sakharov. Sakharov told the press that political officials called him at home to "disinvite" him and the *Vzglyad* team was ordered to cancel the Sakharov appearance. The show that went out on October 13 did not have Sakharov participating in a discussion of Afghanistan and did not, contrary to previous practice, go out live to the Moscow time zone; it had been taped so that censorship could be applied, and the young hosts informed their viewers.

By the end of 1989, *Vzglyad* commanded the loyalty of most television viewers. By a wide margin it was the most popular show in the entire Soviet Union. It was also the top choice for 62 percent of Communist Party members, 73 percent of the college educated (and 71 percent of high school graduates), and 71 percent of viewers under sixty.[21] No official rationale invoking viewer disaffection could possibly be believed.

Official reasons for "suspending" the program scheduled for the end of December 1989 were couched in quite defensible language. Management, mindful of the approaching holiday season and to foster good cheer in the New Year, decided to reduce political programs and put on more smiling entertainment. That temporizing language had little credibility, when, after the New Year celebrations, *Vzglyad* was still a thorn in the side of television officialdom. Individual editions were suspended; the time slot was moved; and pressure was exerted on the youthful team to break up. Utilizing a new and unanticipated weapon, they invoked parliamentary privilege. As a result of the first competitive elections to the Russian parliament, all of *Vzglyad*'s hosts were elected deputies, proving both the value of television exposure for these young activists as well as the importance of parliamentary immunity. Vladimir Mukusev acknowledged that his new deputy status enabled him to defend the guests who appeared on the program to go where as a journalist he was forbidden to enter.[22]

Vzglyad's attention to the tragic events in Tbilisi still rankled officials. With their increasing political influence, the military voiced the opinion that *Vzglyad* should be taken off the air. On the broadcast of December 7, 1990, host Vlad Listyev read a memorandum he said was being circulated to servicemen by Colonel-General Rodionov, commander of the Transcaucasian military district during the bloodshed in Georgia. Rodionov wrote: "The program *Vzglyad* should be taken off the state television channel," and he charged that "the mass information media [that are] engaged in discrediting the army and in the production of provocative and mendacious programs and publications should be brought to book."[23]

The precipitating event did relate to Tbilisi, but from another direction. At a session of parliament on December 20, 1990, Eduard Shevardnadze resigned from his post as foreign minister and parted with Gorbachev in an emotional farewell that warned of approaching dictatorship. The next day, in a separate action, Gennady Yanayev was chosen vice president. For Lyubimov and his *Vzglyad* team, the most important event of the week was the Shevardnadze resignation. The top officials at state television argued that Yanayev's appointment was more important.

Vzglyad put forward a compromise: they would do both subjects. According to Lyubimov, they started working on getting material about the new vice president and found out about Yanayev's alcoholism during his years in the Communist Youth League. The Shevardnadze coverage still was not approved. The *Vzglyad* team threatened to quit. Their hands were tied, and besides, Shevardnadze refused to appear in their studio to do the program about his resignation. The former foreign minister did agree to send his two closest aides: Sergei Tarasenko and Teimuras Stepanov,[24] and the young producers attempted to gain approval for this variant, but at each stage they were stymied, first by the head of news and information, then by the deputy chairman of state television, and finally by Leonid Kravchenko, the chairman. The *Vzglyad* team countered that since they could not get an interview with Shevardnadze they would repeat an earlier program when they interviewed the foreign minister aboard his plane, but Kravchenko disallowed it as a "provocation." *Vzglyad* initiated a lawsuit against Kravchenko. Depositions were taken from officials at state television, including Kravchenko. By the time of the August 1991 coup attempt it was still dragging on, but then it became moot.

During the long suspension, before the final cancellation notice, Vladmir Mukusev was invited by Sagalayev, now combining the presidency of the new Soviet Cable Association with his role as news chief, to produce an alternative *Vzglyad* for the nascent cable industry. As Mukusev put it, the father of *Vzglyad* was still moving his progeny forward. Mukusev credits Sagalayev's administration of the youth department for his own intellectual and moral development. When they did *The World and Youth,* took risks, and had programs canceled, Sagalayev would give them an award. Mukusev described the Sagalayev school: "Fight, draw blood, let them beat you up, I will always cover you."

An acid commentary on the *Vzglyad* controversy came from Pyotr Reshetov. It was Reshetov who, on January 9, 1991, willingly took the heat and officially suspended production and broadcast of the program. As usual, the head of television was reluctant to sign the orders, preferring not to leave a paper trail. Leonid Kravchenko later justified the decision by invoking Gorbachev's television decree forbidding the use of television for partisan political views.[25] As two of the show's hosts, Vlad Listyev and Alexander Politkovsky, remarked, not a single written document about their show had ever been issued by the director of state television; directives had always come orally.[26] Reshetov had no such compunction. According to Reshetov, *Vzglyad* was the last straw for President Gorbachev. "I got orders ten times to close it." Throughout the program's controversial tenure, Reshetov's boss, Mikhail Nenashev repeatedly called and asked: "This time are you going to close it or not?" On Fridays, everyone waited to see if it was canceled.

Reshetov argued that he did not want to close it down, but his approach to saving the program involved censoring it thoroughly. Though *Vzglyad* went on the air live—that was its great attraction in the early days of open-ness—Reshetov attempted to censor it even then. He watched the first orbit and then invited the *Vzglyad* hosts to see him. The conversation always had the same form: he was going to take the program off the air for the next orbits unless changes were made and "problems solved." Reshetov eventually required tapes ahead of time, because, he said, promises to fix the problems were not kept.

When *Vzglyad* was finally pulled off the air, it had become possible to find makeshift alternative, though limited, outlets. Bella Kurkova at Leningrad television's *Fifth Wheel* program offered airtime. The *Vzglyad* team made videocassettes of their programs and distributed them to Lithuania, Latvia, Estonia, Georgia, Armenia, and Siberia, where they were run on small new independent stations. According to *Vzglyad* estimates (probably high), they were still reaching some twenty million households.[27]

Vzglyad continued its underground battle for the attention of the public, and, fittingly, during the siege of the Russian White House in the summer of 1991, *Vzglyad* cameras were turning, and when it was over there was a detailed record for broadcast on a liberated television channel. When more routine times returned, *Vzglyad*'s uniqueness and originality were less and less visible. Their causes had been joined by others, and a weary public was ready for Vlad Listyev's new enterprise, *Wheel of Fortune,*—Moscow style. With shrewd diversification, the *Vzglyad* production corporation (called VID—Vzglyad and Others) had done well, but the show itself faced the kind of competition it had done so much to make possible.

Thinking back, Pyotr Reshetov had no quarrel with Lyubimov's version of the battle over *Vzglyad,* and no second thoughts about the decision to end it. "I did not personally like Shevardnadze's position. I knew him from before, when he was first secretary of the Komsomol of Georgia. I went there. I knew he was a demagogue." Reshetov and Gennady Yanayev (the vice president with the shaking hands) were also officials of the youth organization. About the Shevardnadze resignation story, Reshetov asserted, "I was against the explanation of Shevardnadze's resignation given in the program. We were far from a revolt and also far from dictatorship. The putsch was nothing but a political game involving Gorbachev."

Vadim Medvedev, the Kremlin's ideology chief, had grappled with *Vzglyad,* but was gone by the time it was firmly closed down. He cautiously acknowledged that "there were discussions of balance and accuracy with Lyubimov."[28]

A year after the coup attempt, Leonid Kravchenko remarked that it was still painful to recall the events surrounding the cancellation of *Vzglyad.* He faulted the program's producers for the bait-and-switch tactic of deliberately sending out politically neutral material in the early orbits and then inserting the controversial subjects in the last, Moscow, version. Ruefully,

Kravchenko reminisced, "I made one serious mistake." He did not realize that removing *Vzglyad* from the airwaves would "result in giving VID huge capital." Quickly, Kravchenko added that "Reshetov always convinced me to do the wrong thing."

Eduard Sagalayev, in whose shop the famous experiment began, believed that Gorbachev was involved in the decision to close the program. He was opposed to *Vzglyad,* and wanted to end it. But, typically, he did not want to leave traces or directly make decisions. Instead, said Sagalayev, Gorbachev told his conservative Kremlin partners, "Decide, yourself," knowing which decision it would be.[29]

PROZHEKTOR PERESTROIKI (SPOTLIGHT OF PERESTROIKA)

In 1988, *Braking in the Skies* packed a downtown Moscow theater every night. The title referred both to a plane forced to abort its takeoff and to the stagnation and decay suffocating reform. The plot unfolds in a town beyond the Urals. Mikhail Gorbachev has just concluded a visit to mobilize support for his reform program. The local party and government leaders wave good-bye and then resolve to undermine the reform initiative. They intend to continue enjoying the fruits of their corruption in spite of a young schoolteacher's accusation of fraud and abuse of power. Suddenly two television journalists rush in to claim the cameras inadvertently left behind and rush to the plane to deliver the footage for the next edition of *Vremya,* the prime-time news program. Only a little boy notices that all the while the red light had been on and the camera recorded the whole truth. With great effort, but to no avail, the local obstructionists attempt to order the plane to return.

In this play, the path of reform is ever skyward; the television camera records the truth; the forces of reaction are undone. But the news department did not work that way. It was much more resistant to change than was the youth department. The news was at the center of the Kremlin's attention; it was what framed it and projected the symbols of its rule.

Tampering with the news was therefore a very risky strategy, and Alexander Yakovlev chose to introduce his policy agenda in a short daily show right after *Vremya.* The people in the news department at state television regarded *Prozhektor Perestroiki* (Spotlight of Perestroika) as "completely" the idea of Alexander Yakovlev in order to have a platform for his policies, even when Yegor Ligachev was in charge of ideology and mass media.[30] With some disdain, adversary Ligachev later remarked that Yakovlev was wont to exaggerate his role.[31] Mikhail Gorbachev, in a memoir of over a thousand pages, places Yakovlev at critical times and in critical planning sessions close to himself, but downplays the seminal role of his associate. Yakovlev's refusal to support Gorbachev upon the latter's return from his Crimean captivity was especially bitter to the weakened Soviet leader.[32]

According to those who worked in news at the time, Yakovlev presented a number of story ideas for specific programs. Even though Yegor Ligachev was the secretary of ideology at the time and could "dictate the music," as one official recalls, *Prozhektor* gave Yakovlev the chance to get his views across to the nation even when he was subordinate to Ligachev. Leonid Kravchenko, television's second in command at the time, also took credit for creating the new program "together with" Yakovlev.

In August 1987, the first *Prozhektor* aired, and it produced immediate results. The well-known correspondent Alexander Tikhomirov was host and Alexander Krutov (the first reporter into Chernobyl) reported from Vladivostok. The ten-minute program about substandard housing construction was a concentrated lesson in civic activism, intended to mobilize ordinary people to gain their rights from an unheeding bureaucracy. The first *Prozhektor* showed life in the port city, with housing so scarce and in such disrepair sailors from ships berthed there could not find a place to live and had taken to living on board. To stimulate housing construction, local building officials promised workers they could have 25 percent of any housing they built above the plan. The workers did produce above-quota housing, but were rebuffed by the officials. On the inaugural *Prozhektor,* the workers complained on-camera of their loss of faith in the system. Tikhomirov recalled that the Party reacted immediately and the Soviet minister of construction flew to Vladivostok the next day to explain to local officials that they had to fulfill their obligation.[33]

Alexander Tikhomirov, the public image of the *Prozhektor* project, pushed the rules early. An imposing, magnetic man, he had the title of political observer at state television. There were only about twenty-five political observers (four in domestic news), and they had special status. They could pick their own subjects, form their own production crews and receive larger honoraria. They were the proto-stars in a system that formally eschewed the star system. Tikhomirov had worked at state television since the early 1960s and had covered space issues since the early 1970s. In the spring of 1985, when Konstantin Chernenko, the infirm interim Soviet leader, died, Tikhomirov saw an opening. He went to the television administration with an idea to do a series of news stories from a train as it moved across the country. Since he pitched it as "greeting the twenty-seventh Party Congress," the project was accepted. The minister of transportation provided the train car and Tikhomirov was off.

Prozhektor carried the idea further. The program roamed all over the Soviet Union, identifying grievances of ordinary people and pressing for redress. In one program, a bulldozer was about to destroy a historic building.

The local historian and architect urged the town's citizens to mobilize; the bulldozer operator admitted he had no idea what he was tearing down, he was just following orders.

According to deputy news director Oleg Dobrodeyev, *Prozhektor* ended when Yegor Ligachev had enough and said, "it had began to babble." Alexander Yakovlev lamented that he created the show but the program died without him: "It was closed without me and without asking me." The government had persuaded Gorbachev to cancel it, he said, and Gorbachev did it without even consulting his colleague.[34]

In the fall of 1993, Alexander Tikhomirov, looking back, was inclined to agree with the view attributed to Yegor Ligachev: the program had indeed declined. There were too many hosts of *Prozhektor,* and they all thought they could do the job equally well. And he did not see his level of quality in their work. "A program cannot be eternal," he said.[35]

The end of *Prozhektor* came during Eduard Sagalayev's tenure in the news department. Sagalayev said he canceled the program because it had begun to sound like *Pravda.* The typical "reformist" story in that hard-line paper would identify a "bad shop foreman" who stalls initiative and progress. Then the story would take this low-level example of malfeasance or abuse of power and seek small-scale redress. All of it would stand as a model of self-criticism and improvement. Sagalayev and Tikhomirov saw that *Prozhektor* had become just that. When Sagalayev closed it down, he knew it was Kravchenko's "favorite child," but by then Kravchenko had left television to head TASS, the Soviet news agency. Sagalayev made his case to Mikhail Nenashev, then head of television, saying, "*Prozhektor* is repeating itself daily and there have already been about one hundred shows. All it shows is why the factory works badly." Nenashev agreed; together they ended the program.

TSN

The evening news program *Vremya* had to be handled with great care. Rather than a radical overhaul of *Vremya* (a politically hazardous move), Eduard Sagalayev started a parallel news program broadcast late at night. Far more modern than *Vremya,* it was staffed by and addressed to a more youthful and urbane public. Premiering on January 1, 1990, *TSN* (Television News Service) was a snappy, almost telegraphic, rundown of the news in the style of CNN's *Headline News.* Its broadcasts included as many visuals as possible (much of it CNN footage), young anchors with personable demeanors (if less than perfect diction), and extremely fast-paced styles, a notable change from the measured elocution of *Vremya's* newsreaders. It came on at 10:45 P.M., Monday through Thursday, and at 11:45 P.M. on Friday. The next year the late edition began at midnight. The broadcast averaged from ten to twenty minutes, far shorter than *Vremya*'s forty minutes or more. The tone was chatty and more intimate. News clips often followed each other quickly, with no bridging explanation from the anchor, and a clip from a rock video generally ended the program. For the first time in Soviet newscasts, the single host was seen in tight, American-style closeup, and instead of reading from the typescript on the desk, read from a Teleprompter. (Teleprompters were not in use on the 9:00 P.M. official news, in part because they were new and in part because the newsreaders often had long official documents and statements to read, and any mistake brought disciplinary phone calls.)

The *TSN* anchors also dared to personalize their observations. A story on celebrity gossip began with the anchor's observation: "On my way to work tonight, I noticed they were selling *Playboy* at the subway newsstand." Leading into a story on a fire in Moscow, the anchor said, "Many of you have called asking about the fire. . . ."

Both the choice of stories and the approach were lighter, involved the human interest items so noticeably lacking in the 9:00 P.M. news, and played much more to audience interest. Its young team soon became "news stars" in the Western manner.

Tatyana Mitkova and Dmitry Kiselyov were *TSN* anchors, but most of the program was not talking heads but pictures. In spite of their youthful impudence in providing late-night Soviet viewers an alternative news broadcast, the anchors and writers rarely moved into open political confrontation. Instead, they frequently reported conflicting information from various government sources, and would try to take all the approved information and without their own involvement spread the inconsistencies before the viewers.

When unarmed protesters were killed by Soviet forces in Vilnius, Lithuania, the *TSN* team could no longer tolerate the blinders. They complained, sought to give viewers subtle cues about their dissent from the official line, boycotted individual programs, gave extremely candid interviews to the press—and were fired. En masse, they went to work for Russian Television, the new channel Boris Yeltsin had acquired.

7 DAYS

On November 10, 1989, a stunning new program was launched. Called *7 Days*, it displayed a new look and bold content, but, more important, it occupied the sacrosanct *Vremya* slot: 9:00 P.M. Even in a time of unpredictable reform and tampering with the rules of the game, the symbol of continuity was *Vremya*. Eduard Sagalayev had first initiated counter-programming not in direct competition, but at a time of low viewership. As always, the smaller the expected audience, the more lenient the media watchdogs. According to usual institutional practice, the late-night home for *TSN* was reasonably safe, until, of course, the audience altered its viewing habits. As always, the preferences of the audience came as a surprise to the Party elites. There was a research division at Ostankino, mainly for summarizing the huge mail flow, and its thin survey capacity was used only to rearrange time slots on occasion to accommodate work or school schedules. The notion of audience demand driving program decisions appeared to make no sense in a system designed to educate in the absence of feedback.

Seven Days raised the political stakes dramatically. It was a combination of review-of-the-week summary of news and public affairs analysis. It sought to do this by using experts, but, more important, using the "space bridge" technique Sagalayev had pioneered in his youth program, *12th Floor*. When the coal miners were striking, Sagalayev brought them in live from their locations. They had prime-time airtime to voice their (mainly political) demands. When the walls crumbled as Eastern Europe freed itself, coverage was comprehensive and visually arresting. The Politburo watched *7 Days* and took umbrage. In the eye of the storm was the always-controversial investigative reporter Alexander Tikhomirov. He recalled that in planning the show, Sagalayev proposed that he and Tikhomirov do the program together, alternating the role of anchor. On January 28, 1990, Tikhomirov was in the anchor's chair and he distinctly displeased the Politburo, which gave the order to fire him.[36] Alexander Tikhomirov never hesitated to give his own opinion; his commentary was his trademark, and it annoyed the Kremlin when he went too far.

This time Tikhomirov took on the Communist Party. He was broadcasting from Krasnoyarsk, where a local Party branch based in an aluminum factory had decided that it would refuse to send its dues to Moscow until the *nomenklatura* reformed itself. On air, he asked viewers, "Where do Party dues go?" As Tikhomirov recalled, "That frightened them. While it was about ideology, they could tolerate it, but when it was about money," that went too far.[37] The Party apparatus was giving itself considerable increases in pay and the rank-and-file had never been consulted.[38]

In the same program, Tikhomirov tangled with the army. Just a week before, Soviet troops had been sent into Baku, the capital of the republic of Azerbaijan, to quell rioting over Armenian-Azerbaijani ethnic issues and contests for political power. It was a bloody event in which at least ninety-three people were killed.[39] Tikhomirov argued, on-air, for a frank assessment of the policy and its origin; he noted that because of the Tbilisi tragedy of less than a year before—when a demonstration of unarmed civilians was brutally put down by the army—the Politburo must have been divided.[40] Tikhomirov told the audience that information, unfortunately, was sparse: "We are forced to give TASS bulletins." On the show, to those who charged him with being subjective, he said, "first of all, please allow our correspondents to have their own opinions about the events taking place there. . . . we are often obliged to broadcast TASS reports, without always sharing that opinion, which is considered to be an official one."[41] Tikhomirov recounted that he asked, on-air, why were troops sent so late to Baku? They were not sent when the Armenians were being threatened and killed there, but they were sent when the Azerbaijani political opposition group, the People's Front, appeared in strength in the city. He doubted the soldiers were sent in to save people and thought force was being used to maintain Soviet power facing a challenge. "That was my last show."[42]

The Politburo gave Ostankino an ultimatum: 7 *Days* could continue, but not with Tikhomirov. Tikhomirov was told that "workers needed to receive information" and wanted *Vremya* returned. Sagalayev continued as host in a couple more, but they were paler, less interesting. Tikhomirov later recalled that the program must have seemed to be an unending stream of negative news, with a mine explosion on Monday, a strike the next day, and so on through the week, and all were put together on the Sunday news review show. Perhaps it "seemed too much," Tikhomirov said.

Eduard Sagalayev—author, producer, and alternating on-screen host of the show—said that the Politburo closed 7 *Days* and returned the old *Vremya* to its accustomed slot. Once, not long after, he met with Mikhail Gorbachev, and Gorbachev asked him, why 7 *Days* been off for so long. Sagalayev responded, "you canceled it." In turn, the Soviet leader said, "'No, it's just that *Vremya* was returned.'" Sagalayev asked what he meant, and Gorbachev assured him he was not against the program. Sagalayev took the cat-and-mouse game for just that, a game, but one whose traces would be difficult to follow later. Earlier, Sagalayev asked Kravchenko what the president wanted. Kravchenko's response was direct: "'the president wants to close *Vzglyad* and 7 *Days*. He's had enough of pluralism, and we have to remember that Marxism-Leninism is the basis of our ideology.'"[43]

Just over five years after 7 *Days* was canceled, I asked Mikhail Gorbachev about it. He recalled it as a good program and praised the work of Eduard Sagalayev, saying that Sagalayev "did it with talent." Sagalayev's initiative was good and he "broadcast interesting programs." As for the demise of 7 *Days*, he denied that the Politburo closed it. He understood that there were some "internal problems in the program," but he did not remember a decision about 7 *Days*. Besides, he went on, by that time both the president and the Supreme Soviet were active and it was not so easy, in fact it was "dangerous," to close down a program.[44]

Seven Days began and ended on Mikhail Nenashev's watch as head of state television. He thought the show was not very good, primarily because Alexander Tikhomirov gave his opinion and lacked objectivity. Nenashev thought Sagalayev sufficiently objective, but criticized Tikhomirov for using the anchor's chair to campaign for parliament (something Tikhomirov did do with *Prozhektor*). Nenashev found the show "subjective, compromised—radically compromised" and noted that "some in the Politburo" observed that it was too radical and too subjective.[45]

Tikhomirov did consider his commentary a kind of leverage with which to counter the far greater power of the Politburo and the chief of television. To the extent that the on-air performances of individual journalists encouraged viewer identification and attention, a degree of trust could be established that would, under crisis, act as a counterweight to official deception or silence.[46]

By their intense commitment to alternative positions, television personalities projected a nascent pluralism and depended on wide public recognition to even the odds in the struggle against Soviet institutions. Commentary by television journalists remained controversial into the post-Soviet period, and its advocates argued that such commentary expanded the space for free speech and independence from political power; opponents spoke of professionalism. The Western model of objective journalism argued for depersonalization of anchors, but in the struggle for press autonomy and pluralism, Soviet (and later, Russian) anchors responded that depersonalized newsreaders, the model of Soviet news, only supported a constricted news operation typical of a government's handmaiden. *Seven Days* was not shock journalism, nor did it transmit faked footage—nor was it mired in trivial sensationalism. It did displease political power. There is no doubt that Nenashev wanted *7 Days* closed and did not support the pioneering new look of public affairs reporting. It is on the debit side of Nenashev's mixed record.

After the end of the Soviet Union, Oleg Dobrodeyev, Eduard Sagalayev's deputy in the news department who had risen to head Channel One news in 1992 before moving into private television, said that it was difficult to appreciate what "horrible conditions" Sagalayev had to cope with. Basically, he was told to follow a scheme of "Council of Ministers, Central Committee, Council of Ministers, Central Committee . . . almost daily." Sagalayev succeeded in destroying the "stereotype" of the news programs as ritual. Sagalayev also changed the *Vremya* logo from the forbidding Kremlin tower to more modern graphics and introduced a soundtrack by Alfred Schnittke, the modernist composer whom the West admired but who in his homeland lived mainly by doing music tracks for movies. When Leonid Kravchenko took over, the news returned to its usual martial music. These were all-important political symbols the audience could read.

Oleg Dobrodeyev moved out of state television entirely and built a new kind of choice: the news on private television, in a structure independent of government budgeting and personnel policies. From *12th Floor* to *7 Days,* the news and information universe had expanded far beyond what the youthful experimenters of 1985 had thought possible.

CHAPTER FIVE

Viewers and Voters:
The First Competitive Elections and
the Rise of Alternative News

For most of its history, the Soviet Union produced theatrical elections; the "electorate" performed its role of active supporter of the system and the leadership staged elaborate rituals with mandatory voting. Party activists roused the sick and truculent to go to the polls, and massive media attention was turned on the nominations, platforms, and near 100 percent turnout all across the country.

The rituals had their rationale: they were demonstrations to the international world that the largely fictive Soviet constitution was being implemented. Elections, like the May Day and October Revolution commemorations and the other numerous ceremonies (just about every week had at least one designated "Day of . . .") were also an attempt to persuade the citizenry of the legitimacy of the system. By playing the roles endlessly throughout their lives, it was hoped they would be resocialized, drawn from formalized to authentic support.[1] Then, too, in managing the elections Communist Party leaders were able to configure exactly the mix of gender and social class its rhetoric required, and a seemingly representative mix of elected deputies was the result. If one counted socio-demographic features rather than efficacy of mandate, these elections would have appeared to yield a more balanced social result than, say, later free Russian elections, with no reserved quotas and consequently an abrupt decline in the proportion of women and the less privileged.

The old system of election as theater, with a passive audience instead of empowered voters, was no longer seen as functional by either bold reformers or doctrinaires. Yegor Ligachev, for example, condemned the excessive planning and control regional Party committees exercised over elections and the mere formality such a major civic event had become, but he also acknowledged that the system "did ensure that people of all nationalities, women, young people" were represented in the soviets (parliaments and local councils).[2] In ways that were to become apparent only later, the revised rules for elections would result in massive, unanticipated consequences and a political shift to structures on which to build an alternative power base.

Genuinely competitive elections are the mechanism by which alternation in power takes place in democracies, and challengers and officeholders alike seek public approval to continue in or gain power. True to the notion of contained change, the 1989 Soviet parliamentary election was a hybrid of competition and safeguards designed to maintain the basic shape of the political system while fostering selective change. M. Steven Fish described these elections as "*too sudden and too partial . . . strongly—and negatively*" influencing party development.[3]

The Communist Party of the Soviet Union still held a monopoly over party politics, which would not be given up until the following year, when Article 6 of the Soviet Constitution was repealed. The risk factor of the election was substantially reduced by an arrangement guaranteeing a block of seats in the new parliament for powerful Party-dominated organizations, such as the Communist Youth League, the Party itself, and the trade unions. Some professional groups, such as the Union of Journalists and the Academy of Sciences, had splintered along liberal and conservative lines. In many locales the local power structure restricted the free play of the contest, and outside the large cities the elections were less competitive. Candidates competed on the basis of their platforms, and primarily in the large cities a kind of unifying opposition line emerged. It was the most natural and typical one: against incumbency. The candidate's Party status would turn out to be less important than simply the fact of not holding the office in question.

This first partly competitive election would return a *higher* percentage of Party members to parliament. The fact that members of the Communist Party constituted most of the pool of social activists and that the monopoly it held effectively eliminated competing channels of political mobility made their domination of the election rolls predictable. What the Kremlin leadership had not predicted was the degree to which the Party's salience and legitimacy had become attenuated. The range of views its members held and the passion and directness of the new reformers' speech, even though they were in the minority, would make this a wholly new parliament. On issues of reform, Communist Party members were as divided as the rest of the population.[4]

The elections, set for March 26, 1989, were preceded by a nomination and candidate registration phase, from January to the end of February, and then a month for the campaign proper. For Yegor Ligachev the system needed changing, but to order elections within a month's time was surely excessively hasty and endangered the Party's organizing role.[5] It was incomprehensible that the Communist Party did not take a unified and aggressive stance in the elections, he thought. Nor did setting seats aside mollify him; he rightly saw the risk to the entire system as still too great. He noted that the Central Committee sent out directives to local Party committees to keep their distance from the process. "For the first time, there were no clear directions from the center on how to behave."[6] Instead, he caustically observed, "many unworthy people had announced their candidacies, even former convicts who had committed serious crimes, including murder. As for loudmouths and demagogues who built their platform only on anti-Soviet and anti-Communist planks, their numbers were legion."[7]

The rules for the 1989 Soviet parliamentary election might have appeared to the leadership to guarantee contained change, but television provided an unexpected power-motive for a more profound departure from the past. As before, faulty understanding of the media's effects, coupled with a belief in the power of television to effect *their* and *only their* circumscribed change, led Party officials to underestimate the ability of new political forces to utilize television for careers and platforms.

Under the terms of the law on elections, candidates were supposed to be guaranteed access to the mass media.[8] As Yevgeny Koveshnikov, head of the regulatory Central Election Commission, said, it would now be possible for candidates to campaign *against* other candidates, and therefore candidates must have equal right to equally attractive airtime. But the new permission to oppose others was not to be construed as unlimited license. The constraining provisions of the Soviet Constitution had to be observed and ". . . there must be no digging up of his [a candidate's] personal life or exploitation of any intimate details. It is, of course, totally impermissible to insult opponents. . . ."[9]

The rules set up a partial transition from the old ritual, with no attack option, to a new one with the possibility of genuine opposition.[10] The broad electoral law provided no rules for specific events, no opportunity for paid advertising, and no allotment of free time on the national channels. Boris Yeltsin, a candidate in Moscow, was blocked from gaining airtime on Channels One and Two by a decree that debates and other direct messages from candidates be aired only on local channels. By restricting coverage to locales, challenges to the national leadership would be fragmented.

When Boris Yeltsin finally did meet his opponent, a Moscow factory director, the debate was shown on the Moscow city channel. By that time the Party's Central Committee had formed a subcommittee to investigate

Yeltsin's views and their compatibility with Party membership. Publicly disgraced when he had been removed from his post as Moscow Party boss, excluded from the Politburo, and now hounded by its investigative team, Yeltsin returned as a major political figure. The debate against the dour factory manager displayed his capacity for direct and forceful speech, even though he felt ill at ease in front of the camera. He recognized that television was central to a modern election campaign, but vastly preferred arousing a live crowd to attempting a surrogate version for the "cold glass eye of the camera lens."[11] Reformist politicians were particularly advantaged in these televised contests, since they were often able to perform in front of the camera with considerably greater agility and a much more human touch than complacent incumbents, unused to competing for public approval. With its immediacy, visuals, its live presence, and tremendous audience, television outdistanced what had been a much bolder, more combative print medium.[12]

Journalists themselves ran for the new parliament and retained their jobs in front of the camera while doing so. Aleksander Tikhomirov, advocate of the new investigative journalism, used his program to uncover the Party's illegal—and successful—effort to prevent his election in Voronezh.[13] On his program, he showed "How to do an election campaign—Party-style." He told about the roadblocks they put up and the meeting halls they closed. He said the regional Party organization declared war on him. Tikhomirov finished the tape only fifteen minutes before airtime; his superiors, he said, did not have an opportunity to see it.[14]

The ability of journalist-candidates to use the medium did initiate controversy about ethics, and later electoral campaigns did not permit it. Removal of the reformist journalists from their media pulpits would, as many knew, be the ethical thing to do, but this was an argument mainly advanced by those who wished to close down the pulpit and nullify the advantages the minority reform group could exploit against hostile institutions.

Parliamentary immunity would prove to be a weapon of unsuspected utility for those who would alter the system far beyond contained change. Acquiring parliamentary immunity to ward off the authorities became a deliberate strategy; Bella Kurkova did it to save her *Fifth Wheel* program from extinction.[15] Later, when a number of activist television journalists were elected to parliaments, national and local, they would use the immunity their elected status conferred to protect their antiestablishment forays on television. By subverting long-standing but inactive norms, they invoked immunity.

TELEVISED REBELS: COVERING THE NEW PARLIAMENT

In the middle of May 1989, Alexander Aksyonov was relieved of his duties as head of state television and replaced by Mikhail Nenashev. This was a

critical time to take charge of broadcasting, for one of its greatest challenges was looming. For the first time in Soviet history, a multi-candidate
election had taken place in a new, more democratic process. In spite of the
protections the Politburo wove into the fabric of popular participation,
when the results were counted, some surprises greeted the leaders. Reformist deputies constituted only a minority overall, but in some districts
where only the Party leader was on the ballot, so many voters crossed out
the name that the candidacy failed. In other districts, including Moscow
and Leningrad, the vitally important urban nerve centers of the country,
openly reformist activists running on platforms of change ousted old-time
Party professionals.

How this new parliamentary body would operate was to a great extent
unknown. Perhaps the reformers who were members of the Party would
work within the system to reform it—that was the official expectation.
Procedures were also undefined. Would Roberts' Rules be applied? For the
officials in the Kremlin, the main task of the newly elected Congress of
People's Deputies was the election of the first Soviet president, and it was
to be Mikhail Gorbachev. Few were prepared for the uninhibited outpouring of grievances and furies accumulated for decades.

The first session was scheduled to run from May 25 to June 9. Mikhail
Gorbachev made the commitment to live coverage, and it was a courageous decision. On the evening news the day before the congress opened,
he told viewers: "I don't think we should limit any discussions. We just have
to live through them. Then, everything will have fallen in place and we
would have worked out normal democratic procedures and forms of
work." Although, he added warily, he had met some deputies "who seemed
to me inclined to seek division rather than consolidation," he was quite sure
that "the consolidation line is now shared by the absolute majority of the
people's deputies."[16]

As it turned out, the congress was riveting. According to state television's
research department, some two hundred million viewers tuned in to the
daily eight-hour program during the course of its coverage. The presence of
an electronic rostrum sparked competition among the newly elected and
ambitious deputies, and suddenly the list of requests to address the body
reached four hundred, and was still growing. Said television news director
Olvar Kakuchaya: "'Something is really turning over in our national consciousness. The deputies are realizing the people are watching them, the voters can see them live, and the level of discussion is rising. There's never been
anything like this—people watching how the leadership is changing.'"[17]

Viewers also saw a revolutionary new style of coverage. Oleg Tochilin,
the deputy chief of news, said that in the past, live broadcasts of parliamentary convocations were done quite differently. A solemn camera would pan
across the seated officials on the dais. The hushed multitude listened and
raised their hands in unison, approving the leaders' course. Tochilin remem-

bered the look: "Everything was sort of flooded with red light. You could not make out the faces."[18] In sharp contrast, the tough new coverage featured closeups, often with deadly political contrast, showing, with heavy irony, the rotund figures of officers when the military was excoriated.

Deputies at this first session vented their wrath and, under the protection of parliamentary immunity, attacked the sacred cows and enshrined dogmas. A worker from the industrial city of Kharkov likened President Gorbachev to Napoleon, who led the nation to victory but was undone by sycophants and a scheming wife. Olympic weightlifter Yury Vlasov called for unmasking the terrors of the KGB and its torture of the "cream of the nation." Andrei Sakharov, back from exile in Gorky, called on the congress to do more than talk. Presiding was President Gorbachev, and he was just as freewheeling a moderator as the deputies were legislators. Roberts' Rules were out of order. Emotions in the hall were too powerful to be constrained by the niceties of proper sequencing and strictly focused debate. Once a deputy got the floor (and the television camera), the entire baggage of concerns emerged, including those of Party stalwarts, who were aghast at people "'making a career for themselves soiling the reputations of high-ranking officials by discrediting the Communist Party.'"[19] A female deputy from the economically depressed Central Asian republic of Kyrgyzia poured out a moving appeal for the rectification of a host of political, social, and economic wrongs that women had suffered.

Whether or not the congress actually did anything was less important in those heady days than the display of the legitimacy of views. This dramatization of pluralism was surely the most remarkable yet. Boris Yeltsin recalled that "the entire country was glued to their TVs. . . . Politically, those ten days gave people more than the seventy years of millions of Marxist-Leninist politicians. . . . It was as though the entire nation—well, almost—woke up from hibernation."[20]

Before the end of the session, state television conducted a survey in Moscow. Even though congress sessions were shown during working hours, half of the white-collar people polled watched at least some of the debates. Blue-collar workers were only slightly less likely (42 percent) to have watched them. Moscow's student population were most likely to tune in: 92 percent of high school students and 72 percent of college students said they had watched the sessions. Overwhelmingly, the people interviewed approved of the coverage. A poll conducted from May 7 to 10, 1989, found that among 1,100 people in Moscow, Kiev, Alma-Ata, Riga, Krasnoyarsk, Perm, and Stavropol, over 75 percent were in favor of complete live public airing of the parliamentary sessions.[21] In the factory city of Tula, roughly 120 miles south of Moscow, Alexander Yermakov, deputy editor of a local paper, said that with citizens glued to the television screens, letters to the editor had dropped off from a daily average of one hundred to just twelve. When the congress recessed for a day, Tulans felt deprived.[22]

As for the journalists themselves, they had sometimes bitter recollections of their pioneering work covering that first Congress of People's Deputies. Responding to frequent (and often justified) charges by Party officials that correspondents chose mainly reformist, antiestablishment subjects to interview, Sergei Medvedev, later Boris Yeltsin's press secretary, said: "'Indeed it happens that the same people keep appearing on the air. . . . Certainly, the circle of people we interview needs to be enlarged. However, if a person speaks colorlessly and unconvincingly he will not end up on the air.'"[23]

More often than not, Party officials who reached their positions by playing the game, attaching to the suitable patron and rising in the ranks, had far fewer skills in attracting public approval. They tended to speak in that abstract way that characterized Soviet political discourse, the removal of which was one of the singular achievements of the Gorbachev information revolution. Party officials generally had neither the experience nor the need to speak in ordinary language and solicit support from the public, and the language and manners appropriate to communication inside the Party bureaucracy did not transfer successfully, as few could effectively compete for television time in the parliamentary bazaar. As parliamentary correspondent Dmitry Kiselyov put it, "It is difficult to find a deputy who would defend the point of view of the majority convincingly."

A year earlier, Mikhail Gorbachev himself had been appalled at the inability of his own minister to convey, with minimal intelligence and verbal grace, the policies of his administration to viewers. In connection with a planned rise in state-ordained prices, Gorbachev requested that state television interview the minister in charge of bread production. When the program concluded, Gorbachev called the television station and said, "'Who put that fool [durak] on television?'" Leonid Kravchenko answered, "I didn't make him minister." Just a few days later Gorbachev removed the minister.[24]

It should have been an early warning to Gorbachev that many incumbents were not going to be able to hold their own when television had so decisively changed the rules of discourse. The numbers of the Party's Central Committee in the ruling elite of the legislature were shrinking; Gorbachev had succeeded in creating a presidency which siphoned off legitimacy from the Party, whose professionals were whipsawed. They faced the reduction of their influence at the top and, simultaneously, their inability to compete in the new, more public and freewheeling legislative forum.[25]

Anger and deprivation were creating a backlash. An increasingly outspoken right wing was fed up with the liberalizing tendencies of the Gorbachev administration. In particular, it was outraged by the takeover of the mass media. In June 1989, I observed the formation of a Communist workers' movement at a Moscow meeting. Journalists, professors, workers, a parliamentary deputy, and an official of the Ministry of Communications addressed an audience of 200 to 250 people in a Party-administered building. For leading the takeover of the Party by "petty bourgeois elements," Alexander Yakovlev was the chief target of anger. They have taken over the mass media, speakers said, and there is no real pluralism in the mass media. Speakers were angered by talk of removing Lenin's body from the mausoleum. They said the workers were creating the wealth of society for the consumption of the new bourgeoisie who, led by Yakovlev, subverted Soviet society. There is no milk for our children, the speakers said, misery is our lot. Prices are going up, wages stay low, and a revolutionary confrontation is building. When a woman in the audience asked with studied neutrality if the Party is on the same level as the people or higher, shouting broke out in the hall. She was called a demagogue and the crowd would not let her speak, while shouts of "the army is with the Party," and "the KGB and the Party," were followed by attacks on "Zionists" and "Masons."

The anger and status deprivation of those who opposed the Yakovlev-Gorbachev line, together with frustration and rage at exclusion from an increasingly important media system, were palpable in the days of the first session of the newly elected parliament. The zero-sum notion of television tended, increasingly, to preclude the option of shared time and collective goods.

Television reporters covering the new parliament were not entirely free. Sergei Medvedev put it succinctly: "'When I was preparing materials on the past session I did not once ask my management for advice. . . . Unfortunately, during the ten years of my work at Gosteleradio they implanted an inner censor in me, and it is very difficult to get rid of him.'"[26] Even Vladimir Mukusev, host of the provocative youth program *Vzglyad,* said that he had a little Lapin inside him, referring to the dictator of television during the Brezhnev days, though every day the fellow was shrinking.

As Mikhail Nenashev, head of state television at the time of the elections later observed, opposition to "official powers" was growing and the decline of the authority of the Communist Party accelerated it. "Only this," he noted, "can explain the phenomenon that twelve anchors and television journalists, primarily from those programs which appeared in opposition to official powers, were elected deputies to the Supreme Soviet of the RSFSR [Russian Republic], and three of them were anchors of the program *Vzglyad.*"[27]

In the national Congress of People's Deputies and its subordinate body, the Supreme Soviet, there were nearly sixty journalist-deputies, some of whom had been on a list reserved for the official organizations, and some were competitively elected. The group ranged from acid-tongued, anti-Western ideologue Genrikh Borovik to Yeltsin loyalist, belligerent Mikhail Poltoranin, to reformist *Moscow News* editor Yegor Yakovlev.[28] The journalist-deputies in the Soviet and Russian parliaments retained their jobs in the media, and for some of them the ethical dilemma was a real one. Alexander Politkovsky of *Vzglyad* said that "I understand that fifty journalists in the Supreme Soviet is absurd. In no country in the world can a journalist working on the primary television channel crawl into parliament. But I can't drop it either. So a certain schizophrenia occurs."[29]

The gripping sessions of parliament, telecast live to the nation, proved to be too threatening for the Politburo. On June 26, live coverage ceased. Over the course of three weeks, some ninety-five hours of debate had been covered live. It had, indeed, been a school for democracy. Disparaging the coverage, Politburo ideology chief Vadim Medvedev said that if it was such a school, "it would be as true and self-aware to say that we have only gone through the first stage of this school."[30] The school was in recess because of indiscipline and the energetic and irrepressible promotion of many competing agendas. That was immature and not helpful to the common mission of reform, as seen from the center.

Another rationale for ending live broadcasts came from parliamentary speaker Anatoly Lukyanov, who would be standing trial two years later (and later amnestied) for participating in the attempted 1991 coup. On June 26, TASS reported that there would be no live television or radio coverage of the sessions. Lukyanov, addressing one of the houses of parliament, explained that there had been a 20 percent fall in industrial output because of the attention paid to the televised hearings. Canceling the broadcasts had become necessary in the interests of the common economic welfare. There is no doubt that he was in part correct. Massive attention to the "best show ever" had reduced labor efficiency, but this rationale harmonized only too well with the strains of caution and concern emanating from the Politburo.

Thanks very largely to the extraordinary broadcasts of the sessions, the new parliamentary institutions gained the trust and confidence of broad masses of the population. The summer after the election, Moscow newspaper editors reported that the huge volume of complaint letters they usually received from readers had fallen off sharply. The reason, they said, was that citizens were now taking their concerns to deputies.[31] Contrasting very strongly with the new authority of this parliamentary body were the older institutions associated with decades of Soviet rule. The Komsomol (Soviet Youth League) and the trade unions enjoyed far less confidence. People were more cautious—and less optimistic—about the new parliament's efficacy and the ability or willingness of elected representatives to maintain ties with and accountability to their electors.[32] The notion of parliament as effective institution of democratic governance is quite different from the notion of the legitimacy of holding unpopular opinions and expressing them in public. The latter is the great contribution of the weeks of live coverage in 1989, and it was never equalled.

BORIS YELTSIN'S BATTLE FOR AIRTIME

Boris Yeltsin challenged the ruling regime's monopoly of television airtime, and access to the airwaves became a matter of highest priority. How to cover Yeltsin was a continuing source of pain and anxiety in the Kremlin, and by extension, at state television. The normative impact of institutions and titles, no matter how empty of power they had been, now presented formidable bases for claims on resources.

The bargaining power of the head of Russia had increased exponentially after the elections.[33] In the Soviet system, the component "republics" had operated within a highly centralized system of controls and the power base of the local administration was wholly dependent on Party approbation. In 1989, an alternative source of power—the vote—entered the equation, but the consequences of this change in the institutional rules had not been fully appreciated at the time of their adoption.

As soon as the disgraced Yeltsin gained a political foothold and filled a protocol slot, he could activate the trappings that went with it. Boris Yeltsin was first elected to the Congress of People's Deputies, and in May 1990, after elections at the republic level, he became the chairman of the Russian Federation parliament, which gave him the status of leader of the republic. The Kremlin's strategy was negative coverage of Yeltsin, if possible, and restriction of his unmediated access to the airwaves. If he appeared at all, he was to be reduced to short sound bites, anchor's voiceover narration, or hostile interviews and press conferences. At all costs he was not to have the television audience to himself.[34]

In the fall of 1989, Yeltsin made his first visit to the United States. At a breakfast meeting at Johns Hopkins University, he appeared groggy and spoke slurringly. Some claimed he was drunk; he said he was exhausted from travel and sleeping pills taken to overcome jet lag.[35] *Pravda* was quick to reprint what turned out to be unfounded accusations appearing in the Italian press. State television head Mikhail Nenashev thought *Pravda*'s coverage was reprehensible, tabloid journalism out to compromise Yeltsin. However, the Soviet authorities had obtained television footage capturing the infirmity of the Russian leader. As Nenashev put it to Yeltsin, "I cannot fail to show it or explain why I am not showing it."[36] "They already know about it and not just here."[37]

Yeltsin was offered a private preview of the material. After he had seen the footage, Yeltsin called Nenashev, saying that the tape "did not provoke optimism," and asked Nenashev not to show it. Nenashev refused, but acceded to another request: Yeltsin asked that this footage be included in broader coverage of the visit, balanced by other, favorable, reporting. Nenashev aired it that way. The first part showed a sober and well-prepared

Yeltsin on the *MacNeil/Lehrer Newshour* and the second was the Johns Hopkins appearance.[38]

The forty-five-minute program aired on prime time just before the evening news on October 3. On that program, Yeltsin was also shown arriving in Moscow with the gift of one hundred thousand disposable syringes. Although Yeltsin charged at the time that state television had doctored the tape to make him appear disoriented and drunk (a charge he made in an interview, uncritically picked up by a supportive biography),[39] Nenashev maintained that no such tampering had taken place. Oleg Dobrodeyev, then the deputy in charge of the news and certainly a strong voice for probity and reform, said later, with no hesitation whatever, that Yeltsin did appear drunk on the film taken in the United States. Dobrodeyev was personally opposed to airing the piece (it was not, he said, "correct" to do it) and so was Nenashev, but they were forced by the Kremlin to put it on. It was definitely not faked footage, in their view.

Getting on the mainstream media with his own message was far more difficult. Even before Gorbachev's *glasnost* reform, radio had begun relaxing the strictures against Western-style popular music. *Mayak* (Beacon), with its popular, live, nonstop music and news became the most widely listened to radio program in the country, and thus far the ruling regime's best answer to the intrusions of foreign radio. Overall, radio audiences had fallen off sharply since the introduction of television, and the medium was less strategically important.[40]

According to *Mayak*'s director at the time, Yeltsin thought it the only major communications channel he might be able to use. Director Boris Nepomnyashchy knew he was taking a risk when he had Yeltsin on the program, and soon was called to Pyotr Reshetov's office, a large room dominated by a long, polished conference table. Alone in the room, Reshetov and Nepomnyashchy sat down, facing each other across the imposing table. Reshetov said nothing. Nepomnyashchy waited. After a long pause, Reshetov intoned: "You sold yourself, you sold yourself . . . . to Russia."

After May 1990, when Yeltsin gained the official status of leader of the Russian republic, he advanced his claim on state television. He had the authority and requirement to address the Russian people, as had his predecessors. It was with some justification, then, that he invoked the rules of the past for an agenda of the future. Early in June, parliament requested that Yeltsin address Russia on television. The speech was prepared, taped, and slotted by state television. Without notice, Yeltsin's presentation was pulled. He called it a political provocation. Mikhail Nenashev later recounted the events: Yeltsin's secretariat had requested him to tape the speech to the Russian Congress of People's Deputies on June 8 for broadcast that day, or the next one. Nenashev agreed to tape the speech, but could show it only on June 9 or 10, and Yeltsin would be granted the top prime-time slot, directly before or after *Vremya*.

Nenashev then learned that Gorbachev would be giving a speech on June 9. The television chief knew it would be politically ill advised to schedule Gorbachev and Yeltsin on the same day and delayed Yeltsin's talk until June 10. When Nenashev was summoned to appear before parliament, he first went to see Gorbachev, at eleven o'clock in the morning. Nenashev explained the situation to the Soviet president, and Gorbachev agreed that Nenashev should go to the parliament and take all responsibility himself.[41] Nenashev reiterated to me that he made the decision himself to separate the Gorbachev and Yeltsin speeches by a day and that Gorbachev was unaware of it.[42]

It soon became clear to Boris Yeltsin that until he laid claim to his own television channel, his access to airtime would continue to be managed by his political adversaries. For Yeltsin the fight for airtime was a political necessity, but personal anguish. "When I have to go on TV," he recalled, "I sweat bullets and I hate terribly to see myself on the screen. . . ."[43]

The second national channel had been started in 1982 to develop regional programming. Its signals penetrated about three-quarters of the Soviet Union, and programming was distinctly less popular, featuring repeats or rejects from Channel One, language and science courses, and second-rank sports events. Yeltsin and the Russian parliament advanced the claim that Channel Two should be theirs. There was no doubt that a major television station in the hands of the Yeltsin leadership would be the first truly alternative, competitive television in the nation's history.

On July 30, 1990, Yeltsin ally and parliamentary deputy Vyacheslav Bragin commented that the Russian parliament's decision to press for a Russian channel was needed because "real power is impossible without Russian television and radio."[44] When Mikhail Nenashev left his job as head of state television in the fall of 1990, there appeared to have been an agreement to hand the second channel over to Yeltsin. Nenashev told me that he considered it unfair for every republic but Russia to have its own television channel, and that in the fall of 1990, "after a long discussion," the decision was made to grant the Russian republic a phased access to Channel Two. Initially, there would be two to four hours daily, with the rest available for the other republics.

The prospect of Yeltsin's acquiring his own television channel grew more and more threatening to the Kremlin, and it had second thoughts about continuing to allow him to keep his airtime on Radio Rossia. Radio Rossia had came into being on December 10, 1990, and it was deprived of most of its transmission frequencies early in February 1991. Oleg Poptsov, a combative former newspaper editor and fierce Yeltsin loyalist, took the lead in first operating radio, and then television, for the Russian Federation.

Poptsov recalled that Radio Rossia was allocated six hours on radio, which provided the first truthful information about what was happening in separatist Lithuania. According to Poptsov, those broadcasts "infuriated Mikhail Gorbachev personally." Called on the carpet by the president, Leonid Kravchenko was told to close the radio down, but replied that it would cause a scandal. He was then told to "send them to Mozhaisk" (a provincial town, i.e., send them off to the boondocks).

That December day, Kravchenko offered Poptsov two options: either stay with the channel one radio frequency that reached a huge public and be censored or shift to a frequency that reduces your public by twenty times and do what you want. Poptsov took the uncensored variant and began to work "like the BBC or the Voice of America." We got a "vile [*gadostnaya*] frequency; we went underground, and gained enormous popularity."[45]

In drawing distinctions of scale between smaller and larger publics, the Soviet regime failed to understand that communication is not a unidirectional, fully controllable process and audience preferences may shift to choices hitherto unavailable. Extrapolating from behavior when such choice was absent was likely to be faulty.

It fell to Leonid Kravchenko to work out the modalities of the start-up of Boris Yeltsin's slice of Channel Two television, but the conflict between Gorbachev and Yeltsin "held it up."[46] The transfer did not materialize; new "studies" had to be done and new arguments were advanced against the project. Yeltsin did manage to schedule an interview on Channel One on February 19, 1991, but, according to Leonid Kravchenko, then head of state television, "Each appearance of Yeltsin made Gorbachev crazy." Kravchenko related that Gorbachev pressed him to establish limits about what would be allowed, but Kravchenko said he could not reveal who gave the orders. "I was not to—I did not have the right to implicate Gorbachev."

Gorbachev had been interviewed by Sergei Lomakin and liked his style and looks. And, Kravchenko added, not just Gorbachev liked him; a lot depended on what was decided in "the family." Lomakin was the favorite of Raisa Maximovna. Gorbachev told Kravchenko to "Let Lomakin be there for our side" during the planned interview with Yeltsin on state television.

The president also sent a list of themes to be used in questioning Yeltsin. Although Sergei Lomakin confirmed that questions came from Gorbachev, he denied that he used them on-air. According to Lomakin, before the live interview, Kravchenko came to him with questions from Gorbachev and told Lomakin that there is "a request that Yeltsin be given these questions." Lomakin thought they were not particularly penetrating or controversial ("they could have been asked by anyone"), and, as a professional, he wanted to ask more probing ones. He made up three: Why is Yeltsin against economic reform? Why does Yeltsin want to create his own Russian army? Why are Yeltsin and Gorbachev always in a position of confrontation?

Lomakin's recollection of Gorbachev's questions were that they asked Yeltsin about his relationship with the Soviet parliament and his views of Russia's independence. Lomakin also denied that he was merely Gorbachev's attack dog. "It made no difference for me being Gorbachev's favorite," he said. It just looked to the viewers that way, because his own questions were tough-minded and Oleg Poptsov, the other interviewer, was well known as a Yeltsin ally. Lomakin acknowledged that when the interview was broadcast he appeared to be Yeltsin's enemy, but he asked what interest would viewers have "if the questions had been pleasant?"[47]

Much later, after Gorbachev had left the scene, "his" anchor was marooned on the early morning show. In his heyday as television personality to the political stars, Lomakin certainly had visibility, but there were those who remembered his pioneering work on *Vzglyad*. In February 1991, one journalist reflected on the change in the young reporter after seeing him host a program with television officials: "I felt sorry for the programme's host, Lomakin. Only a short time ago he used to host *Vzglyad*. Today, he eagerly plays up to his bosses. We have lost an ally."[48] Ruefully, Sergei Lomakin complained that he should never have taken on that Yeltsin interview. Because of it, he said, "I still can't do independent programs or be an anchor on the evening news, which I had done before." He thought that day was his creative dead end.[49]

In the winter of 1991, Leonid Kravchenko, as head of state television, had to deal with the agreement his predecessor Mikhail Nenashev had struck with Yeltsin's people. A protocol was on the table for six hours of daily airtime, with ownership and control of the channel to remain in state television. On February 27, 1991, the Russian Federation parliament passed a resolution to instruct the Russian government to ensure the transfer of the television channel and provide all equipment and other property free of charge. The next month, Kravchenko finally gave in to Russian demands for time on the second channel and signed a protocol providing for a start-up date in May, just a few days before the start of the Russian presidential campaign. Kravchenko recounted that Gorbachev called him in and said, "What have you done? You gave Yeltsin an instrument of power. Was it impossible to do it a month later?"[50]

Oleg Poptsov would not countenance use of the word "gave." "No one gave us anything! Everything we got we fought for." He said he had met with Nenashev, a "tired person, charming and smart, an honest person." Nenashev asked why television was necessary at all, but agreed; then he left. Poptsov dealt next with Kravchenko, whom he termed a professional. Poptsov maintained that the decision to launch the Russian Federation airtime was made "in spite of the wishes of M. S. Gorbachev." Kravchenko, according to Poptsov, was not a supporter of Russian television but understood the magnitude of the pressure to initiate it, and Kravchenko's deputy,

Valentin Lazutkin, added his advocacy. But, Poptsov related, those were "tortured relations with Kravchenko and he never kept his word."[51]

In 1995, when Mikhail Gorbachev talked to me about his actions, he stated that the republics of the Soviet Union had a new role as a result of his reforms and that they needed to have some hours on the air for their positions. He also said that he "understood all the intentions." "If I acted differently," he said, referring to his approval of television time for the Russian republic and therefore for Boris Yeltsin, it would constitute a "repudiation of the criteria of democracy." He upheld the grant of time on Channel Two to Yeltsin, although, as he mused later about matters that still rankled, "Yeltsin spoke aggressively on television; he attacked me."[52]

On May 13, 1991, Russian Television finally began broadcasting for six hours a day on Channel Two, not in a block, but in three slices, at midday, early evening, and late at night. Its news program, *Vesti* (News), often had a sarcastic comment about the official and untrustworthy news program viewers would see on its august competitor, Channel One's *Vremya*. Operating from a small studio with obsolete equipment, Russian Television had its troubles. The Ministry of Communications suddenly stripped material transmitted for broadcast on Russian Television news of its priority status for satellite transmission.

On the inaugural broadcast, RTR (Russian Television and Radio) director Oleg Poptsov interviewed president Boris Yeltsin. Acquiring the power to mobilize the population for the implementation of his initiatives was the most important outcome of this long struggle and was the "immense significance that I, personally, attach to Russian Television," Yeltsin said. On that inaugural day, Russian Television also did what the Soviet president dreaded most—it gave the separatist Lithuanian president a chance to reach most of the country.

Just a month later, a survey of Russians found that more people trusted Channel Two news than its competitor on Channel One.[53] In a remarkably short period, in their blocks of time on Channel Two, Yeltsin's supporters had succeeded in establishing an audience and winning their trust. It was also clear that the estimation of television as a key political resource was undiminished from the days of the sclerotic Soviet leaders and was to be a prominent battleground in a zero-sum information struggle.

CHAPTER SIX

Television and Crisis:
The End of Soviet Rule

VILNIUS AND THE DILEMMA OF A DIVIDED NEWS OPERATION

Almost from the beginning, Mikhail Gorbachev's reforms had been put to the test by the Baltic republics, for whom the goal of independence had been submerged, but never effaced, by Soviet rule. A central component of sovereignty in the age of television is the capacity to convey one's messages in one's own words,[1] and bureaucratically, the television of the Baltic republics, as all republic-level television, operated under the direction and control of Moscow. But as the tempo of separatism picked up, local television began to dislodge itself from its bonds.

In February 1988, a small group of Estonians proclaimed the creation of an independent political party. Not a word got on national television news, and local Estonian news was forced to give an official (and negative) account of the party's nationalist demonstrations. In defiance, anchor Urmas Reitelman refused to look at the camera as he read the script.[2] Local Latvian television featured programs about and mobilized support for their nationalist Popular Front; reporters Ojars Rubenis and Edvin Inkens were criticized for coverage of a ceremony dedicated to the Latvian victims of Stalin's repressions.[3] In December 1988, *Pravda* noted with alarm the "inverted pluralism" of Estonian Television in showing an entertainment program instead of a Gorbachev speech.[4] In the spring of 1989, the Lithuanian weekly television show created by Sajudis, the nationalist popular front, was banned because a composer had praised anti-Soviet Lithuanian partisans.[5] That spring, almost two years before Soviet forces took over Lithuanian television, the Latvian Interior Ministry put down demonstrations in Riga against restrictions on journalistic freedom, and in November of 1989, Latvia refused to hold the traditional military parade on the anniversary of the 1917 Revolution.[6] Moscow warily escalated its criticism, which, in turn, did not go unnoticed or unprotested.

The Baltic republics were, indeed, different. Their cultures and religions linked them to Central and Western Europe. They had been incorporated relatively recently into the Soviet Union over the protests of the international community, and the United States continued to recognize the exiled prewar governments. Latvia and Estonia were the most economically developed Soviet region and had the most highly skilled labor force. They were often used as laboratories of reform and were the beneficiaries of special relationships.

Estonia, linked linguistically to Finland, its neighbor across the Baltic Sea, could receive Finnish television. In January 1989, for example, Estonian audiences could see some fifteen hours of Finnish television daily. There were programs from the United States (*Dallas,* for one), Italy, and Japan.[7] The Baltic countries had maintained so much of their prewar, European heritage, that when Soviet delegations headed for the West they were often brought first to a Baltic capital to lessen the culture shock.

Throughout 1990, the Baltic republics moved more certainly and forcefully toward sovereignty and separation and began to take over local television. The change in rules that made contested republic-wide elections possible—and set the Russian republic on an alternative power base—also enabled Baltic separatists to "capture" their republics. Official Soviet news broadcasts elected to show only those who opposed separation and emphasized the insecurity of the Russian minority. Vladimir Molchanov, a well-known anchor for *Vremya,* told a newspaper what he could not say on television:

> I am horrified that I will have to anchor the whole *Vremya* program. What would we say about the events in the Baltics? I, for one, can not say what TASS wants. Let our correspondents we sent there report the story? They won't say anything very clearly. Let the local journalists report? Our superiors don't allow it. It would be much, much easier for me—for my own conscience—to anchor only the international bloc [of news] on *Vremya* rather than look the fool, which says a lot about what is going on in this country, which doesn't have the slightest understanding about all this.[8]

What a narrow slice of intellectuals could read about in a newspaper mattered less; it was their safety valve and would not move the country.[9]

The last-gasp battle for the Baltics began in earnest when the Defense Ministry announced on January 7, 1991, that troops would be deployed to ensure the military draft continued in the Baltics and other breakaway regions. On January 10, Gorbachev's speech to the Lithuanians warned that the standoff had reached a dangerous point and that the bourgeois regime was attempting to reassert itself against the interests of the working class.

Then, on January 13, 1991, in the early hours of the morning, Soviet troops stormed the Lithuanian television tower in the capital, Vilnius, killing some unarmed protesters ouside. It was reported by *Komsomol Pravda* that Soviet state television had called for sound operators, cameramen, and lighting engineers to volunteer for duty in Vilnius, but with little success.[10] Lithuanian television officials left to man a small station in Kaunas.

On January 14, Mikhail Gorbachev told reporters that he knew nothing of these events until that morning and that responsibility lay with the local military commander. Later he remembered that when he heard of the violence in Lithuania he called Defense Minister Dmitry Yazov and KGB chief Kryuchkov. Both assured him that the decision was made locally. Gorbachev recollected that he found it hard to believe the operation could have taken place without Yazov's approval, but at that time he trusted his defense minister.[11] Future coup plotters Yazov and Interior Minister Boris Pugo (who later shot himself and his wife) said then that the local commander, Major General Vladimir Uskhopchik, gave the orders, "under the strength of emotions brought about by anti-Soviet and antimilitary propaganda," in Yazov's words. State television, under the firm hand of Leonid Kravchenko, accountable only to the president of the Soviet Union, broadcast the official point of view.

The Soviet military had its own strong advocate in the person of television star Alexander Nevzorov, whose retrograde piece of unprofessional journalism *Nashy* (Our Boys), was run twice on Central Television. Nevzorov achieved television stardom from the studios of Leningrad Television and the streets of the city. He conceived a new kind of news program, *600 Seconds,* featuring real-life local news. When asked about the genre of his program, he responded, "The genre of the program is truth. The truth about life in the city the day before."[13] Specializing in the sensational, his hard-hitting reporting zeroed in on corruption, crime, and corpses—something entirely new on television.

The imposing and apparently fearless reporter had started out as a hospital worker, a movie stuntman on horseback, and scriptwriter. Nevzorov was the unequalled center of his programs: tall, with black-leather jacket, rapid-fire speech—and the gruesome pictures. His early programs supported Gorbachev's reform agenda, and the star often had run-ins with local officials while trying to root out mismanagement. In one case, he investigated a meat factory producing sausages from spoiled meat. Following up, he and his camera crew tried to film a meeting where the local government council discussed the problem, but instead did a story showing the council denying him entry.

Nevzorov was unafraid and daring; he refused bodyguards and bulletproof vests, and in December 1990 he was mysteriously shot one night on a deserted street. The event was controversial. There were charges that it was staged, and, as always throughout his career, that he was involved with the KGB. Indeed, he had never hidden his cooperation with the "organs."[14]

On the way to stardom Nevzorov became increasingly identified with monarchist and Russian nationalist causes. His views on other social issues were provocatively extreme. When asked whether he would prefer to have a daughter or son from his second marriage, he replied, "well, certainly a son. A daughter—that's just expenditure material. At eighteen, she'd leave—and that's it, and even the name is different. What's the point of it?" And what kind of son? "The duplicate of his father, naturally." And, "Since I'm not a homosexual, human rights don't interest me."[15]

The sixteen-minute film, *Nashy,* began with Wagnerian music and smoking cauldrons. The storming of the television tower by Soviet riot forces and the deaths of local protesters were presented from the point of view of threatened and endangered Soviet Russian loyalists doing their duty among the bellicose and cruel Lithuanian population bent on slaughtering them. Individuals in the anti-Soviet crowds were identified as having worked with United States special forces. The casualties of the violence against Lithuanian citizens were accidental or simply the result of natural causes.[16] The talks with Soviet defenders were static, staged, and dull, in contrast to the hyperactive star and volcanic music.

Nevzorov's television programs were canceled and reinstated more than once, and his political appeal was translated into a mandate when he was elected deputy to the Russian Federation parliament in 1993. From the Chechen conflict, he produced another *Nashy.* As he said at the time, "There is, in principle, no difference between Vilnius-91 and Chechnya-95. The actions of Russian troops in Lithuania were also legal."[17]

If the 9:00 P.M. *Vremya* had virtually no room to maneuver during the events in the Baltics, that was less true for the upstart late-night news, *TSN.* With its team of young journalists who saw themselves not as newsreaders but as engaging, independent anchors, *TSN* was far more rebellious. On midnight, January 13, that first night after the takeover of the Vilnius television tower, Tatyana Mitkova was anchoring *TSN.* With none of her usual polish, her liquid, dark eyes staring into the camera, her voice shaking a bit, she intoned: "what follows is the official version of what preceded the military action in Lithuania, read by Yelena Kovalenko." At the conclusion of the piece, Mitkova came back on to say: "Unfortunately this is the only information from Lithuania that was available to Television News Service."[18]

That was not the preferred scenario at state television. Pyotr Reshetov had hastily penned some four pages of text about Lithuania, but there had not been time to type it in the frantic rush to get it on the air. Just before

TSN was to go on live, Reshetov gave his script to Mitkova and ordered her to read it. She refused absolutely, whereupon the deputy head of state television warned her that if she did not read it, *TSN* would be closed down. Undeterred, Mitkova told him to get his own anchor.

The *TSN* team did manage to slip some subversive messages into the program. They showed a filmclip of a 1988 Lithuanian demonstration in which crowds protested the secret 1939 Molotov–von Ribbentrop pact that had consigned them to Soviet domination. A special soundtrack was chosen, too. Relying on the long-time Soviet practice of playing classical music when high political figures died, instead of its usual upbeat pop music ending, *TSN* substituted slow music of mourning to commemorate the innocent people killed in Vilnius.[19]

The next night almost three-quarters of the *TSN* news program was disallowed, including Lithuanian populist leader Landsbergis's appeal to Gorbachev and the report of the Lithuanian foreign minister's visit to Poland for talks about setting up a government in exile.[20] Anchor Dmitry Kiselyov refused to go on the air because he was denied the right to show a report on a Latvian killed in Riga by Soviet special troops. Censors were moved into the newsroom and applied their scissors, and live broadcasts were replaced by the safer option of tapes that could be previewed and edited.[21]

TSN was in decline. In March the three main anchors were fired. Just days before, some 80 percent of the proposed news program was cut by the censors. After that *TSN* was defanged. Gorbachev's referendum campaign on Soviet unity could proceed without fear of unacceptable messages broadcast from the opposition. Within two months the Russian republic presidential election campaign would begin and Yeltsin would have his own piece of the television broadcast day. The young pioneers of *TSN,* with their style of news reporting and direct, emotional, "modern" connection to viewers, sought refuge at Yeltsin's Channel Two: the repression at Channel One had helped to launch the star system.

In the Kremlin, Mikhail Gorbachev was dismayed by the public reaction of angry journalists and political figures and attempted to turn back the clock. On January 16 the Supreme Soviet took up the issue of media objectivity. Gorbachev expressed his concern about the opposition of some media organs and formally asked the Supreme Soviet to suspend the Law on the Press and reinstate censorship. He asked that body to take over control of the press to ensure "unbiased coverage." This was the same leader who, in the fall of 1989, ordered (but did not enforce) a newspaper editor fired for publishing a poll casting doubt on his popularity.[22]

A deputy immediately responded that he thought that press freedom was the main achievement, perhaps the only one, since Gorbachev came to power in 1985, and that television under Kravchenko had come to resemble a "bad state farm."[23] "I hear you mention here the Law on the Press,"

Gorbachev told the Supreme Soviet deputies. "A decision could be taken right now to suspend the Law on the Press. The Supreme Soviet will ensure complete objectivity. The Supreme Soviet has the power to decide on this matter." In the end, parliament defeated Gorbachev's proposal and he withdrew it, saying he did not "insist."

Leonid Kravchenko came to television in the fall of 1990 with a brief to turn the clock back on the television revolution, dampen controversy, and restrict room for contending views. He did so, obeying his master and ignoring the viewers. Though they could do nothing about these decisions, the viewers were not fooled. Three years in a row they were asked if television programs were getting better or worse, and most saw a worsening. Few saw improvement, and increasing numbers did not want to say anything, perhaps a sign of wariness about a return to repression.[24]

	1989	1990	1991
Getting better	72%	56%	21%
Getting worse	6%	13%	31%
No answer	22%	31%	48%

TELEVISION AND THE COUP ATTEMPT: AUGUST 1991

At six o'clock in the morning on August 19, 1991, TASS announced that Mikhail Gorbachev was unable to perform his duties as president because of a health problem and the government was in the hands of the State Committee for the State of Emergency. The emergency committee took control of the electronic media before the print media, signalling the high priority placed on these powerful communications organs. But they seem to have done it hastily and ineptly, and, of course, the times had changed. An earlier coup—the one that deposed Nikita Khrushchev—had been far better organized. Those coup leaders made sure the media were in their hands and had appointed, in advance, the new heads of radio and television, *Pravda, Izvestia,* and TASS. According to Nikolai Mesyatsev, at the time a high Party official and conspirator, ". . . all basic mass information media were taken under control."[25]

Like everyone else, Boris Yeltsin learned of the coup from television. He was at his *dacha,* he recalled, "sitting glued to the television (I hadn't put on a shirt yet. . . .)."[26] Channel Two's pro-Yeltsin Russian republic programming was canceled altogether; Channel One programs were to be played on all other channels. In a formidable disconnection that stunned the audience, *Swan Lake* replaced news reporting. A year later, Leonid Kravchenko, head of state television, said that he had not interfered with the program schedule, that the ballet had been scheduled two weeks in advance. "I was not about to break up the schedule!" he announced. Other classical music programs and soccer were shown, and between them the decrees and directives of the coup leaders were announced by a faceless newsreader—the demeanor so well known from pre-*glasnost* television.

Kravchenko was roused by the coup plotters around 12:30 A.M., when the Central Committee called to tell him a KGB car was on its way to bring him to Party headquarters.[27] He was ordered to prepare television and radio for the state of emergency. Kravchenko later explained that he thought it was quite likely that Gorbachev was ill. He had recently traveled with the president to Japan and Great Britain and had heard Raisa Gorbachev mention at dinner on the plane that her husband was working to his limit and that she was afraid something "terrible and irreparable could happen to him at any moment."

Arriving at Ostankino with his orders from the coup leaders, he found it occupied by the military and police. Could Kravchenko have refused his orders? Even after the inefficient coup plotters had been arrested and Kravchenko fired, he said on his behalf that the State Television and Radio Company was obliged to carry materials signed by its superiors and, in a familiar rationale, if he did not take charge someone else would.

Vremya director Olvar Kakuchaya remembered that the night of the putsch Kravchenko called him at 1:30 A.M. and told him to get to work immediately. At 3:55 A.M. vehicles carrying armed guards surrounded Ostankino. About half an hour later tanks rumbled down the wide highway to television headquarters.

Meanwhile, Kravchenko telephoned from his car on the *kremlyovka* (the direct line to the Kremlin) and told Kakuchaya that "we are coming; come downstairs; I'll give you the text that must be read." The soldiers kept everyone out, including Kravchenko, whom they did not recognize. Television people came down to the checkpoint to show the soldiers a pass from Kakuchaya for Kravchenko. Kravchenko brought the official texts to the newsreaders Kakuchaya had hurriedly called (he had made sure to call two who owned cars, since public transportation was not available at that hour). Puzzled, Kakuchaya looked at the pages Kravchenko brought. Such bulletins were usually *tassovki*, (official TASS dispatches), and these were unlike anything he had seen before. They were all handwritten. The first ones had Yanayev's emergency directives for the country. Then Lukyanov had written several pages. It was homemade and informal and hurried; no one had even thought to type them, and, clearly, nothing had been prepared ahead of time. The soldiers occupying Ostankino told the newspeople they were prepared to stay there for fifteen days, and they had brand new rubles to spend at the commissary. They were particularly enthralled with the Finnish elevators and made a sport of knocking out the buttons on the panel.

Early on, news correspondent Sergei Medvedev came to Kakuchaya asking to be permitted to go to Yeltsin's White House, where barricades had been put up. Medvedev had wrestled with his conscience about accepting the anchor assignment for the evening news. He knew that if he did not do it, one of the newsreaders would be brought in. From watching CNN, he also knew that an antiputsch campaign had been mounted. The news director agreed to sign a request for newsgathering and called it, disarmingly, "Moscow Today." Kakuchaya feared Medvedev would be killed and told him to stand apart from the cameraman to reduce the risk. He also told his journalist: "We want this for history." He would try to have the story aired, but thought it unlikely. Medvedev then went to pick up the camera equipment and managed to get it out of the building without the signed approval of the KGB chief in charge. Later he ascribed his luck to the incompetence of the paratroopers who did not know which signatures were valid and which were not.[28]

At five o'clock, state television started to work on the emergency committee's press conference. Elena Pozdnyak, a news director, was the best video editor in the business. She used to work on Brezhnev's speeches with a jeweller's finesse. She could excise a single letter from a mispronounced word. Kravchenko passed an order to Kakuchaya for Pozdnyak to take out Yanayev's shaking hands and the derisive laughter from the press corps. She could have done it easily, but she thought it important for the country to see the weakness of the self-appointed leader and refused. She did make one cut: when Yanayev addressed correspondent Sergei Lomakin, using the familiar "you" and the diminutive form of his name, he asked, "Seryozha, repeat it. I forgot your question." Pozdnyak cut that; she knew that if she left it in, "Seryozha" could be torn apart by the mob. Lomakin was lucky that exposure as court favorite did not have worse consequences.

Seeing the young stalwart at the press conference, Kakuchaya was puzzled. He had sent two other correspondents, but he recalled that Lomakin had recently acquired the status of political observer, which gave him the right to develop stories on his own without checking with his immediate superior. Sergei Lomakin agreed that it was his initiative to go to the press conference. He learned of the coup at his dacha and came to Moscow right away. His bad luck, he said to me, was Yanayev's unfortunate turn of speech. Lomakin protested that Yanayev's familiar "you" address was in no way a sign of their close friendship—quite the contrary. Lomakin had seen the coup plotter only once before, with Gorbachev. It was Soviet usage for a more powerful person to address an underling with the familiar pronoun. It was a mark of status, and that is what Yanayev did to Lomakin, who ruefully noted that it "cost him dearly."[29]

At six in the evening, well before the 9:00 P.M. news was to air, Medvedev recounted what he had seen to Kakuchaya, who himself had been following the events on CNN, which played in the offices of every

important official in the building. But CNN was not received by the huge
Soviet domestic audience; that was something only state television could
do. Kakuchaya told Medvedev to pull the story together quickly and "we'll
see if it can be used." Valentin Lazutkin, deputy chief of television, agreed
with Kakuchaya to air the material the latter had assembled from the republics, as well as Medvedev's report. Lazutkin, Kakuchaya said, "saw
everything except the end [of the news piece], because it wasn't ready. He
saw Yeltsin on the tank. He signed it. He knew it would be our heads."

Medvedev said Lazutkin asked only that Yeltsin's speech be shortened.[30]
Medvedev's footage from the streets of Moscow showed people on the
street speaking out against the occupation. Yeltsin was reported as calling
for the committee to permit Gorbachev to speak to the people, for a national strike, and for an emergency session of parliament. Barricades defended the White House, the Russian parliament building, from tanks. One
man said on camera: "We learned from Vilnius."

Film from Leningrad showed massive demonstrations against the emergency committee. Television viewer Boris Yeltsin was as astonished as the
rest of the country, when, in his words, *Vremya* "unexpectedly ran a totally
accurate and truthful report from the barricades of the White House."[31]
Within seconds of airing, Party watchdogs immediately called and denounced Lazutkin.[32] St. Petersburg television, which had been persuaded
by Mayor Anatoly Sobchak to defect from the side of the emergency committee, was broadcasting oppositionist messages, and although the channel
was blacked out in Moscow, many other people in western Russia could
see it.[33]

Lazutkin was told to call the northern city and shut down the television
system. He promised to call immediately and did, but instead of ordering
them to leave, simply inquired how things were going and passed on no orders. Olvar Kakuchaya told Sergei Medvedev to leave town, take time off,
disappear for two or three weeks. We'll hide you, he told the young journalist. On August 20, the emergency committee assigned a KGB colonel to
Lazutkin to prevent a repeat of the previous day's insubordination.

Medvedev's bold report was not the only leak in the television net. The
next day, August 20, the three o'clock news capsule *Novosti* (News) came
on. News capsules normally came on three or four times during the day to
provide updates, often without pictures. Under occupation, the content
was remarkable. It opened with Yeltsin's and Alexander Rutskoy's demand
that internationally-recognized physicians meet with Gorbachev and assess
his medical condition. If satisfactory, he was to be restored to power immediately. They demanded that a state of siege be lifted, that media restrictions
be terminated, and that the Russian republic parliament and president be
allowed to function. Foreign Minister Andrei Kozyrev was said to be on his
way to meet with George Bush, with a stopover in France. Moreover, some

70 percent of the regional governments in Russia were reported to support Yeltsin and reject the appeals of the Emergency Committee.

Just before noon on August 21, the soldiers left Ostankino. The edition of *Vremya* designed to go out live to the Urals' time zones spoke of the "former GKChP" (acronym for the emergency committee), and announced that all press limitations had been removed. State television broadcast a public apology noting that their actions had been the product of orders over which they had no control.

During those days, the impact of the foreign media was enormous, principally for elites. Under house arrest in the Crimea, Gorbachev listened to the BBC; Nursultan Nazarbayev, leader of Kazakhstan, was able to pull down American television. "I might mention," he wrote in his memoirs, ". . . that my only channel of reliable information on events was satellite television. From the morning of August 19 onwards, the television set in my office was permanently switched on and tuned in to CNN."[34] The large newspapers with reputations of political independence were closed down. Eleven outlawed newspapers put out a joint paper, called *Obshchaya gazeta* (Common Newspaper). It was printed outside Moscow and secretly brought in and distributed.

Leonid Kravchenko, the capitulationist leader of state television, was fired on August 16 and replaced the next day by liberal newspaper editor Yegor Yakovlev. Two days later, Eduard Sagalayev was named Yegor Yakovlev's chief deputy and head of television broadcasting. Once in office, Yakovlev restored the banned programs and brought back the dismissed correspondents.

In a move that would create problems for the future, Boris Yeltsin, during the uncertain days of the coup, issued a decree on the media in which all media organs on the territory of the Russian republic became subordinate to the Russian government. He did this to enable his reformist government to grant protection to media organs battered by the rival Soviet government and to replace conservative media officials that his government associated with the reactionary putsch. Between protection and oppression, the line is often thin, especially where legal buffer mechanisms are not yet in place. The budgetary and political impact of this move would be felt for years afterward.

In a wise and thoughtful statement in August 1990, when the crises in the Baltics and Moscow were still months away, television critic Yury Bogomolov despaired of learning what was happening in the Baltic republics from television news. "What can the viewer know about the situation in this region from the broadcasts of CTV [state television]? Only what he can guess without the broadcasts and only within the framework of official approaches and evaluations." The only solution "which many, including liberals" see is that state television, in whatever form, "be placed under the control of a democratic institution, such as the Supreme Soviet of the USSR. But such a 'solution' is pure illusion." Unfortunately, the illusion of putting the powerful resource of television in the "right" hands, instead of protecting it from the grasp of *all* institutional suitors, ultimately proved to be immensely powerful and immensely destructive.

CHAPTER SEVEN

Between Putsch
and Revolt

YEGOR YAKOVLEV AT THE HELM

With great dispatch, Yegor Yakovlev was named head of state television. His was to be the first post-Soviet leadership of the giant institution. Yakovlev, the former editor of *Moscow News,* had used that weekly to press well beyond the limits of *glasnost.* He could do so because his circulation was mainly foreign (it was published in a number of foreign languages and the Russian edition was very limited at first), and his appeal in Moscow was to a narrow swath of intellectuals. Even so, he was frequently called on the carpet. During the 1991 coup attempt, he defied the ban on nonconforming newspapers by publishing the underground paper, *Obshchaya gazeta.*

When the coup was put down, Yakovlev went to head television, a much bigger operation and a much more politically sensitive position. His appointment, he recalled, was a symbol of change. On the second day after the putsch, Mikhail Gorbachev, still president of the still-standing Soviet Union, called, offering the chairmanship of television. Yakovlev knew that it was Boris Yeltsin who was really in charge and made sure the Russian president agreed.[1]

In the wake of the putsch attempt, Channel One was in upheaval. Just before Yakovlev's appointment was announced, television employees jammed into the Ostankino concert hall to learn about their future. Alexander Tikhomirov led the meeting. He strode in like a "commissar"[2] and demanded repentance. He had a list, he said, of those who had collaborated with Leonid Kravchenko. Many in the audience cried. Some, like Elena Pozdnyak, who had courageously refused to edit out the shaking hands of putsch leader Gennadi Yanayev, were simply bewildered by the

wholesale accusations. The next day Yegor Yakovlev was officially presented
to Ostankino by Alexander Yakovlev (no relation), and afterward the two
and Valentin Lazutkin talked privately. Yegor Yakovlev recalled that Lazutkin
told him he should immediately change the name of *Vremya*. The new
head of television agreed and promptly called the old *TSN* team, and that
night they anchored the new news.

Yegor Yakovlev saw his task as carving out autonomy and independence
for television and minimizing the influence of the new monopolist—the
Russian government. Like so many other tragedies in the aftermath of Soviet rule, this one involved a clear perception of the issues and near-total
absence of the resources with which to ward off coercion. The operating
budget of television was in the hands of the Russian government; there was
no significant competition. In a severely depleted economy there was little
hope of raising investment funds to reduce the dependence on government
handouts. The legal system was in flux (an understatement), and no buffer-
ing agencies could guarantee independence from political powers. Yakovlev
did not have much room to maneuver to put autonomous television on a
firm footing.

Television's finest hour had not been in August 1991. Could this institution, so closely allied to political power and so heavily burdened with a
huge, costly, inefficient labor force, rouse itself to independent initiative in
the post-Soviet transition? What exactly did "post-Soviet" mean for television, still operating as a fiefdom of the leadership with no substantial revenue sources of its own? When Yakovlev came on board at Ostankino, the
dozen or so deputy chairmen tendered their resignations. He did not accept them. Four years later, he said "I should have fired them all. They were
infected with the bacillus of intrigue."[3]

Eduard Sagalayev came back to be Yakovlev's chief deputy and operational head of television. Oleg Dobrodeyev came back to be director of
news and information from his post as head of the Channel Two news,
Vesti. Along with them came many of the television stars who had been
working for Yeltsin's Channel Two. The new leadership of perhaps a couple
of dozen faced an old institution of many thousands. Yakovlev announced
his policy on personnel and past partisanship: first, he said, he was not interested in "who did what in Kravchenko's time [everything depends on
how you work now]." Second, he warned them not to gossip and not to
come to him with backbiting and denunciations; and he recalled they didn't,
not to *him*,—but the corridors of Ostankino buzzed with gossip.[4]

An inextricable part of television's past was the security police. The KGB
took a keen interest in the media, and television, in particular. This
medium had enormous influence and reach. It was a near obsession for the
Kremlin, and it had very substantial international networks, especially in its
corps of correspondents all over the world. The failure of the coup created

an opportunity to confront the KGB. KGB leader Vladimir Kryuchkov had been a coup plotter, and the tentacles of the feared organization had spread everywhere, and everywhere opposed the rise of Boris Yeltsin. But the exact nature and extent of the KGB-media connection was difficult to identify. In some cases, among highly placed media officials, it was direct: Alexander Aksyonov had been deputy head of the Belarussian KGB before coming to head television in 1985. When Mikhail Gorbachev came to power, communications officials at the national and regional levels had backgrounds in international propaganda, security and control, and oversight of official youth groups. Little in their careers related to management of the media to which they were appointed.[5]

At the top echelon at state television, Oleg Dobrodeyev estimated, perhaps 10 percent were KGB officers. He thought that perhaps a third of their correspondents were full-time KGB officers. Abroad, in the large capitals, the KGB supplied numerous "journalists." Colonel Mikhail Lyubimov, father of *Vzglyad* pioneer Alexander Lyubimov, was KGB *rezident,* while ostensibly working as press attaché of the Soviet embassy in London. KGB Colonel Yuri Kobaladze's cover in London was Soviet State Television and Radio. Lieutenant-Colonel Oleg Tsarev was in London as correspondent for the newspaper *Socialist Industry.*[6] Onetime chief of counterintelligence, Major General of the KGB Oleg Kalugin began his intelligence career in the United States as an exchange journalism "student" at Columbia University. He recalled the intensive course he took in Moscow to make his cover reasonably plausible, and it served him in good stead when he returned as "correspondent" for Radio Moscow.[7]

KGB influence spread beyond its own personnel in the television network. When a journalist wished to work in the United States, the project had to be approved or shaped by the KGB officers at state television, and, in Dobrodeyev's words, "everyone knew who they were."[8] He asserted that the "organs" did not directly interfere with individual domestic television programs or decree a specific ideological stance, but were involved in news about extremely important events, especially those likely to have international repercussions or which were designed for foreign consumption.[9]

In 1966, the new Brezhnev regime cracked down on dissidents in a staged trial of two writers that attracted notice in the West. The Party's Central Committee published the marching orders for the media: "the Novosti Press Agency and the KGB will prepare articles about the trial for publication abroad," and an ad hoc press group was formed to prepare and monitor both print and electronic media. Included in the press group were two high-ranking KGB officers.[10]

In another sense, though, the KGB was everywhere in the capacity of censors.[11] Overall, one Western report estimated, the KGB (and the Party jointly) had a force of some seventy thousand censors for all mass media.[12]

Eduard Sagalayev called these media-content overseers, "the first department of the KGB."[13] Prohibitions were legion: it was forbidden to show a panorama of a bridge, pictures of Moscow from a helicopter, information about gold mining. Also forbidden were the cupolas of cathedrals, baptisms, marriages, and funerals. Directives were conveyed on the telephone, usually without documentation.[14]

The question "where did they all go?" is intriguing. Some went into newly reconstituted intelligence agencies; some went into the private intelligence business, for which they had accumulated both skills and dossiers. Vladimir Gusinsky, who became a multi-millionaire in post-Soviet Russia and started a private media empire with his banking money, had former KGB officers among his closest advisors. As Gusinsky explained, he was advantaged in foreign markets by the information these specialists provided. "'My ties to the KGB are like the ties of any American corporation to the CIA, any big organization in which high-ranking specialists are employed.'"[15]

Immediately upon his appointment as state television head, Yegor Yakovlev tackled the KGB issue. First, he contacted Vadim Bakatin, the new KGB head, and extracted a promise to recall his people from television and radio. On Bakatin's list of operatives in television was the chief of the correspondents' department. He was fired, as were two others—only three of the much, much larger number in television. Yegor Yakovlev said that it took two years to wind up the work of KGB officers working undercover as journalists in foreign bureaus of state television.[16] How thorough the housecleaning was cannot be known.

What to do about the evening news, the most closely watched indicator of policy and power, was the next item on the agenda. Without substantial and meaningful change in this, the most authoritative source of news and information in the country, a real change from a Soviet to a post-Soviet world would not be perceived. Yegor Yakovlev brought the brightest stars back to Channel One—the rebellious crew of *TSN* and the other young enemies of the Kravchenko-Gorbachev crackdown on television.

At Channel One, the news department, totalling some 800 people in all, was still headed by Olvar Kakuchaya, head of news for two years and in the top news administration for thirteen years.[17] The idea of a wholesale staff dismissal was judged profoundly undemocratic, for it would appear to be a purge, the favorite instrument of the predemocratic past. Yegor Yakovlev wryly noted that ". . . people who were the ideologues of the putsch and whose task it is to stifle democracy have become the most zealous of democrats and . . . oppose any decisive steps by saying that they constitute violations of democracy."[18] Afterward, he told me that he should have done what he did at *Moscow News,* where he fired fifty or sixty people. At Ostankino, the "non-professionals" stayed.[19]

When I talked to Kakuchaya in the fall of 1992, he said that his removal by Yakovlev had been an "undemocratic act," and some 300 of the 470 creative staff of the news department signed a petition that Kakuchaya should continue in his job. He did not conceal his opposition to the *TSN*-style, combative, personalized reporting. The muzzling of *TSN*'s anchors was not a bad thing, Kakuchaya thought. Tanya Mitkova, Dmitri Kiselyov, and Yury Rostov all had irreverent, even insolent, and often inaccurate notions of the news profession, he told me. On *TSN* they gave "very negative information."

Faced with intransigence, Yegor Yakovlev sought a way out. He settled on a contest: let both teams have it out. Two weeks were set aside in September. By lot, *TSN* had the first week for its model, and *Vremya,* the second. Boris Nepomnyashchy was head of *Mayak* radio at the time and moved over to become deputy director of the television news in the middle of the competition. "I was against the *methods*. It was organized quickly, but I was for the concept. They should have talked to the people and not just announced [it] and taken right off." He disagreed with *how* it was done, he said, not that it *was* done. He said there were "deficiencies." It could have been done "more subtly." But, he acknowledged, "there was no time." Probably the "leftism" of *TSN* was responsible, he said.[20]

The noted critic and media theoretician Sergei Muratov also found the whole project too hastily conceived. It takes time, he remarked, to develop two news programs, and why should the Soviet public have only two choices? There were other models. The choice Yakovlev presented ignored a much wider range of possibilities.[21]

The competition was denounced by the *Vremya* faithful as "low farce designed to get rid of the . . . management, in particular its editor-in-chief Olvar Kakuchaya." To avoid this perception, Yakovlev designed the competition with several methods of measurement. Experts—media critics, academics, "opinion leaders"—were invited to provide their judgments and three different surveys were conducted by three polling organizations, two of which were fully independent of the Ostankino system. The three surveys showed a clear preference for *TSN.* It was declared the winner. The name *Vremya* was changed, but returned at the end of 1994 to capitalize on its name recognition in the face of growing competition, Channel One said. The country was beginning the war in Chechnya at the time.

The formation of a new team that would incorporate and conciliate both sides, but award the "prize" to one side, and make no deep or substantial cuts in the other proved to be problematic. The competition was denounced by the losers as fixed from the start. That spring, in a preview of the next year's civil strife, the television center literally came under attack.

When the first violent demonstrations rocked the Ostankino headquarters in June 1992, few had sympathy with the protesters. Led by the thuggish Viktor Anpilov of Working Russia (a tireless campaigner for Zyuganov in 1996) and General Albert Makashov, who had run for president of Russia in 1991, the screaming mob, of sometimes as many as fifty thousand people, called for their own television airtime, a reduction of U.S. influence, and the removal of Jews from television. (Makashov would be much more "successful" the next year, when he led an armed mob to the bloody battle for Ostankino.)

Demonstrators blocked exits and entrances and verbally abused employees braving the gauntlet. Facing a police cordon clearly too thin to protect the television building, the demonstrators easily broke through. Ostankino chairman Yegor Yakovlev promised airtime for the opposition, and on June 28, aired a live discussion with "opposition leaders" in Russia (Communist leader Gennady Zyuganov and Russian nationalist writer Alexander Prokhanov) and, by remote pickup, opposition spokesmen in Ukraine and Kyrgyzia.[22]

The siege of Ostankino ended violently (riot police broke it up), tardily (it had gone on for days and the police had been slow to react in force), and, some thought, with a compromise that only tarnished the television leadership, since it did not placate the opposition in the least. The political forces that attempted, by force, to acquire equal (perhaps more than equal) time on television were arrayed on the extremes. It was a hysterical and frightening group of militants, from whom mainstream leading politicians distanced themselves. But that "mainstream" included many who would themselves, a year-and-a-half later, attack the television center to force *their* way onto the air.

In June 1992, Vice President Alexander Rutskoy contemptuously said on the news: "Let the viewers take a look at the kind of state they are in and what kind of working people they [the demonstrators] are."[23] But in October 1993, complaining that he, too, had been denied access to television, Rutskoy joined parliament speaker Ruslan Khasbulatov and others to attempt to occupy Ostankino and overturn state authority. That spring, in 1992, the much-feared opposition television show turned out to be another of the long-winded talking-heads shows. The old guard had still learned nothing of how to use the medium they sought to influence. That was undoubtedly because, as always, they concentrated on their message, not on the needs and preferences of viewers.

Oleg Poptsov thought the June siege was a dress rehearsal that Russia's leaders, "eternally shortsighted," failed to appreciate, fixated as they were on "the film scenes of the taking of the Winter Palace and the telegraph office" and unable to understand that "times have changed. The targets are no longer banks and the telegraph office or the railroad, but first of all television and radio. Whoever controls the news channels has power over everything."[24]

Russia never really got to see what, if any, true middle-ground approach could have emerged. The prize proved to be too vital to the political interests of the new political leaders, and zero-sum television was in. Shortly, Yegor Yakovlev would be out.

After the August coup attempt, media opportunities for political players had grown substantially. But so had the number of players. As long as there were many contending sources of influence, as long as the parties were disorganized and inexperienced, as long as their claims were naively transmitted, their impact was largely ineffectual and diffuse. And, not to be overlooked, as long as airtime was (artificially) cheap and plentiful there was room for everyone. There is much to be said for weak institutions, when legal protection is in its infancy and the economy is not yet able to support a number of credible contenders operating on their own, independent of the budget of the state.

In the spring of 1992, Oleg Dobrodeyev remarked that in the past, the Party Central Committee's Ideological Department was able to dictate its demands to television, and so did the people around President Gorbachev. Television received what he termed a "colossal number of requirements, depending on who was interested in what." Typically, the Central Committee added up all the demands and requests from all of the ministries and the regions. Then they were prioritized and passed on to television. At the highest level of the Communist Party, each powerful player dictated his demands in his functional area. As the centralized system disintegrated, the people at television could see that the linchpin had disappeared. The result was an explosion of telephone calls. Erosion of power at the center meant that there were more contending parties. Dobrodeyev said that when he headed the news operation for Channel One under Yakovlev, the competing requests were not only for coverage, but for a particular political spin on each story. Though he generally acceded to the demands for coverage, he refused to include political bias. It was not difficult, he said, to expand coverage. After all, there were *seven* daily editions of the news—every three hours. In addition, there were two hours of news and music on the morning program—plenty of time to satisfy all claimants. As a result, the news director was exhausted brokering all of the demands and constantly trying to relieve pressure on the evening newscast, the plum everyone sought. Yegor Gaidar had his press people badgering television, and so did Gennady Burbulis, counsellor to President Yeltsin. Pugnacious Ruslan Khasbulatov, chairman of the increasingly oppositionist Russian parliament, had his press department attempting to put the squeeze on Ostankino news.

In March 1993, Dobrodeyev said that he had to deal with attempts to pressure him into broadcasting what he called "purely propaganda materials" fifty to sixty times a day, since every party and every political structure considered it a duty to go on the air.[25] In this battle for the spoils of airtime, the only moderating element was the scattered character of the demands. The greater the plurality of sources, the greater the ability to withstand them. The broadened arena for editorial autonomy was not a result of legal guarantees or chastened political practices. Rather, it resulted from the fragmentation of executive political power, begun in the early years of *glasnost* and moving jaggedly forward in its aftermath.

In 1992, it appeared that Channel One, unlike Russian Television over at Channel Two, might actually have acquired a kind of political buffer derived from its transborder activity with the non-Russian republics. At meetings of the Commonwealth of Independent States, when a "common informational space" was referred to with great approbation, it was always the first channel that the heads of the republics had in mind. It penetrated all their borders and retained viewing audiences despite the new nationalisms.

But rhetoric about the desirability of transborder television as an integrative force was easy. More difficult was determining who had ownership and control and who paid what. Coffers were declining rapidly, and television was expensive. At the Uzbek capital of Tashkent, the CIS signatories made the realization of a shared television space somewhat more likely. The different republics would "own" the company through the mechanism of a stock company, begun by but not limited to the founding republic governments. Russia was to pay the most, providing the technical base and the lion's share of the costs.

At the time, many treated this internationalization of Ostankino as a hopeless idea. The majority of Russians polled thought the commonwealth existed only on paper, and some observers were not impressed that the board of directors of the new multi-national organization included member states hardly qualifying as democracies, a fact certain to adversely influence the channel's news policy. Some of the directors were at war: how, for example, would Armenia and Azerbaijan agree about a "common information space" with respect to issues of the disputed Nagorno-Karabakh region?[26] At first President Yeltsin backed the idea, but trouble with parliamentary speaker Ruslan Khasbulatov, his former ally, turned opponent, was brewing, and Yeltsin's advisors convinced him that he should not order a reorganization putting Ostankino under the jurisdiction of the privatization ministry, then headed by a Khasbulatov ally.[27]

During that important postputsch year, it appeared that the commitment of the non-Russian republics to a joint television company was fairly wobbly, economically limited, and perhaps only transitional, like the commonwealth itself. Whatever the strength and prospects of the multi-national company, the participation of Channel One provided a measure of insurance, a kind of extra-territoriality, that, in Dobrodeyev's words, would enable it to say, "Russia can no longer claim that Ostankino equals Russia's investment in it." He believed that because of the number of "owners," or directors, "nobody can really dictate." This insurance policy was virtually the only structural protection Ostankino would have in the battle for political control of television, but it was entirely too weak and too removed from the reality of rising nationalisms and declining economies.

On October 21, 1992, President Boris Yeltsin fired Yegor Yakovlev for "crude transgressions in covering ethnic conflicts. . . ."[28] The edict removing Yakovlev, signed by the president's national security council secretary, cited the television chief's role in exacerbating ethnic conflict as a violation of the Law on the Press as well as the Constitution.[29]

The act in question was the broadcast of a documentary film on a conflict in the Caucasus area of south Russia, scene of persistent unrest among the many small ethnic groups. An Orthodox Christian people (North Ossetians, traditional Russian allies) uprooted, drove out, torched the homes of, and, in the process, killed many of the Ingush, a Muslim people with whom in Soviet times they had lived side by side. The film was well done; it was not tendentious. It did reveal that the Russian army, in the words of its own leaders, inappropriately favored the Ossetians. And it also showed Yegor Gaidar on a fact-finding mission to the area, his round face frozen with fear as he walked slowly down the street, surrounded by infuriated demonstrators, one of whom, a woman, slapped him in the face.

The film was not biased propaganda; it showed that all ethnic conflict is tragic; misery and death have no ethnic exclusivity. It was one of the few programs that successfully contextualized and explained the roots of ethnic conflict, and in so doing brought down the wrath of the Ossetian leader, Akhsarbek Galazov. After Yakovlev was replaced, Galazov stated with satisfaction that he had asked President Yeltsin to fire the television chief,[30] or at least take "appropriate steps."

In an open letter to President Boris Yeltsin, Yakovlev deplored the method Yeltsin used to fire him publicly without informing him in advance, saying it was Yeltsin's style.[32] But the letter also raised a legal issue. Yakovlev objected to Yeltsin's decree "indirectly accusing me of fanning up national [ethnic] hatred. . . . Such charges need to be proved. According to the Russian Constitution this can only be done in a court of justice."[33]

Yakovlev announced he would take legal action against the president unless the decree was "corrected to comply with the law." Yeltsin did so, removing any reference to illegal acts. He then appointed Igor Malashenko, Yakovlev's deputy, to replace him, and Malashenko promptly announced that he owed his position to Yakovlev, that he had no policy disagreements with Yakovlev, that he would hold Ostankino to the Yakovlev policy, and that he had previewed and approved the offending program. "And I would do it again," he said.[34] Later, Yakovlev told me that he had not seen the documentary before it was broadcast, but if he had, he would have approved it.[35]

Yakovlev's sudden departure pointed up the sensitivity of ethnic relations and the inevitable role that television played for leaders of ethnic groups. It was a powerful asset for ethnic groups in making their arguments and mobilizing their adherents, and because the Yeltsin administration dominated state television, it was always implicated in the content of programming.

The proximate cause of the firing was layered over a more serious set of differences. Yegor Yakovlev said, "they were right to fire me." He would never do what later chairman Vyacheslav Bragin did—produce extremely partisan electoral coverage. Yakovlev said that during his time there was some television criticism of Yeltsin (though nothing like what emerged later) and the Russian president was distressed. There was probably something still deeper: Yakovlev noticed that Yeltsin spoke sharply to him at meetings with journalists and that the president never trusted him because of Yakovlev's relationship with Gorbachev.

At one meeting with Yeltsin, Yakovlev told the president that he had gone to Gorbachev's *dacha* for dinner, but he also wanted Yeltsin to know that from the time of the violence in Vilnius until the putsch he had not spoken to Gorbachev, and it was he, Yakovlev, who had been the first journalist to approach Yeltsin after his humiliating dismissal from the Moscow Party post.

Yet, for all that, Yeltsin was not comforted. He asked Yakovlev if he would like an ambassadorship—anywhere. Yakovlev declined, saying he could always go back to *Moscow News*. Then, Yeltsin asked, "Why did Gorbachev invite you to dinner instead of me?" Yakovlev remarked that given Yeltsin's position, it was he who had to invite. But Yeltsin only said, "He never calls."[36] Yeltsin and Gorbachev were still filled with bitterness and intense dislike for each other and still smarting from real or imagined slights.

Yakovlev's regime at state television was short. The first post-Soviet television policy was not smoothly crafted or administered. Yakovlev had a notorious temper and was not given to low-key, consensual discussions. Much was left undone: mass firings were avoided; most of the top-heavy, flabby structures were left, while financial support drained at an alarming rate. And, in parallel motion, corruption penetrated. Political pressure was exerted as always, but could be warded off by a complex balancing of forces. The attempt to ensure autonomy by devising a new institutional-structural base was doomed by internal Russian politics and the fragile external world of a barely existing commonwealth of nations whose information policies diverged dramatically.

Yegor Yakovlev's successor was his deputy, Igor Malashenko, a thirty-eight-year-old graduate of Moscow State University's philosophy department who had studied Dante because medieval thought tended to be well off the radar of political correctness, Marxist-Leninist style. A tall, thin man, whose face was dominated by large glasses and a bemused air, Malashenko had worked for twenty years in the U.S. and Canada Institute; he been a functionary in the Communist Party Central Committee's International Department and in Mikhail Gorbachev's press office. In short, he was no stranger to media politics, but he did not stay long. For a month and a half he took over as acting director until the appointment of Vyacheslav Bragin, and then went back to the number two position; he left a month later.

Bragin came in with a mandate to make sure the Yeltsin administration won the coming referendum, and, under him, in Malashenko's words, "what balance there was has been destroyed irretrievably."[37] Malashenko charged that Bragin and President Yeltsin's close advisor and media point-man, Mikhail Poltoranin, had made professional news operations very difficult, if not impossible. Anchors were receiving instructions about how to shade the news.[38]

In his open letter of resignation to Bragin, Igor Malashenko argued on behalf of a silent and much put-upon majority: the viewers. "You intend to transform yourself into a gung-ho patriot . . . but why must the viewers pay for it? . . . Of course, programs have to be changed at short notice from time to time, but these decisions have to be very carefully considered, because the viewer finds sudden and bewildering program changes extremely annoying. These kinds of instructions pour out of your office as out of a horn of plenty—neither the data of the sociologists nor the opinions of people in television interest you. Any negative consequences are secondary as far as you are concerned, compared with the possibility of earning a few points in the political game. But I hope that your tenure as chairman of 'Ostankino' will be brief and that you will not do too much damage to television and its viewers."[39]

THE PRESIDENTIAL-PARLIAMENTARY STANDOFF

The constitutional crisis of post-Soviet Russia's first year was expressed most vividly in the conflict over television, the most important political asset for a deeply divided political class. To be sure, the larger context related to the entire course of political and economic reform, which increasingly antagonized a legislature viewing, with concern, the president's ability to constrict its powers.[40]

The tension was temporarily released by the referendum in April 1993, a plebisiciatary safety valve soliciting support for the president and rejection of parliament's position. But since that confusing vote could not possibly sort out the claims of polarized political power, the pressure again built until the storming of television in October. Much of the constitutional crisis was not only played out on television, but was shaped by the contest over control of the medium. Each side—presidential and parliamentary—used its different constitutional powers to take control, and there was little room for compromise. Zero-sum television was most acute, even surpassing the intensity of the Gorbachev era, when intra-elite competition was limited ultimately by the ruling of a single leader.

On December 25, 1992, President Boris Yeltsin decreed a new structure to oversee the media: the Federal Information Center under the chairmanship of the president's old ally Mikhail Poltoranin (previously Yeltsin's press and mass media minister). He also appointed the respected jurist Mikhail Fedotov to be minister of the press. Much public discussion would take place to clarify the distinctions between the two, with Fedotov insisting that he had full freedom to grant subsidies and protect the autonomy of the press, even though the new FIC and its politically powerful director had overwhelming influence and few scruples about using it.

The uneasy division of duties did not last long, nor did the principals' amity. Fedotov and Poltoranin soon clashed and Fedotov lost, denouncing Poltoranin in the process. Later, Sergei Yushenkov, Poltoranin's deputy, assessed Fedotov rather harshly as a good jurist and a "very bad administrator" who could not handle relations with the FIC. As examples of Fedotov's mismanagement, Yushenkov cited the subsidies Fedotov allocated to the communist press.[41]

About a month after the creation of the FIC, Yeltsin again took action with respect to television, unpredictably issuing a confusing decree on state television, suddenly switching the frequency and resources of Channel One to Channel Two.[42] Though the decree was shortly rescinded, it was evidence of Yeltsin's scant concern for the requirements of laws on the books, not to mention the preferences and viewing habits of the public.

The mobilization of parliamentary forces in the clash over television was accelerated by President Yeltsin's appointment of his wholehearted supporter, Vyacheslav Bragin, to head Ostankino. Bragin had been chairman of the parliamentary committee on the media. With his removal, the way was clear for that committee to appoint a chairman of a far different political stripe. On January 22 Vladimir Lisin, formerly correspondent for the Communist Party paper *Pravda,* was elected head of the committee, which would now assume primacy as the parliamentary counterweight to Yeltsin's FIC. The conduct of the April referendum, when the anti-Yeltsin opposition justly complained of inequality of access and quality of coverage, motivated parliament to step up its campaign to gain access to television and deprive Yeltsin of what appeared to be an extraordinarily effective television monopoly. Under the aegis of parliament, Lisin moved to create a new body, the Federal Oversight Council, to monitor state radio and television programs and appoint and dismiss "leaders of state television and radio companies."[43] If this were to take place, it would mean that Yeltsin's hold over television would at last be broken, and the opposition would gain a commanding influence over both Channels One and Two, the content of programs, and the personnel. Moreover, such a parliamentary-based council was to spawn local councils to do the same thing with the dozens of regional television and radio companies in the state system.

Yeltsin's media chief Mikhail Poltoranin warned of violent seizures of television stations: "It is in the television studios and the television companies . . . that confrontations, armed confrontations, are possible. . ."[44] Lisin rejected the charge of censorship: "What is involved here is not political censorship but a balance between the influence of the executive and legislative branches of power on the state mass media."[45]

Ruslan Khasbulatov, leader of parliament, paid a visit to Russian Television and, in telling them not to fear the new federal council, asserted that "Parliament has always been and remains the most reliable defender of all those who do not violate the laws and the Constitution."[46] Mikhail Poltoranin countered that the new watchdog councils were unconstitutional, "the result of the deputies' struggle for monopoly over the mass information media."[47]

The takeover of television was delayed by the pro-Yeltsin parliamentary deputies' appeal to the constitutional court. But the rhetoric continued to heat up. Lisin's deputy, Viktor Yugin, said the mass media "are far stronger and more frightening in their activities and influence more people" than the KGB, the Ministry of Defense and the Ministry of Internal Affairs.[48]

It is difficult to imagine a more hyperbolic notion of the effects of television. By early July the law establishing the Federal Oversight Council was working its way through parliament. Since the April referendum, Yeltsin had been pushing hard for a new constitution that would end the standoff between the two centers of power. The parliament (accurately) saw its own demise in the success of the project. The terms of the distribution of power were about to change, but not if the mighty tool of power, the "troops" of television, could be put under parliamentary control.

To counter the parliament's move to take control of state television, on September 7 Boris Yeltsin issued a decree privatizing enterprises providing services to state radio and television by turning them into joint stock companies. With this, the jurisdiction of the parliamentary watchdog would be reduced, though not eliminated. Parliament immediately suspended the Yeltsin decree as a transparent subterfuge foreseen by its resolution of July 8 making it unlawful for state television and radio companies to be reorganized, liquidated, or privatized.

There was some parliamentary presence on the small screen. In the spring of 1991, the Russian parliament ruled that its chairman, Boris

Yeltsin, be granted Channel Two. Those six hours of daily airtime had become anti–Gorbachev opposition television. Legally, some or all of Channel Two still belonged to the parliamentary body and its chairman, Ruslan Khasbulatov, leader of the anti–Yeltsin opposition.

In the spring of 1993, Channel Two began broadcasting the weekly *Parliamentary Hour.* Each week the legislative body produced a videocassette and handed it over to Russian television. Just before *Parliamentary Hour* began, Channel Two announced it was going off the air and returning at the conclusion of the show. Oleg Poptsov, head of Channel Two, said he had no idea what was on the cassette he was handed.[49]

Parliamentary Hour was remarkable for the depth of its enmity toward reform leaders and its language of bellicose threat. Take, for example, the July 12 program featuring former Soviet journalist Iyona Andronov, who had worked in Europe, Cambodia, Laos, Vietnam, Nicaragua, and Afghanistan and written books about the CIA and the FBI—a likely KGB-linked background. On the show, Russian Foreign Minister Andrei Kozyrev was said to be in the pay of the United States: "It is absolutely clear that he does not work for Russia." After discussing Yeltsin's submission to presidents Bush and Clinton, Andronov concluded that "the minister traitor is in charge of the foreign policy. . . ."[50] Another edition of *Parliamentary Hour,* which aired very shortly before the October rebellion, called television and radio journalists the "chief instruments of the information psychological war" and warned of trials to come for treason.[51]

On July 20, Ruslan Khasbulatov formally opened Parliament's new television studio, "RTV-Parliament," a technically advanced operation financed by an allocation of two million dollars.[52] From now on, Channel Two would be required to broadcast *Parliamentary Hour* five days a week. A month later Poptsov received a letter from Khasbulatov informing him of the decision of the Committee for Mass Media of the Supreme Soviet to have *Parliamentary Hour* broadcast *seven* days a week. Poptsov was also told to move the program into a more desirable time slot, from 6:45 P.M. to 8:20 P.M. According to the ratings, the parliament's program attracted between 5 percent and 6 percent of the population, not bad for daytime, but low for prime time.

Rescheduling the program threatened to preempt the popular American soap opera *Santa Barbara* and feature films, and would deprive the station of advertising revenues for its most attractive time slots.[53] Poptsov flatly refused to comply with the rescheduling demand and, as was its habit, the news program *Vesti* editorialized in the broadcast. The anchor told the public, "Only the CPSU Politburo used to have the prerogative of upsetting broadcast schedules in contempt of viewers' interests."[54]

Khasbulatov also started looking at commandeering time on Channel One. As always, most important were the broadcasters' preferences, not the viewers. How their message was received was of absolutely no interest to the political power players, and there was virtually no financial dependence on viewers.

As the showdown between parliament and the president approached, the role played by television head Vyacheslav Bragin became increasingly important. Bragin was the sixth head of state television in seven years. When Yeltsin, in his desperate battle with parliament, needed television more than ever, his own politically loyal steward, in his zeal, undermined the effectiveness of the medium: Vyacheslav Bragin brought a political, cultural, and economic agenda to state television. Regarding politics, he understood his mission as the promotion of President Yeltsin's policies. To this end he gave government officials airtime on demand, even if it meant suddenly disrupting scheduled programs. In one week alone, three such unscheduled addresses by officials were broadcast. Bragin never saw it as a policy dilemma, asking rhetorically: "to whom did we give the floor? . . . We gave the floor to major state officials. Such things used to and will take place." He was convinced that the political lectures he arranged for viewers were a great success, and well he might, since he measured popularity by the reactions of Yeltsin-led party supporters who shared his views.[55] As Vyacheslav Bragin told me, he wanted an "independent centrist position" for Ostankino, but they would not hide their democratic position.[56]

On the cultural front, Bragin wanted television to bring Russia back in. He was appalled by the growing dominance of foreign influence, especially from the United States, and vowed to "retain and reflect our Russian reality, to return to the screen ordinary . . . peasants and workers. We have to bring back the province, the small Russian town, and people with natural gifts.[57]

His first contribution to the renaissance of (probably anachronistic) Russian culture was a new program, *Russkii Mir* (Russian World), a trip into the serenity of unspoiled folk life. Bragin's office symbolically displayed his pledge to return to the past. Over his desk hung an old-fashioned, real Russian landscape: "the sun, spring, the shore of a Russian lake. And I thought: now I have the symbol of Ostankino—this flowering apple tree."[58] He had replaced a modernist rendition of Noah and the flood.

Bragin's financial problems could not be solved by changing interior decor. With over 80 percent of the government allocation for state television going to the Ministry of Communications for transmission and satellite services, the financial underpinning of state television was weak. In the spring of 1993, Bragin could pay one of his most popular shows only 120,000 rubles for a production that cost 2.5 million. As a result, Ostankino had effectively broken down into dozens of independent revenue centers, with each production studio and each program selling its own advertising and retaining most of the revenue, while receiving airtime at no or nominal cost. It was estimated that the companies were bringing in some three hundred to six hundred million rubles a day, most of which stayed out of the reach of the parent, Ostankino.[59] That was *overt* financing; the greater danger was *covert* financing. Viewers would not know of the kickbacks and payola determining whose songs were played, whose firm was covered as a news item, and whose business telephone number happened to crawl along the bottom of the screen.[60]

Bragin vowed to end these corrupt practices by closing down the independent production companies and studios operating within Ostankino. One night in March it was done. When Andrei Kozlov, host of the popular quiz program *Brain Ring* came to his office to get his tape for that day's scheduled show, he found it locked and sealed. And so did the producers of another favorite quiz show, *What, When, Where.* In giving the order, Bragin had said he would "throw all these private deals (*lavochki*) out of state television." Bragin had been at his job for two months. He was unaware of the chaos that would ensue if the most popular shows were withdrawn without notice from the most watched channel. The seals were broken and the shows were broadcast. Kozlov kept his seal as a souvenir, and the viewing public was once again an afterthought in Ostankino's policymaking.[61]

Bragin ran television with the assistance of two close associates: twenty-six-year-old lawyer Kirill Ignatyev, a leader of the pro-Yeltsin parliamentary political bloc, and thirty-year-old Oleg Slabynko, whose only experience in television had been as Bragin's press secretary for two months. Slabynko never tired of telling people "I understand very little about television."[62] Three years later, when he had become a television producer, he was murdered in his home. The two new recruits effectively replaced the first deputy, Valentin Lazutkin, an experienced veteran of television who had once been its interim chief. Lazutkin contemptuously referred to Ignatyev as Bragin's "boy" (*malchik*).[63] After all this mismanagement and incompetence, the passive board of directors of Ostankino, which had not met once in the past eight months and had never been much of an independent managerial voice in the company, "rose like a phoenix from its ashes" and declared no confidence in Slabynko.[64] Bragin, the faithful political lieutenant, was no Sergei Lapin. To their surprise, the Ostankino people found themselves longing for the days of that Brezhnev-era television dictator who knew production values when he saw them.

Taken together, all these professional blunders were still of less importance than Bragin's growing political intrusiveness and his reintroduction of censorship. In his fervor of political loyalty he drove out the best newspeople. It recalled an earlier time only two years before, when Gorbachev's man, Leonid Kravchenko, drove the news talent to Yeltsin's new channel. In 1993, as civil conflict approached, the president of Russia could ill afford the loss of credible and trusted on-camera faces. Oleg Dobrodeyev, head of news at Channel One at the time, said it was "indecent" to work there. Bragin was a "clinical case," a "small-time party apparatchik from rural Tver district." Young people came who did not know television, and "frenzy" ensued.[65] "If the situation doesn't change," he said, "information as a category will inevitably disappear from state television. . . . Information as such is not needed by the powers; they need an instrument of instantaneous influence and rapid reaction."[66]

Dobrodeyev and his best anchors walked. A new television station was starting up, a private one that began by paying for time on the St. Petersburg channel (which could be received in Moscow and the rest of European Russia) and then took over the evening hours of Channel Four when the old educational channel was privatized. Bragin minimized the walkout, saying it involved only tens, not hundreds, of television people, but his worsening news programs had been dealt a tremendous blow, and so had President Yeltsin as the fall of 1993 approached.

Yeltsin and his close advisors did not fully appreciate how ill served they had been. In March of 1993, Sergei Yushenkov, Mikhail Poltoranin's deputy at the Federal Information Center, apparently demanded equal time at Ostankino because Ruslan Khasbulatov had been interviewed, and Bragin put the pro-Yeltsin talking head on.

Later, Yushenkov bitterly told me that the story that he had suddenly gone to television to demand airtime was not true. It was not without warning and he was invited. It was Bragin's idea; he called five people he thought could provide the response to Khasbulatov. Yushenkov was the only one who answered the phone and had actually seen the Khasbulatov material. He had refused at first, but then agreed. From the television people, he met hostility and criticism and concluded that "interference with television is not successful; it is better to refuse than to go on the air." Besides, he added, the dollar was driving programming. Yushenkov said that he often asked television to show press conferences, with the result that the news would show a bad caricature. "I then said we'd pay, and the next press conference showed us dazzlingly."[67]

Vyacheslav Bragin thought it entirely correct and effective for Yushenkov and others to break into the programming schedule to give the government's views. In June 1995, Bragin said that although things were "not so serious now . . . *then,* there was a crisis!" It was Khasbulatov who struck the tone of aggressiveness that called forth the "sharp reaction of the democratic powers," such as Yushenkov and others. Yushenkov was also a parliamentary deputy. It was not unusual, Bragin maintained, to have opposing views in a news story, and it was natural to include unscheduled interruptions. How many times, he noted, did anchors say, "this just came in" or "this is the latest news." Those appearances of Yushenkov were "fresh political reaction" to Khasbulatov.[68]

Perhaps President Yeltsin himself did not sufficiently comprehend the way his own team made him look on television. On March 25, with the referendum vote a month away and the fate of the country hanging in the balance, Boris Yeltsin came into the living rooms of his nation. It began well, but when the second camera was switched on, Yeltsin was still addressing the first one. Viewers saw their president talking on and on, not to them but to some other, unseen audience. Then the camera focused for some reason on the foreground, leaving the president a blurry background. The center of the camera's attention was then the teacup on Yeltsin's desk. The picture was so insistent that the viewer might have asked if there was something out of the ordinary about this teacup. Throughout all this, the loud whispers of the camera crew could distinctly be heard, urgently directing each other in hoarse sotto voce. It was not the first time. Yeltsin had been publicly criticized for an important televised speech in which he fixed on the wrong camera for almost a full minute, thus giving the impression that he could not look his viewers in the eye.[69] Yeltsin should have pondered the utility of control that ultimately subverted his own interests.

When President Yeltsin abolished the parliament by decree on September 21, 1993, the daily *Parliamentary Hour* was taken off the air, and so were voices of opposition. In those days, critic Irina Petrovskaya did not hear a single proparliamentary position except for an interview on the Moscow city channel. Instead, the order of the day was one-sided portrayal of the rising tension and sarcastic comments about the "so-called deputies."[70]

THE STORM OF TELEVISION: VYACHESLAV BRAGIN'S WATCH

When the battle of Ostankino was over, 143 people were dead and 735 were wounded, Moscow's Department of Health announced, though unofficial estimates were much higher.[71] The forces loyal to Ruslan Khasbulatov, Alexander Rutskoy, and their allies in parliament had failed to take the television center. On September 21, when President Yeltsin issued Decree No. 1400, suspending the Congress of People's Deputies and ordering new elections, the parliament, from its stronghold in the White House, ordered Yeltsin removed and named his vice president and archrival Alexander Rutskoy acting president. On September 28, the Ministry of the Interior cordoned off the building with barbed wire and placed troops around its perimeter. October 4 was the deadline for the rebels inside to surrender and leave. On October 2 hundreds of demonstrators outside the building assaulted the police cordon and, from the White House, the rebels urged them on. The cordon around the White House broke easily and the anti-Yeltsin forces of Vice President Rutskoy, Speaker Khasbulatov, and the forces they mobilized from the provinces swarmed out first to occupy the neighboring glass skyscraper that housed the Moscow mayoralty, and, incidentally, the offices of new private television stations, and then they started off for Ostankino, the nation's nerve center of television broadcasting.

Just before 6:00 P.M. the first group of rebels arrived at the center and the battle began. The next morning President Yeltsin ordered the troops to take parliament by force and the tanks fired their shells into its white marble face, setting off the flames that blackened the facade of the same White House that Boris Yeltsin himself defended two years earlier.

When the brief and bloody rebellion of October 1993 had been put down, and before the blackened marble had been replaced, in Moscow it was often said that television saved Russia. Indeed, Boris Yeltsin himself said that "the Russian channel, the only one that stayed on the air was what saved Moscow and Russia."[72] And the first vice chairman of the Russian Council of Ministers, Vladimir Shumeiko, said to Channel Two, "You achieved a heroic feat; it is you who to a great extent rescued the situation."[73]

Attributing national salvation to television is a tall order and evidence not only of the critical role television played, but also of the continuing obsession with the medium and the power imputed to it. The events surrounding the complicated role television played in this crisis also underline the profound problem of zero-sum television to serve the cause of reform and democratization. In the absence of new structures and institutions of law and government—and with continuing government monopoly of the technological resources of signal dissemination—it was television that bound the nation after nearly fatally betraying it.

The two buildings of state television face each other across a wide boulevard. Virtually mirror images, they are city-block-sized concrete boxes with broad glass fronts. The newer building (ASK3), dating from the 1980 Olympics, houses a number of studios and technical areas. The older building (ASK1) is the administrative nerve center, where offices and some studios are quartered. On duty that night in October were only about a third of the station's police security force. With about 40 percent of Moscow's police living outside the city, without telephones and out of touch, it took time to alert them to emergency duty.

October 3 was also a Sunday, a favored time for police officers to moonlight, and the defending force was especially light.[74] The mob surged to ASK3, rammed a truck through its front and, a little while later, a grenade launcher was fired at the front entrance. Volleys of gunfire were returned by the security forces stationed at the television center who had been told to engage in defensive actions only. Outside, in the flat, treeless, parking lot and on the concrete apron of the building, a crowd gathered. They would have nowhere to hide and dozens would be killed. Several corner rooms of the bottom floor of the television center were set on fire with Molotov cocktails.

Across the street, from his office on the tenth floor of ASK1, Ostankino chief Vyacheslav Bragin gave an order: suddenly, at about 7:20 P.M. in the middle of a soccer game, a nervous and shaky anchor came on to tersely tell the viewers that due to the threat, state television was shutting down, about an hour-and-a-half after the first attackers arrived. That was all. Nothing more. Suddenly, the screens went dark all across the country. As one observer put it, on the night of October 3, the total information vacuum was a clear signal that the orderly process of government had failed and the leadership had vanished.[75]

Bragin later said he took the action in order to save the lives of Ostankino's personnel and to prevent the powerful medium from falling into the hands of the opposition. Channel Two (Russian Television) then began transmitting on the frequency deserted by Channel One, and it broadcast all night. It was the thread of information that connected the spellbound, apprehensive citizenry.

It was Channel Two that Yeltsin, Shumeiko, and millions of viewers thanked in the aftermath of what might have been a larger civil war. With the military uncertain and hesitant to act, the continuing emblem of the legitimate government that was sent out over television may well have been a critical factor in the eventual outcome.[76] For Boris Yeltsin, his authority, and the credibility of his government were severely threatened by the television blackout. In his words, "When state television went dead, a large portion of the population perceived it as a disaster. Even I felt as if I'd been knocked out of the ring." In Yeltsin's view, when Channel Two came on, "it was a significant turning point," and he checked the television screen periodically throughout the violent hours.[77]

The conduct of the head of the biggest network in cutting off television channels was heavily criticized.[78] In his defense, Bragin said that he called all the ministers who could supply armed force: interior, security, and defense. He was "bounced around to their deputies" and, when he finally reached the minister of the interior, was told that troops were on their way, and not to panic. Bragin added that he spoke that night to Prime Minister Viktor Chernomyrdin *fifteen to twenty times,* and talked to Shumeiko as often. He talked to Yeltsin's chief of staff and to Mikhail Poltoranin, the president's close counselor. He called every member of the government, and all of them told him, "just hold on, hold on." In desperation, he called Moscow mayor Luzhkov, who sent a hundred men. "The others promised," he told me about his many desperate calls, "but they did nothing." At Channel Two Oleg Poptsov thought it "unimaginable" that the militia failed to stop the mob that surged to Ostankino.[79]

At Ostankino that night, extremist General Makashov demanded cameras and correspondents to prepare stories for broadcast. Bragin told his assistant: "Give him everything he asks for—correspondents, camera . . . Stretch out the time; film him all night, even, it doesn't matter, we won't let even one frame on the air." Finally, Bragin said, it was Chernomyrdin who told him to pull the plug. According to Bragin, when he phoned that the mob was advancing to the entrance of the broadcast area, the prime minister said, "Enough, turn it off." Russian Television head Oleg Poptsov said later that if someone called in panic that armed rebels were advancing down the corridors and about to take over broadcast studios, he, too, would advise closing down. But Bragin, much less Chernomyrdin, did not know that the rebels had not even got to the first floor. Bragin did know that his news director was calling and saying that a man had been killed in front of him.

The decision to close down Ostankino was probably based on an erroneous assumption. There were ample resources to continue broadcasting. In his own building, Bragin had studios; he was not dependent on ASK3. Even if he wanted to evacuate both television buildings (which the level and zone of fighting did not warrant), he still had at least twelve mobile units to broadcast programs from any location. Beyond that, there were full broadcast facilities at the Bolshoi Theater, the Palace of Congresses in the Kremlin, and a host of other places, including at least one that was so heavily fortified it could withstand nuclear attack.

A year and a half later, Bragin said that of course he knew about alternative broadcast resources and was prepared. From September 21 on, when Yeltsin decreed the end of the parliament, Bragin worked day and night at Ostankino. He slept in his office, and that in itself showed how perilous the situation had become. But, he said, "no one thought there would be a storm of Ostankino." As for consultations, Bragin's previous "number two," the seasoned professional Valentin Lazutkin, said to me that from September 21 to October 3, Bragin held no meetings with senior television people about what to do and what could happen. Lazutkin said that there was not a single meeting about "reserve possibilities" for broadcasting. Ostankino was particularly weak, Lazutkin recalled, because it was built to withstand war from foreign sources, but there was no planning for protection from unthinkable internal threat.[80] Lazutkin said further that he, not Poptsov or Bragin, initiated the plan to switch the button to enable Channel Two to be seen on the deserted frequency. Bragin, in turn, denied Lazutkin's statement about meetings and said that there were meetings and he thought perhaps Lazutkin was present at some.

How did Channel Two manage to take over Ostankino's frequency and keep Yeltsin's government connected to its public? Again, stories differ.[81] The leadership at Channel Two were professionals, and the pattern of their behavior differed from Bragin's. Oleg Poptsov thought there would be an outburst on Saturday or Sunday and had moved to emergency footing. He instituted night brigades and arranged personnel shifts to cover a twenty-four-hour day, and within fifteen to twenty minutes three auxiliary studios had been converted for broadcasting. Channel Two was preparing its evening newscast, *Vesti,* when Ostankino and all the other channels went off the air. Moving quickly to an in-town auxiliary studio, program preparation continued. Anticipating trouble, Channel Two received from the Ministry of Communications access to the all-important "button" to transmit signals.

Sergei Torchinsky anchored the entire night of emergency programming. He began at nine o'clock in the evening of October 3 and finally went home at ten o'clock the next morning. He recalled that he heard about the events at about 7:00 P.M. and right away went to Oleg Poptsov and Anatoly Lysenko, his deputy. Poptsov gathered staff, engineers, producers, directors, and anchors in a downtown auxiliary studio. If they came under fire, they were fully prepared to relocate to still another studio somewhere else in the city. At 2:00 A.M. an attack was expected and the women were told to leave, but they stayed on and Russian Television's most famous and loved face, anchor Svetlana Sorokina, went on the air. From his post in Paris as deputy director of UNESCO, former Soviet state television deputy chairman for technology Henrik Iushkyavichius telephoned RTR to tell them where the backup studios were located and how to access them.

Again, Bragin's story angrily differs. He called Poptsov a "fake hero" (*geroi lipovy*) and what he said was "deceiving prattle" (*trepnya*). It was not Poptsov, but Bragin who had the plan. The switch was *his* work, and he labored at it for four hours, from three in the afternoon until seven. "It was *our* initiative; not Poptsov's," he said, and he talked to Poptsov about twenty times during the course of those four hours to iron out the technical questions in the switch plan. Poptsov just as angrily denied this version, telling me "*We* had the plan. *We* told Bulgak [minister of communications, to switch the frequencies]. *We* decided." Bragin had absolutely nothing to do with the plan. His story was "nonsense" (*chepukha*). Professing circumscribed sympathy for Bragin, Poptsov also said of Ostankino's chief: "People didn't do a damn thing for him; he had no one to talk to." There he was, secretary of a rural Party organization, all alone.

The "button" to switch the frequencies, letting Channel Two go out over the country on the frequency that Channel One had abandoned, was part of the political design of the technology the previous system left behind. Political control of television had been a matter of highest security. As Valentin Lazutkin remarked, even if the entire complex of Ostankino had been taken, the rebels would not have got on the air. The command over signals would have been asserted from "another source." "Ostankino took itself off the air," he said, but "from another place, they also could have taken it off the air."

Evaluating from afar and in safety the steps taken by individuals in times of crisis is hardly fair. One has to imagine the information each of the actors had or ought to have had. One has to imagine the difficulty of extracting reliable information from a city thrown into chaos. Most important and most difficult, one has to imagine the emotional impact of death and combat. But one telling point weakens Bragin's argument. After he described his actions and sketched his plan for switching the frequency to ensure continuity of signals, I asked him why, if he had planned it all, had he not told the viewers that television would be coming back up on Channel Two? Why did he not reassure the public (presumably the purpose of the switch) instead of cutting them off tersely and shakily? He answered with indignation and pathos: "That's easy to say over coffee and cookies," but people were shooting; they were using *grenade launchers,* they were fighting with *machine guns; dozens of corpses* could be seen from the windows, he said. He referred to his conduct as having been judged "correct" by the government and he was kept on at his post to oversee the coming elections. He was shifted to a post in the Ministry of Culture after that.

When embattled Channel Two went forward with its all-night crisis programming, it had no idea what would be shown. Streams of well-known people came, despite the gunfire, to the makeshift studios to talk to the nation. The continuous vigil of commentary was varied: parliamentary deputies, trade union leaders, writers, actors, artists, and television personalities all appeared. One extraordinary moment surpassed the rest. Three young men were arguing about the political import of the civil strife surrounding them. To their left, at the end of the table, an actress, a mousy dejected blonde woman, stared almost vacantly ahead. She made no effort to join the debate; she seemed hardly aware of it. Finally, when the anchor called on her, she appeared to wake from her inner vision and began to speak directly to the people of Russia. She said, uncertainly at first, that she had been quiet because she did not want to be objective. She said that whatever happens, we showed that we have learned nothing these seventy years— just look at those bestial faces of the mob. Her emotion grew as she called on Russia to wake to the replay of 1917. We must not, she implored, be like those people who thought that *then* we had sausage. You were shot for being late to work, but people worked well and we lived well. It wasn't important that millions were shot to death or ended in concentration camps. She urged viewers to think beyond individual well-being and self-interest and listen to conscience.

In the dark, early hours of the morning, it was a galvanizing moment. Boris Yeltsin was moved, as was the nation. He said: "For the rest of my life I will remember the anxious but resolute and courageous expression of

Liya Akhedzhakova . . . I see her image before me now; her hoarse cracking voice remains in my memory."[82]

If Akhedzhakova's role was the glorious call to moral courage, the old *Vzglyad* team presented a very different view, for which they were later disciplined. Earlier that night, at 9:00 P.M., First Deputy Prime Minister Yegor Gaidar made a plea on Channel Two to the citizens of Moscow. By calling out popular support, it was reasoned, the fence-sitters would be convinced to intervene on the side of the president, and that included the armed forces most of all.

Sergei Yushenkov recalled that when it became clear that troops were not being deployed and "nobody was bringing anything," the decision was taken to call for a show of support from Moscow citizens.[83] *Vzglyad* stars Alexander Lyubimov and Alexander Politkovsky told their fellow Russians to disregard Yegor Gaidar's call to rally in support of freedom. With studied nonchalance, they told Russian viewers to let the armed forces do what they, not unarmed citizens, could do, and to follow the television stars' example and go home to sleep.

Lyubimov and Politkovsky were fired. The programs they hosted were pulled off the air, an action they intended to take to court, but then Bragin was replaced.[84] In his defense, Lyubimov later said that "'To call civilians onto the streets when there are armored vehicles standing by is simply immoral'"[85]

Talking with media officials from both private and state companies, I found few who actually disagreed with what Lyubimov and Politkovsky counselled. Gaidar's call to the citizenry was risky. The mobilization of support for the president in an uncertain time might have been a symbolic asset, but the presence of unarmed civilians in the midst of a war professionals would have to fight made for a messy battlefield. Gaidar's appeal was unsettling for many, not just the young television stars. Where the critics faulted the *Vzglyad* pair was in the tone, the patent absence of partisan fervor, and the almost mocking, uninvolved view from the sidelines. In crisis, there are no sidelines, only the front. Sergei Lomakin, Gorbachev's favorite interviewer, said that Lyubimov and Politkovsky were "absolutely wrong in tone." They adopted a "playboy tone, an indifferent disdain."[86]

The state of emergency President Yeltsin decreed during the rebellion and in its immediate aftermath included prior censorship of the press and a ban on certain newspapers. On October 5 and 6, some Moscow newspapers appeared with blank spaces left by the censors. The next day, censorship prior to publication ceased, but the ban on some of the most extreme opposition remained. Two papers, including the venerable *Pravda,* were told to change their editors. In St. Petersburg, the militarist-nationalist Alexander Nevzorov was again temporarily banned from television. At the time Sergei Yushenkov was deputy to the head of the Federal Information

Center, the powerful coordinating body for media policy for the Yeltsin government.

Just after the state of emergency decree had been lifted, Yushenkov remarked that his center did not support censorship (the Ministry of the Press did that, he said), but that aggressively fascist papers advocating pogroms should be shut down. He personally regarded Communist rule as no less vicious than Nazi horrors, and given the many years of their repressive force, the Communists were guilty of a larger scale of atrocity. That no process analogous to de-Nazification, with its international tribunals, had cleansed and renewed Russian political life left a profound instability in the system. Yushenkov thought the president's decision was fully in accord with the press law: it was against the law to propagandize war. The procedures required by the law were not followed: there must be two warnings before a media organ is charged in court. Speaking about his own views, Yushenkov angrily said that he would prohibit *all* Communist newspapers for a defined period, because "Too much blood has been spilled." The courts ultimately should decide that, he said, but they were not yet in a position to act as an independent force.[87]

The world outside Russia watched live coverage of the violent rebellion provided by Cable News Network, but at this point CNN could be received only by a very small fraction of Moscow residents and the country at large. Oleg Poptsov made the decision to carry CNN on his frequency. He did so only when the army was in plain view, waiting to attack parliament. Poptsov did worry that the pictures might mobilize some civilians to join the opposition, but, with the military there, he noted, "Only a crazy person would get into a fight with the army."[88]

A curious footnote to the civil war, in which television participated as a high-profile political asset, was the evolution of Alexander Tikhomirov. The pioneer of television investigative reporting, the man who scandalized the Politburo with his withering commentary and hard-hitting stories on *7 Days,* supported the parliamentary opposition and Alexander Rutskoy's bid to take over the country. While covering Afghanistan he had met General Rutskoy. When both of them were elected deputies to parliament Tikhomirov became a close friend and trusted advisor. Their views were especially close on issues of war, and, therefore, national identity and political change that had gone too far. They shared a view of the Second World War and the contributions of the Soviet military, a devotion to Russian history (and Soviet history), much of which had been "nullified now by the reform," in Tikhomirov's words.

Rutskoy had been charged by Yeltsin with oversight over agriculture and understood, according to Tikhomirov, how unfairly the Russian people, particularly the elderly, were treated and how the liberalization of prices and the "storming" reform of shock therapy had forced the nation into misery. Tikhomirov had done an interview on television with Rutskoy in which the general had decried the "Americanization of society." Tikhomirov would have been in the Russian White House when the artillery attacked if a temperature of 104 degrees had not made him leave that fortress early.[89] The embittered former reformer had been denied the grandest of gestures.

In large part, the contrasting behavior of Bragin and Poptsov can be laid to the difference between degrees of professionalism, but also to a difference in that much more elusive and important concept, leadership. Certainly, no one who had followed the course of Poptsov's battle to create a television channel for Yeltsin-led independent Russia could think of the combative Poptsov as politically neutral. He was a fierce and loyal supporter of Yeltsin and his reform program.

Bragin was also a loyal political appointee but with no experience in television, and he did not have time to acquire it before crisis overwhelmed him. In 1991, when the Kravchenko crackdown drove the new stars to Yeltsin's channel, the most reform-minded were also the most effective and famous media performers. In 1993, many of the most professional television news figures had moved out of Bragin's constraining reach and had sought refuge beyond the state system altogether, in newly developing commercial television.

Not much more than a year later, in the fall of 1995, it was Sergei Yushenkov, then head of the parliamentary committee on defense, who exposed the Yeltsin government's cover-up of the Russian military's camouflaged, covert incursions into Chechnya before the open conflict began. By then, he had moved into one of the many oppositions that war engendered within Yeltsin's original reform team.

CHAPTER EIGHT

Pictures, Parties, and Leaders: Television and Elections in the New Russia

The pattern of television coverage of electoral campaigns in Russia was basically set in December 1993. In that and subsequent elections, television played a critical role in affecting turnout and influencing voters' party preferences. Whatever the merits or demerits of the way television coverage was designed, to a large extent the scheme came into being as a particular kind of reaction to an earlier use of television in a major national campaign—the referendum of April 1993. It was a referendum to settle the parliamentary-presidential question of the constitution: Who had power over whom? Would the future look like the communist past or take a new, more democratic shape? The referendum did not resolve the distribution of power, but, what is sometimes forgotten, it did decisively affect the role television was to play in elections ahead. In an important way, the April 1993 referendum was the first part of the two-part effort to settle a revolution peacefully. It did so only incompletely, and the presidential election of 1996 was its continuation. In the intervening three years much had happened in Russian society and politics, and two parliamentary elections had taken place. But the stark choice of 1993 was much the same one as 1996.

ZERO-SUM CAMPAIGN COVERAGE: THE APRIL REFERENDUM

The referendum of April 25, 1993, was an attempt by the Yeltsin administration to break the deadlock of the two-headed power structure pitting the president against an increasingly recalcitrant parliament, the Congress of People's Deputies, and its smaller, more continuously operating body, the Supreme Soviet.

From the outset, the Yeltsin administration charged that television ". . . secure the passage of the referendum."[1] The Russian people were asked four questions: about confidence in President Yeltsin, support of his economic reforms, the desirability of holding an early presidential election, and support for early parliamentary elections. Equal access to state-owned media was supposed to be guaranteed for campaigning for or against referendum questions, but that did not happen. The Yeltsin side campaigned for a "yes" vote on the first question, "yes" on the second, "no" on the third, and "yes" on the fourth. Boris Yeltsin noted that he personally put together the catchy campaign slogan emphasizing the positive: "yes, yes, no, yes." He believed that people were fed up with negativism, always saying no to war and imperialism; it was time to affirm.[2]

Like its Soviet-era predecessors, the Yeltsin leadership perceived the impact of television in the most extreme and unambiguous terms, but so did many others. Writing four days before the event, one observer called "[t]elevision a propaganda apparatus of monstrous 'thermonuclear' force, **mass medium No. 1** [emphasis in the original]."[3] The exaggerated prominence given to television by leaders and observers alike was related to the continuing weakness of other channels of mobilization. Like earlier examples of the electoral process in Russia, the referendum campaign on television was carried out in the absence of a developed party system with competing organized party structures.

The president's control of television produced some clear and worrisome signals well in advance of the referendum. On February 4, an unscheduled interview with presidential aide Sergei Filatov disrupted the entertainment programming schedule on Channel One to advance the president's positions. Television critic Elena Chekalova presciently asked "where is the guarantee that a whole chain of officials and political leaders with their declarations will not stretch out [over airtime] . . . ?"[4] Nor were there guarantees of equal time. Yeltsin opponent Vice President Alexander Rutskoy protested that he could not get airtime shortly before the vote because he was told the programming schedule could not be altered, though it was altered for others.[5] Offers of time on national television were made to the political opposition, but always for controlled, mediated time, mainly on talk shows that had reputations for independent thinking, sharp questioning, and reformist views, like *Vzglyad*.[6] There was no opportunity to buy time or receive free-time allotments. Access to television and its vast audience was wholly controlled by the Yeltsin administration.

A systematic content analysis of television messages related to the referendum on news and public affairs programs on channels One and Two and the Moscow city channel between April 5 and 15 showed the heavy hand of editorial bias. There was a clear preponderance of propresidential positions on news and public affairs programs on the state-run television channels.[7] On Russian-Federation-wide channels One and Two, support for the president was voiced in 23 percent of the news stories, while support of the parliament's positions, by contrast, was recorded in 8.5 percent.[8] Editorializing was common: a presumably neutral news story instructing the public about voting procedures showed a sample ballot with the pro-Yeltsin responses clearly marked.[9] On the air, news anchor Sergei Medvedev (later Yeltsin's press secretary), said of Ruslan Khasbulatov's charge that Yeltsin raised television salaries to one hundred thousand rubles: "I don't know such people. It would be nice if the Supreme Soviet took it under consideration."[10] On the news, Boris Yeltsin often had the opportunity to speak for himself. His own words were transmitted as he gave speeches and performed his duties, but when speaker Khasbulatov was shown, an off-camera voice usually summarized his statements.

The arguments in the televised referendum campaign were usually couched in extremes. Then-Foreign Minister Andrei Kozyrev cautioned that if Yeltsin lost, a "Yugoslav-style scenario would threaten Russia."[11] Of his opponents, Yeltsin said, "It is either us or them. That is how it is. They will implement their threats—if we lose."[12] The positive arguments positioned Yeltsin as guarantor of democracy and freedom, and the negative ones saw a Yeltsin defeat setting loose the forces of reaction. For its part, the parliamentary opposition referred to the ruin of the economy toward which Yeltsin was leading the country, the corrupt influences derailing production and trade, and the dangerous fracturing of society Yeltsin's policies had produced.

Of all the newsmakers in stories relating to the April referendum, the most frequently covered by far was Boris Yeltsin, who appeared in nearly one-fifth (18 percent) of the stories on Channel One; 12 percent on Channel Two; and 11 percent on the Moscow Channel. In comparison, Vice President Alexander Rutskoy was the newsmaker in 2 percent of the referendum stories on Channel One, 5 percent on Channel Two; and none on the Moscow Channel. Ruslan Khasbulatov was on 6 percent of the referendum stories on Channel One; 5 percent on Channel Two; and 3 percent on the Moscow Channel.

The pro-Yeltsin partisanship of the news and public affairs programs made television journalists a campaign target of the president's opponents, who resorted to other methods of getting their (increasingly extremist) views across. A leaflet circulating in Moscow urged voters to respond no, no, yes, no "if the ATTACKS OF LYING PROPAGANDA OF THE HIRED television-radio-BABBLERS prevents you from forming a definite opinion."[13]

Communist Party leader Gennady Zyuganov said that he thought no one supported the president of Russia "except for radical journalists," whom he likened to the agitators and propagandists of the 1930s.[14]

Almost all of the referendum messages on state television were placed in news and public affairs programs, but some constituted unexpected, even bizarre campaigning. During the April 6 show *Musical Sound Track,* the host called on young people to vote for the president so that they could continue to hear the latest rock and not go back to the old boring stuff. At halftime in a Spartak soccer game, a telegram was read on television from the coach and team supporting President Yeltsin. Participants in a popular quiz show referred to the lack of professionalism of parliament, saying, in a parody of Lenin's dictum, that when a cook runs the state, everything turns into total Communist borscht.

By all accounts, perhaps the most popular public affairs program, one that broke new ground by personalizing the president and his family, was the seventy-minute "A *Day in the Life of the President,*" aired just before the vote.[15]

Directed by the well-known film director Eldar Ryazanov, it presented to Russian viewers an unaccustomed look at the family and home life of their leader. Done in an intimate style, with hand-held camera following the director and Naina, the president's wife, the program began with her visit to church to collect blessed Easter eggs. Her small, round figure, clad in a dark cloth coat, her unpretentious, modest, and candid remarks seemed wholly without artifice. A crowd of women gathered at the church to praise the president and give her eggs for him. Naina, tearful, tells them what a "fighter" Boris is and how "committed." To the accompanying Ryazanov, she says that "God has always been present" in her home. Inside the car going to the Yeltsin apartment, she talks about her education, how she met Boris, and she remarks with pathos that she still is not at home in Moscow and goes back to her family in the Urals to "gain strength." Handkerchief to her eyes, crying, she acknowledges that so much "filth" has been dumped on them in Moscow.

At home, in the same apartment they had since they moved to Moscow—the usual Central Committee issue, she says—she displays unfeigned simplicity. The children and grandchildren gather, and Naina remarks that Boris never yells, never raises his voice, and, contrary to rumor, he is not impulsive and "thinks everything through." President Yeltsin drops in, to the director's apparent surprise, and sits in the kitchen with both granddaughters on his lap. Over tea (Naina and his daughters have receded into the background) Yeltsin, in shirtsleeves, and Ryazanov talk about ordinary things, avoiding, as has the entire program, the overtly political. At the end Ryazanov wishes him victory. Naina and her daughters join Boris to begin dinner and the program ends. Quite a contrast to Raisa Gorbachev! Naina's simple human agenda would be heavily covered in 1996.

Ryazanov was only one of the many intellectuals and artists who publicly and vigorously supported the president. Yeltsin defended this outpouring of praise, saying that "many criticized . . . Ryazanov for a show about me and my family, thinking it was indecent and that he was sucking up and trying to find favor . . . he was really fighting for democracy to win . . . [as were the] other artists and writers of Russia who supported me."[16]

The use of celebrity campaigners combined a historical understanding of the "intelligentsia" in Russia and modern, imported campaign techniques. The tradition of the intelligentsia in Russia made them the carriers of the conscience of the country, and when free expression was severely circumscribed they had the obligation to use their talents and craft to right the balance. It earned them popular deference and burdened them with an everlasting tension between civic obligation and artistic detachment. The intelligentsia had also been the chief beneficiaries of Gorbachev's and Yeltsin's reform, which granted them the psychic gratification of free speech, international contacts, and reintegration into world culture. In some ways, as political analyst Igor Klyamkin pointed out, they represented the most available alternative, or counter-elite, with which to oppose the Communist system. Many had become dissidents or "internal emigres," cautiously waiting out the long winter of repression.[17]

On the other hand, the long wait on the sidelines and habits of theoretical analysis tended toward moral absolutism and an inability to compromise.[18] In the 1990 Russian republic elections, this "prestige elite," was notably successful in their parliamentary races.[19] Until Chechnya most were on Yeltsin's side, and their appearances on his behalf also represented a new media savvy. Yeltsin's advisors developed events specifically to attract media coverage, what in the United States has been termed "pseudo-events," such as the president's meeting with the celebrity artists and intellectuals in Moscow's Bolshoi Theater.[20]

Khasbulatov also had "his" intelligentsia, "not the stateless intelligentsia with whom Boris Yeltsin had been meeting, but those who have inherited the spirit and morality of Russian traditions," a supporter said.[21] The use of the word "stateless" deliberately recalled Stalin's anti-Jewish campaign against "rootless cosmopolitans." In the referendum campaign, as later that year, the supporters of Khasbulatov once again drew the line between upstart-usurpers, marginal ethnics, and "real Russians."

How effective the celebrity endorsements were was another matter. Notwithstanding the politicians' intuition, it appeared that ordinary Russians did not identify with the famous intelligentsia. A survey conducted a few months after the referendum asked whether the Russian intelligentsia spoke for the majority of Russia's population. Forty-five percent of those interviewed said no; only 24 percent said yes, and the rest found it hard to decide.[22]

Later, in the 1995 parliamentary election campaign, celebrities (writers and actors) were used again in long perorations looking out from leather wingchairs with the same stuffy self-satisfaction—and probably the same scant effect. In contrast, a wholly new kind of celebrity joined the fray that year. Our Home is Russia, the Yeltsin-backed political party, understood that to survive it had to encourage young people—a group with usually low turnout rates—to vote to offset the solid support that mobilized older people gave to the Communist Party.

The Yeltsinites targeted youthful voters with extravaganzas featuring the American rapper M.C. Hammer (who had no idea he had become involved in an election campaign or even that an election was taking place) and Claudia Schiffer, the supermodel of the moment. On election eve, Channel One staged a huge outdoor rock festival on Arbat Street in central Moscow. Billed as a public service to get out the vote, it showed favored candidates dropping by to plug their programs. A 1996 campaign tour by Russia's leading rockers was again designed to bring out the youth vote, and outdoor rock festivals were held just off Red Square. The pictures television sent to the county conveyed the urbanized, privileged, Westernized youth culture as the beneficiaries of change.

In the televised campaign of the April 1993 referendum, as before, and as would be the case in the future, the great heartland of the country was ignored by television. In the coverage of this campaign, state television followed the traditions of Soviet television: excessive concentration on the capital city, with only cursory attention to the rest of the huge and highly differentiated country. About three-quarters of all coverage was centered on Moscow, less than one-fifth related to other places in the Russian Federation. And just under 10 percent of the stories were generated by former Soviet republics and more distant foreign locales.

To be sure, the seat of government always generates more politically newsworthy stories than the provinces, and the drama of the dispute between president and parliament played out in the capital city. Nonetheless, the referendum was to be a national vote. The Soviet period saw an exceedingly Moscow-centric pattern of news coverage, one that was criticized by those concerned with the disaffection of the rest of the country. Little had changed by the time the referendum came around in the spring of 1993. Through its neglect of provincial cities and the countryside in general, state television and, therefore to some extent, the political elite of which it was a part, was deprived of needed information about and communication with a very large constituency. It also projected a notion of the nation that effectively excluded both geographic and ethnic regions.

Television revolutionized campaigning when political advertising was introduced to boost Yeltsin's chances. Gennady Burbulis, Yeltsin's campaign manager, invited Ben Goddard, of the California-based Goddard+ Claussen/First Tuesday advertising agency, to help.[23] Some fifteen days before the referendum, Goddard and design specialist John Ridgway arrived in Moscow.[24] It was a time of intense, round-the-clock activity. Goddard and Ridgway spent twelve to fourteen hours in meetings each day and then returned to the bar of the elegant Metropol hotel to do the advertising work, sketching it out on paper cocktail napkins. The final products were sent from the home base in California. Scripts were translated into Russian and faxed to liberal playwright Alexander Gelman, who made them "culturally correct" and faxed them back to the United States, where the computer work was done and the tape edited.

One "glitch" provided an unexpected "bonus," according to Goddard: the satellite feed sending the finished spots back to Moscow had to be routed through London. When Yeltsin's opposition complained of U.S. manipulation, they looked for the source in London without success.[25] The Yeltsin team was unified, Goddard observed, by their stake in the outcome and the clarity of the issues. People were forced to work together, he said, because unless there was a *da-da-nyet-da* vote, everybody lost.

Although Mikhail Poltoranin was the senior man on media issues, it was Burbulis who controlled the campaign.[26] Gennady Burbulis, the former professor of Marxism-Leninism in Yeltsin's home town of Yekaterinburg, and later close aide and strategist for the Russian president, met Goddard when he visited the United States. Burbulis, called the "gray cardinal" for his analytic gifts and backstage political influence, had aspired to be the vice president but was passed over.[27] Instead, he became Yeltsin's chief governmental strategist until they parted ways. As head of his own think tank, Strategy, Burbulis continued to work on elections, was in charge of the April referendum, and one of the managers of the December 1993 parliamentary campaign for the president's favored Russia's Choice party.

Burbulis's review of the events stressed the Russians' input. He said that it was not correct to say that the Californians "carried out our referendum." He saw a partnership, with his team explaining their understanding and the Americans translating it into visuals. "The use of unconscious information—that was done with the help of the Western company."[28]

In Goddard's view, the "fundamental guiding principle in producing political television is the premise that everyone always votes their own self interest," and the key to winning is aligning your position with the needs of the electorate so that they see your position as in *their* self-interest. In the referendum spots, Goddard said, he showed the Russian people in a positive light and the message was that parliament was the problem, the Yeltsin team was the solution.[29]

Burbulis saw three elements critical to the success of the campaign ads: they very precisely "framed the psychological idea of the referendum," so that people knew the consequences of saying yes or no; for the first time, the leading figures in the arts voluntarily came to work on their side and carried the trust of the people with them; and finally, the harder parliament pushed against the referendum the more "we [the Yeltsin campaign] got in favor."[30] The second point is debatable; the rest are exactly right, and marked a telling difference between this campaign and the ones that followed.

To this viewer, the spots forcefully framed the zero-sum dichotomy Goddard was after. The old way (shot in black-and-white) was the parliament with its feral ways: the leaders' grimaces of anger and violence; placards brandished like weapons; symbols of the old, like the statue of KGB chief Dzerzhinsky regaining its pedestal. The new way was suddenly visible in brilliant, sun-drenched colors, where life was "normal" not under occupation. Mothers and babies, young people—the future—dominated each frame. The spots were brief, but the entire message was there—return to the past and the fallen statues righting themselves in that gray world contrasted with the individual stake of each person in a many-hued future. At the end of each spot came the familiar drumbeat: Yes, yes, no, yes.

It was reminiscent of the *franjas* in the 1988 plebiscite in Chile. In a television system controlled by the Pinochet regime, those who favored the restitution of democratic government were relegated to short bits of time after 11:15 P.M. on week-nights and at noon on weekends. The ruling regime never imagined that the spots would play to such large and deeply affected audiences.[31] The most symbolically effective showed horses penned up, crowded together, and then set free to gallop in the countryside, manes flying—unencumbered, unrestrained beauty. It was a brilliantly devised message to propagandize freedom as positive, seemingly risk-free, good and decoupled from the divisiveness and negativity of a decision rejecting Pinochet's rule. The Russian campaign emphasized the contrast.

For their work, the Americans were partially reimbursed for their expenses with money from Western sources supporting the cause and partially covered their own costs. Their help was contributed to the Russian campaign. The involvement of U.S. firms and U.S. money in political advertising for the Russian election proved to be extremely controversial in Russia. The opposition, which did not have access to political advertising at all, was angered by what it regarded as potent foreign interference in violation of election laws. Boris Yeltsin recalled that as soon as the first results of the referendum came in, "almost the first words out of Khasbulatov's mouth were about the Poltoranin-Goebbels television station."[32]

The Yeltsin administration's attempt to fence off television from the opposition was to have repercussions far beyond the referendum. Right after the vote, Ruslan Khasbulatov, soon to be the leader of rebellious parliamentary forces, did indeed charge Yeltsin and his minions at television with conspiracy with foreign forces. He praised the millions who dared to express their lack of confidence in the president "in conditions of information terror, up to and including the use of means of psychological warfare banned under the Geneva Convention; up to and including direct and blatant participation in the organization of the referendum not only of foreign citizens but also of their funds, which, as you know, is forbidden by law. . . . The dirty information war, according [to] the specifications of Western consultants which was directed by Burbulis and Poltoranin, provoked natural opposition from citizens. This opposition will grow."[33]

Vowing to end Yeltsin's rule over the most powerful medium and attain his rightful place, Ruslan Khasbulatov said that "the monopoly over the mass media should be ended, and will be ended. . . . The Supreme Soviet and the Congress must continue to act as a force to curb destructive, antistate trends, leading to irrevocable consequences . . . [among which] are . . . the threat to freedom of the press and the threat of one-sided *diktat* in the media and above all in Central Television."[34]

Khasbulatov had identified a real issue: the laws on the books prohibited contributions to political parties by foreigners, even when diverted through philanthropic foundations, according to Valentin Lazutkin.[35] Vyacheslav Bragin, who was head of Channel One, said that this whole issue was a "sharp *(ostry)* question." Ostankino *was not allowed* to use foreign money. He personally had no recollection of seeing particular foreign advertising spots among all the campaign information he saw. Rather, he remembered that his assistants for political programming informed him that the ads "had an objective, constructive character, supported the democratic process, and were not biased." He knew that foreigners were advising about some spots, but said that his trusted "number two," Kirill Ignatyev, dealt with many of these questions. "I thought they were Russian ads," Bragin told me. He said he had to trust his colleagues and their proposals. "I didn't investigate where [the ads] came from."[36]

Gennady Burbulis said more. The law was in effect and it prohibited such contributions of expertise, just as it did money. And Goddard was not the only expert assisting the Yeltsin referendum campaign. Mark Malloch Brown, at the time a partner in the U.S. firm Sawyer Miller, stated that he had provided "a little free advice," to the Yeltsin campaign, though he forcefully noted that he had "no involvement" in the subsequent parliamentary campaign.[37]

Burbulis expected Goddard to be tactful, but instead the campaign was used for publicity in the United States and it "hurt their effort."[38] Ben Goddard recalled that he did have some discussion that his effort might be a contribution to the campaign, but his position, and that of the Russians, was that "we were providing advice and not a product," which he understood to mean that he and his American associates did not buy airtime. He said he was told by an American attorney participating in the Moscow discussions on a volunteer basis that therefore his contribution was acceptable. Goddard said further that he never talked about this particular issue directly with Burbulis. The attorney, who was characterized by Goddard as bilingual and in the employ of a respected U.S. firm, was said by Goodard to be "involved in many meetings" as "interpreter" and "facilitator."

Interestingly, when Goddard returned from Moscow and told the U.S. media about his work, he got what he termed a "very anxious phone call" from the attorney. Goddard noted that the attorney "lectured" him, telling him that it was "not helpful" to let anyone know what had been done.[39] This collaboration and the ensuing outcry made a later dispute between a U.S. firm funded by the U.S. Agency for International Development and the Russian government much more controversial, and many in Russia would say that in December the outcome was more than ever a function of television's influence.

Televised campaigns brought in televised opinion polls to Russia, as they did elsewhere. Survey results showed support for the president's agenda, as did the final tally. Before the polls closed, exit polls were being discussed on the Sunday news program *Itogi* (Results). The relatively great predictive power of these surveys helped to legitimize and accelerate their use in future political contests. Equally, the apparent belief in the power of television to decisively affect the electoral outcome contributed to a sense of confidence among the president's advisors and some of the new political parties that Western-style advertising and televised appeals to the electorate were adequate substitutes for effective party-organized voter mobilization.

The turnout for the referendum was high—65 percent of the registered voters (virtually the same as it would be for the 1995 parliamentary elections). Still, this was a decline from the 87 percent in the Russian republic in the 1989 Soviet parliamentary elections[40] and 75 percent in the 1991 Russian presidential election.[41] It would go up to 70 percent for the first round of the 1996 presidential elections and was only slightly under 70 percent for the second. As for the outcome of the questions: 58 percent of those casting votes indicated confidence in the president; 53 percent approved the social-economic policies of the president; 50 percent voted for early presidential elections; and 67 percent for early parliamentary elections. Because the last two were considered to be political mandates of a constitutional nature, it was required that they attain the support of at least 50 percent of the eligible voters. Calculated on that base, 32 percent wanted early presidential elections and 43 percent wanted early parliamentary elections.[42]

Just a month and a half before the referendum, a survey asked Russians if it should be held. Thirty-one percent said yes, but nearly one-fifth (18 percent) did not know what the referendum was about; more than one-fifth (23 percent) had no answer; and over one-fourth (28 percent) said no.[43] Yeltsin's—and television's—task, which they performed with great success, was to move a good number of this 69 percent to take part in the referendum and vote the Yeltsin formula. The results were controversial and indeterminate; they mandated no specific policy and achieved no solutions. Boris Yeltsin could justifiably claim that in the parliamentary-presidential standoff, the people of Russia had come down on his side. What he could not extract from this plebiscite was the institutionalization of a procedure to which both sides would agree and that would represent a true consensus for a specific policy course. With growing, not lessening, polarization, he faced greater, not reduced, intransigence from the opposition. They, in turn, were determined never again to submit to their exclusion from the fount of power—television.

Because of their perception of the power of television (beginning from an already high plateau in Soviet times), the leaders on both sides of Russian politics focused on what they thought was its unique impact. They were also all too aware that the elections of 1993 were being held against the backdrop of wrenching economic, political, and social change. They understood that the economy was grinding a large proportion of the population into poverty, especially the elderly and others on fixed incomes, as well as those who could not adapt well to the market. Industrial production was still declining and prices were rising twice as fast as incomes. Large-scale bankruptcies, though still in the offing, were drawing closer and threatened significant numbers of state employees with unemployment. Ethnic tension was increasing within the Russian Federation and on the borders with other former Soviet republics, and the strains between the center and geographic and ethnic regions were increasing. Organized and opportunistic crime was on the rise, with little apparent opposition from law enforcement, and there was widespread belief that economic success was in large measure not due to the workings of the market but to the unlawful appropriation of collectively-owned state property and officially tolerated corruption. The health care delivery system had disintegrated and male life expectancy plummeted. In no small measure the polluted environment was to blame: it had become deadly and regulations were not enforced. On the international scene, former clients had decamped, the West exhibited caution, and the hugely populous neighbor to the east was rapidly gaining.

In riven Russia the Yeltsin team could also identify sources of optimism: they could see the effects of a privatization program that spelled the end of the institutional base of the Soviet regime and initiated new relations, especially with the Russian regions oriented toward trade and innovation. Yet in this maze of variable and interacting forces, this leadership, as those before it, ascribed decisive influence for the results of the referendum to the media—television, in particular. For them, it was still the syringe ready with the ideological injections.

THE PATTERN OF CANDIDATE-DOMINATED CAMPAIGN COVERAGE: THE 1993 PARLIAMENTARY ELECTION

In the Russian parliamentary election of December 1993, the many strands of an evolving pattern of campaign coverage came together. This pattern was to shape the televised campaign in the future. Public opinion polling, political consultants, "American" and "counter-American" strategies, and a piercing new mode of political discourse were ushered in and remained. The fortunes of individual candidates and parties shifted over time, but both were constrained by the basic parameters established in that first fully competitive election.

In contrast with past elections, this was to be the first multi-party parliamentary election. Though the earlier 1989 and 1990 elections had been multi-candidate, formalized parties with a reasonably coherent structure of local organizations were few. Three parties stood out in the field: the Communist Party, Zhirinovsky's Liberal Democratic Party, and Russia's Choice, the party of Yegor Gaidar's reform democrats, favored by the Yeltsin government. The Communist Party had the organizational advantage derived from its past and had retained many of its networks across the country, and Vladimir Zhirinovsky's Liberal Democratic Party had done surprisingly well in the Russian presidential election of June 1991. That last Soviet-era election presented to Russian republic voters about a half dozen candidates, all of whom (including front-runner Boris Yeltsin) were much better known than Vladimir Zhirinovsky.

At the beginning of the 1991 campaign, according to his principal image-maker, Vladimir Berezovsky, Zhirinovsky had the support of no more than one-half of one percent of the people polled. Therefore, a media strategy was devised to enable the marginal candidate to get into the race. He developed, in short, an "attack strategy" against hostile television interviewers, sound bites contrasting powerfully with long-winded bureaucratese, and the "daring" personal mannerisms of a maverick. Though the cards were stacked against him both by the Yeltsin faction and prime minister Nikolai Ryzhkov's faction, backed by the Communist Party, Zhirinovsky knew how to hold his own. During a televised round table with journalists, a hostile state television interviewer attempted to pin him down, and Zhirinovsky harshly told him: "'I am an official candidate for president of Russia and I will answer as I consider it necessary.'"[44] The interviewer was speechless. Finding the right voice to counter Zhirinovsky eluded just about all of his television interlocutors then and later, just as moderate, thoughtful responses were so often hopeless and helpless on American talk shows.[45] In 1991, Zhirinovsky finished with six million votes. (In the second presidential contest five years later, he got 4.3 million.)

In 1993, the parties of the extreme right and left had been proscribed. Directly after the Rutskoy-Khasbulatov-led revolt was quelled, a number of hard-line parties were banned for complicity. Four, including the Russian Communist Party (the largest, claiming half a million members), were legalized within days, but six nationalist and communist groups were banned, thus leaving the "red-brown" field of support mainly to the Russian Communist Party and Vladimir Zhirinovsky, while the democratic forces were divided among four parties.

The campaign period was once again short—one month—and especially difficult for parties with little organized infrastructure, limited funds, and a transportation and communications system particularly unreliable in the winter. The elections would fill the parliament's lower house (the State Duma) with 450 members (half to be filled by proportional representation nationwide by party or bloc and half from single-seat constituencies on a first-past-the-post basis) and an upper house (the Federation Council) with 178 members (two from each of the 89 republics, regions, and provinces). The ballot would also be a plebiscite on a new constitution advocated by the president.

Boris Yeltsin declared himself above party politics and took no public position on the party lists, but concentrated his energies on pushing for the new constitution, which would significantly enhance his powers while reducing those of the elected legislature, whatever its political coloration. The size of the turnout was vital; passage required that at least 50 percent of the 107-million electorate take part. But overall, turnout was on the decline and would be 54.8 percent that December.[46]

The periodic holding of elections is critical to the institutionalization of the democratic process and of the development of party politics based on programmatic competition.[47] When Russians turned out that December, they were being roused for the *sixth* time in *five* years to participate in critical national votes. They kept on going to vote and by mid-1996 would have done so some *nine times in eight years*. The glut of elections, swiftly following one another under conditions of crisis, may also have attenuated each one's impact on the voter's understanding of the usefulness to be derived from voting. In December 1993, voter fatigue was the likely result,[48] but with a respite of two years when the election season began again in 1995, turnout rose. At the end of the contest in 1993, the Constitution was declared victorious, but, tellingly, turnout figures were controversial and less than fully documented.[49]

The results appeared to differ radically from the strong support Yeltsin got earlier in the April referendum. The December election lacked the simple and powerful polarized choice of a backward-looking parliament versus a future of freedom and economic reform.

Some thirteen parties made it to the ballot for the 1993 parliamentary elections by presenting the Central Electoral Commission with petitions containing the required one hundred thousand valid signatures. These parties were mainly loose and sometimes new entities defined by leaders rather than political or economic programs. A number of existing parties reorganized, formed coalitions, and renamed themselves, thus making Russian voters disoriented and poorly informed about their political options.[50]

The new parties suffered from a relatively short history, poor internal communications, a low degree of party discipline, and much fission, occasioned by the inability of leaders to compromise and form winning coalitions. (Two years later forty-three parties were on the ballot.) Nor was there any real possibility of resurrecting pre-Soviet parties, with their symbols and platforms. The Constitutional Democrats, the Monarchists, and confessional parties seeking to revive a pre-Soviet past enjoyed no organizational and only the vaguest programmatic continuity. The legacy of communism had left a public distrustful of parties and government, and they were, in a sense, exercising their newly-won freedom "*not to participate* in party politics."[51]

Gradually, over the course of future elections, voters' economic preferences could be matched to parties, but political trust was slower to develop. Ensuring the accountability of elected officials to their constituents was especially difficult when presidential decrees were replacing laws and neither were consistently implemented. Given the headlong downward spiral of the economy and the traumatic political changes, the task of the fledgling parties would be all the more difficult.

The summer before the December election, *more than three-fourths* (76 percent) of the Russian public could not name a single political party or movement and only 18 percent correctly paired the best-known party, the Communist Party, with its leader.[52] The following June, with new parliamentary and presidential elections again looming in the next two years, the majority of Russians could not identify themselves with a position on the political spectrum. Fifty-two percent said they did not identify with any political direction and another 12 percent had no answer. Only about one-third spoke of communists, democrats, socialists, and other political positions.[53] To complicate the task of the parties in the December 1993 elections, the person of the president was not engaged; he was viewing his office in a de Gaulle-like posture, standing above party politics and representing the nation as a whole.

In Western electoral experience, political parties increasingly detached themselves from the popular roots from which they grew, and candidate-based fund-raising (largely through television) tended to replace the party-generated patronage of the past. In Russia, the parties were also detached, but, importantly, without having first established grass roots. It was thought television might be a substitute for the historical process of slowly aggregating local demands and loyalties into a national fabric of party identification. The prominent exception, the Communist Party, exploited the old structures and the old economic levers of the Soviet system by continuing, wherever possible, to monopolize or adapt instruments of local power.

In the absence of a functioning legislature, presidential decrees made law. On October 29, Yeltsin signed one on media access, in force from November 22 through December 8, after which televised campaigning officially ended. Public opinion polling could not be published or announced by the media from December 2 through December 12. A special Information Arbitration Tribunal was set up to monitor fairness in media coverage of the campaign. Composed of leading figures in the law and the press, its deliberations were advisory to the official Central Election Commission. Equal amounts of free time would be available to all registered parties on Channel One (Ostankino Television), Channel Two (Russian Television) and on state-owned radio. The rules did not apply to privately owned stations. Parties petitioned the commission for their time slots and indicated whether they wished to break up their allocation into smaller portions and what kind of format they wished to use.[54]

They drew lots for the schedule. The pattern set at this time—of equal amounts of free time drawn by lot and oversight by a council advisory to the election commission (and appealing to the court of public opinion)—continued in subsequent elections.

Once again, television personalities were out on the hustings; the political activism of the journalists, so important in the first competitive elections in 1989, continued through the 1993 election but tapered off thereafter. The constitution adopted in 1993 had made parliament a distinctly less powerful organ and therefore less attractive to liberal journalists, and the political climate there did not favor their reform-minded agendas.

An early government attempt to restrict the subject matter of the campaign failed. Boris Yeltsin and his First Deputy Prime Minister, Vladimir Shumeiko, made a bid to quash candidates' criticism of the draft constitution, and Shumeiko's letter to the Central Electoral Commission asked the body to exclude any party or movement that criticized the draft Constitution. Both the commission and the Information Arbitration Tribunal rejected the attempt to limit speech. Party leaders, including those of pro-Yeltsin Russia's Choice, joined in the attack on the Shumeiko initiative.

Although equal amounts of free time were made available to registered parties, the requirement for equality or balance in news coverage remained, as in Western democracies, a purely editorial decision.[55] What was worthy of coverage was left up to the news department of each station, and the lion's share of the amount of time devoted to the different parties went to Russia's Choice, the party favored by the president's administration. The dramatic change was in removal of editorial partisanship, not in allotment of news time. The imbalance in time was partly the advantage of incumbency; many Russia's Choice candidates held responsible governmental posts.[56] The Gaidar party was strongly advantaged with a huge allotment of coverage especially, on the larger network of Channel One.[57]

Had it not been for the tremendously skewed and blatant coverage by state television that April, the pendulum of campaign coverage practices would not have swung so far in the other direction of passive, uninformative journalism in December. Correspondents and anchors were forced to maintain scrupulous neutrality, not by equally probing questions to all, but rather, by near silence. It would be the same story in 1995, and they did not kick over their traces again—with partisanship this time—until the second great, defining national referendum: the 1996 presidential election.

The provision of free time guaranteed that candidates in Russia, as in Western Europe, could present their messages directly to the public on state television, whatever the size of their party's coffers. Journalists were ordered to remain above the fray. Neutrality was to be so strict that television journalists were reduced to traffic police. They were not allowed to provide commentary, analysis, or even searching questions. In short, their training and roles as journalists were to be nullified; they would not be posing questions about the reliability, feasibility, consistency, or desirability of any of the views and claims put forward by the candidates.[58] That, in turn, left the viewing public to listen to a succession of platforms without any assistance in the assessment of their comparability or even of their exact meaning. Vladimir Zhirinovsky squarely faced the viewing public and said with deliberate mystification that "I use Aesopian language. . . . I could say other things. . . ." "I will say more about what I think about the former republics. . . . Sometimes I speak more softly than I think and than I want. . . . After the election, we will fully show our cards."[59]

For most communities of journalists, statements as provocative and deliberately obfuscatory would have called forth the most vigorous criticism and pressure for the candidate to reveal hidden plans. In this campaign, the journalists were ordered to refrain from such probes. Valentin Lazutkin, who was in charge of election coverage at Channel One, was deeply dissatisfied. He said his proposal for "*no* monologues, just collisions and debates, always with opponents," was turned down flat by the Central Election Commission of the government."[60] By the time of the December 1995 parliamentary elections, when state television attempted a course correction and proposed making the candidates' allotment of free time into a multi-party confrontation, the candidates rejected the proposal out of hand, preferring solo appearances. Almost all stayed with their unmediated time slots.

The glaring—and illegal—exception to this pattern of the prohibition of partisan editorializing was a desperate reaction to a rapidly accelerating swing of undecided voters to the Zhirinovsky side in the last days of the December 1993 campaign. State television violated clearly stated rules prohibiting campaigning just before election day. One of those violations was the broadcast on Channel One of a prime-time documentary film called *Hawk*.

Hawk was a television film presenting Vladimir Zhirinovsky in his own words. It showed him making speeches, talking to his entourage of sullen youth, haranguing the crowds. Vyacheslav Bragin, head of Channel One, ordered the broadcast of this film strategically placed directly after the hysterical, fictional film *Stalin's Legacy,* which showed the madness of a hypothetical return to Stalinism. Valentin Lazutkin said that Bragin insisted on showing *Hawk* over the objections of his chief of programming and others, but Bragin said he had orders "from above." All night, Lazutkin recalled, Bragin searched through Ostankino's archives to find the place in Shostakovich's seventh symphony where the music portrays the advancing Nazis. Lazutkin said he told Bragin that splicing in the score would create technical problems and told him to keep it soft. Bragin made it louder.[61]

Bragin later refused to disclose if anyone ordered him to show the film. He looked at me and said whimsically, "something happened to my memory," and then "I can't tell the entire story of this film." He did describe his state of mind and his strong support for the film. He said that he became concerned, well before others, that Russia's Choice was in trouble and the extreme right might actually come to power. He said that on October 16, he told top officials that they should not think that Russia's Choice will gain a majority. But "there was euphoria," and no one would listen. When I asked whether he had based his conclusions on survey or other data, he said that he felt them, from his "intuition as a person," from his trips to his old city, Tver, and from contacts with "simple people. . . . I did not believe the sociological data."

Invoking the crisis of the time, he explained that he had to defend democratic institutions from the threat, and broadcasting the film was effective and took votes away from Zhirinovsky.[62] To the contrary, Valentin Lazutkin said that sociologists attributed a 12 percent *increase* in Zhirinovsky votes because of the broadcast. Neither of these propositions can be tested, but it is true, as discussed below, that among people who voted for Zhirinovsky a large number decided late in the campaign. It is also true that the polls had it wrong and failed to predict Zhirinovsky's triumph. But that votes were swayed *away* from Zhirinovsky by the broadcast is most un-likely.

Bragin denied that the broadcast was in violation of the deadline for ending campaigning. Five days after *Hawk* was shown, the Information Ar-bitration Tribunal ruled that "legal requirements and ethical norms" had been violated by Ostankino.[63] After the elections, the tribunal became the permanent Judicial Chamber for Information Disputes, and two years later its chairman, jurist Anatoly Vengerov, told me without hesitation that the showing of *Hawk,* had been a violation.[64]

Astonishingly, during the entire period of the 1993 election campaign, there was not a single news story about a political party set in a rural loca-tion. Only one story involved the countryside at all, and it provided only general election information. As before, Moscow generated far more sto-ries about political parties than did any other location in Russia. St. Peters-burg also became a player, but the rest of the country was spottily covered and quite invisible. Before the elections, the chairman of the state-owned Sverdlovsk Radio and Television Company, from the home town of Boris Yeltsin, complained that regions were getting short shrift. He noted that the various "national" channels were not Russian, but "Moscow television. More than 90 percent of broadcasts for and about Russia are today pre-pared within Moscow."[65]

The degree to which television campaign strategies personalized the cam-paign is an important element of "modern," television-dominated, Ameri-can-style campaigning. One could argue that Yegor Gaidar, the torchbearer of Russia's Choice, was drowned in the sea of faces of his party's many na-tional leaders and, when personalized, proved hopelessly out of touch with the television age. Even though the party of Yegor Gaidar had the over-whelming advantage in news coverage and purchase of advertising time, the party's strategy chose to spread out the appearances of the many candi-dates it fielded. Russia's Choice was a kaleidoscope of the faces of famous politicians, which was both the advantage and disadvantage of incumbency. The party could be seen in the faces of literally dozens of its candidates, while its leader, Yegor Gaidar, appeared in only a fraction of stories and programs about the party. In cinema vérité–style campaign ads, he ap-peared distinctly uncomfortable.

Vladimir Zhirinovsky's Liberal Democratic Party had no such problem. Out of power, staffed mainly by people little known to the public and without substantial political influence, the focus was on the energetic showman and his extreme ideas, and he chose to fill his paid and free time (he was barely covered on the news) by spending most of it talking directly to the public. As Vyacheslav Bragin remarked, Zhirinovsky divided his time into pieces and was always at the center of attention. He gave the impression that he was always there on the television screen, while Gaidar be-haved "democratically" and gave time to others, diluting his effect.[66]

The new Women of Russia party brought together a number of women candidates who were politically aligned more with the Soviet past than the feminist future, and many had ties to the Communist Party. Try as they might to play the new game of politics, the old condescension was still alive. At one televised round table of candidates, the Women of Russia's participant was absent. The moderator, going around the table making in-troductions, noted the empty chair (she was caught in traffic) and said that we hope she will arrive "and, as a woman, decorate our meeting."[67]

How well candidates fared in the free television time they were granted depended, as ratings do, on the competition in the time slots drawn by lot. When the Mexican soap opera *Just Maria* played on Channel One, the pre-election program on Channel Two could not compete. On the other hand, with weak competition in the time slot and strong campaigners, the ratings shot up. On November 25 Zhirinovsky, and on November 26 the Women's Party candidate Natalya Gundaryova, a well-known actress, appeared on the Channel One program *Voter's Hour.* On those two days, over 40 percent of the people answering a Moscow telephone survey reported they had watched those two programs. In contrast, for the previous two days, the re-sponse was under 30 percent each day.

Perhaps the most important innovation in the Russian coverage of elec-tions was large-scale political advertising. Although advertising time was initially limited to a half hour of paid time, that ceiling was later revoked by the government and replaced by no ceiling at all. Airtime was to be made available at favorable rates, much like the lowest unit rate in U.S. elections, and was to become a major source of revenue for the stations.

In future elections the prices shot up, though the stations still claimed they were offering a bargain. In 1993, for the first time, huge sums had to be raised for an electoral campaign, and although a disclosure law was on the books there was very little prospect that the actual donors and the amount of their contributions would be precisely identified. Funding for the parties' campaigns came in part from a uniform grant from the Central Election Commission. In addition, Russian private donors contributed large sums, often to a number of parties.[68] Most of this money, in turn, came from the banking and finance industry, some of whose numbers would be bankrupt by the next election.[69]

Two years later, candidates were speaking in terms of around one-third of a million dollars to mount a parliamentary campaign. It was natural, one campaign investor remarked, that entrepreneurs, having contributed to campaigns, would expect a kind of "guarantee" that there would be "regu-lar meetings of deputies with us to discuss bills or amendments or supplements to [laws] in force."[70] In the elections of 1993, campaign financing and regulation of contributions emerged as issues and as features of the future.

POLITICAL ADVERTISING

Much has rightly been made of the innovation of political advertising and political consultants. During the referendum campaign, advertising was restricted to pro-presidential messages. When the fires in the White House had been put out, and the parties most directly involved in the uprising proscribed, new and fairer television campaign rules were decreed. President Yeltsin's October 1993 ruling (ratified by law subsequently) provided for two ways registered political parties could use television to communicate directly with the electorate. All parties had an equal amount of free time and could purchase advertising time at reduced rates.

In the United States, it has been customary to link frustration with the intractable issue of campaign reform to the pervasive dependence on televised political advertising, although research shows that ads do provide information about candidates, especially in the absence of free-time allotments.[71] This component of campaigns accounts for a large proportion of total expenditures, and proponents of reform have suggested voluntary (and sometimes required) limits on advertising buys, or supplementing paid advertising with the provision of free time for candidates. The phenomenon of well-heeled candidates buying their way into prominence virtually entirely on the basis of enormous advertising expenditures, as in the 1994 senatorial race in California and the 1996 Steve Forbes presidential candidacy, was sobering, but projects for reforms invoking limits inevitably confront free-speech arguments.

Political advertising could play a very different role in a radically different political context. Where airtime was monopolized by an authoritarian government, there was no guarantee of opposition access to state television (the only available choice). This was often the case in countries beginning the transition away from dictatorship. With scant likelihood of forcing their way into state-controlled programming (or with the deck unfairly stacked against the opposing candidate on interview shows or news coverage), candidates and parties challenging the system found that paid political advertising provided the only significant opportunity to shape their own message.[72]

In the 1993 Russian elections, parties had varied advertising strategies. Government-backed Russia's Choice outspent all the other parties by a very wide margin. The Party of Unity and Accord (which did not survive the next election) and Zhirinovsky's party came next.[73]

A number of parties failing to reach the 5 percent cutoff to get into the Duma outspent parties that did pass the threshold. The highly visible Civic Union (a centrist party of large state-sector industrial interests stressing managerial skills and stability), did not elect a single deputy. It was handicapped by the role played by its most prominent leader, Alexander Rutskoy, in the October revolt and altered its name slightly to dissociate itself from the former vice president. Similarly, the Movement for Democratic Reforms, with some highly visible senior political figures of the *glasnost* era (now hopelessly passé, though only four or five years had passed), paid for a total of one hour and forty-five minutes of ads and did not qualify for representation. Nor did a strategy succeed that was adopted by a new party, New Names/Future of Russia, to rely almost entirely on television to achieve name recognition and mobilize the electorate. Two parties that succeeded in electing deputies bought no advertising time at all: the Communist Party, led by Gennady Zyuganov did very well, as did the new Yabloko party, led by Grigory Yavlinsky. The Communists had their organization at work and Yavlinsky had a very well educated, highly informed constituency, particularly in St. Petersburg.

In the December 1993 elections, the participation of foreign political consultants, especially those who did television ads, was such a contentious issue that the parties made sure that very little surfaced in the media and that foreign political consultants kept a low profile. Some campaign strategists made it a point to publicly reject any foreign input. Tossing aside a U.S. National Democratic Institute book called "How to Win at Elections," a Russia's Choice candidate told the *Christian Science Monitor* correspondent: "'We didn't need any Western ad agencies to help us. . . . We know what we're doing. Some Americans and Brits offered their consulting services, but when they came here and saw what we had accomplished, they said, "Bravo."'"[74]

Ben Goddard of California-based Goddard+Claussen/First Tuesday was back in Moscow, but this time he only gave "substantive advice on a very informal basis." He did not become directly involved. He certainly concurred with the Russia's Choice leaders that it was not a good idea to have "direct and visible links with Western political consultants."[75] As Goddard observed, the opposition had learned from the referendum campaign; they had become more sophisticated campaigners and were raising issues of kickbacks and illegal payments. Contributing to the disinclination of Russia's Choice to collaborate—and to be seen to collaborate—with U.S. consultants was a notorious flap.

The U.S. consulting firm Sawyer Miller Group (later Robinson, Lerer, Sawyer, Miller), had an $11.8 million contract from the U.S. State Department Agency for International Development to assist the Russian Federation privatization ministry (the State Committee on Property—in its Russian acronym, GKI) create support for the reform process.[76] Its most visible effort was the implementation of the massive voucher program, which involved distributing to millions of ordinary citizens certificates they could cash in, use to invest in privatizing companies, put into investment funds, or keep for future action. The effort was complex, confusing, and utterly new. Sawyer Miller used AID funds to develop television public service announcements and other public events promoting and explaining the government's program. In mid-November, about a month before the elections, the Sawyer Miller spots, which had carried the tag line "Your Voucher, Your Choice," were somehow changed to say "Your Choice, Russia's Choice." U.S. Government funds now appeared to be supporting the campaign of a political party in the Russian elections. The ads ran for about a week before a national uproar forced the Russian government to pull them.[77] How this came about was subject to dispute.

At the time Mark Malloch Brown was a Sawyer Miller partner in charge of the company's international practice. He maintained that the Russian government ordered his Moscow office to change the tag line, and when the American company refused to do so the Russians removed Sawyer Miller from the task and took over the materials. The Russian privatization ministry (GKI) replaced Sawyer Miller with another U.S. public relations company, Burson Marsteller. GKI, on the other hand, charged that it had been unhappy with the quality of Sawyer Miller's work for some time and denied it had applied pressure to alter the ad. GKI's deputy chairman, Dmitry Vasiliev, later argued that Sawyer Miller's work was a failure and simply did not relate to Russian culture and Russian circumstances: "What works in Texas is completely inappropriate for Russians. . . ."[78]

Malloch Brown disagreed, stating that the Russians reedited the spot and changed the graphic. "We didn't make the changes; they did," he stated.

It is true that conflicts were brewing between Sawyer Miller's methods and Russian government expectations, which Malloch Brown laid to problems of the "tremendous growth" of demands and an office that was staffing up hurriedly, as well as an "in-your-face" management team. From the beginning, the Russians and the American firm seem to have had different conceptions of the assistance project, but when, in November 1993, a long-delayed tranche of AID funding came through, GKI gave first priority to Sawyer Miller.

Mark Malloch Brown recalled that it was Arkady Yevstavyev, press officer for Anatoly Chubais, head of the privatization ministry, who instructed Sawyer Miller to change the tag line, which Sawyer Miller refused to do.[79] (In 1995, Yevstavyev took over as head of news at Channel One and, when his patron Chubais was removed, Yevstavyev lost his position too.) At the same time, Malloch Brown said, he was "absolutely certain Chubais was unaware of and did not initiate it."[80]

The new U.S. partner, Burson Marsteller, came in to manage the privatization campaign, but according to Executive Vice President Kirby Jones, who arrived after the tag line had been changed, it was involved in neither the creation nor the placement of the altered ad.[81]

Denying the charges, Russia's Choice leader Yegor Gaidar told a U.S. newspaper that "Russia's Choice does not need to use such funding sources."[82]

Although it was a small flap in the United States and did little harm to the privatization assistance program, which developed clearer procedures and considerable experience, it was a much more significant issue in Russia because it related to the role of foreign political consultants, extending the fallout from the April referendum campaign. The political arena was increasingly polarized, and one of the issues on the political agenda was precisely the intent and influence of the "enemy," or "partner," depending on where the party stood in the political spectrum. Citing reports from the American press, rival party leaders charged that Russia's Choice had violated electoral regulations by "using funds from foreign sponsors," in this case, AID.[83]

The press and the surveys of public opinion spoke of a strong lead for Russia's Choice, but the campaign strategy was fraying. The Gaidar, Burbulis, and Poltoranin factions developed tensions as the period wore on,[84] and the Russia's Choice campaign was far too concerned with organization and personnel and too little with the message they would use to mobilize their electorate. Burbulis said that the campaign did not have a "single center" to work out "ideology and agitation." (At times his constructions had the flavor of the Marxist-Leninist style.) Several groups worked simultaneously on political advertising spots for television, and they did not have close links to his group. Burbulis flatly stated that the ads were "worthless" (*bezdarnye*). They exhibited the "maximum distance from assimilation by voters."[85]

A further complicating factor in the use of political advertising in the December 1993 election was the context of television advertising for consumer products. The impact of Western-style product advertising on Russian television had been problematic at the outset. Even for domestic products, ads looked Western: the rock music, the connection between glamorous seduction and impossible dreams. And the viewers were also divided about *what* was advertised—particularly Western items. Expectations were raised and then dashed either by unavailability of the product or, more frequently, astronomical pricing that put it out of the reach of most people. People who did like televised ads were especially the privileged of the new order: between thirty and forty years old, with high incomes and working in the private sector.[86]

Surveys were also revealing a backlash. A large number of Muscovites, especially older and less wealthy viewers, were reacting to advertising with considerable irritation.[87] In the spring of 1994, a survey of Moscow viewers' reactions to product advertising revealed that more than half (53 percent) reacted to ads with irritation.[88] Another survey found that 60 percent of those interviewed across Russia found ads irritating or disturbing, and 51 percent saw no utility in them.[89]

Mainstream newspapers featured complaints about the morality of advertising: "Advertising can be not only vulgar, but also immoral. Here is an example. A foreign company offers natural juice . . . and the text [says] 'Natural juice will extend your life six years.' And what's a person to do who doesn't have the money—die?"[90] Most disturbing were these ads for foreign foods, an impossible luxury for a population whose basic health needs were unmet. A respected Russian television critic wrote in the fall of 1993: "How many parents are pushed to rage by the daily whining of their offspring and curse this intrusive advertising of foreign sweets for which most of the adult population of the country simply lack income?"[91]

The decision by Russia's Choice to fashion its ads in the style, and sometimes the setting, of Western product advertising was at the time a costly mistake. It is likely that those ads cued, among viewers, the same dissatisfactions as the ads whose style was borrowed. On the other hand, Vladimir Zhirinovsky's strategy to craft advertising that did *not* resemble product advertising was a much more strategic, and under the circumstances, a more effective choice. Zhirinovsky chose a deliberately "old-fashioned" way, shunning jump cuts, jarring images, and the fast tempo of Western-style product advertising. In fact, a plank of his "platform" vowed to take ads for American-made, heavily advertised Snickers candy bars off the air.

Zhirinovsky's ads were long homilies. He sat in front of the camera on a modest set, speaking without notes and without pause about a selected subject announced in advance. He spoke, in turn, to religious believers, to the military, to youth. He promised each group resources and support and he held out the promise of the return of the empire. His points were often disjointed and absurdly egocentric, but his enormous energy and urgent, emotional tone held the audience's attention and made him a (relatively) gripping figure on television.

Early in the campaign, when only 2 percent of the people polled in urban Russia were saying that they intended to vote for Zhirinovsky, some 28 percent said that Zhirinovsky would make the best "actor." He had been noticed and it had to be his television performances that, for better or worse, made people think that this man played his role with consummate ease.[92]

Zhirinovsky also eschewed the abstract language of his competitors. When he appeared with competing candidates, his voice was often the only direct and forceful one; when he appeared occasionally with candidates from his own party, all deferred to him. He rejected the appearance of the "Americanized" model of political campaigning while adapting its advantages to his campaign and his targeted electorate (what Gennady Burbulis and others called *adresnost*—aiming at a particular address, or targeting).

In one of his ads, addressed to "young Russians," he said he understood their problems, and turned to sex. He drew parallels between stages of Soviet history and sex: the October Revolution was rape (of the country); the purges were homosexual behavior (within the same party); the time of Nikita Khrushchev was masturbation (he satisfied only himself); the time of Mikhail Gorbachev was impotence (he wanted to effect change, but nothing happened). Sexual life was "covered up" before, but now it is public, but in a "vulgar form," while it should be in a "special place and a special time." Product advertising on television distressed people and should also be relegated to special places—to offices or shops. Let people watch their television films in peace. When the state takes over the economy, it is equivalent to rape.

Other "sermonettes" addressed the need to nurture religion, but he made it clear that by "believers" he meant Orthodox Christians only. With popular young television talk show host Dmitry Dibrov, Zhirinovsky sat in the studio to take questions from a crowd live in Red Square and on the telephone. While Zhirinovsky continued to make his unsupported, rabble-rousing charges and promises, Dibrov, in keeping with the prohibition on journalistic intervention, only smiled foolishly—a depressing picture that showed how unprepared the young telegenic star was for serious political contests.[93]

Was Zhirinovsky a brilliant media star? A superb manipulator of the most powerful medium? A master tactician of the airwaves? Gennady Burbulis, for many years one of Yeltsin's most powerful strategists, called Zhirinovsky a "virtuoso" in his use of airtime, a talented populist who "intelligibly stated his ideas," and said he was the only one whose appeal to his audiences was not abstract.[94] Burbulis was certainly right about the competition, but Zhirinovsky also rambled and ranted. His sets were tacky and shopworn; his entourage appeared to be mainly pasty-faced young louts scraped from the bottom layers of the dispossessed and angry. His advantage lay in the energy with which he spoke and his ability to speak aggressively without stopping and to exaggerate irresponsibly. He did not hesitate to grab attention with verbal shock tactics, scooping up discourse from a world banned from all mass media for seven decades. Zhirinovsky's exhortations did liberate and magnify elemental urges, as fascists had done earlier. He breached the wall of separateness that people had built to protect themselves from an intrusive Soviet political elite that attempted to substitute its language for normal discourse and thus stamp out private thoughts altogether.[95]

Zhirinovsky's words reached down and freed that private world and legitimized it as sovereign, and he perhaps, instinctively, understood how out of touch "normal" television discourse was with viewers. He sought to re-integrate the long divided selves of the viewers and to confirm the validity of private life driving public choice.

Every other campaign did the reverse. The other candidates presented lofty images of a remote leadership (for experts and outstanding people are always above the common plain), the authority of which ordinary people were to acknowledge, and because of which, pledge fealty. Daily cares, urges, and anguish had no place in this high-minded world, and nor did the language in which people understood their inner drives and passions. That was "low politics." Maybe so, but the democratic candidates failed to understand the implications of such information as that produced by an October 1992 survey of nearly a thousand Russians that found 53 percent of those interviewed agreeing that people who appear on television "often express their points of view incomprehensibly and that television journalists abuse words and terms the viewer does not understand."[96] Had Zhirinovsky been competing with even moderately down-to-earth politicians who could use normal speech instead of bureaucratic, Soviet-tinged abstractions, his shock value would have been greatly reduced.

Zhirinovsky's innovation transformed Russian televised campaigning and, predictably, his inventions were later appropriated. As one Russian observer remarked, in the December 1995 campaign "Misfortune befell Zhirinovsky—he was robbed. Intellectually. Most of his slogans, it seems, were eaten up by other parties and blocs. . . ."[97] In spite of the competition, Zhirinovsky's party finished second that year, behind the Communists and ahead of the two democratic reform parties passing the 5 percent threshold. He drew most of his support from particularly depressed regions and on the borders, where his message and his distinctive persona, amplified by television, still found its constituency.

Yegor Gaidar was leader of the Russia's Choice party in 1993. His stewardship of Russia's transition to the market economy had inflicted pain but launched the radical market reform project. A short, plump, shiny, moon-faced man, he was distinctly uncomfortable on television.[98] Nor was he particularly good at explaining why he should be elected, lacking, as he did, the common touch. His party chose to craft its ads to emphasize how *unlike* everyone he was, how brilliant an economist and how intellectually fit to lead the country out of its disastrous economic plight. Valentin Lazutkin, in charge of Channel One's election coverage, thought the Gaidar ads the most "worthless" (*bezdarnye*).[99] Viewers were lectured about his eminence, and the conclusion to be drawn was that he must be deferred to for his clear superiority to the rest of us.

One bit of "spontaneous" unpaid advertising occurred in the studio when a popular quiz show was in progress. To the host's groveling delight, the government's minister of privatization, Anatoly Chubais, dropped in on the show. With Chubais listening with pleasure, the host praised Gaidar's intelligence and noted that many spoke of his mental gifts. "This is a compliment," he said, and "this is the first time I've heard it as a compliment and not an insult. . . . We will all vote for intelligent people, for intelligent Gaidar and his intelligent team, and I personally will do this." Chubais, now appearing a bit uncomfortable, wisely said that the important thing was for people to take responsibility for their choices, whatever they are.[100]

The longest and most ambitious Gaidar television piece was a twenty-minute, cinema vérité–style documentary that attempted to humanize the intelligent Gaidar while all the while stressing what an exceptional being he was. It showed the Gaidar family at home, his wife bathing the children and talking about her extraordinary husband and his full absorption in important things for his country. It showed Gaidar and his wife sitting on a couch, the wife looking adoringly at her husband. It must have been quite unintended that the prominent cello solo accompanying the image of spousal affection was the introduction to the aria in *Don Carlo* in which the king laments that his wife never loved him.

The camera went to the home of Gaidar's parents, who told of their son's lack of interest in his suits or ties and his insistence on dealing with complex issues, even though people tell him to simplify his message for the common folk. Gaidar comes in to join them for a family get-together and watches a television program showing *Izvestia* economics editor Mikhail Berger praising Gaidar for his brilliance as an economist and manager of the country's fate. Gaidar's face, in extreme tight shot, fills the screen. The camera lovingly lingers while Gaidar tries to show delight at the tribute, but it is all strained and unconvincing.

Gaidar did not "personalize" very well. Valentin Lazutkin said that he was portrayed rather like the young Lenin ("Russia goes forward!") or a caricature of Stalin.[101]

Other *Russia's Choice* ads looked like Western ads, indeed, so much so that viewers must have wondered what country they were in. Lazutkin talked of this kind of television as provocation, since 93 percent of the population were living badly, with 57 percent officially under the poverty line.

The disconnection of the Gaidar team from the travails and misery of the country could not have been more apparent than in the boy-and-dog ad. This short spot showed a child sitting on the polished wood floor next to a huge St. Bernard and surrounded by piles of fluffy toys. Yuppie, narrow-jeans-clad legs go by. One pair stops, a hand comes down and pins a Russia's Choice button on the child, who hugs the massive dog and says, "They won't let us vote for Russia's Choice, because we're little."

Clearly targeting the new, young beneficiaries of the economic reforms, the ad in effect said that this lifestyle—whether one had already arrived or hoped to get there—depended on a Russia's Choice victory. But this was a small, very small part of the population that December, and the ad went out through the whole country.[102] Most would have seen an alien life of unimaginable wealth, for just feeding a giant dog was beyond the means of many. Some viewers could also have concluded that only corruption and special favors produced a life like this, and as the party in power, Russia's Choice must have gained its wealth in unsavory ways.[103] For Valentin Lazutkin, this ad was "removed from the mentality" of the Russian people. He said Russia's Choice—and Vyacheslav Bragin, along with his deputy, Kirill Ignatyev, who worked so hard on this campaign—overestimated their capabilities. Although they had funding and technology, and though there were plenty of textbooks, he said "classic mistakes were made." They thought they were geniuses, and they were very proud of this ad, Lazutkin recalled.[104]

Most of the other candidates in their free or paid time stared at the camera (or resolutely faced an interlocutor with not a glance at the camera), and delivered their messages learned by rote without the inflections of normal speech. The Agrarian Party, the Communists, Women of Russia, Charity and Dignity, and the Constructive Ecological Movement of Russia (CEDAR) all produced uniform, gray, featureless speeches, full of the abstract, bureaucratic language of an earlier day. As television-era candidates, they were obsolete. Sometimes the ads showed pictures from a candidate's childhood; sometimes they showed scenes of pastoral Russia and the peaceful, picturesque life of a landscape of unrecognizable perfection.

The remaining parties mixed snappy soundtracks, usually with pop music, and wordy statements by their leaders. Sergei Shakhray's were unusual for their clear appeal to nationalistic values not much remarked upon in a Western press fixated on Zhirinovsky's use of this card. Stressing the *volk,* Shakhray appealed to traditional Russian values of unity and pre-Communist collectivism. One spot showed the exploits of the Soviet hockey team in past years as examples of the formidable effect of unified, passionate, national effort (in a sleight of hand Russian, not Soviet). Yet, unlike Zhirinovsky, Shakhray diluted this appeal by long statements, again in the usual mold, but with rather more focus on Shakhray's person. He, too, was shown to be a most unusual person. In one ad, when asked by an interviewer if he believed in God, he drew attention to a car crash (news footage shown) that only he survived. "There must be something," he said, his mustachioed face filling the screen.

Turnout for the December 1993 election was officially put at just under 55 percent (54.8 percent), though that was later disputed. The highest vote-getter was Zhirinovsky's party, garnering some 23 percent of the party-list votes. Next came Russia's Choice, with 15 percent; the Communist Party, with 12 percent; and Women of Russia, the Agrarian Party, and the Yavlinsky bloc all hovering around 8 percent.[105] Unity and Accord (Sergei

Shakhray's party) won 7 percent and the Democratic Party of Russia (Nikolai Travkin), 6 percent. The constitution was judged to have been adopted, with 58.4 percent of the electorate casting votes.[106] The failure to publish detailed results in a timely manner—as required by law—cast doubt on the question, as did reports of fraud, but the results held.[107]

Did television affect the outcome of that election? The Communists did well and bought no advertising, and in their free television time performed as woodenly and monotonously as always. Russia's Choice, heavily advantaged by huge advertising-time purchases and *the* preponderant news coverage, turned in a disappointing performance, and in the next election, two years later, did not even cross the 5 percent threshold.

Political advertising on television did appear to make a difference. Before the election, at the end of November, the results of a public opinion survey on ad effectiveness were broadcast on a popular news program. The ads were ranked as follows: Russia's Choice was first; Zhirinovsky's party was second. Even at this early date, Zhirinovsky's ad campaign was achieving a success that should have raised concerns among his opponents.[108] According to a study by Alexander Oslon and Elena Petrenko, television affected the outcome, especially for particular kinds of voters: the waverers who could not make up their minds and decided on their candidate close to election time.

Many of these voters ultimately chose Zhirinovsky. One estimate from survey evidence found that about two-thirds of Zhirinovsky voters made up their minds during the campaign, and most of them in the last week.[109] Forty percent of the women voting for Zhirinovsky made their decision either during the last week of the elections or at the polling place itself.

The late-deciding Zhirinovsky voters were on average older and less well educated than other voters. The urban voters who supported Zhirinovsky told interviewers (two to four times more than did other voters) that it was the mass media that changed their initial intentions, and 32 percent of the people interviewed overall said the media motivated them to vote.[110]

Each evening, beginning on October 23 and ending on December 3, people were interviewed in Moscow about their campaign viewing on television. Recall of ads for Zhirinovsky's party was more prominent than for any other, and more than others' ads, Zhirinovsky attracted the undecided.[111] Of television viewers polled, some 21 percent recalled the Zhirinovsky ads, while 20 percent recalled the Gaidar ads. Fifteen percent recalled Nikolai Travkin's ads, and only 10 percent recalled those of Sergei Shakhray (who at this point was spending more on ads than Zhirinovsky).[112]

In television, the biggest loser was Vyacheslav Bragin, head of Ostankino. Within days after the election results were known, he was removed. Sergei Yushenkov, deputy chief of the Federal Information Center at the time, said the fault for the outcome lay with the wrongheaded rules the government had devised, according to which "journalists were prohibited to comment on the speeches delivered by leaders of parties and blocs." Yushenkov was irritated that "Candidates were able to speak lies both free of charge and for pay."[113] Democratic forces were splintered and squabbling among themselves. Russia's Choice conducted a "sluggish" campaign, and economic hardship implicated the government.[114]

The first television-dominated electoral campaign had come to an end. With some permutations and adjustments, the basic, typically "modern" campaign continued into the future.

THE DECEMBER 1995 ELECTION

Two years later, in the parliamentary election campaign, some lessons had been learned, but not many. Just as Russia's Choice, the Yeltsin administration's favorite, dominated the airwaves in 1993, so did the new favorite, Our Home is Russia, in December 1995. This party, led by Yeltsin's prime minister, bought the largest amount of advertising time (Zhirinovsky's party was also a heavy buyer) and was granted by far the most favorable treatment on state television news broadcasts. One ad spot, repeatedly presented in prime time, showed Our Home's most visible candidate, movie director and actor Nikita Mikhalkov, as a cosmonaut, looking down at Russia and musing with affectionate warmth about the homeland and its charms. The spot carried no identification or attribution and was done by state television itself, which absorbed all costs. As the official rationale went, the ad was a public service announcement intended to instill optimism in viewers.

Sergei Shakhray's airtime looked much as it had done before—his attachment to his Cossack origins, his inspirational goals. CEDAR—the ecology party—changed its tactics. Their television spots showed a flaxen-haired girl playing happily in a pristine forest, while camouflaged terrorists—a metaphor for the lethal environment—bore down on her. For this viewer, recalling the imagery of the famous daisy ad in the Johnson-Goldwater campaign, the CEDAR spot (unlike the daisy spot) simply did not connect to either policy or candidate distinctiveness.

That year CEDAR and thirty-eight other parties (including Sergei Shakhray's), did not pass the 5 percent threshold to elect deputies to parliament. Most had bought airtime for their political ads (but not the Communist Party, with its well-organized party structure), and all had availed themselves of free time on the state channels.

Vladimir Zhirinovsky's message was straightforward—why should Russians vote for generals who lost wars and bureaucrats who were responsible for the economic debacle? He stressed his signature themes. The newly created Our Home is Russia party, headed by Prime Minister Viktor Chernomyrdin, was the administration's favorite, heavily advantaged in state-controlled media, but few could forget what had become proverbial by then. In describing a policy initiative on television, Chernomyrdin said, "We wanted it to be better, but it turned out as usual."

Neither the president nor the prime minister could solve what had become a huge problem for large numbers of their potential voters: wage arrears. People were simply not being paid—for months and months. Teachers, civil servants (still an enormous sector), scientists in research institutes, the military, and miners urgently demanded what they were owed and what their families desperately needed. Saddled by responsibility for much that had gone awry, the freshly minted party did surprisingly well, passing the 5 percent barrier to gather slightly more than 10 percent of the party-list vote. But it did not attain the wildly optimistic 20 percent that Yeltsin had expected (which was, in fact, close to the Moscow results). Our Home was not only the party most heavily covered in the news but was also by far the leading buyer of paid time. Zhirinovsky's party was in third place among the top buyers, and General Alexander Lebed's party, rapidly gaining notice, was second.[115] The Communists bought no time. Although television exposure could not reliably be directly related to the success or failure of many of the forty-three contending parties that year, it did seem to boost the candidacies of individual party figures: "It gave the leaders an advantage in the competitive single-member district races. Sixteen leaders from 14 parties won in single-member districts, while their parties . . . failed to cross the 5 percent barrier. This shows that, at least on a local level, Russian voters were attracted to well-known figures."[116]

The reform vote was to some extent eroded by the contending forces of numerous small parties built around a single public figure. Even though polls showed well in advance that most of them had no chance to advance past the 5 percent mark, they stayed in the fray until the end. In this way they commandeered attention to themselves as individuals and a large number returned to parliament as independent candidates (not from party lists). By not withdrawing, they had reduced the vote for the democratic reform parties and contributed to the Communists' decisive victory and Zhirinovsky's solid second place. A study by British scholars found that because of the fragmentation of parties and the 5% threshold requirement, about half the voters favored parties that failed the 5% test. They concluded that "[T]he 1995 Duma produced the most disproportional election result of any free and fair proportional election. . . ."[117]

The relatively great predictive power of public opinion surveys before the April 1993 referendum helped to legitimize and accelerate their use in future political contests, though doubts had been raised about the real intentions of people who responded with a "no answer" or "no opinion."[118] In December of that year, because of the harshly adversarial parameters introduced by the armed rebellion of October, the extraordinary volatility of the electorate, and the outlawing of certain political parties, analysis of pre-election public opinion surveys became much more problematic. What would appear to the reformist party leaders to be an overwhelming lead in the survey results actually masked both the instability of the electorate and the hesitancy with which many acknowledged they would vote for the antigovernment opposition.[119] Whether or not these polls were accurate and reliable, they were what the government believed to be true, and fueled what turned out to be their overconfidence. Vsevolod Vilchek, head of public opinion research for Ostankino, recalled becoming concerned early in the campaign when public opinion questionnaires began to come back to him with the "no opinion" responses checked, but crude and inflammatory handwritten comments added. He began to see a pattern and believed that the "no opinion" or "no answer" response was masking a great deal of anger.[120] Polls taken before the December 1995 election had to ask relatively small samples about choices among forty-three parties. The results were mainly wide of the mark.

Gennady Burbulis ascribed much of the debacle of the 1993 election to Boris Yeltsin's passivity: "This was the fault, above all, of Yeltsin, who took a sideline position that was uncalled for when he needed to side with the democrats and present a strong front against the fascists and revanchists."[121] As Burbulis told me, Yeltsin "distanced himself from the democratic wing" and played the role of "referee," and he hoped that Yeltsin would have the courage (muzhestvo) to remove himself from the 1996 presidential elections early so that alternative candidacies could gain strength.[122]

Less than a year after this conversation, Boris Yeltsin declared himself a candidate. In turn, Yeltsin looked at Burbulis anew: "I began to notice that features in Burbulis's character . . . [that were typical of the] love of the provincial for the attributes of power in the capital." Burbulis had been the first in the Yeltsin administration after August 1991 to order himself a government limousine. He awarded himself a large security guard. He dogged Yeltsin's footsteps, even turning up in the sauna. And Yeltsin noticed that Burbulis had "an overweening pride and an inability to present himself to the public."[123]

The true victim in all of these recriminations was the concept of the political party—a construct vainly struggling against the power of personalism. Neither Yeltsin nor his former chief strategist understood the importance of party-building for the durability of their reform program. In 1992, Gennady Burbulis complained that "our deputies are highly politicized." They were not elected by parties, he argued, and should not take on the trappings of parties.[124] At the time, it was the Communist Party against which he was inveighing, and it appeared that he eschewed the idea of the political party too long. In a conversation in 1995, Gennady Burbulis said their greatest mistake was not founding a political party. That should have been done in 1991 to take advantage of the "momentum" of Yeltsin's victory over the coup attempt. But Yeltsin did not do so; said Burbulis, "He did not want to."[125]

In December 1995, only four of forty-three parties made it past the 5 percent mark: the Communist Party, with 22 percent of the party-list vote; Zhirinovsky's Liberal Democratic Party, with 11 percent, the new pro-Yeltsin Our Home is Russia party, with 10 percent; and Yavlinksy's Yabloko party, with almost 7 percent. The same pattern of free and paid time was in force, the same preference for unmediated, direct speech to the viewing public obtained. Journalists were once again told to refrain from analysis and probing questions. This time they could be marginally more active when candidates did not have prepared video spots and preferred to have a studio conversation with a neutral host.

Only on private NTV were a half-dozen or so debates between pairs of candidates arranged during the last week of the campaign. Host Evgeny Kiselyov expertly conducted the programs and asked probing questions. Overall, in 1995 the shape of the televised campaign differed in few important ways from the pattern established in 1993, when the first competitive party elections took place. The public, old and young alike, said in the fall before the 1995 election that it was television—by a very wide margin—that would be most "useful in influencing" for whom to vote.[126]

Just after the election, a survey found that Russians thought seeing party leaders on television was most effective in influencing their vote for a party. They rated televised ad spots second, and only third, the advice of friends and family. At the bottom of the list were placards, flyers, public meetings, and other campaign activities.[127] Still, it is important to note that self-reported reactions understate or simply ignore the complex and not fully conscious process of individual decision choices. Indeed, in this survey about a quarter of the people interviewed said that nothing influenced their decisions (I made up my mind by myself) or didn't answer.

THE RACE FOR THE PRESIDENCY

Standing alone, without a political party, was actually an advantage. So thought the strategists in Boris Yeltsin's camp in the spring of 1996. He would campaign above politics; he would be a member of no party and above all parties; he would be the president of all the people. He was also the president of the other candidates, and to drive this point home, the television campaign kept his face out of the ad spots until the last day of the campaign for the first round. The Yeltsin team had a formidable problem to solve for their candidate.

As economic problems burgeoned and Chechnya, bombed to ruins, was still not pacified, Boris Yeltsin's approval rating had dropped to 4 percent by December 1995 and was only up to 8 percent early in 1996. The Communist Party had become the dominant party in a legislature of limited authority and was heavily favored to take the presidency, where the true power lay. Though there were nearly a dozen candidates in the running in June 1996—when no candidate gained more than 50 percent of the vote, a run-off was scheduled for July 3—the real contest was about unfinished business left over from the April 1993 referendum: Should Russia go back to communism or break with it? The two parliamentary elections in between had not resolved that fundamental question. Only the capture of the presidency could. It would be difficult to overestimate the importance this election had for Russians.

Not everyone saw the first round of this two-part election as a Boris Yeltsin–Gennady Zyuganov fight. Partisans of liberal, Westernizing economist Grigory Yavlinsky complained about Yeltsin's two-camp strategy, saying that their candidate was the only genuine reform alternative to a Yeltsin whose credentials had been soiled by corruption, the war in Chechnya, an increasing reliance on hard-line advisors, and his own infirmity. Leading human rights advocates Yelena Bonner and Sergei Kovalyov supported Yavlinsky against an increasingly harsh Yeltsin, apparently, like Gorbachev at the end, the thrall of undemocratic advisors. At the end of the first round, Yavlinsky had gotten his usual share of the vote: a little more than 7 percent. Most Russian social scientists doubted that he could have done much better, since his base of support tended to be limited to highly educated, urban entrepreneurs, especially in the two largest cities, Moscow and St. Petersburg. On television, he stressed issues intelligently and lucidly, giving examples of strategies to lift the country from depression (saying that he was following Franklin Roosevelt's ideas), and tried to add heart to the brain he projected. He showed clips of his parents (father: an orphan, a soldier, a lifelong volunteer helping orphans; mother: a chemist), his childhood, his youthful boxing championship. He told viewers that in boxing it is not the stronger who wins, but the one with more stamina. Other Yavlinsky spots showed rapping youngsters, mothers dancing with prams, and other cartoonish jollities, particularly unsettling on the last day of the campaign, when earnest appeals were usually the order of the day. The vote for Yavlinsky came out roughly the same as it had the last December and the December two years before that.

Television was partisan in this election, and in Russia and the West, there were bitter recriminations. There are many layers to this complex question of objectivity and partisanship in the 1996 presidential election. The partisanship of television was based on an evaluation that a return to power of the Communist Party did not mean a basically democratic administration of a populist or social welfare complexion, but a regime seeking monopoly power and likely future cancellation of free electoral choice. These broadly differing visions depended on one's frame of reference. Some Russians still remembered the horrors of the purges, the repression of religion, collectivization of agriculture, assassinations in the Katyn Forest, the millions killed by avoidable famine. Russians had been reliving this repressed past with vivid retrospective clarity, for history had, in a sense, come to life again during Gorbachev's *glasnost,* when mass burial grounds were unearthed and previously untold stories documented the effect of Communist Party rule.

Gennady Zyuganov had been an active Party functionary, who doggedly rebuilt the Russian party after the parent Soviet one had been banned. The people around him had been much more important than he in the old Party. One was Anatoly Lukyanov, key participant in the 1991 putsch. Another was Nikolai Ryzhkov, once Soviet Prime Minister. Still another was Viktor Anpilov, who led the bloody 1993 revolt and whose special target was television, the portfolio he hoped to acquire in a Zyuganov administration. Of a different stripe, more nationalist than socialist, Alexander Prokhanov was a close Zyuganov advisor. Throughout this campaign, Zyuganov did not criticize any of his alliance partners or in any way dissociate himself from their views. It was extremely difficult to pin the candidate down and extract concrete plans from him. He portrayed himself as a fully collective leader.

The Russian Communist Party that Gennady Zyuganov rebuilt were mainly people who did not like what they saw of Russia's reforms—or were incapable of flourishing in the changed environment. Many of the talented and enterprising in the old Party had left to take up jobs in the new Russia. The solid core of the Party were people who were often too old and too rural to take advantage of new opportunities and desperately looked for any way out of the hard-scrabble, hopeless life they now led. The Communists promised help precisely to them and also to the ones who remembered with longing that Russia had been a vast empire and had anchored one end of the bi-polar confrontation that humbled the world.

Television officials thought they had to remind their viewers about the lessons and memories current hardships had pushed aside, and they believed their medium was a particular target of Zyuganov and his party, not only because of the Communists' past doctrinal aversion to plural speech, but also because of their current campaign statements criticizing television and promising to exert control over its content. During the second round of the presidential campaign, Zyuganov charged the big three networks with inciting civil war. His ally, Viktor Anpilov, repeatedly vowed to remove Jews from television. And the Communist-controlled Duma was once again considering how to get control of the state channels. One deputy contributed to a hearing on "information security for the population" the following formulation: "Russian Federation central mass media have turned into the basic sources of threats to national security of the country and continue to lead an 'undeclared war' against their own people."[128]

Faced with the looming threat they saw—the return of Communism and potential shutdown of speech pluralism—what should the press do? The way of the democratic press would oppose speech with more speech. Only in times of crisis could that right be qualified by restrictions on words that cause immediate and specific harm. An independent news operation also is a much more trusted one; its message more effective; its audience broader. In Russia, at this stage, viewer choice in national news coverage ranged from the state stations to NTV. There were important differences, but the choice of nonpartisan television was not among them.

There seemed to be a *permanent crisis* in Russia and permanent crisis chills free speech. For over seventy years, the Soviet regime had invoked crisis to proscribe what it regarded as dangerous behavior. In 1991 and 1993 there had been violent attempts to overturn the government and there were so many contract killings (with no arrests) for economic gain and political advantage, that private armies of bodyguards were seen everywhere, at restaurants, clubs, receptions, around buildings, in waiting rooms, on the street, in cars. In this atmosphere, calls to suspend rights were frequent. Ultimately, invoking crisis and limiting speech narrowed the forum for and range of potential solutions and excluded opponents, who would themselves contemplate zero-sum solutions to muscle their way into television. The art of governing *after* a victory would not be made easier by this strategy.

It was said by some that the partisanship of television in the 1996 presidential election was not so much about the larger issue of return of dictatorship or even protection of free speech, but about private advantage. Few of the well known politically aware television figures would find a home in a new Communist-led information world. The big television magnates would see their nascent empires fall apart; the on-screen stars would likely be back at lower pay and impersonal performances. It is difficult to separate short-term personal material gain from long-term or broader devotion to principles and philosophical goals for society at large. Idealism can itself be construed to be in one's interest, formulated as psychic gratification, and put into the calculus of individual benefits. The equation was a complex one and the reductionism of labeling the decision to declare partisanship as solely for immediate, personal profit vastly oversimplified the interaction of many short-term and long-term, material and moral, facets of the question.

Of the three television networks reaching large numbers of Russians with news and public affairs programs, one, Russian Television (Channel Two) was state-owned; a second, NTV, was privately owned; and in the third, ORT (Channel One), the state was the majority stockholder. Channels One and Two were in the president's camp from the outset; their brand of news had always been partisan at election time. In part, the president so over-whelmingly dominated their news broadcasts because he personally took the reins of government in his hands. Previous election campaigns had identi-fied a whole range of newsmakers in the administration and spread the time around; this campaign was about a single human dynamo, the president.

NTV's motto was "News is our profession," and in a short time, it had established a reputation for trusted and credible news, even though it did not have the reach of the state channels. It took on an embattled Yeltsin ad-ministration over Chechnya, but in the 1996 presidential election, its pres-ident, Igor Malashenko, signed on with Yeltsin as chief media counselor for the duration of the campaign. Like the other channels, NTV did not con-ceal its pro-Yeltsin position. Malashenko's political move from adversary to advisor was startling, considering Yeltsin's reaction to NTV's coverage of Chechnya (see chapter 11). Some critics asserted that he had gone over to the president to get a reward. NTV had a license for the prime-time hours of the fourth channel, an educational channel. The daytime hours were owned by Channel Two, which used them for exceedingly boring and lit-tle watched instructional programs. Malashenko wanted those hours to build his audience. Would he now receive them as an "honorarium"?

Malashenko acknowledged that he wanted the channel but was not at all sure that he had improved his chances. He was concerned that Yeltsin's peo-ple, the ones who had been around him for the first term, would be back in after the election and "'again, it begins . . . Kiselyov [NTV anchor] is an enemy, *Kukly* [Puppets—political satire] is ideological subversion. . . . Yes, I myself even now sometimes hear the same thing from those same people. And documents are read [at campaign meetings] where the word "anti-presidential" with respect to NTV is the kindest [thing said].'"[129] Mala-shenko feared especially the revenge of Yeltsin's personal security chief Alexander Korzhakov, who had voiced dislike of NTV and had publicly announced, after he apparently ordered a raid on the offices of Vladimir Gusinsky, NTV's backer, that he was of a mind to go "goose hunting" [*Gus* is goose]. In any case, in the fall of 1996, Malashenko's station did finally get the rights to the rest of the broadcast day.

When Malashenko joined the president's campaign team, he was allied with Yeltsin advisor Viktor Ilyushin and former privatization minister (later, chief of staff), Anatoly Chubias. Korzhakov and his hard-line allies were be-coming marginalized and apparently struck back between the first and sec-ond presidential election rounds, when the security service detained and interrogated (allegedly for removing large amounts of foreign currency from the Russian White House) two Yeltsin campaign aides: one was the advertising tycoon, Sergei Lisovsky, and the other was Arkady Yevstavyev. This was the same Yevstavyev who had been Chubias's press secretary and a key player during the controversy with the U.S. Agency for International Development over a violation during the 1993 campaign. The deep divisions in the Yeltsin campaign staff were making the second round campaign difficult.

With the lines drawn as they had been in April 1993, the television channels were all in Yeltsin's camp. There was a critical difference though between the television campaigns of '93 and '96: in the first, the opposition had no right to air time of any kind, paid or unpaid. In 1996, all candidates had equal amounts of free time on the state-supported channels to address viewers as they wished with no interference from the station. Time was appointed by lot—ten minutes each morning and ten each evening from May 14 through June 14. For the second round, it was ten minutes a day. Stations could not censor or otherwise alter the televised material. All parties used their free television time. In addition, candidates had the right to buy time for their paid spots. In these candidate-centered presentations, the incumbent president was often criticized and viewers were reminded of all of the mistakes and miseries the current administration had inflicted on its citizens.[130]

Gennady Zyuganov used his free time far more effectively than he had done in the last two parliamentary election campaigns. He combined shots of rallies, huge crowds of supporters (among whom were many young, rapt faces), vigorous speeches, triumphal music, and heroic shots (from below) against impressive national monuments. He spoke forcefully, but deliberately without charisma, of problems of the economy and society and called for a return to Russian greatness. The editing was smooth; the tempo fast, not jagged or confusing. In between the first and second round of voting, he chose to sit at his desk facing the viewer, speaking without visible notes and in a direct and simple way told of what he had seen in his travels—of the misery of families, the poverty, the decline of the army. In his last message before the decisive second round of voting, Zyuganov's message was affecting and well presented, speaking again directly to viewers without news clips or sound track. He again invoked the sad conditions of life for many people, especially children. In addition, there were newspapers to carry Zyuganov's message. Even though the market had declined overall, Zyuganov's party still had *Pravda, Sovetskaya Rossia,* and other sources.[131]

As always the controversy was over the bulk of the broadcast day: entertainment programs and, more important, news coverage. On all of the Moscow-based networks, entertainment programming was heavily loaded with exposés of the Communist past and films about Stalinism. What was covered on the news was an editorial decision. The sitting president always has an advantage; news is made in that office. What made the 1996 campaign so extraordinary was the sudden change in the candidate himself. Before the campaign, it was not an exaggeration to say, as a Russian sociologist did, that Yeltsin was a "living corpse." Weakened by heart problems, puffy faced, slurring his words, stumbling, canceling or flubbing meetings with high officials, moving woodenly and uncertainly, Boris Yeltsin had become a faint copy of the man who had stood on a tank to defend freedom five years before. When he made trips, he was surrounded by security and greeted by officials before being whisked away. It all looked like past Soviet times: remote, barely alive leader cordoned off from his subjects.

At Boris Yeltsin's side, more and more visible, was his personal bodyguard Alexander Korzhakov. By the time of the 1995 parliamentary election campaign, Yeltsin's distance from the public had acquired a sinister veneer because of Korzhakov's influence. The chief of security had inflated his role of protector of the president's person to gatekeeper of the flow of political participants. A stocky, blunt, faithful watchdog, Korzhakov appeared to be acquiring power over the weakened president, and in the absence of evidence to the contrary, the rumor mills were operating at full steam. To reduce suspicion, just before election day that December, Korzhakov was offered to television. Vladimir Pozner recalled getting a call from Boris Berezovsky, the businessman who had become decision maker at Channel One, asking if the correspondent would be interested in interviewing Korzhakov. Pozner thought it "somewhat frightening," that Korzhakov saw his role as protecting Boris Nikolayevich from "all the different kinds of shysters who want to get in to see him." When Pozner asked why that was the business of a security guard, Korzhakov said that he had to protect Boris Nikolayevich morally and not just physically. The television program was a heavily cut version of this long interview and consisted virtually entirely of softball questions and equally uninteresting answers, mainly about the "human" Korzhakov. On one point only did Korzhakov provide politically intriguing views. He criticized the way Defense Minister Pavel Grachev was handling the Chechnya war. Even that was a pallid reflection of the uncut tape; there Korzhakov said that if Grachev were an honest man, he would resign or commit suicide.[132]

This Yeltsin and his faithful Korzhakov were not a winning combination for the 1996 presidential campaign, and the first task of the campaign committee was to refashion their candidate. According to Igor Malashenko, it was not easy.[133] The campaign team was at first polarized. The group that took over the campaign included Chubais; Ilyushin; Vasily Shakhnovsky, from Moscow mayor Yury Luzhkov's staff; Georgy Satarov, presidential advisor; Vyacheslav Nikonov, a well-known political analyst; Sergei Shakhray; Sergei Zveryev, from MOST bank; Alexander Oslon, head of public opinion analysis and director of surveys; and Igor Malashenko. This team succeeded in ousting the first campaign team, headed by the hard-line Deputy

Prime Minister Oleg Soskovets and Alexander Korzhakov. They fought for rights over Boris Yeltsin, and after the first round of the election, Yeltsin removed Korzhakov, Soskovets, and Mikhail Barsukov, head of internal security, successor to one part of the KGB.

Malashenko recalled that when he was appointed in March, well before the first round, he and the rest of the "outsider" group working on the campaign decided to substantially increase television coverage of Yeltsin. To do so, they had to convince Korzhakov and others to draw up a schedule for Yeltsin's trips and photo-opportunities, a schedule they would have to stick to. That had not been done in the past. Second, they had to convince Korzhakov and Soskovets to break up the security wall around Yeltsin and move him closer to ordinary people. Third, they had to do something with Yeltsin's wooden delivery, his head bent down reading his speeches. NTV and MOST bank owner Vladimir Gusinsky hurriedly shipped a Teleprompter from New York, and for the first time, Yeltsin was looking directly at the people he addressed.

Finally, they had to keep in touch with Yeltsin and convince him of their strategy and for this an invaluable ally was added to the team: Tatyana Dyachenko, Boris Yeltsin's daughter. Malashenko called her a "born manager." A computer engineer with no political experience, she traveled with Yeltsin and conveyed messages to him. According to Alexander Oslon, she attended the daily two-to-three-hour-long campaign staff meetings and listened carefully. She understood the concepts but "was always quiet." She played a "huge role" because as a trusted family member, she could convey the staff's ideas to her father.

In an article in *Time,* a group of Americans appeared to take a good deal of the credit for pulling off Yeltsin's victory, acting primarily through Mrs. Dyachenko, who later told the *New York Times* that although the Americans did some work, none of it was central to the campaign. The response to the claim in Russia was naturally quite negative, especially about the implications of some ambiguous points in the story. For example, the *Time* article said the Americans proved a point about the effect of a Yeltsin speech with an audience of Russians wired to a "perception analyzer." Said one of the Americans, science "'won the day again.'" From that day, the article continued, their influence increased. In the context of the magazine's story, it seemed that the Americans had brought in a new technology and the Russians were bowled over. In fact, the perception analyzer the Americans used belonged to the Russian polling organization, Public Opinion Foundation, whose director, Alexander Oslon, said it had been in operation since September 1995. During the elections that year, the technology had been extensively used for the Yeltsin-backed Our Home is Russia party, testing reactions to political ads for television and other campaign materials, often several different versions of a product.[134]

Richard Dresner, one of the American team, acknowledged that the equipment was already in place at the Russian polling agency when he arrived, but said that Mrs. Dyachenko had never seen it before. According to Dresner, it was she and "the family" who were his sole clients in the election campaign. That arrangement had been made by Oleg Soskovets, the hard-line backer of the disastrous war in Chechnya who was then in charge of the reelection campaign. Soskovets and Dresner had only one meeting; at the end of it, the American team was hired and told to work with the Yeltsin family, but that turned out to be Mrs. Dyachenko only. Dresner further noted that Mrs. Dyachenko was disinclined to share with the official campaign staff the survey and focus group data and memos Dresner and his team were generating. Apparently, according to Dresner, two separate streams of campaign strategy advice went to the president: one from the officially appointed campaign team and one from the Americans through his daughter. Dresner said that at one point, Mrs. Dyachenko asked the Americans to take their names off some memos, because she wanted to distribute them to the campaign staff without revealing their origin.[135]

Igor Malashenko had a very different view of the impact of the Americans. He told me that sending memos to Boris Yeltsin was not the way things worked in Russia. Strategies were determined in private meetings with the president. Malashenko had one-on-one meetings with Yeltsin, and with Yeltsin and a few others—Chubais or Shakhrai or all six (Ilyushin, Chubais, Shakhrai, Shakhnovsky, Oslon, Malashenko) in the inner core of the campaign staff. The campaign staff did not send memos to Yeltsin. Malashenko said, too, that when he joined the campaign staff in March, Mrs. Dyachenko told him about the Americans who had been hired by the ousted Soskovets. The campaign team decided to honor the commitment made earlier, because they wished to avoid a "scandalous" disruption. Mrs. Dyachenko, Malashenko noted, did share the Americans' memos with the campaign staff, and when the memos were anonymous, Mrs. Dyachenko identified them as coming from the American advisors. From time to time, the campaign staff read them, although Malashenko called them "useless," and the Americans continued to be paid.

Mrs. Dyachenko's role as member of the campaign staff was to deliver messages to her father at the request of the campaign team. Malashenko declared he "was not aware of any instance when she delivered a message [to her father about the election] other than as a member of the campaign." He absolutely rejected the notion of Boris Yeltsin's daughter as transmitter of two separate flows of advice to her father.[136]

When Richard Dresner was asked about Tatyana Dyachenko's statement in the *New York Times* downplaying his role, he said: "Nobody spends two million dollars and passes four hundred pages of memos to her father and says 'you really didn't do anything for us.' That seems impossible to me."[137]

Some of the funds supported Dresner's work with "Video International," the campaign's advertising agency that made ample use of his survey data.

Igor Malashenko, in recalling with asperity the claims made about the Americans' role in Boris Yeltsin's victory, raised a sobering question about the impetus for their invitation. Malashenko drew attention to the comment in the *Time* article indicating that Soskovets and his associates requested the Americans to inform them when they saw Yeltsin losing in the polls. That determination, according to Malashenko, was to be used to "justify cancellation of the elections." In fact, Soskovets, Korzhakov, and Barsukov were removed precisely because they were considering such a cancellation. They apparently tried several pretexts: the war in Chechnya, terrorist bombs in Moscow, the Communist-led Duma's attempted nullification of the break-up of the Soviet Union. Whether the subplot utilizing the polls of the American consultants was also part of their larger chess game remains conjectural.

The Yeltsin his campaign staff unleashed was a formidable candidate. He used the power of the presidency to sign all manner of decrees and agreements. He promised new support for teachers, for people with unpaid wages, for miners. He ordered the bank to make good on his promises. He met with the presidents of Armenia, Azerbaijan, and Georgia to sign agreements; he signed a kind of merger with the president of Belarus; he signed a truce with Chechen leaders and then without notice flew off to the battleground in Chechnya to praise the soldiers and crow about victory. He went barnstorming around the country, with television covering each stop and being rewarded with pictures of the president dancing with folk dancers, bogeying with rock stars, swinging on swings with children. He was funny and, most important, radiated life. Addressing schoolchildren on the last day of the school year, he said that they would soon have exams, but he had an exam coming up, too, and it was the hardest one of his life.

Boris Yeltsin was all over the television screens, making the most of the power of his office and a newfound energy and passion. When a Communist debated a Yeltsin partisan on television, the Communist said that Yeltsin was weak and needed help, to which the Yeltsin partisan said, "just turn on television" to see how strong the president is.[138] The downside of this strategy was the contrast when, ominously, Yeltsin was suddenly absent from the screen between the two rounds. The vacuum led Zyuganov to charge that the president was not able to serve another term, but television did not treat this disappearance of its favored candidate as the campaign issue it should have been.

On the campaign trail, Yeltsin exhibited an unaccustomed interest in and knowledge of local issues. His advisors knew well that the strength of the opposition was in the small towns and countryside. Before each trip, surveys and focus groups identified the citizens' most serious concerns. One survey conducted by the campaign's public opinion advisor, always included an open-ended question asking people what they would ask the president if they had an opportunity to address him. People in the eastern city of Khabarovsk had on their minds questions about the wage arrears, crime, disorder, poverty, the war in Chechnya, housing, medicine, children's welfare, education, the army, and Yeltsin's personal life. They were asking: "What hasn't been sold off yet in Russia?" "When will bribery end?" "When will this mess end?" "When will we begin to live normally?" "Could you live on 275,000 rubles?" "How can one decently bury loved ones?" "Let him say how many boys were killed in Chechnya; he wouldn't send his children!" "Does he know what's really going on?" "How do you feel about alcohol?" "Does he believe in God?" "Do you watch television?" "Why did BN [Boris Nikolayevich] sleep so long and not work all these years and only works before the election?" As the survey report concluded, the "totality of the questions on the impoverished material situation, social sphere, wage arrears and pensions can be characterized as a *'cri de coeur'* [*krik dushi*]."[139] Yeltsin was a newly expert campaigner, but with much to apologize for.

For the first time, the Moscow-based networks began to take the locales seriously. Moscow-centrism was tempered by attention to the candidate's campaign stops. Backgrounders accompanied stump speeches and rallies. Vast Russia, from yurts and snowshoes to grimy miners, from the countryside and cities and small towns, a mosaic began to appear. One of the most inventive and moving programs was the invention of Eduard Sagalayev at Channel Two. Called "Open News," it was a conversation from a number of remote locations with the Moscow studio hosted by Sagalayev himself and star anchor Svetlana Sorokina. These were conversations with families, with ordinary people, whose wisdom, concerns, and humanity were not taken lightly. The studio hosts achieved a rarity: they erased the status barrier between themselves and their guests, just as the technology eliminated the physical distance.

It fell to Igor Malashenko to coordinate network coverage of the presidential campaign. He said there was no problem with Channel One and his own station, but Channel Two posed a problem. Eduard Sagalayev had replaced Oleg Poptsov there. The circumstances of Poptsov's firing had angered the news staff, insulted by Yeltsin's summary action. The new appointee Sagalayev was respected as a professional, and there was little opposition to him, though he made it clear that the change was due to the coming election. Sagalayev remarked that the crisis of the election and the hostility Poptsov engendered made him ballast: "You are forced to jettison it in order to avoid tragic consequences."[140] He brought in his old colleague from state television, Boris Nepomnyashchy, to be news director and fired the one who was there, Alexander Nekhoroshev. According to

Nekhoroshev, Sagalayev offered him the job of correspondent in Brussels. Just two hours after Nekhoroshev cleaned out his office, Sagalayev rescinded his order, but kept his new appointee on as well.[141] It was not clear who was doing what.

The Communists complained to the Central Election Commission about Yeltsin's domination of the news, but the Commission disallowed the charge, saying that the incumbent was doing presidential things. According to the polling organization, Public Opinion Foundation, about a third of the viewers seeing Yeltsin and a third seeing Zyuganov on television came away with a favorable impression, but 52 percent of the viewers had seen Yeltsin and only 36 percent had seen Zyuganov.[142]

The president's campaign team and their newly invigorated candidate were pumping out coverage in impressive volume, some of it incumbent activities, some, clearly campaign material, much, as to be expected, a blend of the two. Did Zyuganov have an opportunity to be covered in news programs in addition to his free time? It was by no means an equal opportunity. On the state channels, the heavy hand of editorializing was present in Zyuganov's coverage and these channels had the greatest number of viewers. The Zyuganov side did have other prime-time opportunities to get its message across even on state television. For example, on June 6, Alexander Lyubimov brought on to his Channel One show *Odin na odin* (One on One) Zyuganov supporter Yury Ivanov to debate Yeltsin partisan Boris Fedorov. Ivanov forcefully and rudely attacked Yeltsin, to the applause of many in the studio audience. The same program on June 27 had the candidates' top advisors debating, this time a much more low-key, droning conversation. Channel Two produced a series of candidate-surrogate debates with the advisors of each of the candidates and mounted a mini-debate of minor candidates (including Zhirinovsky); the big four—Yeltsin, Zyuganov, Lebed, and Yavlinsky—refused to debate. But these were small islands of television opportunities in a sea of negativity and attack on the state channels.

NTV still produced the most serious and most comprehensive news coverage. Where Yeltsin was most vulnerable, and NTV, most critical, was on Chechnya. The war was still covered the NTV way, usually leading the newscast and reminding viewers of that tragic blunder. Because Malashenko had gone over to advise the president, and the people at NTV made no secret of their political preference, it was common in the Western press—and in Russia, too—to speak of the death of press freedom in this Russian election campaign. Gennady Zyuganov routinely charged that he had been frozen out of television, and it was generally taken at face value. But a close look at NTV's coverage shows a system of news presentation that did permit the Communist candidate access to news coverage; he had the opportunity to put his platform before viewers with his own words.

There was little outright editorializing on the part of NTV's news anchors, but that practice did change toward end of the first-round campaign, when anchors presented biased statements and on the last day of the first-round campaign, NTV eliminated Zyuganov from its coverage altogether. The much more serious suspension of objective and fair coverage was the news operation's tough, professional questioning of Zyuganov's, but not the favored candidate's, promises and claims. Stories examined Zyuganov's promises (such as his hoped-for alliance with democratic candidates); analyzed his economic programs; scrutinized his plans for ending the Chechen war. This searchlight was not turned on Yeltsin's abundant campaign promises, decrees, and projects, nor the precarious health of the candidate.

As Gennady Zyuganov's campaign swung into action (and before he had the benefit of free time on the state channels), here is what NTV's coverage did. In virtually all of the stories reported here, the candidate or his supporters, often both, spoke in their own words, not replaced by the anchor's voiceover. On NTV's evening news program, *Segodnya* (Today), on March 29, there was a story about Zyuganov campaigning in the Altai region. On April 1, Zyuganov was interviewed about the war in Chechnya. On April 2, Zyuganov announced that dozens of smaller parties and organizations were allying with him. On April 4, a Zyuganov supporter explained why he favored the candidate. On April 5, Zyuganov and his leading candidate for vice president (Yeltsin had abolished the office) spoke about their platform. On April 9, Zyuganov's meeting with the "creative intelligentsia" was covered and he discussed his meeting with Poland's new Communist president. On April 12, Zyuganov was shown in Voronezh and Lipetsk, speaking at a rally and visiting a church. On April 16, he was in Bashkortostan, visiting factories, meeting with local deputies, rallying his supporters, and laying flowers at the Lenin monument. On the 17th, NTV covered Zyuganov in Chelyabinsk; on the 22nd, Zyuganov and the head of the Agrarian Party celebrated Lenin's birthday and addressed supporters; on the 23rd, Zyuganov spoke about the elections, his likely victory, and his platform; and on the 27th, Zyuganov went to St. Petersburg to talk to veterans and speak about party unity.

On the weekly *Itogi,* on March 31, Zyuganov and his allies were covered, as was Zyuganov's charge that Yeltsin was planning to impose emergency rule. The next week a story of more than three minutes gave Zyuganov and his potential vice president, Aman Tuleyev, the opportunity to speak at length. *Itogi* on April 14 ran a story about Zyuganov's campaign. The correspondent spoke of the "warm reception" the Communist candidate received in the heartland, and Zyuganov spoke of the loss of the "fatherland Russians created with the work and torments of a thousand years," and warned that with Yeltsin's plan to legalize the sale of land, "tomorrow we won't be a people but [individuals] who wait on owners." In Voronezh, the correspondent noted, Zyuganov, supported by the local leadership, taped an hour-long program to be broadcast uncut during the week and in Lipetsk Zyuganov spoke live on local television. On April 21, Zyuganov was invited for a 26-minute live interview on *Itogi*. He had time to speak at considerable length about his economic platform, his plans for governing, his solution to the Chechen war, his view of Lenin ("any cultured person" would observe Lenin's birthday, he said), and about his charges that NTV was excluding him from the air. Anchor Yevgeny Kiselyov noted that he had invited Zyuganov two weeks before, that NTV covered his campaign, that this was a lengthy, live interview—why the charges? Zyuganov repeated that NTV's president was an advisor to Yeltsin.

Zyuganov got another chance for a long, live interview with Kiselyov on June 6 as the guest on NTV's *Geroi Dnya* (Newsmaker of the Day), right after the evening news. It should be noted that the pre-election interview show typically featured lively and incisive questioning. Kiselyov was evidently determined to get some concrete answers to the questions Zyuganov was very good at evading with general statements and canned rhetoric. When asked if he would form an alliance with or had offered a post to Vladimir Zhirinovsky, Zyuganov responded, "let's wait and see"; "we are conducting broad consultations"; "the door is open to all." The most contentious part of the interview came when Kiselyov asked him about the "radicals" in the party, in particular Viktor Anpilov and General Albert Makashov. Zyuganov asked why he called them radicals and countered that the radicals were Yeltsin's people who destroyed the economy and didn't want an honest election. Kiselyov, looking at Zyuganov in ironic frustration, said that he just wants an answer and that another correspondent remarked that if you ask Zyuganov what time it is, "he answers thank you, I've already had dinner." Zyuganov then warned Kiselyov that he was violating the electoral law. "The journalist can ask questions," Zyuganov stated ponderously, "and answer questions, but you are obliged not to comment. It is strictly written in the law." Kiselyov, rejecting the intimidation, said that it's an interview, not the candidate's free time, and he can ask questions. "I am asking if you control your allies," Anpilov included. Zyuganov responded that they all agreed to form a coalition and abide by its terms. Kiselyov showed a tape of the prognathous Anpilov saying that people who can't speak Russian properly, who have an accent, should be removed from the screen. Real Russians should be on the screen. "We see those Jewish faces and it insults us," Anpilov concluded. Zyuganov replied to Kiselyov that it is a multinational country, there should be friendship of peoples and equal rights. Any person has the right to appear on television, he said, but went on to comment that traditions of people, including the Russian people, must be respected. Kiselyov asked what Zyuganov thought of anti-Semitism.

The Communist Party and the lesser parties grouped around it in the coalition, whose candidate was Gennady Zyuganov, had been running on

Victory Day, Red Square, Spring 1990. (Ellen Mickiewicz)

Russians gather in Red Square to question parliamentary deputies elected in first multi-candidate competitive election, 1990. (Ellen Mickiewicz)

The October 1993 revolt. (© by Vladimir Vyatkin, by permission)

The Russian White House in October 1993. (© by Vladimir Vyatkin, by permission)

Bullet holes, the view from the Mayoralty Building, the offices of TV-6, October 1993. (Ellen Mickiewicz)

Mikhail Gorbachev. (Collection of Ellen Mickiewicz)

Yegor Ligachev, second in command in Gorbachev's Politburo. (Ellen Mickiewicz)

Alexander Yakovlev, architect of *glasnost* on Politburo and opponent of Ligachev. (Ellen Mickiewicz)

Mikhail Nenashev, head of State Television, May 1989–November 1990. (Ellen Mickiewicz)

Leonid Kravchenko, head of State Television, November 1990–August 1991. (Ellen Mickiewicz)

Pyotr Reshetov, top television deputy under Nenashev and Kravchenko. (Ellen Mickiewicz)

Oleg Poptsov, head of State Television Channel Two, 1991–1996 (Boris Yeltsin's channel in his battle with Gorbachev, and the second national channel). (Ellen Mickiewicz)

Yegor Yakovlev, head of State Television, August 1991–October 1992. (Ellen Mickiewicz)

Vyacheslav Bragin, head of State Television, January 1993–December 1993. (Ellen Mickiewicz)

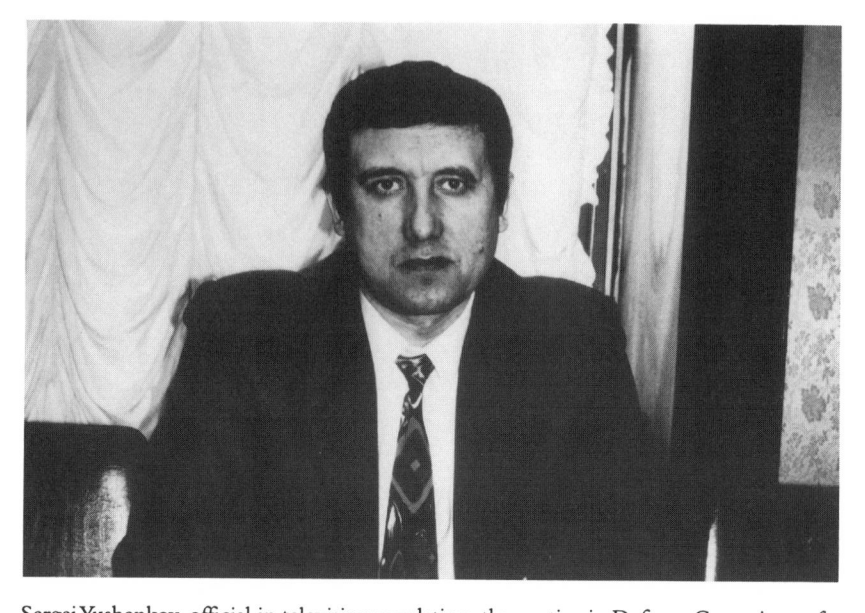

Sergei Yushenkov, official in television regulation, then active in Defense Committee of State Duma. (Ellen Mickiewicz)

Sergei Blagovolin, head of Russian Public Television (ORT), Channel One, 1995–1997. (Ellen Mickiewicz)

(*Left*) Eduard Sagalayev, founder of TV-6, first private television broadcasting station in Russia, then head of Channel Two. (Ellen Mickiewicz) (*Right*) Valentin Lazutkin, head of television regulatory body and former high official in State Television. (Ellen Mickiewicz)

Alexander Tikhomirov, famous investigative reporter of Gorbachev period, later advisor to rebel Vice President Alexander Rutskoy. (Ellen Mickiewicz)

Sergei Lomakin, favorite television journalist of the Gorbachev family. (Ellen Mickiewicz)

(*Left*) Oleg Dobrodeyev, news director of private television station NTV. (Ellen Mickiewicz) (*Right*) Evgeny Kiselyov, NTV partner and anchor of Russia's most watched news analysis program. (Ellen Mickiewicz)

Elena Masyuk, NTV's best reporter in Chechnya, pictured here in Grozny, 1995. (© 1995 by Elena Masyuk, by permission)

Freshly dug graves, Chechnya, 1995. (© 1995 by Elena Masyuk, by permission)

Raisa Gorbachev and Eduard Shevardnadze. (© by Vladimir Vyatkin, by permission)

Boris Yeltsin with former security chief Alexander Korzhakov to his left, Moscow Mayor Yury Luzhkov (under Korzhakov), and to Luzhkov's right, his wife. (© by Vladimir Vyatkin, by permission)

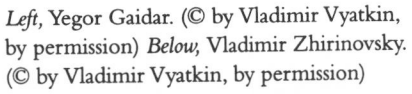

Left, Yegor Gaidar. (© by Vladimir Vyatkin, by permission) *Below,* Vladimir Zhirinovsky. (© by Vladimir Vyatkin, by permission)

Grigory Yavlinsky. (© by Vladimir Vyatkin, by permission)

Alexander Lebed. (AP/World Wide Photos)

Gennady Zyuganov. (© by Vladimir Vyatkin, by permission)

Scenes from the 1996 presidential campaign: A Communist demonstrator with a Stalin button. (© by Vladimir Vyatkin, by permission)

Communist demonstrators argue with spectators. (© by Vladimir Vyatkin, by permission)

a platform of nationalism, with an admixture of socialist populism. The target of the venom of many in this coalition was Russian Jews. Zyuganov called anti-Semitism a cruel thing and said he was for equal rights. Kiselyov probed further: "then you discuss anti-Semitism?" Zyuganov responded that they discuss nationalism, including anti-Semitism, as a phenomenon. The program, in spite of the charged subject matter and Zyuganov's earlier irritated riposte, was low key and cordial on both sides. Near the end of the program, Kiselyov observed that many fear catastrophe if the Communist Party wins, and Zyuganov, quick on the uptake, answered "Zyuganov didn't give the command to bomb Grozny." "Zyuganov didn't carry out thieving privatization."

With tension building toward the first-round vote, here is another sampling of coverage of the Communist candidate during a week on NTV news, the next to the last before the first round of the election. On June 3, *Segodnya* showed Duma Speaker Communist deputy Gennady Seleznyov stating that Yeltsin violated balance-of-information norms, that other candidates did not have reasonable access to the news, and that the Central Election Commission was silent on the issue. On June 4, *Segodnya* had a story on Zyuganov's charge that election returns were likely to be falsified and his notion of bringing the three centrist candidates (Lebed, Yavlinsky, and Fedorov) into his cabinet. On June 5, Aman Tuleyev withdrew his candidacy in favor of Zyuganov, and Zyuganov spoke to crowds in Siberia about Tuleyev's decision and reiterated his wish to have the moderate middle in his cabinet. The anchor added that Zyuganov's position might be "shaken" by a disclosure from presidential aide Georgy Satarov, who charged the Communists with preparing armed volunteer militias. The Communist Party, in turn, announced it would sue Satarov, who responded that he had proof and identified his source. Another story in the newscast showed Minister of Defense Pavel Grachev proclaiming what he said was a unanimous vote for Yeltsin from sailors in Far Eastern ports. The story went on to say that the Central Election Commission regarded it as a violation of the law and Grachev corrected his statement, saying that it was his own subjective opinion, not fact.

On June 7, Zyuganov was shown in Siberia, speaking about the economy. The anchor noted that notwithstanding Yavlinsky's rejection of the proposal the day before, Zyuganov continues to say he wishes to include Yavlinsky in his cabinet. Anchor Osokin editorialized by saying that observers think that perhaps what was important to Zyuganov was not Yavlinsky's presence in his cabinet, but rather showing voters that he was willing to include the political center. The story shifted to others in Zyuganov's electoral alliance, focusing on Viktor Anpilov, who had a lengthy opportunity to say that there were no plans for mass uprisings in the event of a Yeltsin victory. He argued that the media had been usurped by the current government (this comment was made into a bank of television microphones with a salad of logos). He noted that Zyuganov understood the importance of re-establishing socialism in Russia. Finally, Anpilov showed the cameras a picture: one of the many posters of Yeltsin shaking hands with Moscow mayor Yury Luzhkov (who was also running on June 16), but this one had been doctored so that both men appeared to be wearing yarmulkes. Anpilov explained "here is something very witty." "They are in Jewish caps." It's the story, he explains, of the ruin of Russia under Yeltsin. Anpilov closed this long piece professing his joy in working for communism. "I am prepared to do anything," he said, "I'll sweep the floors."

Anpilov's message required no editorializing. Did he truly represent Zyuganov's thinking and plans? If not, he was never disavowed. (Later, after the first round of voting was over, Zyuganov announced his shadow cabinet, and Anpilov was absent. Had he done so earlier, the media would not have had a target like Anpilov.) *Segodnya* anchor Mikhail Osokin told viewers that on June 8, Zyuganov had "curiously" referred to his party as producing new ideas and new people. On June 8, there was more on Zyuganov at a rally, and Anpilov again (this time he was screaming that all of Russia and its past were with them, "with us are Stenka Razin [the seventeenth-century peasant revolutionary] and Pushkin."). It's difficult to imagine anything in common between the limpid poet and the rabble-rousing fanatic.

The election was drawing near. On June 12, four days before the election, the daily news program *Segodnya* led with the Moscow metro bombing that some thought was a terrorist act to stop the election. There was also a story about the unveiling of a complex of monuments to victims of Stalinism in Magadan, home of labor camps. Some survivors spoke, as did the sculptor Ernst Neizvestny, moved by the product of his long years of work on the monument. At the end of the story, the NTV correspondent editorialized, telling viewers: "whether there will be monuments or camps will become clear on Sunday." The next story was about a rally in favor of the Communists, led by Viktor Anpilov, shouting his usual slogans and urging people not to celebrate this day of Russian independence. The next evening *Segodnya* covered Zyuganov's invitation to Yeltsin to debate, but anchor Tatyana Mitkova mentioned that the president's plan to be in Yekaterinburg that day had been well known long in advance. Zyuganov was shown saying that he was confident of victory and stood ready to include in his administration a broad representation of all political forces, including experts from the current government and economic leaders around the country.

On the last day of the campaign, June 14, *Segodnya* had no coverage of the Zyuganov campaign. Other candidates were covered and there was a long story on Belarus's secret service, which had accumulated frightening power and threatened the press. Anchor Mitkova reported that Reuters quoted European economists to the effect that if Zyuganov won he would nationalize the grain trade industry, since "if he does not give bread to the people, he will be out of power in two months." A story on financial markets noted that money was leaving the country because of uncertainty about the outcome of the election and an expert explained that the money will come back and production rapidly increase with a Yeltsin victory. Finally, in a last bit of heavy-handed coverage, pop singer Alla Pugachova, comfortably settled on her lakeside terrace in Switzerland told viewers that she intended to go home to vote for Yeltsin and urged everyone to vote for him.

The other candidates were covered less on the news, but one, General Alexander Lebed, became increasingly prominent. After the first round, he joined the Yeltsin administration. In his allotment of unpaid time, Lebed praised the early Yeltsin, but declared that he was no longer *svoi* (one of us). Lebed promised to remain *svoi* and to champion rectitude. He often wore his general's uniform on the campaign trail, something he had given up during parliamentary elections, when he had a disappointing finish. His short spots stressed his integrity and reliability and his ability to get things done, in contrast to the civilian candidates.

Former Soviet president Mikhail Gorbachev complained that he was prevented from gaining air time on the media, but he was a very minor candidate. In his free time, he showed clips of his meetings with foreign dignitaries, told of his plans for Russia, and criticized the current government's departure from his policies. He also told viewers that no one knew the Communists as well as he and they were the least capable, the dregs of the party.

Vladimir Zhirinovsky was suddenly a more sober and serious figure, having been made so by contrast with the clownish forty-nine-year-old pharmaceuticals tycoon, Vladimir Bryntsalov. Bryntsalov and his much younger wife, Natalya, were a comic duo, bathed in vulgar luxury. Their house was a movie set, with servants, nannies, cooks, crystal chandeliers, a huge white piano. Natasha knew she could be first lady because she was running this vast house with all this help. Bryntsalov, a guest on Alexander Nevzorov's show on Channel One, took the correspondent to a riding ring to show off his excellent health. Mounting a horse for the first time, the candidate took off, his horse tethered to the instructor in the middle of the ring. Bouncing along inexpertly and inelegantly, Bryntsalov became a foil for the anchor, who, with trained seat, followed on a cantering horse, one hand holding the video camera. Nevzorov, who had been a movie stuntman on horseback, owned this show. This fringe candidate was given coverage on the state channels in the hope that he would take votes away from Zyuganov.

Vladimir Zhirinovsky continued his themes, stressing patriarchal values, ethnic enmity, and nationalism of the bellicose type. Svyatoslav Fedorov, the well-known eye surgeon famous for his assembly-line techniques, projected a conservative competence but garnered few votes. Two other candidates were virtual ciphers, extreme nationalist and former Olympic weight lifter Yuri Vlasov and Martin Shakkum, a former Soviet functionary.

The results of the first round put Yeltsin at 35 percent; Zyuganov, at 32 percent; Lebed, at 14.5 percent; Yavlinsky, at slightly more than 7 percent; and Zhirinovsky, close to 6 percent. The rest had less than 1 percent; Mikhail Gorbachev had only one-half of one percent of the vote. Just 1.5 percent availed themselves of the option of crossing out all the names in protest, pretty much in the range of previous elections. It was obvious that the very alienated were staying home.

It was not all television, of course. Yeltsin had concluded an end to the Chechen war, although it was still seen on NTV every night exacting its price in human life. A huge number of social remedies were promised and signed into law, if only they would now trickle down fast enough to affect the vote. The military was reformed once again on paper, and between the two rounds, the laconic, rumbling General Lebed (together with his electorate, it was hoped) joined Yeltsin's administration to stamp out crime and corruption, remake the armed forces, and, perhaps, its doctrine, and, maybe, while he was at it, take a stab at foreign policy, *tout compris.* He later went to Chechnya and put an end to the war that had confounded all the others, and he began to champion the armed forces, calling attention to their disastrous plight and impoverished lives. He went on to restructure military planning and personnel and soon clashed with opponents in Yeltsin's post-election administration. The president, who had withdrawn to a sanitarium to await heart surgery, mustered his strength and went on national television, slowly and woodenly signing the decree to fire Lebed. It was unseemly, Yeltsin said, for his rebellious appointee to be running for president. Lebed was surely in the next race for presidency, whenever it opened up.

Because the vote in the first round had been so close, the Yeltsin television advertising strategy shifted from "positives"—warm and reasoned testimony of ordinary people praising new ways—to a confrontational attack campaign. The new spots showed old, black-and-white footage of labor camps and mass hunger and urged voters not to return to those troubled times. Others showed old footage of brother against brother in civil war and switched to news clips in color from the much more recent armed revolt in Moscow, all the while urging voters not to let it happen again. Still other spots showed ordinary people who had worked hard to make something of their lives, pleading not to let the Communists take it away. When Zyuganov charged the three networks with inciting civil war, their heads issued a response denying the charge and stating that they were doing all they could to stabilize the country and Zyuganov was attempting to intimidate the media.

Between the rounds both Yeltsin and Zyuganov had exhausted the whistle stop campaign. Both were staying home. Yeltsin became ill, disappeared from sight and canceled important meetings. Igor Malashenko was later to say he could see the president was very sick, but decided to conceal the information in order to win the election. Gennady Zyuganov tried to make the vanished leader the campaign issue it rightly was, but television was not interested in exploring it. What follows is a sampling of NTV's coverage of Zyuganov during the second-round campaign.

On the June 26th edition of the daily news program, *Segodnya,* a long story (nearly four minutes) covered Gennady Zyuganov playing volleyball and demonstrating his excellent physical condition. He then told reporters that he was putting together a very broad government of many party and regional leaders and, criticizing the media, noted that "not one has refused [contrary to what] you reported." This long story displayed Zyuganov talking at considerable length but at the end, the young correspondent noted that Zyuganov, having taken advantage of the "information pause," had launched a number of initiatives and then had little to add. The next story featured a press conference of several of the politicians whom Zyuganov had invited to serve under him. They all categorically rejected the offer and some said that they had first heard about the invitation from the media.

On June 26, *Segodnya* ran a roughly three-minute story about Zyuganov with no editorializing. He was celebrating his fifty-second birthday and attacking the media for inciting civil hatred. He named the three network heads twice. A second part of this story showed the hard-line Union of Officers which claimed that only the "machinations" of the administration could convert a Communist victory into a Yeltsin one. The next story, about as long, was devoted to Communist deputy Viktor Ilyukhin's analysis of dangerous conflicts inside the Kremlin. He identified in some detail the warring factions and the economic sectors they favored and referred to General Lebed's action in moving against Yeltsin's security chiefs as burnishing his image of "savior" of Russia.

On June 27, *Segodnya* carried two stories of about two minutes each, without editorial comment. The first showed Zyuganov's meeting with Orthodox clergy. A priest voiced his alarm that mothers were no longer respected and children were no longer protected. The next speaker approvingly noted that the Russian language had no word for "sex." There was only love—sinful and pure. Film director Stanislav Govorukhin said with disgust that in two or three years Russia could become as "stupid and uncultured" as America. Zyuganov, calling himself an "optimist," said he believed in Russia; he believed in fate; and he believed in the future. He promised full rights for religion. A second story showed Communist deputy Svetlana Goryacheva on a campaign trip to her home town of Vladivostok. There, the NTV reporter commented, "she enjoys the respect of both ordinary people and officials," and, indeed, she was shown surrounded by enthusiastic citizens. She told viewers that she was disturbed that the Party could not send election observers all the way to this eastern port and that she thought it would be "difficult to get an objective" vote count.

On July 1, the last day of the campaign, *Segodnya* began its newscast with a meeting between Boris Yeltsin and his Prime Minister, Viktor Chernomyrdin. This marked, the anchor announced, the return of the president after four days of absence from view. Anchor Mikhail Osokin told viewers there was no reason not to believe Chernomyrdin's statement that it had been only a cold, that Yeltsin's grip was as strong as ever. That was the sum of the station's investigation. Yeltsin himself produced a stiff, formal statement about the importance of voting. He looked alarmingly like the incapacitated leaders of the Soviet past.

Following came a story about Zyuganov, which Osokin introduced by saying that evidently the Communist candidate had "obsolete information." Zyuganov told the press that he was very concerned about the state of the president's health and recommended that a medical commission examine him. Zyuganov next warned of likely falsification of the vote count, and asserted that if there was an honest count, his "chances of winning were huge." Finally, he attacked the bias and alarmism of the press and said he would return to the matter after the election. A later story on that last day of the campaign was about a Communist deputy who denied that there had been any dissensus in the Communist camp. The anchor corrected the assertion, saying that there was evidence of such conflict, and that the deputy should have spoken about his own views but not claimed to invoke others' as well.

A final story about the Communists covered Aman Tuleyev, the presidential candidate who withdrew in favor of Zyuganov. In this story, Tuleyev argued that it was time to implement what was promised. "Enough of red and white," he said. There should be a coalition of all representatives of all sectors of the economy and "whatever the people choose should be supported by every honest person." Other coverage spoke of election day security, of plans to stop Communist demonstrations in Moscow (illegal after the end of campaigning), of preparation in election districts. This was a much more low-key end of the campaign on NTV's news than had been the case before the first round.

The second round brought out nearly 70 percent of the Russian electorate and Yeltsin finished a convincing thirteen percentage points ahead of

Zyuganov. People (4.5 percent) voted against both candidates three times as much as they had in the first round.

Boris Yeltsin's blizzard of activity during the month-long campaign before the first round could not possibly have been brought home to the millions of voters spread across the eleven time zones had it not been for television. Yeltsin's remake of himself as candidate and leader could work only if television amplified with very rapid response and thorough penetration the energized, conscience-stricken head of state converted to social welfare as his first order of business. It was television, too, that could provide incontrovertible proof to Russians that what appeared to be a moribund, absentee president some few months earlier, had recovered his combative energy. Conversely, when he canceled appointments and disappeared from the screen, as he did between rounds, the old suspicions surfaced as a campaign issue but appeared to have had little effect, perhaps because this phase of the campaign was so short, and the Yeltsin-Zyuganov choice so clearly framed.

In the 1996 election campaign, NTV, whose "profession was news," had much more than the state-controlled stations a Hobson's choice of failing to help the president (and possibly seeing an end to the rights by virtue of which it existed) or signing on with his team (and undermining the credibility, authority, and independence it had worked so hard to build). The membrane separating civic engagement from Western-style journalistic objectivity was not impermeable, especially in a crisis. And this election, it was hoped, would be the final chapter of the end of Soviet rule. That narrative of transformation had not yet been completed and would take a much longer time. Profound cleavages still marked the body politic. As the next chapter details, there were very few people in post-Soviet Russia who were willing to see views on television that seriously questioned their own bedrock convictions. On several of the most well-known issues of politics, society, and morality, people were deeply divided and little inclined to hear opposing advocates talk about their positions on the most powerful medium, television.

The extension of the franchise was achieved early in the life of the Soviet regime. The transformation of the franchise from nominal to real, was a profound change. Genuinely competitive elections for parliamentary representatives and the president dramatically altered the political map of Russia. This change was accomplished over the span of less than five years, and even if no other change of note had accompanied it, electoral reform, by itself, might well have been dislocating. However, the transformation of the franchise was accompanied by other changes of enormous magnitude: the very definition of the polity was altered suddenly, and citizens of the Soviet Union became citizens of other countries or, in some cases, foreign nationals. Together with this thoroughgoing reassessment of individual identity

and culture, the disintegration of the economy created hardships for dependent populations and those on fixed incomes. The move to a market
economy resulted in rapid, uncontrolled changes in prices and real wages,
while the security provided by the old state sector disintegrated. Some
people had the skills and adaptability to gain substantial psychological and
economic rewards from the new system, while others were deracinated and
déclassés. With few able to predict the course of internal or foreign politics,
Russia repeatedly went to vote.

The legacy of the Soviet regime was manifest also in the absence of secondary associations, which had been proscribed for many decades. The
prerevolutionary political parties, community associations, religious con-
gregations, societies, clubs, and lodges were all gone. At the same time, the
network of relationships the Communist Party built up during their years
of monopoly rule, particularly among older people and outside the two
dominant cities of Russia, proved to be quite durable. The new age of televised electoral campaigns ushered in personalization—the candidate-centered style of modern, American-style televised political campaigns—a
kind of cultural overlay that amplified the traditional Soviet focus on the
individual leader.[143]

Communist Party doctrine had been ambivalent about "great men," saying, as Marx did, that the collective was all and that the more-or-less random distribution of "great" leaders canceled each other out over the course
of history. The doctrine also had its voluntaristic side. Even before Stalin let
loose his disastrous "cult of personality," and even though Lenin abjured devotion to his person, there was an ominously powerful place for the great
leader. In post-Soviet Russia it was going to be more difficult to build party
structures and grass-roots organizations when personalized, candidate-dri-
ven groupings vied for attention, split, and reformed as the leader migrated
from one political formation to the next.

Television has been a key factor in the changing politics of the Western
world. In Russia, this has been equally true, and perhaps more singularly so
because of the deterioration of its national newspaper market and the erosion of its communication networks, both personal and institutional. That
left television as the primary structure for dissemination of information, including that critical flow of information about candidates, parties, and elections. The concentrated brevity of the official campaign period enhanced
the influence of television.[144]

The massive social, political, and economic change Russia experienced
came with the end of socialism and the introduction of the market. Democracy and market economics were twinned in the pronouncements of
the reformers, though that consonance may be problematic.[145] The enormously ambitious reform project was seen by many as modernization in
the American mode. That meant not just the introduction of the market,

but a startling change in a hierarchy of values and symbols that separated generations. The Americanization of the electoral campaign, then, was a subset of a more thoroughgoing process, the manifestations of which were clearly American. To the extent that political advertising was linked to this larger revolution—*a l'américaine*—a whole host of cultural and political cues was triggered. Positioning oneself closer to the "Americanized" end of the spectrum, or moving in the direction of the older, more durable elements of the Soviet legacy produced markedly different campaign strategies. Determining how to represent specifically, distinctively *Russian* pre- or non-Soviet values and images, given the mode and tempo of change, was even more challenging.

In the Western world, television has had the effect of nationalizing elections. The old whistlestops, when candidates could craft their messages only to limited groups in the population, are a thing of the past. Television standardizes and magnifies. Television coverage of electoral campaigns in Russia did the same, but without popular consensus on the definition of the nation. Who actually *belongs,* who is *really* Russian was still the stuff of contention.* Whether the ethnic republics within the Russian Federation belonged there or not was the casus belli in Chechnya.

In the West, the tendency of politics in the television era to weaken parties, with their attendant networks of patronage and local support organizations, has been remarked on with some concern. In Russia, television electoral politics, with its emphasis on personalization drawing from both Soviet traditions and Western imports, played to a nation uncertain of its future and lacking the secondary associations that can act as brakes or firewalls. Though it is only one factor in this complex model, television, the most powerful medium and desired political asset, could well have retarded the development of the very political parties that render the electoral system effective.

---

*In the Russian language, there are two forms of the word "Russian" used in political reporting. One is *Rossianye,* which identifies citizens, whatever the ethnicity, of the political unit known as the Russian Federation. The other, *Russkiye,* refers to ethnic Russians.

CHAPTER NINE

Room for Views: Television and the Play of Controversial Positions

W hen Alexander Yakovlev proposed to the ruling Politburo and Mikhail Gorbachev, the newly installed General Secretary, that the media begin a campaign to legitimize pluralism—contending points of view—he was urging a way of thinking that the Soviet system had decisively rejected. After all, the basis on which information was strictly controlled was the belief that only one view merited attention—that promulgated by the Communist Party leadership on the basis of its superior knowledge in achieving the economic and social goals the Bolshevik Revolution promised.

At first, the introduction of contending points of view was couched in terms of reform and revitalization of the socialist system, but Yakovlev favored making the way clear even for those views that challenged the past more dramatically. From the spring of 1985 on, Yakovlev and his allies, among whom Gorbachev figured for some of the time, worked to remake Soviet culture from one that admitted only one legitimate point of view to one that could grant space to several. The media were to serve as the primary vehicle for this deliberate, if partially concealed, policy, and as time went on and the national newspapers fell victim to the declining economy, it was television that would increasingly take on the task. It would be left to a later time to wonder whether a market economy could generate the range of views—the marketplace of ideas—that in theory democracy required.[1]

The course would be difficult; official Soviet doctrine energetically disseminated an official inventory of tabooed views, taught unrelentingly in schools and in the media.[2] Some of them related to the slightest hint of criticism of the Communist Party's power position; some related to what was morally or socially acceptable. Since official doctrine purported to extend to *all* facets of life, including the secret life of the mind and heart, no position of any kind could be fenced off as apolitical. A speech code of very considerable scope was in force.

In my discussion of the room for views in Russia, I am interested in the overall play of four key controversial positions for the people who run television and for the many more who watch: whether people should be allowed to voice views on television that Lenin was implicated in Stalin's excesses; that the Communist Party should return to monopoly political rule; that prostitution be legalized; and that one ethnic group is inherently superior to another. How much latitude was there for television to challenge the icons of the past and the present, in the minds of both viewers and policymakers? The "yes" answer to a question about the permissibility of airing a view does not separate the tolerant from advocates. Then, too, some of these views represented a real threat to certain people, and we cannot ignore the connection between a sense of threat and a willingness to keep public statements off limits. In the roiling atmosphere of change in Russia, attitudes toward these views were not "academic," and considering how controversial the questions were, it is surprising that relatively few people—especially in the early days of the opening of speech freedoms—gave a "don't know" or "no opinion" answer.[3]

People who favored permitting advocates of the four marker positions to be seen and heard on television included both those who agreed with the position and would gladly see it aired and those who, while personally disagreeing with a position, were tolerant of it. One pair of positions evokes opposed values and does provide a glimpse of the tolerant viewer.[4] The positions decanonizing Lenin and supporting a return to monopoly rule by the Communist Party do not coexist within a single ideological framework. People who say that *both* should be heard on television are those who, though they probably disagree with at least one of the positions, think that access should be accorded it.

The discussion below is based on seven public opinion surveys (Russia, 1989; Russia, 1992; Moscow, 1993, just after the national referendum; Russia, before and after the parliamentary elections in 1993; Russia before and after the parliamentary elections in 1995)[5] and on interviews with the people who ran television, both state and private. The questions are fundamental markers of the Soviet system, key canons of the Soviet past and post-Soviet present. They provoked real, engaged responses, as opposed to rote answers to abstract hypotheticals. Because the content of the position was clear to the people interviewed, we may have seen a more realistic picture of the issues than would have been available from answers to questions asking about adherence to speech freedoms in the abstract.[6]

Each of the four positions, or markers, I examine has a long-standing connection to primary aspects of the legacy of Soviet society. One of them—the advocacy of single-party rule by the Communist Party—was off limits for the first survey, but joined the battery of questions in 1992. The responses provided insights into the play in the system for widely understood and truly disputed stances.

DESANCTIFYING LENIN

People were asked if they thought it permissible for someone to give an opinion on television that Lenin was as culpable as Stalin for the inhumane Stalinist system. The use of Lenin's name on television had been carefully guarded: Eldar Ryazanov's respectful but unorthodox anecdote involving Lenin was cut out by the censors, creating an incident at state television in 1988 (see chapter 3). And playwright Mark Zakharov's discussion of even the *possibility* of Lenin's burial in the ground on *Vzgylad* set off a firestorm in 1989 (see chapter 4), culminating in the public penitence of the soon-to-be-fired television boss.

It took some five years for the Russian government to begin the process of demystifying Lenin. Not even the 1991 attempted coup was judged sufficient cause for risking confrontation with Lenin loyalists. Within days after Yeltsin vanquished the October 1993 armed revolt, he ordered the goose-stepping honor guard removed from service at Lenin's tomb on Red Square. The next month, the Lenin Museum, just off Red Square, was closed. Only in January 1994 did the proposition of Lenin's complicity in the bloody repressions of the Soviet era achieve political and public prominence. Yeltsin officially rehabilitated the troops of the Kronstadt fortress who were crushed by the new Bolshevik government in 1921 for opposing, from the *left,* the imposition of what they regarded as a new dictatorship.

This 1994 decree marked the first time that Lenin was officially linked to terror and repression. Tellingly, Alexander Yakovlev, who had just become head of Channel One state television, said at a news conference: "All the repressions, camps, hostage-takings, mass deportations, executions without trial, even the execution of children, were not invented by Stalin. . . . He was just the Great Continuer of Lenin's Task. It all began under Lenin."[7] The attack was a warning not to turn the clock back, but it may have rested on a false assumption of massive popular support for this still-controversial view—a mistake the Muscovite intelligentsia often made.

President Yeltsin and the military chose Lenin's mausoleum from which to review the parade marking the grandest event of recent time: the fiftieth anniversary of victory in Europe at the end of the Second World War, the one remaining unifying event in the depleted store of commonly held and revered symbols. The issue of Lenin was one that stretched the conscience and understanding of Soviet and post-Soviet citizens.

THE COMMUNIST PARTY'S POWER MONOPOLY

The other side of the political coin was single-party rule by the Communist Party. This question asked if people who believe the Communist Party should regain its monopoly of political power should be able to advocate that view on television. Until 1990 the Communist Party, according to Article 6 of the Soviet Constitution, held a political monopoly, and the removal of Article 6 was a momentous decision. It is worth recalling that a literary journal had published the first public criticism of the Party *only two years before.* The Leningrad literary and public affairs monthly *Neva* ran an article calling for a multi-party system.[8] Even after the dissolution of the Soviet Union, the legacy and power of the Communist Party were still politically explosive. The attempted coup of August 1991 was carried out in the name of the Communist Party of the Soviet Union to restore its primacy, and Boris Yeltsin banned that party and its most loyal publications.[9]

Armed with the support given him in the nationwide referendum of April 1993, Yeltsin attempted to break the backbone of the Communist Party organization. He issued a decree banning the creation and operation of party organizations in the workplace—the key to the coherence and centralization of the Communist Party for over seventy years.[10] It was a repeat of an edict issued in July 1991 which alarmed the then–Communist Party of the Soviet Union and in no small measure was responsible for its attempted comeback by force the next month.

The looming threat of the Communist Party culminated in civil strife in October of that year. At the conclusion of the attempted violent overthrow of Boris Yeltsin in 1993, the newspapers loyal to the communist cause were again outlawed. Subsequent modification of the decree permitted reopening if new editors were named. Only two months later voters sent enough Russian Federation Communist Party deputies to the State Duma to make it the third largest party (and now legal, as opposed to the outlawed Communist Party of the Soviet Union).

After two years in parliament, the Communist Party headed for the polls again, this time upholding the political rules of the game. In the December 1995 campaign, Communist Party head Gennady Zyuganov told the public that he would not engage in witch-hunts or turn the clock back. He promised to obey laws strictly and adhere to "international norms." He addressed the Party's past: "You can be calm: the communist-patriots' party guarantees that there will be no repeat of the tragic pages of history and repressions of all kinds."[11] At the same time he spoke of renationalization of key parts of the economy and reconsition, by voluntary means, of the Soviet Union. The two parts of the message coexisted in an uneasy tension and tended to divide when Zyuganov distinguished between domestic and foreign audiences. This time the party came in a decisive first, with 22 percent of the party-list votes (yielding ninety-nine seats), and added another fifty-eight seats from single-candidate districts.

The next spring the Communists ran Zyuganov for the presidency. In this critical election, he easily won the right to challenge Boris Yeltsin directly in the second round. With only four percentage points separating them, the second round turned out to be exactly the kind of campaign the Yeltsin people had framed: a referendum on the past versus the future. Zyuganov could not break out of this frame, even though his rhetoric was designed to stress nationalist populist, rather than socialist, themes. He was not aided by the heavily reported pronouncements of Viktor Anpilov, a much more radical communist, whose comments Zyuganov would not disavow.

LEGALIZING PROSTITUTION

A completely different dimension of controversy and the degree to which television ought to allow it related to a moral issue. People were asked if supporters of the legalization of prostitution ought to be allowed to air their views on television. In part, this was an issue related to standards of indecency and obscenity, and in part to public health problems and crime.

In the mid-1980s, it had become politically possible, for the first time, to acknowledge the existence of prostitution and wonder publicly what caused it. Until then prostitution was considered one of those retrograde practices of corrupt bourgeois societies. Although articles sympathetically probing its causes appeared in research journals, there was also a good deal of concern that the very discussion of prostitution made it all too desirable. Two professors in the Interior Ministry's institute criticized a popular film for "colorful images" and "vivid advertisements," and lamented the lack of attention to "stories of destitution, venereal diseases," the involvement of crime, narcotics, alcoholism, and the disintegration of the family.[12] At the opposite end of the spectrum, arguments for legalization were presented in research journals in 1988 and 1989.[13] At the same time, secondary schoolchildren thought foreign-currency prostitution was among the most desirable professions. Hard-currency prostitutes, the "inter-girls" of the movies, were rarely detained or even fined. Foreign tourists in Moscow hotels could easily observe the way the ring worked, with the collusion of the militiamen supposedly guarding the hotel, and the floor-concierge, the keeper of the keys.

Trying to keep up with rapidly changing views about prostitution and a law enforcement system that deteriorated when the Soviet Union broke up, the Russian Interior Ministry created a new squad for sex crimes. The "morals police" had a mandate they could not, and did not, fulfill. Over two thousand pornographic video parlors were operating in Moscow alone.

The question of prostitution's legalization was given new currency by Vladimir Zhirinovsky's 1993 political campaign. One of his more attention-getting "talks" with the television audience was addressed to the sex lives of young people. He deplored prostitution, and though he acknowledged that it was as old as history, and understandable that sailors on leave should resort to it, he claimed it was a degradation of the womanhood of Russia. Back from a trip to Europe, he told an interviewer on Russian television that "all the brothels are full of Russian women. What have we brought up our daughters for? . . . This is a shame!"[14]

The legalization controversy was also complicated by increasing public awareness of AIDS. What, then, did people think about talk of the legalization of prostitution on television? Even though this issue, compared to the other three, had been the subject of fairly frank public debate, approval of televised pluralism did not expand, but contracted. As the environment of public morals visibly disintegrated, the public was less willing to countenance advocacy of legalized prostitution on television.

INHERENT ETHNIC SUPERIORITY

The last disputed position we asked people about was the most sensitive of all: Should people who believed that certain ethnic groups were inherently superior to others be allowed to voice their opinions on television? A yes answer could run afoul of the rather broadly and vaguely worded strictures of the law. Such advocacy was considered a violation of the Soviet Constitution in its time, and post-Soviet Russian laws on the press. Article 29 of the Russian Constitution, adopted by referendum vote in December 1993, qualifies freedom of thought and speech by saying that "the propaganda of social, racial, national [ethnic], religious or language supremacy shall be prohibited."[15] Rhetorical devotion to this precept was very widespread.[16]

Inflammatory speech remains a thorny issue everywhere, and democracies differ in their approaches. As Timur Kuran has written, "no human law is immutable, and in unusually threatening times pluralism might appear luxurious. In any case, even the most liberal legal system allows exceptions to freedom of speech."[17] In the United States, limitations are justified by reference to "clear and present danger," difficult to define but requiring proof of the likelihood of specific harm or injury within a narrowly drawn time frame. In society in crisis—for example, one teetering on the brink of civil war—restricting speech that ignites disorder may be necessary. At the same time, the regime in power may define crisis as virtually permanent, in effect, permanently restricting speech. That was certainly true of Soviet leaders in their seventy years of power. The Soviet past left a legacy of expansive interpretation of hate-speech restrictions, despite the regime's own glaring violations (explained away by reference to hair-splitting doctrine) of those prohibitions. In post-Soviet Russia, Vladimir Zhirinovsky quickly discovered that expressions of inflammatory speech could now cross the boundary into public discourse, with little or no official penalties. As a perverse and unfortunate consequence, the market of ideas operated very imperfectly, rewarding bold bigots for their breakthroughs and disadvantaging self-censoring moderates. The importance of Zhirinovsky, then, lay not so much in his person or platform but in the coup de grâce he gave to the code.

As the Soviet Union broke up, the tempo and gravity of inter-ethnic conflict increased, as did the number of instances of overt discrimination and threats against ethnic groups. One expert noted that in the spring of 1994 most of the dozens of extreme nationalist groups in Russia were anti-Semitic (Jews being defined by ethnicity, rather than confessional attributes).[18]

Officially, however, the prohibition on such talk in public fora was maintained. It was one of the charges the Party made against Boris Yeltsin when it removed him from the Moscow leadership in 1987 and accused him, among other things, of anti-Semitism. Moscow city boss Yury Prokofyev said at the time: "If we speak about Yeltsin's political literacy, I witnessed his meeting with the members of the [anti-Semitic] Pamyat society. You know what that society is. They were invited to the Moscow City Soviet and comrade Yeltsin spoke to them. And he ceded them one position after another. And to whom? To hysterical people and members of the Black Hundred."[19]

The anti-reformist view mandated strict interpretation of the prohibited speech law ostensibly to prevent racism and bigotry, while advocates of political liberalization favored free speech, even at the price of speech seeking to spread ethnic hatred. Yegor Yakovlev was prescient in 1990 when he opposed prosecuting Pamyat because "then tomorrow we won't be around either."[20] Two years later he was fired by Boris Yeltsin from the directorship of state television on precisely the grounds of disseminating ethnic insults by scheduling a documentary film on ethnic conflict within Russia. While high-mindedly rejecting public adherence to the position of ethnic superiority, the Communist Party also, of course, had a history of purges of ethnic groups, large-scale deportations of peoples, and systems of discriminatory quotas, all couched in the oblique language of coded speech that everyone understood. On the question of anti-Semitism, throughout Soviet history the Party line insisted on differentiating its official anti-Zionist stance (directed against an "international" threat said to emanate from the state of Israel) from its opposition to anti-Semitism. But for the many Soviet Jews victimized by the policy and the high-ranking and petty officials who energetically implemented it, the distinction hardly mattered.[21]

Hate speech by political candidates, especially Vladimir Zhirinovsky, was rarely punished swiftly or with serious fines, but it was, nonetheless, frequently under investigation or review. The Russian government attempted without much result to prosecute him for propagandizing war and ethnic hatred in his book published before the 1993 parliamentary elections.[22] During the 1995 campaign, the Judicial Chamber for Information Disputes, the official oversight organ, sent to the chief procurator (prosecutor) several cases involving candidates' hate speech. Zhirinovsky had proposed on television a war termination strategy: napalming Chechen villages in retaliation for wounding or killing a single Russian soldier, and another extremist party leader had offered viewers a plan to end crime in Russia by removing people from the Caucasus and Central Asia.

The chamber's charge was to flag violations and notify law enforcement. The confused interpretation of the antihate speech statute and the political forum that such a case would give to the flamboyant extremists made state action unlikely.

Especially sensitive were attempts, no matter how low key, to deal frankly and responsibly with ethnic tension on television. When two correspondents for Russian Television conducted a "space bridge" between Moscow and Almaty about Russian-Kazakh tensions, Kazakhstan authorities charged the program directors with chauvinism and "inflaming interethnic differences."[23] (The program was apparently a fairly tame effort, offering talking-head intellectuals and data on Russian emigration from the Central Asian republic.)

The political potency of television had always made it a special target, and in 1995, when the upper house of the Russian parliament considered the law to reorganize state television, much of the discussion obliquely referred to the Jewish origin (usually clear from names) of several of the new directors, and warned of a conspiracy to deprive television viewers of seeing ethnic Russians on the screen.[24]

In matters regarding television policy, the ethnic issue of greatest immediacy was anti-Semitism. The two most powerful media magnates, Boris Berezovsky and Vladimir Gusinsky, were both Jews, and after many years of absence, Jews were assuming on-air and off-screen prominence. Just before the 1995 parliamentary election campaign began, Sergei Blagovolin, the head of state television, said, "'Like any Russian intellectual, a person's ethnicity is of absolutely no importance to me. But it is impermissible to have on the channel all Russia watches ladies and gentlemen Deich, Borovoy, Albats and Minkin as the only opponents of Zhirinovsky and Zyuganov.'"

The names in question were decidedly Jewish and Blagovolin's relegation of them to marginality in his country was, he thought, merely good practical sense when threatened by the likes of the Communists and Zhirinovsky.[25] A government official of Central-Asian descent tried to answer the thinly veiled complaints of Duma deputies about Jewish television figures by emphasizing the importance of equality for all Russian citizens (*rossiyanye*) whether or not they were Russian (*russkiye*). At the same time that coded speech and discriminatory acts were plain to see, the official doctrine and its normative prohibitions remained on the books, its vaguely worded prohibitions to be manipulated by those in power.

Rising rates of crime and widespread fear and personal insecurity affected the way many people felt about ethnic groups, particularly those from the Caucasian regions of southern Russia. In Russian cities the dramatic increase in crime was linked to the increasingly public presence of Caucasian—especially Chechen—"mafia" organizations.

In the wake of the October 1993 revolt, President Yeltsin declared a state of emergency and curfew and used the occasion to crack down on crime in the capital. Police were given a free hand to detain and deport people from the Caucasus—identified by their looks—because, as police inspector Andrei Shchavlev remarked, "Most of our crimes are committed by Caucasians . . . They have dark complexions, large noses, so they're easy to spot and detain. . . . They go into bars or restaurants, beat up men and steal their women . . . They bring girls into a dorm, force them to take drugs, then turn them out to the streets as prostitutes. These people drive all the best cars . . . but they have very low culture."[26]

Before the breakup of the Soviet Union, people inteviewed in polls were in the main indifferent to intermarriage (slightly more than half polled), but did name people from the Caucasus as the least desired ethnic group to marry into one's family.[27]

The crackdown on the darker-hued ethnic groups persisted beyond the October 1993 state of emergency. According to a reporter of Armenian extraction, "Today the hunt in the streets on the basis of 'color' has become a norm of life." She heard Muscovites say that "We are fed up with these blacks. All the markets are filled with them."[28]

When the Russian government went to war with its rebellious secessionist republic of Chechnya in the winter of 1994–95, the reason most often stated was the urgent necessity to clean out the den of thieves that was destroying the country. In that unfortunate operation, the Chechen republic and the Chechen people were criminalized. It is noteworthy that in spite of these attitudes on the part of some, or perhaps many, Muscovites did not support the war largely because of the way private television (NTV) and then Russian Television (Channel Two) framed[29] the coverage of events, displaying Russian victims of their commanders' errors, horrifying scenes of the sacrifice of young men incinerated in their tanks, and civilians (many of whom were Russian) devastated by bombing. This prevented the Yeltsin administration from bolstering support for the war by exploiting the insecurity and fear with which Moscow's citizens regarded Caucasians in their city.

THE TOLERANT POSITION

Intolerance is the more reflexive response. Unless the political culture teaches citizens to preserve rights for those they oppose, the rationale for one's own benefit will not be immediately apparent. It is difficult to link one's future benefit to a less than optimal preference today and to calculate the costs of today's intolerance that will come due in the future.[30] Generally speaking, political tolerance is in fairly short supply, even in Western democracies. One study found a consensus for *intolerance* in twelve Western European countries, when people who were not favorably disposed to fascists were asked about their willingness to grant them a legal basis for existence—to run candidates for office and to hold public demonstrations.[31] In the United States, too, it was found that only a small percentage of the public was willing to grant a group they most disliked the same political rights as others.[32]

In the late Soviet Union and post-Soviet Russia, studies found that of all the foundation blocks of democratic values, political tolerance was least solid. One study found that in Russia the majority of people interviewed would not let members of groups they most disliked run for office, and another found support for democratic institutions, but *only if* defined as political rights of the majority.[33] Tolerance needs some degree of basic shared values, as do the institutions of democracy. "A stable democracy requires general agreement on fundamentals because such a consensus gives people the security to grant others expressive freedom."[34]

With the violence of the October 1993 events still fresh in his mind, Russian television critic Alexander Aronov pondered the meaning of the tolerance position ascribed to Voltaire and concluded that for *Voltaire,* the best polemicist of his age, to assure his opponents a right to speak presupposed the presence of Voltaire himself, that is, the right to disseminate unpopular, controversial, or even dangerous positions must be balanced by the capacity to refute or counterargue at a level of effectiveness that Voltaire evidently possessed.

Quite the contrary occurred when ill-prepared Russian television hosts assembled representatives of the communist and nationalist-fascist positions, and the medium provided long-distance amplification. The moderators and hosts of these public affairs programs were "much stronger than poor Voltaire"; they communicated with a huge instantaneous audience. Moreover, Aronov continued, "Voltaire, by the way, says nothing about free expression for those who have no argument other than knives and bombs, that is, applying it to our conditions, the communists-fascists."

In Aronov's mind, the danger in encouraging a free play of positions resulted in real-world outcomes that were frightening, as his hyperactive, frantic commentary claimed:

No one else but you, gentlemen Voltairians-bamboozlers from "Vzglyads,"
"ViDs," "Red Squares," and all the Politburo [programs], led us to this point.
Equally amicably chatting with these people and those people. . . . It is you
who invited Zhirinovsky and appeared[35] that one can talk to him as to a de-
cent person.

   You preferred cheap professionalism to social responsibility, [the cheap
professionalism] of a fire reporter who, basically is interested in only one
thing, that if there is a fire, it produce not 20, but at least 40 lines in his next
paragraph.[36]

Aronov here raised the specter of threat: how can one be tolerant of
those who would destroy one's very life and most certainly the fledgling
democratic system? Letting Nazis and Ku Klux Klan members advocate
their programs in America really may be seen as a threat to potential victims, who, therefore, give the less "tolerant" answer when queried about
what political freedoms to accord disliked groups.[37] Threat tightens the
boundaries of one's own group and increases ethnocentrism.[38] That is one
reason why Zhirinovsky ran particularly well in Russia's border regions.
But insecurity and deteriorating economic conditions also appear to trig-
ger intolerant responses.[39] In the United States, prolonged economic stress
has been linked to reduction in ethnic and racial political tolerance.[40]

   Support of speech codes, particularly with respect to ethnic, religious,
and racial differences, is everywhere fraught with difficulties and contradictions, and the subtext of threat lends a certain urgency to it. Consider the
following statement: "What is new is the reach, impact, and audacity of all
sorts of what is loosely termed communication, combined today with ner-
vous-making economic difficulties and social strains in big cities and small
towns, with . . . political fragmentation and religious fragmentation. . . ."
This observation referred to the United States in the wake of the 1995
bombing in Oklahoma City.[41]

   In the United States, the rise of hate radio and the use of the Internet to
disseminate the previously unsayable led some to conclude, as Rabbi Abra-
ham Cooper of the Simon Wiesenthal Center did, that "'. . . today it is
O.K. to express bigoted, racial ideas in public . . . Is that related to the new
ability to communicate hate? I don't know. But people feel much more
comfortable now letting it all hang out than they once did.'"[42] He was
speaking of the legitimation of extremist views in public discourse, something that was very much on the minds of Russians in the pathbreaking
and pattern-setting 1993 electoral campaign.

   Among media professionals interviewed in Russia—as among the pub-
lic-at-large—the connection between threat and televised speech was repeatedly made. From the words of the ordinary men and women we surveyed at the beginning of the slide toward dissolution of the Soviet state, to
the often bitter comments of the men who ran television in the aftermath

of the October 1993 revolt, the cloud of threat often obscured the space for contending views. We start with the words of ordinary people and their reactions to letting the first three positions be aired on television: Lenin's repressive policies, legalization of prostitution, and ethnic superiority.

DAWN OF CONTENDING VIEWS: 1989

At the end of 1989 the Soviet Union was moving uncertainly along the path toward a liberalization that was to result in its demise, but the inexorable logic of the end was far from evident. The Communist Party still held a political monopoly; it was not until the next year that its hold would be loosened. On television, new examples of genuine debates and pluralism of views were broadcast daily. The past was being unearthed and revered authorities toppled.

Television audiences saw what they had never seen before. Some were insulted or appalled; some were relieved and energized. Some worried about the effect on their children; some saw it as all of a piece with the economy declining and reduced attention to law and order. What follows are the reactions of ordinary people, part of a national random sample, to questions about televised free speech. These people took part in a nationwide survey and in their homes gave their views to local interviewers. The responses show how divided people were in their own minds and their groping confrontation with a world in which contesting views were suddenly made legitimate and contended for the public's approbation.

In the small town of Klin, Tchaikovsky's home, some two hours by car from Moscow, a forty-seven-year-old Russian father of four grown children sat on his living room sofa across from the large television set centrally positioned in the bookcase. He was a member of the Communist Party and thought television a mighty force, the most objective and comprehensive medium, but not everything it did was for the best. He worried that "the Russian language might be lost, because television just shows music in foreign languages." He had no hesitation in saying that legalization of prostitution could be talked about, but not nationalist claims to superiority—that was off limits. About Lenin's responsibility, he could not understand: "Why mix Lenin and Stalin?" And he rejected the idea that the view could be talked about on television.

A seventy-seven-year-old retired university administrator in Klin greeted the interviewer on a cold day in November. Dressed in a sweater-jacket and wearing fur slippers worn through at the toes and heels, he settled in to a long talk. He hadn't had a chance to talk quite so much in a long time and was eager to say what was on his mind. He thought Stalin, and then

Brezhnev, had "destroyed Russian habits of honesty" by encouraging denunciations, and now that people had been "spoiled" they would have to be reeducated. He sat at his desk in the living room, in front of the television set in the corner and across from his ample bookshelf, piled high with books and down the wall from the piano. On the walls were his framed butterfly collection and other souvenirs he had brought back from Vietnam and Cuba. He, too, believed television to be the most objective and comprehensive of all media, but he came down hard on whether or not it should allow advocates of extreme nationalism (he called it fascism) and legalization of prostitution to talk on television—decidedly no. Thinking more, he began to qualify his prohibitions. Perhaps, after all, the Lenin and prostitution issues could be talked about on television, but only if "strong opponents" joined in the discussion.

One young woman did not live well in the "dormitory" (an apartment building with shared—and limited—amenities) in Klin. She had a one-room apartment (a communal kitchen was down the hall) whose narrow length accommodated her five-year-old son's crib, converted in the daytime into a small couch. On the opposite wall was a bookcase and a desk, on top of which a very large television set surveyed the cramped quarters. The young woman was twenty-three and divorced. She spoke softly but firmly and answered questions while the television flickered with the sound turned off. She, too, favored television over other media. She did not think the controversial view of Lenin should be permitted, nor the one about ethnic superiority, but she was willing to hear arguments for the legalization of prostitution broadcast.

The gentle bearded man greeted the interviewer in his stocking feet, then sat back in his chair in the corner of his living room and comfortably stretched out his legs. Married, father of three, with a high school education, he was a believer in the Orthodox Christian faith, but embittered: "I want to trust and I used to trust, but now in this period nobody trusts anybody. They believe only in the ruble." He longed for ideals he could still believe in. He rejected the notion of televised speech on all three questions. About Lenin, he said that such views could not be permitted, "or else we'll get anarchists. We have to have *some* ideals." About ethnic nationalism, he called the provocative position "fascism."

In Kiev, the twenty-year-old Ukrainian was interviewed in the presence of her partner. Dressed in a short black dress, pink tights, and clogs, she gave firm answers and did not look to her partner for approval. He smoked incessantly and fingered his pack of cigarettes nervously as he stared intently at the local interviewer. She had a high school education and worked as a technician in health services. She praised television, saying it was the most objective of media, and that now that there was much more information on television it was easier for her to make up her mind. She never hesitated on the marker questions: yes, permit all the opinions on television.

The forty-nine-year-old widow in Alma-Ata, capital of Kazakhstan, was Russian. She loved television, but found that it was actually harder for her to make up her mind when she saw positions presented from many different points of view. Though she said she had no free time whatever, supplementing her work as an engineer with extra work "done on the left," she did manage to see about an hour and a half of television daily and six to seven hours on the weekend. She declared she had no confidence whatever in the Communist Party, the Young Communist League, or the government. She wanted reform to move as rapidly as possible, but she was concerned about the right to strike and engage in political demonstrations; people should "speak out, but not destroy order." She approved of airing the Lenin and prostitution issues, but not inherent ethnic superiority—absolutely not that.

The Kazakh telecommunications security man was forty-two, father of two, with a vocational high school education and one year of college. During the first part of the interview his mother mopped the floor and put on the kettle for tea. Entranced with the survey, she forgot about the kettle, left boiling furiously in the kitchen. When her son was asked his age, she broke in: "I'm sixty-two and feel one hundred." Seeing multiple points of view on television was disconcerting for the man. He found more information now, but it was harder to make up his mind. He said the controversial view of Lenin should not just be permitted, it was *necessary* to disseminate it publicly. The views of prostitution should also be permitted. As to ethnic superiority: "yes, why not, if they are good specialists."

The thirty-eight-year-old Kazakh conservatory musician certainly did not share this notion. When asked about Lenin, he said, "This is the first time I've ever heard such a question." Organizing his thoughts, he replied, "Well, since there is democracy, it can be published in newspapers and shown on television." As to advocacy of ethnic superiority on television, yes, he would permit it. On morals questions he was strict: no advocacy of the legalization of prostitution in any forum. He, too, found it more complicated making up his mind since more information was provided on television. He was comfortable when authoritative institutions provided direction. His confidence in television was very high and he called it objective, but was concerned that it had begun to show programs children should not see. His own television watching, he said, included weekend cartoon shows, which he watched with his little daughter, though he admitted that he "absolutely" liked them too.

For many of the people interviewed, questions such as these had never been put to them before. They were trying to find their way in a rapidly changing environment of officially sanctioned values. What was remarkable was the willingness of these people to countenance views that were absolutely off limits for television at the time they were interviewed. Just a few months before, the head of state television was forced to resign and publicly take responsibility for far less than the question about Lenin asks.

In 1989 it was a different country, not only because the Soviet Union was still intact, but also because *perestroika* was in full flower. For ordinary citizens, then, the world was opening up, including the long-suppressed world of their own past. The costs and missteps were as yet unknown and the limits untested. Some were uneasy with the suddenly decreed incertitude, but people would say then that they were more open to seeing television tackle the marker controversies than they would be later.

Prostitution, for example, came to be associated more and more with the crime that was destroying cities all over Russia. The play of the legalization position on television was to narrow over time, as would the play of the ethnic superiority position. The latter, like the former, was associated with the tensions and troubles that plagued post-Soviet Russia. The blush of discovery and a kind of openness to experimentation was in retreat.

While acceptance of the controversial positions on prostitution and ethnic superiority was reduced some after 1989, the case of the two political markers was somewhat different. The question of Lenin's complicity tended to divide the nation in half, and that split continued over time and roughly in the same proportion, with small fluctuations but not big reverses. Attacking Lenin on the most pervasive medium (to use a term from U.S. law) was still out of the question for a very large number of Russians. On the Communist Party question, which was not asked before early 1992, the "yes" answer declines from two-thirds of the respondents to about 20 to 30 percent. The Russians interviewed were no longer willing to see the Communist Party as the single monopoly party with no competitive elections and no pluralism. As we shall see later, Communist voters were considerably more likely than others to support televised speech advocating such a monopoly, but many more people, even those who were faring poorly in the new system, were unwilling to turn the clock all the way back, and that is how they viewed the central question of the presidential contest of 1996.

TELEVISION POLICY MAKERS: DECIDING FOR THE PUBLIC

In post-Soviet Russia and in post-revolt Moscow, eleven of the top decision makers involved in television policy gave their views about how much room for views television should permit. They were interviewed between

late October 1993 and mid-June 1995, and included the heads of important television stations: Vyacheslav Bragin and Sergei Blagovolin, when
each was the head of Channel One; Oleg Poptsov, when he headed Channel Two; Igor Malashenko, president of private NTV; Eduard Sagalayev,
president of private TV-6 before he moved to replace Poptsov; two officials
in television regulation policy, Valentin Lazutkin, the head of the Federal
Radio and Television Service at the time, and Sergei Yushenkov then-
deputy director of the Federal Information Center; Evgeny Kiselyov, Russia's top anchor and NTV partner; Mikhail Nenashev, a Soviet-era head of
state television; and two political figures whose oversight function included
television: Yegor Ligachev, Mikhail Gorbachev's second in command and
Gennady Burbulis, Boris Yeltsin's former counselor and campaign manager.

To a man, they supported the notion that people with the view that
Lenin was as responsible as Stalin should be allowed to express their opinion on television. Mikhail Nenashev dismissed even the notion that such a
position could still be considered controversial, calling it a "senseless question." Hard-liner Yegor Ligachev was not so sure and gave a qualified answer: "Yes, that may be a factor, but it would need argument [on the air]."

On the doctrinal opposite: letting people say on television that the
Communist Party should be returned to monopolize political life, there
was some disagreement. Sergei Blagovolin and Sergei Yushenkov were
doubters who would bar the airwaves to such views. Yushenkov responded
with warmth: "Certainly not!" Much troubled by the question and pointing to the violent events of the October revolt just days before this interview, he said that in Russia something like de-Nazification should have
taken place and should still take place. The Communist Party had committed more crimes and was responsible for more deaths than the Nazis. Allow
a view supporting their return to uncontested power to be heard on television? The Communist Party was "like Nazism, even worse." The threat they
posed made televised advocacy of the position truly dangerous.

On the other side, Yegor Ligachev, who strongly believed that the Communist Party infrastructure of rule had endured and that the Party would
return to power, agreed that this view could be permitted on television but
made the point that he did not share it: "I like the multi-party system."
When he had been a powerful member of the Politburo, Mikhail Gorbachev recalled, Ligachev supported the notion of a multi-party system,
but only one dominated by the Communist Party of the Soviet Union.[43]
The remaining eight officials, opposing Communist Party monopoly rule,
were willing to grant access to the view on television. One, Mikhail Nenashev, noted the danger in the position but was not willing to proscribe the
view. "There will always be extremists," he said philosophically. "But," he
cautioned, "it should not be a sermon for fascism. Each leader, inside,

thinks that his party is the most important; one might as well show it. But I am not for dictatorship."

Most of the officials interviewed clearly did not personally support a Communist Party monopoly of power but would permit that view on television. Vyacheslav Bragin said, "yes [viewers] can laugh at it." Oleg Poptsov thought an advocate of such a view would be perceived as mad, "and I can say that I'm Peter the Great." In June 1996, television people did not regard advocates of a resurgent Communist Party as so quaintly loony. The degree of perceived threat had changed drastically.

Nine of the eleven top officials agreed on the "tolerant" position of airing diametrically opposed views—condemnation of Lenin and advocacy of Communist power monopoly. In this they were far in front of the mood of the Russian public, and even of the Moscow public. They were closer to the views of the public in their mixed (largely negative) reception of the issue of the legalization of prostitution. Government official Sergei Yushenkov did not have a firm opinion: "I haven't thought it out; more yes than no, but I haven't thought about it."

Of the remaining ten high media officials, only four thought it permissible for the legalization of prostitution argument to be on television. Heads of both of the big private stations said no. Yegor Ligachev said, "Absolutely not: this is immoral." Though he would give this position airtime, Mikhail Nenashev tended to downplay the salience of the issue and wanted to limit viewership. Yes, he thought it could be permissible, but "not for young children." Besides, he did not consider it "the most important theme; it is not a real problem now."

It was on the issue of permitting views advocating the superiority of an ethnic group that all of the officials agreed without hesitation or qualification. None would allow advocates of this view airtime. Responsible under the law, they were undoubtedly aware of legal prohibitions and the political risks they would incur. Some of their comments also suggested a real personal revulsion. Mikhail Nenashev answered: "No, that has elements of fascism. People are not at fault if they belong to a nation [ethnic group]. Television is such a huge force in forming public opinion, that it [airing such a view] is not desirable. It can provoke genocide." Yegor Ligachev rejected the view as "racism and fascism."

THE PLAY OF POSITIONS OVER TIME: THE RUSSIAN PUBLIC

For ordinary Soviet viewers in 1989, the country's slide into severe, protracted economic crisis and eruptions of violence was foreshadowed. In subsequent years and surveys there was a certain contraction in their will-

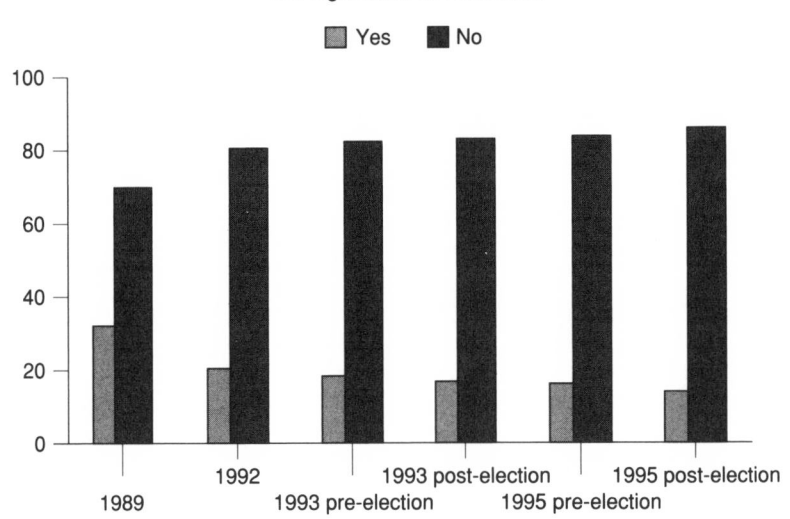

Allowing Views on Television: Russia

On Legalization of Prostitution

☐ Yes ■ No

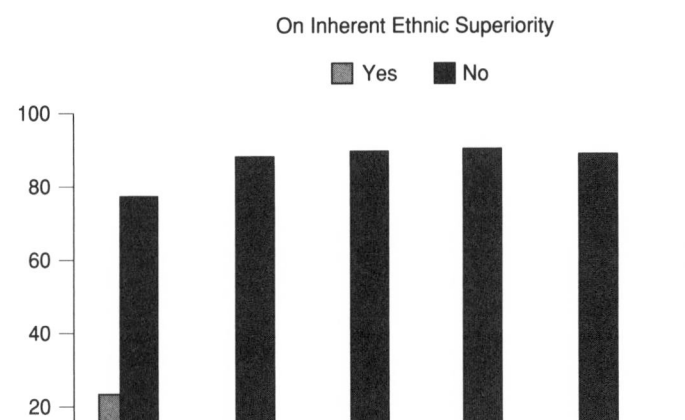

Allowing Views on Television: Russia

On Inherent Ethnic Superiority

☐ Yes ■ No

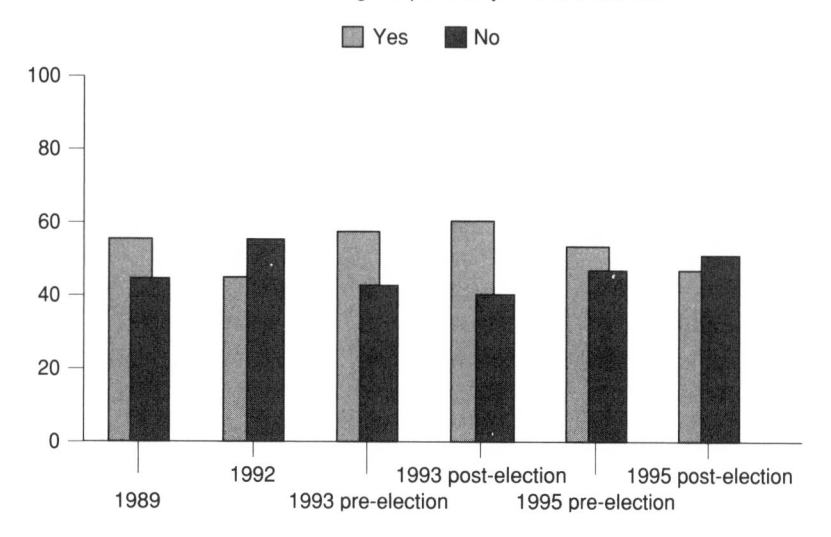

Allowing Views on Television: Russia´

On Lenin's Sharing Responsibility for the Stalin Era

☐ Yes ■ No

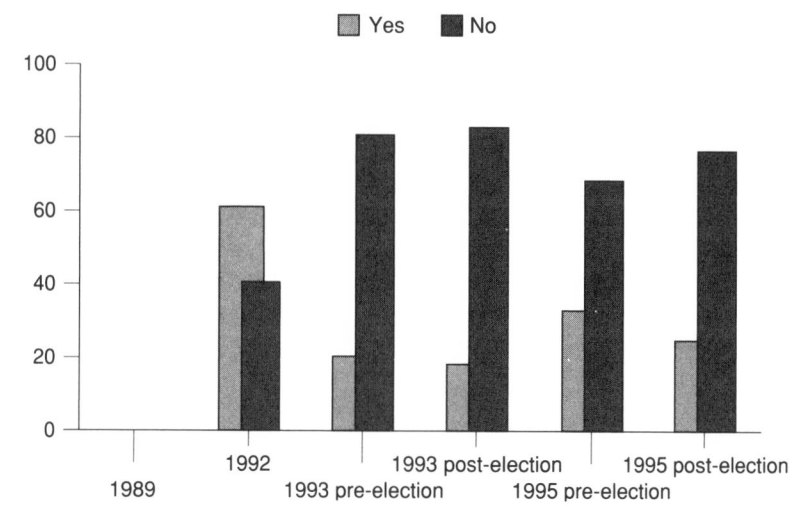

Allowing Views on Television: Russia

Advocating Return to Communist Party Monopoly Rule

☐ Yes ■ No

Allowing Opposing Views on Television: Russia

Both Criticism of Lenin and Advocacy of Communist Party Monopoly Rule

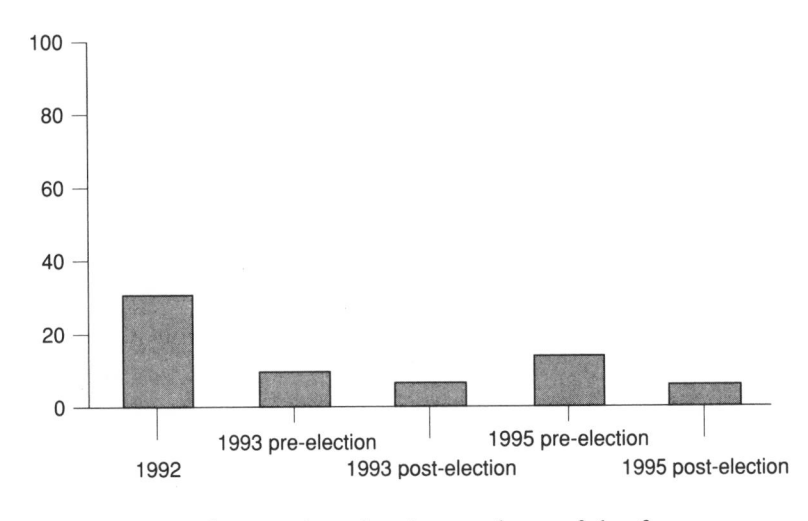

ingness to open television broadcasting to three of the four controversial marker views, and a continuing, near-even division on the fourth. The graphs above tell the story.

Over time, people became less inclined to grant advocates of the legalization of prostitution airtime. Support of inherent ethnic differences was also still largely off limits for most people, as it was for all the television officials. As for the directly political questions about Lenin and the Communist Party, they remained highly controversial. The Lenin issue still split the Russian population virtually down the middle, except in Moscow, where anti-Leninism was strong. The figure of Lenin had not been lost in the mists of the past, and a significant number of people polled would not allow his image to be desecrated in words.

In the capital, the picture was very different. Muscovites (seven in ten) were much more willing to hear the view about Lenin than was the rest of the country. Perhaps that is why Moscow-based elites were often in error about the rest of the country. In the 1992 survey of Russia, although support of the Lenin responsibility question was very strong in Moscow, where some 69 percent of those interviewed said yes, it was much lower in rural areas (39 percent), but lowest of all in the small cities (31 percent).[44] As a British study observed, these small towns were often really company towns, whose economy depended on a single factory in the state sector, usually in heavy industry or defense.[45] And it was these firms that were the likely victims of the wrenching transformation from a state industrial base to a post-

Soviet, consumer-driven, market-related base. Here there was neither the busy, relatively information-rich atmosphere of larger cities nor the traditionalism of rural life. The Russian small town was caught in the middle and proved to be least adaptable and most resistant to the coming change. These sharp differences made it perilous to generalize the views of one's friends and family as so many of the political elites in Moscow did.[46]

Among Russians in 1992, those who favored airing the view that the Communist Party should be the sole political power were not distinguished from others by education, age, or sex, but they were more rural than urban. As virtually mirror images, the questions about Lenin and the Communist Party were associated with directly opposite views of other aspects of Russian life: those who answered yes to the Lenin question favored foreign investment in Russia to expand the economy and create more jobs; while those who said yes to the question on the Party rejected foreign investment as leading to loss of control over the economy.

Support for permitting advocacy of Communist Party monopoly rule on television declined powerfully over time in Russia, perhaps accelerated by the violence in October 1993 that partisan attachment to the old ways caused. In public opinion surveys there was general consensus that the public, sobered by economic hardship and political failures, was still not willing to return to the old system, even if, especially among the old and those who depended on the state sector, there was a good deal of nostalgia for the world status and guaranteed, if limited, standard of living of the Brezhnev era.[47]

The question incriminating Lenin and the question about advocating Communist Party monopoly power represented ideological antitheses; a person who believed in one part of the pair would find the other objectionable. In Russia, of those who had opinions on both of these questions (75 percent of those interviewed) in the 1992 survey, only 28 percent took the tolerant position of allowing both. In Moscow, right after the April 1993 referendum, 66 percent of those interviewed responded to both questions, and 15 percent could accept both positions being aired on television. In Russia before the December 1993 parliamentary elections, 62 percent answered both questions and only 10 percent would grant airtime to both marker positions. In the postelection poll, when 66 percent answered both questions, a mere 9 percent were willing to see both positions on television. Finally, just a week before the December 1995 parliamentary elections, 68 percent of the Russians polled answered both questions and 14 percent said they would permit both positions on television, while just after the elections (with 62 percent responding to the two questions), the figure was back down, to 7 percent. Since 1992, the willingness to hear both sides of this hotly contested, absolutely fundamental argument about the Soviet legacy had shrunk from just over one-fourth to around one-tenth.

THE PLAY OF POSITIONS AND VOTERS' CHOICES

The April 1993 referendum provided the first opportunity to line up the play of views and political choice. Voting behavior involves many factors, but I am concerned here with the relationship between the four marker positions and voter preference, and between voter preference (and nonvoting) and the television campaign, irrespective of demographic characteristics. We know that the elderly, the less well-educated, rural people, and women (depending on their work obligations) watch more television than others. We also know that the different political parties draw disproportionately from certain age and status groups. For each of those social-demographic groups, was following the campaign on television related to party preference or failing to vote?

REFERENDUM, 1993

In the April referendum political advertising was used extensively for the first time. Leaflets, posters, and television ads all spelled out the responses to the four referendum questions supporting Boris Yeltsin: yes, yes, no, and yes. The referendum took place around Easter, and a joke made the rounds that the traditional Russian Orthodox Easter greeting and response among believers: "Christ is risen." "Indeed, He is risen." had been transformed into "Christ is risen." "Yes, yes, no, yes."

The pervasiveness of advertising and television coverage was especially pronounced in the Moscow area. Never before, and not again, until the June 1996 presidential election, had the choices been as neatly and starkly divided. April 1993 started and June 1996 continued the contest over the fundamental definition of Russia and the legitimacy of the reform project that overthrew communism.

That spring in 1993, less than two years after the statues had been toppled, we asked people in Moscow their views. Were Yeltsin backers more willing than others to accept the airing of the marker positions on television? In the postreferendum survey of Moscow residents, we asked those who said they had voted about their willingness to allow all four positions on television.[48] And we did this for those who had faithfully voted the complete Yeltsin formula as well as for those who voted the weaker version (yes on trust of the president, regardless of their other answers).[49] Independently of age, education, or gender of the voter, both the full-formula loyalists and the less rigorous presidential supporters,[50] strongly backed televised advocacy of Lenin's criminal complicity and strongly opposed television time for advocates of Communist Party monopoly power. On these dimensions they differed from other Moscow voters.

Allowing Views on Television: Moscow

(Post-Referendum May 1993)

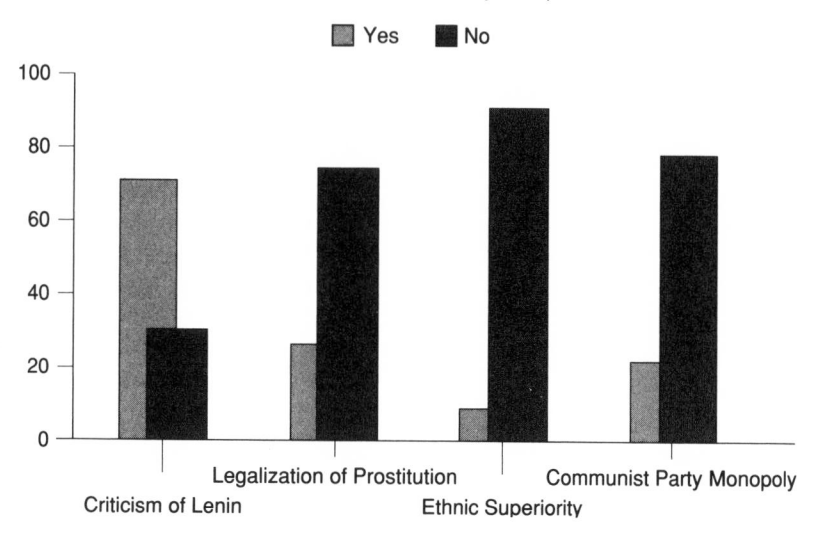

With television so widely available and increasingly the source of information, Yeltsin's strongest backers in the capital would grant television airtime for a political view they believed in and would deny airtime for the one they opposed.[51] Even among the more highly educated and information-rich of the Russian capital, the polarization of Russian political life and the urgency of crisis conditions, almost a constant given, reduced the space for the tolerant middle.

PARLIAMENTARY ELECTIONS, 1993 AND 1995

Surveys representative of the Russian Federation were undertaken to look at these controversial positions and voting intentions shortly before, and voting choices shortly after, the 1993 and 1995 parliamentary elections. Before the 1993 elections, when a number of parties had been outlawed and a revolt of the far right and left had been put down, people might have been uneasy about indicating their preferences. Therefore, the electoral victory of Vladimir Zhirinovsky might well have been an important factor in legitimating the kinds of views he emphasized most forcefully; postelection it was acceptable to be a Zhirinovsky supporter. To be sure, taking polls after elections may generate a different distortion. People interviewed may assert that they voted when they did not and chose winners when they had not. For these reasons it is useful to look at the paired before-and-after results.[52]

The surveys also permit us to judge whether or not following the campaign on television was associated with certain partisan preferences—and with voting itself—independent of the demographics.

Following the Campaign on Television and Voting Choice

In the 1993 and 1995 surveys, both before and after the vote, people intending[53] to vote Communist were distinguished from others who said they were likely voters by their greater attention to televised coverage of the campaign, and this is quite independent of their demographics. Regardless of age, education, sex, or urban or rural residence, the Communist faithful were also unusually faithful consumers of television campaign coverage. This was consistent with the pattern of exceptionally high political media consumption that characterized Communist Party members from Soviet times forward.[54]

Communist Party leaders disdained paid political advertising on television. They refused to spend money on it, preferring to support local canvassing—organizing rallies, distributing leaflets, and fanning out to persuade ordinary people. Their structure of local organizations benefited from the experience of decades. Compared to them, other parties were all upstarts hurriedly forging thin organizations under the pressure of critical elections. For the convinced Communist electorate, attentive to the television campaign, a little coverage and a little free time went a long way. For challengers seeking to forge a new brand name and convert the passive or perplexed, the media mission was much harder. In December 1995, without television, the new pro-government party led by President Yeltsin's prime minister may not have been able to establish its trademark as well as it did, even if the outcome did not meet the (unrealistic) expectations of the party's leadership.

Permitting Controversial Positions on Television and Voting Choice

Likely Communist Party voters were much more willing than other voters, whatever their demographics, to respond negatively to allowing criticism of Lenin on the air and positively about televised advocacy of their party's monopoly power. After the 1995 parliamentary elections, which returned the Communists as the largest political party in the Duma, the four marker positions explained nearly one-third of the Communist Party vote.[55] Communist voters were decidedly against permitting the ethnic superiority, the legalization of prostitution, and the criticism of Lenin positions access to television and they strongly supported airtime for the advocacy of monopoly rule of their party. The table below shows the differences among parties, grouping together those of related tendencies. Communist Party adherents had a coherent, durable, and consistent pattern of attitudes.

Political analyst Igor Klyamkin was undoubtedly right in saying at that time: "Electors opted for [Vladimir Zhirinovsky's] LDPR, singling out of the torrent of its leader's words two ideas—the 'Russian' and the idea of authoritarian 'order.'"[56] On a number of questions about attitudes toward non-Russians, Zhirinovsky voters displayed an "aggressive nationalism."[57]

The election returns showed that strong support for Zhirinovsky came from Russia's border regions; five of the seven provinces casting more than one-third of the votes for Zhirinovsky's party faced foreign lands in the new post-Soviet world,[58] and these regions were particularly sensitive to the "ethnic question." In the presidential election of 1991, too, Zhirinovsky had run well in areas of Russia where ethnic tensions were high.[59] He did so again in the 1995 parliamentary elections, again picking up substantial support in Russia's Far East, and especially in economically depressed regions. It is not surprising that in the survey taken a week before the 1995 elections, Russians who said they would permit talk on television of inherent ethnic superiority were also significantly more likely to say they would

Party Type and Permitting Politically
Controversial Positions
Post-Election December 1995 (% voters)

		Democratic	Centrist	Nationalist	Communist
Criticism	yes	69	52	66	23
of Lenin	no	31	48	34	77
Communist monopoly	yes	11	12	13	62
rule	no	89	88	87	38
Legalized	yes	16	13	16	6
prostitution	no	84	87	84	94
Ethnic	yes	9	10	17	8
superiority	no	91	90	83	92

support candidates who favored a military solution to the Chechnya war—then a distinctly minority position.

Zhirinovsky was the most outspoken of such candidates, using his television time to advocate taking vengeance in Chechnya. Zhirinovsky was not prosecuted for these proposals, repeated on several different television channels, although it was noted as a violation of the law by the official monitoring body and passed along to the procurator general for possible action.

Caught in the dilemma of aiding Zhirinovsky by giving him still more publicity in a trial or aiding him by failing to prosecute, the government effectively chose the latter. In this way the worst outcomes of outlawing hate speech were achieved: the looseness of the statute's wording permitted intrusive governments to manipulate its provisions; public discourse by responsible officials was inhibited by the uncertainties of legal interpretation; and those who openly flouted the provisions of the law were hardly punished at all, and their continued flow of hate speech proceeded undiminished.

Following the Campaign on Television and Turnout

People who told interviewers before the election that they did not intend to vote and who later said they had not voted, no matter what their age, sex, education, or whether they lived in cities or in the countryside, were clearly distinguishable from potential voters by their extremely low attention to the televised electoral campaign.[60] In 1993 and 1995, nonvoters were far less likely to follow the campaign on television, quite apart from the fact that they were also less well educated and younger than the average voter.[61]

As in most countries, "lower social classes are disproportionately left out of the electorate,"[62] and these nonvoters were people likely to be more "socially rootless."[63] A 1996 U.S. study found nonvoters not particularly different from voters on questions of alienation (both were fairly mistrustful of government), but quite different in their calculation of the importance of their vote. Nonvoters, more than voters, thought their votes—and elections, too—did not make a difference. Nonvoters were also ill-informed about their choices.[64] In the United States, nonvoters receive much less information about electoral campaigns from television than do voters, and if they do not get that information on television they simply do not get it at all. "This reaffirms the pivotal role of television as *the* campaign medium."[65]

Thirty-two percent of the urban Russians interviewed in one survey said they made up their minds to vote because of media campaign programs.[66]

That figure came from the voters' self-assessment. Not all viewers consciously unraveled the varied, often unnoticed, influences on their decision to vote, but nonvoters definitely stayed away from the televised campaign.

At the opposite end of the range of turnout potential were the Communist voters. The particularly high attention paid to the television campaign by Communist voters suggests that this was, after all, still a highly mobilized part of the population. Communist Party voters were significantly more likely to belong to a political party than were other voters, and they still had their habit of consuming media output.[67] Older and more rural they were, but the Communists were still activists to be reckoned with and their propensity to vote made them a constituency not to be discounted.

The most revolutionary change made in campaign discourse came from Vladimir Zhirinovsky. His unexpected victory in 1993 made it legitimate to publicly espouse belligerent and exclusivist views of ethnicity. In the past, legal prohibitions on such speech had imposed a thin lid on public advocacy of what were usually called fascist views. It is telling that in the 1991 Russian presidential candidate debate, the extremist nationalist candidate, General Makashov, obliquely objected to Jews in Stalin's code word "cosmopolitan," contrasting them to "true" Russians. In the 1996 presidential campaign, Communist Viktor Anpilov, speaking much more plainly, was shown on the news calling for a purge of Jews from television. The feeble performances of Zhirinovsky's critics severely inhibited the presumed positive effect of the "marketplace of ideas." That he presented his views in the most fearful, anxious, and bellicose fashion was his innovative contribution to television's virtual monopoly of national campaign discourse. The flamboyant candidate fused public and private worlds, and made it possible to put on the public agenda what for years had been, by convention and law, off limits.

CHAPTER TEN

The Media Market:
Politics, Commerce, and
Press Freedom

When the official Soviet censorship agency was abolished, Communist Party monopoly rule removed, and pluralism in media ownership and content permitted, issues of press freedom in Russia began to resemble those of other countries. In other words, as direct political intervention receded (but certainly did not vanish), much of the conflict began to take place on the economic front. Politics and economics were tightly intertwined, but masked by a very nearly unregulated and economically crippled media system, still hostage to the legacy of over seventy years of information control. The institutions of the Soviet system had created pathways, and the footprints of the past were everywhere. Every Soviet regime had been obsessed with the mass media, beginning with Lenin's revolutionary use of newspapers to mobilize activists and radio to support his new order, and ending with Mikhail Gorbachev's bold and unpredictable media innovations. The regime's conviction that the mass media held the secret of mass persuasion could be seen in the very nuts and bolts of the rusting infrastructure left in post-Soviet Russia.

In every town there was a single television tower receiving signals from Moscow and adding some of their own. Rooftop antennas designed to pull down the signals were constructed to point *only* at the state-controlled broadcast tower. In the United States, typically, there are a number of transmitters in towns and cities all delivering signals to individual home receivers. In Soviet Russia by political choice and institutional design, that could not happen, and the nascent private television sector in post-Soviet Russia had either to use the transmission facilities of the government (with the attendant dangers to autonomy) or replace each antenna (at considerable capital investment under difficult economic conditions).

The capital-poor legacy of Soviet management also meant that the state could no longer afford the upkeep of its precious political asset, television. In the spring of 1994, the government budgeted only 25 percent of state television's needs.[1] With the withdrawal of state subsidies from these formerly "budgetary" organizations, many of the most prominent players in the rapidly privatizing media market spiraled quickly downward into worsening economic conditions. The hybrid private/public entity that soon emerged at state television combined the worst features of both. As for the other media, there was of course radio, but the political class had fixed its sights on television and the older electronic medium barely showed up on their radar, even though in 1994 prime-time state radio (still offering the most popular stations) had an impressive twenty-five-million-strong audience, and private stations had multiplied. That year, there were over thirty in Moscow alone. But politicians were not interested. Unlike their American counterparts, who had discovered the powerful new instrument of talk radio, Russian politicians and other opinion leaders concentrated on television, sometimes bribing their way to get on.[2] The national newspaper market simply collapsed.

TENSIONS IN THE NEWSPAPER MARKET

With the 1990 Law on the Press, the legal foundation was laid for the founding of print entities independent of state direction. By and large, these were paper transactions in which the newspaper brought together a group of "founders," who, together with the senior newspaper staff (but mainly its editor-in-chief) determined the policy and content of the paper. Existing assets were ordinarily simply claimed by those in charge.

In the beginning, "public organizations" and local government bodies, now adapting to the new system and diversifying their assets, were usually the founders. Until its disbandment, the Communist Youth League was one such organization, using its bank account, particularly at the local level, to convert to new activities. Local governing councils (soviets) were also active in gaining participation in new media enterprises (or conversions of old ones). The new "independent" media came about through declaration of a new mode of administration and, effectively, the seizure of assets. Investments were sought, but with a heavily state-owned economy, the monies had to come from the institutions that already had discretionary bank accounts for social programs. This permitted elites with initiative to adapt to change and convert their resources. On the output side, newspapers had to produce newsprint and distribute it to subscribers (most of the circulation was to subscribers).

Unfortunately, these stages of the newspaper economy had not undergone the same process of privatization; they were firmly in the hands of the state, particularly the printing presses and paper supply. It was impossible, the newspapers found out, to produce a paper simply with writers and editors sitting in newly appropriated offices. Further, the assets the new private entities claimed were often obsolete and required repair or replacement.

It is not surprising that the removal of subsidies affected the costs of newsprint and distribution services so dramatically, and threatened the survival of many of the most widely read newspapers. Many Russians regarded the sharp increase in charges as an ill-concealed plan for the state to curb the expression of speech which it had initially encouraged but which had exceeded its expectations. From 1990 to 1991, the price of newsprint escalated five to seven times. In 1992, the Moscow-published newspapers with the largest circulation in the former Soviet Union lost about eighteen million subscribers. *Pravda,* the flagship of the Soviet period, went from 10.5 million subscribers in 1985 to 337,000 at the end of 1993.

Other papers, particularly those that did bolder reporting, enjoyed peak circulation between 1988 and 1990 before rapidly declining later. The weekly *Argumenty i Fakty* (Arguments and Facts) was the leader, with over thirty-three million subscribers in 1990, but 5.5 million by 1994. The daily *Izvestia,* which struck out on an independent path, peaked at 10.4 million in 1988 (but was down to 435,500 in 1994), and the feisty *Komsomol Pravda,* at twenty-two million in 1990, was down to 871,000 in 1994.

Not a single major daily, including the ones that were not holdovers from the Soviet era, exceeded 1.5 million subscribers in 1993, and most were under a million.[3] By the summer of 1995, only four newspapers could properly be called "Russian" in the sense of a national circulation: *Trud* (Labor—the trade union paper), *Komsomol Pravda, Argumenty i Fakty,* and *AIDS-Info* (a paper devoted to erotic material and "oriented to young people who are most interested in sexual relationships"[4]). The rest were Moscow papers, with little distribution nationwide.[5]

The Moscow-based papers, too, were having difficulty: in the spring of 1995, two prestigious ones, *Nezavisimaya Gazeta* (Independent Newspaper) and *Kuranty* were announcing bankruptcy and looking for buyers, while large-scale banking and investment businesses were expanding their media empires. The decline of the central market aided the impressive development of the regional press, which, at the beginning of 1992, had pulled ahead of the central press in the preferences of Russians. Nevertheless, ahead of both was television.[6]

Advertising did not nearly cover operating costs, and although advertising did help to support press independence, it was far less available outside Moscow, thus leaving the provinces more in the grip of local political forces.[7] If subscriptions and advertising revenues did not adequately assure the operation of many of the newspapers, there were other ways. The most common strategy was to approach the government once again. Editors and publishers framed freedom of speech arguments in terms of demands for governmental grants to maintain their voices in the media market. In turn, with government subsidies sustaining large numbers of media organs, there were inevitable calls for oversight. After the October 1993 violence, Sergei Yushenkov, deputy chief of the Yeltsin government's media office, criticized what he considered flabby policies of the Press Ministry in granting aid to politically repugnant papers.[8] In sum, as might be expected, those who subsidized the pipers intended to call the tune.

Alternatively, some newspapers sought either private Russian investors (the MOST bank group brought out the newspaper *Segodnya* (Today), while *Nezavisimaya Gazeta,* together with the magazine *Ogonyok,* became part of the rapidly expanding media empire of industrialist Boris Berezovsky) or foreign partners. The latter often met with disappointing results, such as the Hearst organization's roller-coaster attempt to bring out *My* (We), a jointly produced *Izvestia* supplement. With the newspaper market in disarray, television was capturing more and more of the media market.

COMPETITION FROM THE PRIVATE SECTOR

Political pluralism within centrally controlled institutions is virtually oxymoronic—but not entirely. Such a counter-intuitive process had launched *glasnost* in 1985, but only in the spring of 1991 did the opening of Russian Television introduce the possibility of a genuinely competitive television system, in which fundamentally different political points of view would be disseminated from quite different institutional perspectives. The pro-Yeltsin and the pro-Gorbachev channels faced each other over a tense political divide. When the divide closed after the attempted coup of August 1991, both national television stations were in the hands of a single political leadership. Pluralism and press autonomy would be on a solid footing only when legally enforceable and predictably operating buffer arrangements were in place. Until that time, competition and diversity of political views were most likely to emerge from the workings of the market.

The state channels, though retaining a very significant national audience, increasingly faced an erosion of viewers in competition with the new private stations, particularly in Moscow, St. Petersburg, Ekaterinburg, and other lively local markets. All over Russia—in locales, in apartment buildings, in pockets of homes linked by cable—small television stations began popping up. By the spring of 1994, there were about two hundred of them in Moscow alone.[9] Local private television stations across Russia—broadcast and cable—soon outdrew the local state television system. At the end of 1994, some 38 percent of the viewers were watching programs from these new stations, as opposed to 17 percent who watched local state stations.[10] Overall, the number of choices for average Russians, though increasing, would take time to grow. In 1995, nearly three-quarters of the population could choose from three to five channels (broadcast and cable), and just over 1 percent had a choice of eight or more.[11]

Independent (nonstate) stations generated their capital initially from investments of "founders," just as newspapers did. Then they charged viewers subscription fees and advertisers airtime assessments. Beginning with mainly entertainment programming, some then added a modest local newsgathering capability. Audiences were often attracted to these small-scale stations by the prospect of seeing pirated Western films, mainly from the United States.

Jurassic Park was playing on Russian cable while it was still opening in movie theaters across the United States; a hand-held video camera version rapidly made its way onto the Russian small screen. At the annual film market in Voronezh, where television executives picked their programming, it was impossible to detect the provenance of the movies.[12] The central state-run channels and larger private stations usually made their deals directly with international distribution firms and observed rights protections, but the small, new companies often did not. A successful private station in Siberia was able to broadcast twenty-four hours a day and buy its own transmitter. In 1994, the owner of the station estimated that about one-third of his programs were pirated, down from 100 percent when it had started up, just a year before.[13] Pirating was certainly lucrative, and it is doubtful that the most impressive provincial success stories in Russia could have been achieved without it.

Russia finally signed the two principal international agreements protecting copyrights in 1994, but enforcement in the "Wild West" of regional arrangements was problematic. For Americans, it meant the collision of two aspects of foreign economic policy: protection of intellectual property rights and support of privatization. This flow of purchased and pirated American films and series on local and national television was part of what I term the "problem of America," and part of a larger syndrome of images and messages that had a profound impact on political life.

In Moscow, as the military gave up some of its many frequencies, new entrants in the media market appeared. CNN broadcast its international twenty-four-hour news in English to an expanding market that was limited by transmitter power and the adaptability of television sets.[14] Moscow viewers could also see private television on the 2X2 Channel, which used the Moscow city television channel's broadcast frequency. This channel included English-language news programs from CBS and Russian-dubbed news from the BBC in its programming. The new private ventures pierced the state monopoly and, depending on where they lived, gave viewers some real options.

Two ventures represented major moves on the part of former state-television officials and the will to take on the state system in head-to-head competition. Both were out to create something entirely new: national networks. On January 1, 1993, TV-6, the first independent broadcast television station in Russia, began operating under the direction of Eduard Sagalayev. "The era of monopoly TV, which lasted decades, is coming to an end," said a prominent television critic.[15] Sagalayev, who had been in charge of youth programming at Ostankino when Alexander Yakovlev and Mikhail Gorbachev began loosening the strictures of speech, received a license for a low-powered frequency released by the military.[16]

Sagalayev's shop at state television in Soviet times had launched the famous programs *Vzglyad* and *12th Floor,* and he began *TSN,* a CNN-like late-night news program, and *7 Days,* the news analysis program the Politburo closed down. At first, received by fewer than a million viewers (due to problems of transmitter power and television set adaptability), the new station, TV-6, expanded rapidly through the use of satellites and, by late 1993, reached some thirty million viewers in thirty cities of the former Soviet Union.[17] In 1995, about 85 percent of Moscow received TV-6, and it claimed it could reach more than seventy million potential viewers, in 168 cities in most of European Russia, Ukraine, the capital of Kazakhstan, the Baltics, the Urals, and parts of Siberia.[18] Actively promoting partnerships all across Russia, TV-6 was determined to build a network of affiliated stations, not owned and operated by TV-6, but joined by contract.

The TV-6 initiative began as a joint venture with the Turner Broadcasting System, but in 1994, Turner and TV-6 dissolved the partnership. It had been an uneasy marriage. The arrangement splitting ownership down the middle, with no majority partner, meant that neither side could take the lead in shaping the new station, and they were at cross-purposes about what it should be. Sagalayev parted with Turner when Russian mega-entrepreneur Boris Berezovsky became a new backer. This was a notable move away from dependence on foreign investors and foreign products to an indigenous enterprise developing its own programming capacity. After the separation from Turner, TV-6 sharpened its focus and image. It was to be a family-viewing network with strong roots in Russia, even the filmic Russia of the old Soviet black-and-white films it had begun to show with great success.

The second heavyweight entrant into the broadcast television market was NTV, led by Igor Malashenko, who had briefly run Channel One.

NTV set up shop first on the St. Petersburg channel, buying time for a few hours daily. The heavy backing of a big investor, Vladimir Gusinsky, made the difference. Cash-strapped, state-run St. Petersburg TV was eager to lease some airtime, so eager, in fact, that Malashenko confidently remarked that there was very little likelihood that his programs could be shut off. "We pay a lot to St. Petersburg TV; they need cash; that's why we won't get thrown off the air." Besides, there was a provision in the contract that if NTV was denied airtime, the station would be obligated to pay a substantial fine.[19] This temporary arrangement was soon superseded in 1994 when the prime-time hours of Channel Four, formerly the educational channel, were granted to NTV.[20]

Vyacheslav Bragin's rule at Ostankino had a direct effect on the creation of the new channel. Once again, some of the best talent on state television fled political pressure and censorship (and low salaries) by going over to another channel, this time one finally outside the boundaries of the state-owned system. Malashenko made Oleg Dobrodeyev, the respected head of news for Channel One, his news director and partner. He also brought over the immensely popular Evgeny Kiselyov, anchor of the Channel One weekly news analysis program *Itogi* (Results, or Wrap-up), and the well-known news anchors Tatyana Mitkova and Mikhail Osokin. While at state television, Kiselyov had made his Sunday evening show the single most popular news program in the country, and it was the drawing power of *Itogi* that enabled Ostankino to charge advertisers its top fee.[21]

Malashenko assembled an all-star team, and by the end of 1993, the new *Itogi* was outdrawing the competition in Moscow. NTV also began its own daily news show, *Segodnya* (Today) and broadcast a rich diet of attractive foreign and domestic films. At the time of its debut, newspaper critic Galina Chermenskaya thought the NTV formula unbeatable; it had "the combination of big capital . . . plus high professionalism, plus, one hopes, real independence."[22] By January 1995, NTV reported that it could reach a potential audience of seventy million viewers, extending from Belarus to the Urals and from Arkhangelsk to Belgorod and part of the Caucasus in the south. But this audience, like TV-6's, could be tapped only with improved receiving technology.[23] NTV had begun with a number of outlets: the educational channel in Moscow and its counterpart in a number of other locations. Building a network would require greater penetration and, like TV-6, NTV had to construct a system of local affiliates through partnerships with local private stations. Tapping the new technology, NTV also designed an array of direct-broadcast satellite channels, with backing from MOST and a new investor, the same governmental natural gas agency that was reputed to be considerably less financially generous as a board member at Channel One.

The popularity of NTV news shows roused critics to warn of an unhealthy nexus between commercial television and press freedom—a new issue for Russia. Majority partner Gusinsky and his MOST bank had enabled NTV to put up over thirty million dollars for its frequency.[24] A few months later, assets had grown to fifty million dollars.[25] Would the politics of Gusinsky now replace the policies of the government? NTV's leaders repeatedly asserted that the bank considered television the most important source of social stability, an environment vital to long-term economic health.[26] Not everyone was so comforted. As with many of the huge fortunes of the "new Russians," Vladimir Gusinsky's rise to prominence elicited suspicion and a flurry of conspiracy theories. NTV's spin in its news coverage was often ascribed to orders from Gusinsky, a supporter of Moscow mayor and, before they closed ranks in 1996, Yeltsin opponent Yury Luzhkov. On December 2, 1994, President Yeltsin's security guard attacked the heavily guarded headquarters of MOST Bank in Moscow, and Yeltsin's chief security man, Alexander Korzhakov, told a newspaper that he was interested in "goosehunting" (a play on Gusinsky's name).

The extent of Gusinsky's personal involvement in NTV and whether or not he secretly shaped news coverage was largely a matter of conjecture. According to Oleg Dobrodeyev, the person in charge of news at the station, the bank did not interfere with its coverage: "It is cheaper and better for them to do it on other channels. None of their investors was ever interviewed on NTV. Gusinsky knows our position."[27] Malashenko, president of NTV, identified Gusinsky's interest as the financial side of the station, and during the Chechnya conflict, when NTV came into its own as a major, even leading, news source, Gusinsky was in London.[28]

Gusinsky's probable distance from the content of his media properties was further supported by the independence that his newspaper *Segodnya* wielded in criticizing Kremlin economics, possibly costing MOST a great deal of future business. Like the NTV leadership, the newspaper people talked of their free hand in editorial content decisions.[29] Nonetheless, Gusinsky was a partner in NTV, and even from London was in close communication with the station. Evgeny Kiselyov said that on Fridays he discussed the content of *Itogi* with Gusinsky, whom he considered a partner and friend. The "big problems, like Chechnya" were discussed, and Kiselyov talked to him frequently while Gusinsky was in London and the Chechen conflict was at its height.[30]

In a remarkably brief time, NTV succeeded in creating a reputation among viewers: by mid-1994, 51 percent of those polled in the European part of Russia said that NTV programs were the most interesting; 35 percent said Channel One's programs were. Just two months earlier, the proportions had been reversed. In April 1994, of the six top-rated news programs, four were from NTV, one from Channel One, and one from Russian Television.[31] Some programs, like Channel One's *Field of Miracles* (the *Wheel of Fortune* lookalike), had great staying power.[32] Under new management after 1995, Channel One strengthened its entertainment programming, adding old and new movies and name-that-tune quiz shows, and its audience numbers improved. Technology helped: it was still the most widely available channel in the country. NTV was expanding, building a national network, but it would take time to develop the penetration of its older competitor. Then, too, NTV had two important features—it was deliberately elitist and it was uniquely trusted in times of crisis—that required a more critical look at the aggregate ratings numbers. From the beginning, the station's identity derived from its heavy fare of news and public affairs programs, done in Western style. There was little of the emotion and homey-ness of the other channels. Elite opinion-makers responded. If NTV attracted better educated viewers to its regular news coverage, during crisis that base broadened. At the height of the war in Chechnya, the ratings rose suddenly and substantially because of the trust and authority of NTV's news operation. This phenomenon suggests that, for NTV, much like CNN, there are peaks and valleys for average viewers and sustained, concentrated attention from heavy-consumption opinion leaders. NTV—like its unsmiling daily news anchor—demanded more of the audience.

BUFFERED POLITICS AND REGULATORY LAW

The government's inability to provide adequate subsidies led television stations to seek revenues in a new television market at first fragmented, then increasingly dominated by a few "new Russian" media barons, mainly bankers and industrialists. Relying for defense of pluralism on the declining fortunes of the government or the rising ones of a limited number of entrepreneurs was a precarious position. A more convincing and durable defense of pluralism would ultimately have to come from a consistently predictable and efficacious legal framework. A provisional commission on licensing could hardly handle the rapidly mushrooming new media outlets. It was estimated that by the fall of 1994, eight hundred broadcast entities were lined up seeking licenses, though many were already operating without them.[33]

The number of applicants was growing "not by the day, but by the hour," and they were competing for frequencies, especially around election time.[34] The provisional licensing commission was routinely bypassed by broadcasters and the political executive alike, and was replaced with another commission, pending the adoption of a broadcast law and still *another* commission to award licenses. (Two licenses were actually needed during this period of private television's development, and that greatly complicated life for the struggling new stations. One license authorized the frequency on which to broadcast, and the second gave the station the right to disseminate programs. Different bureaucracies, different processes, and cumbersome procedures made for many roadblocks along the way.)

The legacy of Soviet institutions again came into play: state-monopoly transmitters and communications satellites were often the only way to deliver signals. To make matters worse, rapidly climbing inflation resulted in repeated rate hikes the new media outlets could ill afford. That some of these increases were dictated by political interests is undeniable. Price breaks were routinely given to state television stations not only for satellite time, but also on import duties for the foreign-made equipment on which all stations depended.

A number of government agencies both helped and hindered the quest for press freedom. By decree, Boris Yeltsin introduced three controversial organs: the Judicial Chamber on Information Disputes (a successor to the Arbitration Tribunal set up for the December 1993 elections); the Committee for the Press (replacing, at nonministerial rank, the Press Ministry); and the Federal Television and Radio Service. The first was a kind of watchdog group appointed by the president to monitor the press and speak out on fairness in the media. The "court of public opinion" was its only forum. The Committee for the Press was far more problematic because it controlled government subsidies to newspapers (111.4 billion rubles, about $55 million, in the fall of 1994), an addiction without which many would have perished.[35]

The hand of the state was also present in the presidentially appointed Federal Radio and Television Service, which held both budgetary and personnel authority for the nearly ninety state-owned local television stations across the country. This body was to "coordinate broadcasting in the country and protect the interests of the viewing and listening public," in the words of Alexander Yakovlev, the veteran of *glasnost* who, for a while, was head of the Ostankino television company, and chairman of the board of both its new parent, ORT (Russian Public Television Company), and the new Federal Service, all while forming a political party for the upcoming parliamentary elections.[36]

The service had additional jurisdiction over the increasing numbers of private stations; some seven hundred were operating in Russia by the summer of 1995. According to Valentin Lazutkin, head of the service, his duty was to monitor conformity with license provisions and adjudicate competing claims to frequencies in the regions.[37]

The Press Law for Russia, published on February 8, 1992, continued to support the freedoms won earlier. It also included some troublesome articles that opened a Pandora's box of problems. The appointment of a censorship body was strictly forbidden, but certain kinds of speech were prohibited, expecially speech calling for:

- changing the existing constitutional structure by force
- arousal of religious differences
- social, class, or ethnic intolerance
- war propaganda

Vaguely worded and overly broad, these were significant exceptions to the removal of censorship. The ouster of Yegor Yakovlev was initially justified as a sanction for exacerbating ethnic intolerance. The vagueness of the law left room for a rash of defamation suits by public figures seeking to intimidate and stifle the press. Choppy waters were ahead for journalists. Vladimir Zhirinovsky alone was reported to have filed nearly one hundred lawsuits from late 1993 through the summer of 1994.[38]

Much time was spent on defining the prohibited categories of speech, for example, what "fascism" was in any given case and whether an individual really was a "fascist." As former reformist KGB chief Vadim Bakatin noted, "there is no precise definition of fascism" in the law and "not a single fascist party or organization considers itself fascist."[39]

War propaganda and hate speech prohibitions were more familiar in the European Convention on Human Rights than in American law, but given the characteristics of the Soviet system from which Russia was emerging, one wondered whether this was the most useful model to adopt. The vagueness of the law and underdeveloped legal institutions meant that guarantees of political pluralism were vulnerable, and it was not sufficiently appreciated that models of media regulation do not exist outside political and cultural contexts, and that a component of that context is the legal culture.

Culture, in general, was also at issue in television regulations. As in many other countries, quotas were in force for foreign programs. After the collapse of the Soviet Union, the dilemma for Russia was more acute than for its European neighbors, but basically similar. The French, the European Union, and others moved to support local values and local production through quotas. (Was this respect for indigenous, threatened cultures or economic protectionism for uncompetitive industries? Or probably both?) Canada's MAPLE system detailed every possible definition of what *national* meant, but erecting fences to safeguard "domestic" production and "domestic" content rarely kept the intruders out. American media giants were quick to invest in the European market, and the growth of the audience for direct-satellite-delivered programs threatened to overwhelm the Maginot-line rules.[40]

For some countries, at issue was not so much preserving local cultures but the quite different question of preserving oppressive censorship, which was more easily evaded with the new technology. Broadcasts of foreign origin so easily received by increasingly miniaturized dish antennas spelled problems for national censors in countries devoted to information control. The looming convergence of telephone and cable delivery systems and the rapid advance of the Internet created even greater problems for outmoded methods of censorship in the modern world. The government of Singapore's strict antipornography policy prescribed roaming randomly through the files of Internet users, but policing the Internet promised to be a Sisyphean task.[41] In still other countries a growing concern was a looming gap: in the new technology, some were starting late; would worldwide "redlining" create or perpetuate disparities? A South African official reminded the most industrialized countries that "the reality is that there are more telephone lines in Manhattan, New York, than in the sub-Saharan Africa."[42]

In this rapidly moving transitional period, global technology tended to overwhelm national barriers—mowing down censorship controls and local distinctiveness—and heightened the controversy over the very meaning of the nation-state. Was a nation a unique cultural and political collective worth preserving, or an obsolete and retrograde passing phase? Would information gatekeepers develop meaningful local products designed for local traditions and customs, not to mention languages? Who should rule on the values and practices to be protected? Should the channel-surfer be deprived of choice by paternalistic elites? For most of the world outside the United States, the target of the limitation was clear: the largest, most competitive producer of television content—the United States.

As technology developed, so did information politics, and it would be a mistake to think of the process as wholly technologically determined. As Jill Hills cogently pointed out, the race for technology was for economic advantage, and in Europe the concept of broadcasting as a public good, and therefore a place for the free market of opinions, gave way to a free market for advertisers; cultural bias gave way to economic bias.[43]

Opponents of government regulation pointed to the explosion of choice provided by digital delivery systems and argued that it was outmoded to protect viewers' access to programming alternatives. Added to this antiregulatory, technologically-based argument was the view of many in politics, from Helmut Kohl to Newt Gingrich, that the content of public-sector programming was biased and unrepresentative, and government should cease to fund it. These arguments supporting the elimination of regulation due to technologically expanded choice depended on a fairly robust economic system that could provide a wide range of choices, and access to the public. Once that choice was assured, whether the economics of the market would then follow a strict policy of profit-maximizing and excessive concentration and limit choice and access again was still a question, but not yet for the vast viewership of Russia. There, the choices were still limited and national values in great flux. (On Russian Independence Day, celebrated in June, it was common to hear people from all walks of life ask, "independence from what?") The market brought with it real problems for this culture, but the power to "protect" the medium in the underdeveloped legal system could also mean a return to the unwelcome hand of the state.

With overlapping jurisdictions of regulatory bodies, competition among the bureaucracies, and the very uneven application of vaguely worded laws, the security of broadcast autonomy was not most effectively lodged in the judiciary of post-Soviet Russia. Journalists were also increasingly at risk, not only in zones of conflict, but also at their desks. The death of a young investigative newspaper journalist who opened a booby-trapped suitcase in his office in the fall of 1994 was a warning to all that investigators of corruption were at risk. The murder of the country's most popular television personality, Vlad Listyev, shocked and sobered the country the following spring. The imperfect workings of the media market—rather than the law—very likely provided the best available guarantor of political pluralism.

THE DILEMMA OF STATE TELEVISION

Though initially limited in their viewership and program production capacity, the new stations did represent an outlet for political pluralism, helped to a considerable extent by the unprofessional administration of Channel One. In 1993, Vyacheslav Bragin had become so partisan and so devoted a micro-manager at Channel One that journalists attempting to uphold professional standards fled to the new broadcast options. But the problem was not only political. Ostankino, like the Russian economy in general, was in deep financial trouble. At the end of 1993 the channels attracting the majority of viewers, Channel One (Ostankino) and Channel Two (Russian Television), were state owned and state run. Politicians had fought over control ever since the first cracks of pluralism appeared after 1985, and Moscow went to war over Ostankino in 1993. These two channels, especially Channel One, were thought to hold the fate of the country, to save or lose Russia in election after election and in crisis after crisis. Television was still the obsession of the administration in power and its adversaries. That had not changed since the days when Mikhail Gorbachev, Yegor Ligachev, and Alexander Yakovlev discussed the medium with their fellow Politburo members at every meeting.

By the end of 1993, the government was doling out to Russian Television only 18 percent of what it needed to operate, and to Ostankino, about 25 percent. State television also owned and operated a huge network of local stations whose operating costs were enormous, in no small measure because of the drain of satellite transmission payments to the state monopoly Ministry of Communications. Employees of the distant Chita station near Lake Baikal had to turn off the radio transmitters serving eastern Siberia because no payment for their electricity bills was received from Moscow. As of June 1993, they were owed some four hundred million rubles.[44] By July 1993, Ostankino owed eight billion rubles in transmission costs, and by September 1994, state television owed its regional affiliates some 410 billion rubles.[45] In December 1993, transmitters in such regions as Kaliningrad in the west and Kamchatka in the north were turned off; communications ministry workers were demanding their wages, and the state television and radio companies were not paying.

In February 1994, half of the small screens in Russia went dark. Television was shut off from St. Petersburg to Sakhalin, at the extremity of the eleventh time zone: the striking communications workers had received no wages in several months.[46] Millions of viewers across the country were deprived of news and soap operas. This was not a trivial action. Television had become the principal informational lifeline and connection to the outside world for many now stranded in deprived communities. The crisis of newspapers had accelerated the public's dependence on television, so that as early as May 1991 some 83 percent of the Soviet Union's population named television as their principal source of news and information.[47] The relatively narrow, well-educated managerial class retained its interest in newspapers, but the rest of the status pyramid turned mainly to television.[48] Television was also the only affordable escape from the grinding conflicts of everyday life—it was free. Prime Minister Viktor Chernomyrdin stepped in to order the finance ministry to pay the overdue wages.

Budget cuts were having an effect on news reporting. Channel One began closing foreign news bureaus to save money, as did the U.S. networks in the 1980s, and like the U.S. networks, Russian state television began to rely on purchased footage much more than it had in the past. Under such conditions the contribution of a station lies in what an anchor narrates while the tape rolls, but the local angle, the specific cultural meaning of a story, depends on the construction of the visuals and the probing of interviewers, and that was often absent. An all-purpose product from an international vendor rarely succeeds in speaking to the nation, especially about a civil war on its own territory. As politics enabled television to speak more freely, economics was putting it on an "information diet." In 1993, in what television people increasingly began to recall as the glory days under Brezhnev's television dictator Sergei Lapin, television was handsomly financed by the state. (Yes, freedom of expression was severely limited, but he certainly understood production values and the money was there.) Like other favored enterprises in the planned economy, television then had absolutely no incentives to maximize labor productivity or effect savings in any department. As a result, the television labor force grew until it was a bloated giant. Massive layoffs were in store.[49]

The Russian president's solution was the "privatization" of Ostankino Television in 1995. Ostankino was transformed into ORT (Public Radio and Television Broadcasting). Fifty-one percent of its shares was owned by various government agencies, including components of the television system. That left 49 percent of the stock of the new public television entity in the hands of the biggest banks and industrial giants. The largest single shareholder (at 8 percent) of this group was Boris Berezovsky, head of LogoVaz, an industrial conglomerate. Berezovsky was also the major investor in TV-6. His investment in ORT earned him a top slot in the organization's board of directors and a commanding influence on the station, as well as the burden of raising money. By the spring of 1996, the majority-shareholder Russian government was supplying about only $30 million a year to cover $220 million of expenses.

To launch the new concept, the operational head of television (the general director) was to be Vlad Listyev, an alumnus of the old *Vzglyad* team. Since those early days on the bold late-night show he had gone on to copy the American game show *Wheel of Fortune* by making it into the hit show *Field of Miracles,* and then, suspenders and all, to copy Larry King on the popular *Chas Pik* (Rush Hour). In between, he had started the highly regarded political talk show *Theme.*

Overseeing the operation was a board of trustees, with President Yeltsin as its chairman and the speaker of the State Duma as his deputy. The arrangement separated airtime from program production. ORT controlled the former; Ostankino was reduced to production. Only news production was transported into the new ORT, and the government intended special treatment for it. Gennady Shipitko, then head of news and information, remarked that the government had an interest in three types of programs in particular: news, children's programs, and culture. If the government provided the budgets for them, it "can influence the content."[50] As for the private sector's expectations, one of the investors, the Inkombank, issued a statement that naturally they wished to help "our television to survive and develop." How easily that would be done was less clear. The bank's statement went on to describe a preparatory meeting Ostankino held for the major (specially invited) potential stockholders, and Inkombank concluded that "already at that preparatory meeting it was understood how contradictory were the desires and the intentions of the potential stockholders."[51]

There was division among the oligarchs and Inkombank pulled out soon after the organizational meeting.[52] A year later all of them had dropped out, with the exception of Berezovsky, two banks, and the government's natural gas monopoly agency.[53] Berezovsky himself left in the fall of 1996 to join

Boris Yeltsin's administration. State television's unstable transformations began with Mikhail Gorbachev's *glasnost*. Before, Sergei Lapin had ruled television for sixteen years; afterward, the average time in office as head of Channel One was 1.4 years. As state television cycled through different variants of funding and administration, its days of monopoly were over.

State television had become a hybrid of commercial and governmental interests. Private investors looked to make programs pay dividends. The government maintained its interest in news and public affairs and interfered as it thought necessary. The result was neither the public interest focus of noncommercial television nor the independence of commercial television.

ADVERTISING, OPEN AND HIDDEN

Though downsizing was clearly in order, it would not solve the deep financial problems. Revenues from the new private sector had to supplement the state's declining contribution. Advertising was the most logical step, and what had been a very limited effort soon mushroomed. During the decades of Soviet rule advertising was extremely limited: since the planned economy had been substituted for the market, advertising—a bourgeois machine to manufacture unnecessary wants—presumably had no place. The few exceptions to the rule were limited ad campaigns to guide distribution systems gone awry and alert consumers to oversupplies of time-constrained products.

Channel One ran its first ads in 1988. Television officials, at the time unaware of the potential importance of advertising, made no attempt to regulate the process or, even more serious, ensure its receipt of revenues. Only when the business had burgeoned and become indispensable to a badly starved state television sector did Ostankino's leaders attempt to assert control, which then proved illusory: ads were multiplying. In the eight months from February to October 1993, adtime on Channel One increased by 83 percent.[54] By 1995, both newspapers and television companies derived from 30 to 50 percent of their budgets from advertising.[55] Valentin Lazutkin, head of the Federal Radio and Television Service, said that before Vlad Listyev's death there were as many commercials on state television as on commercial television.[56]

The ratings system, an essential element of the media market, was fraught with difficulty in terms of reliability and in the degree to which it did—or should—guide programming decisions. Ratings in the U.S. television industry are the station's vital link to the advertising market on which it depends. Through ratings, potential viewers are "sold" to advertisers, and as the ratings systems gained in sophistication, increasingly detailed characteristics of viewers could be targeted.

The existence of the market and the availability of consumer products for which demand exists or can be created are essential, and this took surprisingly little time to develop in Russia. But how to gauge viewing habits, which would presumably drive advertising revenues, was not simple. Foreign firms—the British branch of the American Gallup organization and the French Médiamétrie—were providing information for foreign advertisers in Russia early. Domestic operations sprang up, but there were difficulties: telephone surveys were effective only where near-universal service was available (such as in Moscow); reliability of diary-type surveys asking viewers to pencil in television channels watched in each fifteen-minute time slot suffered from a general lack of awareness of the channel (as opposed to the program). Asking about programs required large numbers of individually tailored diaries, since program choices varied so greatly across the country. The precipitous rise of crime made conditions for face-to-face surveys more problematic, even though middle-aged and elderly women were the unthreatening interviewers. As sociologist Vsevolod Vilchek noted, at the beginning of 1995 some 40 percent of the people he randomly chose for interviews refused, as compared to only 10 percent in the past.[57] A Nielsen-type box transmitting information directly from a television set required foreign capital investment, which was in short supply at the beginning of the advertising market, and, for some Russians, evoked old fears of daily domestic life overheard by the listening devices of an oppressive state power.

In the post-Soviet advertising market, as in the economy in general, perceptions of corruption were so intense that ratings were widely believed to be manipulated.[58] The independence of companies providing ratings had to be proved, not merely asserted. At the end of May 1996, the Russian National Association of Broadcasters (Eduard Sagalayev was its first president) took a step toward minimum uniform criteria for ratings by gaining the agreement of forty television companies, fifteen advertising agencies, and fourteen polling firms to abide by a set of research standards.[59]

But the *function* of ratings continued to agitate Moscow intellectuals. Long accustomed to regarding television as the supplier of programming disseminating the nation's traditional culture, they wondered if the lowest common denominator should govern choice. Vsevolod Vilchek believed that ratings should not drive programming, but should be "corrected" by the judgments of experts.[60] Could the public adequately identify and serve its own interest? Should the state guarantee what the market failed to provide? Ratings began to show that the people who guided state television had been out of touch with their audiences. The choice of programs reflected the preferences of the television company but not the public, on whom many of the broadcast officials still did not consider themselves dependent. Sixty percent of the nonnews Channel One schedule was watched by an audience of less than 4 percent of the population.[61] The new chiefs of the reorganized Channel One quickly moved to drop nearly fifty programs and establish expectations about ratings for all nonnews time slots.

Viewers preferred serials first (especially imported soap operas), then movies, then news, then entertainment, such as game shows, musical programs, sports, and talk shows. Leading the top ten programs in Russia at the time of the December 1993 elections were an American soap opera *Santa Barbara, Field of Miracles,* and a Mexican soap opera, *Just Maria.*[62] The soap operas were so popular that in 1993, when asked to name the most important events of the year before, Russians put as fourth the televised Mexican soap opera, *The Rich Also Cry* (just after the freeing of prices, issuance of vouchers, and indexation of incomes).[63] The soap opera fascination continued as one serial replaced another, as Mexico's *Wild Rose* followed *Just Maria* in the public's preferences. Feature films continued to attract large audiences, as did talk shows such as *Theme,* especially when Vlad Listyev hosted it.

In news and public affairs Russians were turning inward after the Soviet period. Before Gorbachev, international news and coverage of foreign affairs had always been first in their preferences.[64] In part that was the result of official concentration on the foreign threat—and curiosity about the forbidden fruit. Perhaps in larger part, it reflected viewers' dissatisfaction with the lacquered uninformative coverage of domestic affairs. Later, preoccupied by volatile economic and political conditions, news of Russia claimed first place in viewer interest, and foreign news and Russian foreign policy stories were at the bottom of the scale.[65] News and public affairs programs continued to float near, but not at, the top of viewer preferences.

The clash of commerce and public interest, of new values and old, of foreign and national images all became part of the post-Soviet ratings debate. With still limited choice among channels and offerings, whose values should be paramount? How could the emerging Russian national identity be detected in the plethora of foreign-made television shows? Because of budgetary constraints the television stations could at first only afford the cheapest imports, and, as a noted television critic said, "'. . . in the global space we are entering by the back door.'"[66]

The dramatic and sudden change from Communist Party-ruled, standardized television to one in which commerce, ratings, and advertising were ubiquitous and, moreover, looked and sounded like the culture of the United States, was unsettling. In a very few years, the look, tempo, and function of the most powerful medium had been transformed. But the onslaught of the new images and pounding beats was not always welcome and was often confusing. In some ways the new market approach that television trumpeted in its programs, but even more in its advertising spots, represented a new type of propaganda for an exhausted public. Snickers, the American-made candy bar, soon came to symbolize the "problem of America"—the overwhelming dominance of U.S. commerce and values in a country attempting to sort out the meaning of the loss of great-power status. (But it was also a more affordable piece of the dream of a prosperous future than many other blandishments hawked on television.)

In the spring of 1994, the deputy chief of Channel One remarked, "it is annoying that Russian television is beginning to speak primarily in English."[67] Others there thought airtime and investment should be redirected from programs about America to programs about "the lives of miners, metallurgy workers, farmers, and teachers," and go into the depths of Russia's territory to tell the story of "how people live there."[68] On this, Yeltsin loyalist Vyacheslav Bragin would have agreed with Communist Party leader Gennady Zyuganov, who, during the 1996 presidential campaign, said he was for national television channels "where citizens of the country can see how a miner from Kuzbas, a fisherman from the Far East, or a peasant from Kaluga lives and breathes."[69] Even the head of Channel One, Sergei Blagovolin, who, with his powerful board member industrialist Boris Berezovsky, had a close association with Western news corporations, said in the spring of 1995 that "we want more of *our* films" on television. There's a danger, he said, when one's own culture disappears, and he intended to right the balance to something like 50 percent foreign and 50 percent domestic from what he estimated was 80 to 90 percent foreign and 10 percent domestic.[70] The Communists wanted to go further. Their 1996 platform had a plank restricting foreign-made entertainment programming to no more than 20 percent of the schedule.[71]

Vyacheslav Bragin, looking back on his direction of Channel One from the vantage point of 1995, questioned who would provide for the "education of the coming generation, the revival of Russia, its spirituality?"[72] The channel was no longer an expression of national priorities, and the public would be moved to make it different. "Whoever reconstructs television," Bragin said, "will never make peace with this." He had tried to reform television, to take off American and Latin American soap operas—"this nonsense" (*chepukha*). "We are a great country," he said. "We have our own programs. If they hadn't overthrown us, we could have made national Russian television."[73] Communist Party Leader Gennady Zyuganov, during the 1996 election campaign, was more negative about the "'endless killings, destruction, violence, quasi pornography, and rudeness. All this together destroys the psyche, especially of children. This is a completely Americanized type of TV, its worst variant.'"[74]

Vyacheslav Bragin could not decree a return to national values, but, to a certain degree, the surfeit of low-quality Western products did so. Old Soviet films, even the ones in black-and-white, with their sentimentality and echoes of a vanished fantasy, steadily gained on, and in many cases outdrew, the American competition on state and private television.[75] When asked to express agreement or disagreement with the statement, "Old Soviet films are not in accord with today's life; on the television screen they often seem false and lying," people in Moscow overwhelmingly disagreed (64 percent to 18 percent, with the rest not answering).[76] As new Russian-made soap operas and series came on line, they began to challenge the dominance of the foreign product. A March 1996 Moscow survey saw *St. Petersburg Secrets* (on Channel Two) outdrawing the American-made *Dynasty*. Russian mini-series had also placed first in January and February; viewers preferred the setting and familiar accents. That spring 60 percent of the films shown on Channel One were Russian, but most of the new films were foreign ones.[77]

Mixed up in this confusion of images and advertising were the shreds of a grandeur many had known at the time to be hollow, but in retrospect acquired density. As a late-1993 article in the main Russian television guide complained:

> We hated the evil empire. However, in this evil there was greatness. Deformed, but there was. And now in this same arena that spilled the blood of gladiators and viewers, as in a madhouse, soap operas thunder like crazy . . . Finally we ran up against what we fought. We reached capitalism. The way we did it turned out to be deadly boring. And I know why. The private detective Mike Hammer, hardboiled man, pronounces as the curtain comes down, the stunning American saying: "You get no greater satisfaction than knowing that your ass belongs to you."
> In our borrowed garbage of Columbia Pictures not even this part of the body belongs to us.[78]

Russian national identity and culture were still fragile, and change was unexpectedly drastic and confusing. Democratization and the market arrived with a suddenness and scope that were entirely new, and much of it looked American. A 1994 study of ads running on Channel One found that fully 67 percent were for foreign products.[79] For those able to benefit, the future was a welcome replacement of the straitjacketed past. For those unable to benefit, the new ways seemed to be expressed in imposed trappings. And there were certainly those who did personally benefit but found themselves in an alien culture, having lost the status of a superpower.

When the European Union gave money to start a television program on Channel One called *Window Onto Europe,* it was greeted by one television critic as a welcome "counterweight to the wave of American influence on our television."[80] The host Dmitry Kiseleyov, of the old, reform-minded *TSN* news team, remarked, "We want to show that the orientation to America, to American culture, to American dollars, to the American dream is not completely natural for Russia. Russia was always together with Europe and not with America."[81]

As chapter 8 showed, the *forms* of political advertising adopted by the candidates in December 1993 differed quite substantially, and Vladimir

Zhirinovsky clearly made the strategically correct choice—for his constituency—in utilizing political advertising but making sure that it did not appear to relate to product advertising. He deliberately eschewed the rapid tempos, jump cuts, rock music, and modern graphics so characteristic of Western-oriented product advertising and opted, instead, for simple homilies of a spontaneous, personalized, and traditional type, in a setting of little artifice.[82]

Campaigning for taking Snickers' ads off the air, Zhirinovsky understood that the context of advertising and its appeal to a U.S.-inspired market ideal with particular cultural dimensions had sharply divided generations and social strata. In 1993, the Mars company so overwhelmingly dominated the field of candy advertising on television (taking up 87 percent of all adtime for sweets, down a year later to 63 percent because of a very aggressive Cadbury campaign), that one observer remarked, "It is not by accident [*nedarom*] that Snickers and Mars entered into folklore and that communists frightened us with the attack of well-armed Snickers."[83] The Snickers campaign had been formidable. According to a U.K. Gallup poll, only 5 percent of Russians knew the Snickers name, but a year later, after the marketing campaign, 82 percent recalled the brand.[84]

Ads were particularly appreciated by children. One-third of all children under eight and 20 percent of young Russians from eight to seventeen "enthusiastically" watched all ads that came on while they were watching television, a February 1993 survey showed. Predictably, the most popular were for Snickers, Mars, and Bounty candy bars, and chewing gum. But also among the top ten were Camel cigarettes, Coca Cola, and Pepsi Cola. (Rasputin and Smirnoff vodkas emerged after the top twenty.)[85] Alcohol and tobacco advertising on radio and television was later banned, causing some to protest damaging state interference in the advertising market so essential to private television, but others supported the protection of a vulnerable population of young people hooked on ads.

When the product advertised was an investment firm, the problems were magnified. What should viewers do with their privatization vouchers at a time of spiraling inflation? Where should they (quickly) put their increasingly worthless savings? The MMM investment firm, a paper pyramid scheme that collapsed in 1994, had an offer with which it saturated the airwaves. These ads, by "Russia's chief advertiser," were the most frequently broadcast and the most watched on television; some 2,666 spots aired in March, April, and May 1994.[86] They held out the prospect of huge annual dividends, vacations in California, and apartments in Paris. A share bought in February 1994 for 1,600 rubles fetched 81,800 rubles in August of that year, according to MMM's ads.[87]

In the wake of the MMM debacle, the Russian government and later the parliament issued regulatory edicts about false and misleading advertising.[88]

State television was largely responsible for the name recognition and financial success of a dubious enterprise against which the government of the same state had repeatedly warned the public. The straitened circumstances of the media, both print and electronic, meant that when paid in advance by MMM to run its ads, the money was soon spent. When MMM came back on the air in 1995, its chief had gained the immunity that came with his election to parliament and the ads no longer made explicit promises.[89] They did continue to show images of high living and seductive wealth, but, alluring though they were, they did not engage in false and misleading statements. Russian investment companies were such heavy advertisers—being the leading domestic product advertised—that their domino bankruptcies deprived the stations of much needed income and exacerbated the problems faced by the growing private sector. Advertising from these investment firms accounted for 25 to 30 percent of the budgets of all television companies.[90]

The introduction of product advertising also created new, mainly unregulated, channels for the acquisition of influence in the television world. Program production companies and advertisers concluded their own agreements and then the production companies gained airtime on state television, which saw very little of the advertising revenue. In mid-1993, Channel One said it ran only nineteen minutes of advertising a day. However, a study of programming showed about one hundred minutes of advertising during the day. Estimated at the lowest rate, that produced a revenue flow of at least sixty to seventy-five billion rubles annually,[91] but a government audit found that Ostankino received only 11.2 billion rubles of it.[92]

These figures related only to *overt* advertising. Much more television airtime was bought by private parties, but it was extremely difficult to identify. Sometimes "sponsors" paid for programs; sometimes they were identified, sometimes not. Alexander Tikhomirov's program on Channel One was financed by his friends.[93] In addition to "sponsors," advertising sources included people who bought favors from state television. Bribery and payola made this a dangerous game. Vlad Listyev's murder was probably related to these corrupt practices, and earlier, the head of music programs at Channel One, V. M. Kruzhiyamsky, had his skull crushed with a brick. A head of music programming at Russian Television said the big pop stars were tied to organized crime pushing bribes to have videos shown.[94] On a gala New Year's Eve show on Channel One, a man in a red jacket appeared on-screen, standing next to President Yeltsin. He had reportedly paid the official advertising rate for a minute, fifteen million rubles, and an additional bribe.[95]

Sometimes covert advertising bought newspeople, a practice much more damaging to the viewing public. Eduard Sagalayev termed it "jeans television"; television journalists were bribed to report stories favorable to a

business, product, or political figure.[96] At the beginning of 1993 it was estimated that some 82 percent of all television airtime had been sold or "ordered" by interested parties. Sergei Yushenkov, when he was the deputy
head of the media oversight Federal Information Center, remarked that
there were no independent journalists; they all had "sponsors," only some
admitted it and some didn't.[97]

The deputy head of Channel One at the beginning of 1995 agreed in
part with this negative assessment. Gennady Shipitko said that in the
"global sense" news was free from commercial interests; it was not official
policy. If, as he put it, most stories are the result of daily planned news
agendas, then there was little room for unplanned puff pieces for private
buyers. He maintained that "corruption did not define the broadcasts" and
"did not define objectivity." That said, Shipitko also acknowledged that "in
individual stories, there can be perhaps commercial influence, corruption,"
but it was the individual correspondent, not the channel, who sold news
stories to commercial interests.

His example suggested that even in centrally planned news stories, such
as legislative coverage, there was room for corruption. In the past, he said,
State Duma deputies "paid to be shown on television." Basically, Shipitko
concluded, it was simply not possible to control the correspondents' hidden
ads, and, unfortunately, they were driven to corruption because they were
paid "miserable wages."[98]

At private NTV, news director Oleg Dobrodeyev told a different story.
Out of hand, he rejected the notion that hidden ads might have appeared
on the private station's news programs, where correspondents were paid
much more than at state television. When asked how he could detect the
hidden purchase of news, he replied categorically, "It's as clear as black and
white to a professional." Did his reporters ever turn in paid stories? "Yes,"
he replied tersely, "one, and he was fired."[99]

Effectively, state television was operating in large part on an unregulated
and partially concealed commercial basis within a state-owned framework.
Each head of Ostankino in post-Soviet Russia, from Yegor Yakovlev to
Alexander Yakovlev, attempted to take control of the situation, stamp out
corruption, and centralize advertising in all its forms. Network presidents
found it difficult to bring to heel the increasingly freewheeling, almost elemental abandon with which the departments and subdepartments of the financially strapped institution sought funds. A minuscule fraction of these
revenues went to support the institution of government television.

Channel One tried creating an agency to handle its advertising and develop new rates based on program popularity, but the venture, *Reklama-
Holding,* had no leverage over the big program production companies who
preferred to keep things as they were. Though reducing the scope of corruption by some, the centralized agency appeared to have introduced its

was squirreling away eight thousand of every twelve thousand dollars of airtime it sold.[100] When state television was restructured as a public/private partnership (Russian Public Television–ORT), it temporarily suspended advertising altogether, throwing the advertising market into a transient tailspin. It then concluded its own deal to sell its airtime through the largest advertising firm, which was working both for itself and for Channel One. (The conflict of interest did not go unnoticed, just untouched.) By separating production companies from control over airtime, the new majority-state company began to resemble Western television companies more, but how truly that business approximated a market with reasonably open access to competition remained, at this stage, problematic. Very few players dominated this game.

In the quest for financial independence, the notion of reinstating a subscription or license fee was frequently advanced. There had been subscription fees until 1962, when they were abandoned in favor of a value-added tax on television sets. Some people were obviously willing to pay for subscribing to the new cable systems, but for many, especially the elderly (for whom television had the most important social function), incomes were so inelastic as to preclude the possibility of even token fees.

A second argument calling into question the utility of subscription fees related to the extraordinary importance national television had achieved in the turbulent and anxiety-ridden life of the new Russia. As the only institution reaching most people, and as the main source of information helping to make an unpredictable and often threatening everyday reality intelligible, television performed a social and political role that few, if any, institutions could duplicate. No government or contender for power wished to deprive itself of this asset. None considered it desirable to risk a "social explosion" by pricing the free good out of reach.

In post-Soviet Russia the state could no longer afford the rich offerings the old, luxuriously budgeted television industry produced. As it turned into a public/private hybrid full of internal contradictions and tensions, a fully private sector came into being. The rise of a real television market through advertising and private investment provided the foundation on which to achieve more pluralized programming, and even though this pluralism was tainted by the pervasive corruption that affected other sectors of Russian society, the fact remained that alternative channels and alternative views of the news finally became possible.

During the war in Chechnya—a most critical juncture in the political life of the country and the fortunes of its president—it was that private sector that told the truth most effectively and most visually. The course of pluralization was by no means a smooth one, and fateful elections pressured the fragile system, but in the period of uncertain rule-making and rule-application, without an alternative structure or sources of funding, it would application, without an alternative structure or sources of funding, it would have been nearly impossible. Yes, a judicial system that enforced a buffer arrangement to assure press autonomy from the state and a widely accepted canon of journalism that defended the news from commercial intrusiveness were certainly desirable, though not yet in place. The wobbly Russian market supported a great deal of change in post-Soviet years, and its achievement in information reform must be counted as a major break with the past.

CHAPTER ELEVEN

Television at War:
Private Television News
Under Fire

In August 1991 Dzhokhar Dudayev, a Soviet Air Force general, came home from his post in Estonia. He was one of the most prominent sons of Chechnya, but not the only one. Ruslan Khasbulatov, his fellow countryman, had higher ambitions—to lead all of Russia—but that would come two years later. Dzhokhar Dudayev came back to Chechnya when its last Communist Party leader, Doku Zavgayev, was overthrown (a political housecleaning given tacit support by Boris Yeltsin). Dudayev had been invited, without a proper election, to be president by one of the contesting Chechen factions.

As Soviet power crumbled, the army beat a hasty retreat, leaving behind storehouses of weapons. Chechnya, a fierce foe in tsarist times, had been subdued but never truly pacified, and its ritual, warlike spirit was never extinguished. It was also an oil-rich province that was especially important for oil refining and was a strategic railroad node for Russia. At the end of the Soviet Union, Chechnya was on the likely route for an important oil pipeline, though other potential routes had also come into play.

Chechnya was not a foreign province or department. Russian was its language; before the war over a third of the population were Russian, and Russians made up around three-quarters of the population of the capital city, Grozny. The central government building in Grozny, what came to be known as Dudayev's palace, looked like a copy of the White House in Moscow—the familiar Soviet-style architecture seeded all across the country and a display of the once highly centralized political system. So what was happening in Chechnya was not happening in a far-off exotic land, but in the Russian Federation itself.

When Dudayev returned, the process of sovereignty-grabbing had been playing out all over the former Soviet Union. Dudayev sought the same for his republic. His notion of president brooked no opposition, and he dissolved the elected Chechen parliament in the spring of 1993. From then on, local opposition groups clashed repeatedly with Dudayev and each other. Some were large-scale: in June 1993, supporters of the dissolved parliament fought with Dudayev's guard in Grozny and fifty people were killed. The fault lines in the opposition were in part based on tribe and geography—plains Chechens versus the highlands Chechens—and in part on the old, familiar, but deadly jockeying for power of competing bases of power, such as the chief of Dudayev's praetorian guard, who went after power himself.

One pretender, especially, provided what appeared to be a promising opening for Russia, which began asserting in the spring of 1994, after much indifferent behavior, that Chechnya had gained too much autonomy. Umar Avturkhanov set up a "provisional council" in the village of Znamenskoye, near the border. He asked for and received substantial support from Russia. It must have seemed an easy call for Russia: Dudayev was opposed in bloody strife by his former cronies, by Khasbulatov, and now by a rival government. Znamenskoye would be a corridor through which Russian troops could easily and rapidly overpower what to them might have seemed the shaky regime of a fantasy-ridden, bantam dictator.

During the three years before, Moscow did very little to crack the wall of Dudayev's sovereignty after a failed military expedition in 1991 and stood by while human rights in Chechnya were routinely violated in the most flagrant way. Moscow did not collect taxes or otherwise assert its rights vis-à-vis what it continued to regard as a constituent unit, even though in December 1993, when a new constitution was adopted, the Chechen "foreign ministry" declared: "'The Chechen state recognizes only the constitution of its own country.'"[1] Lawlessness, gun-running, money-laundering, and granting asylum to gang leaders made Chechnya a refuge for crime. Investigations would later show that the gun and oil trade Dudayev lived on had likely allies in Russia itself.

In November 1994, the opposition mounted an unsuccessful attack on Grozny, supported "unofficially" by Russian troops, several of whom were captured and returned to Russia. It appeared the covert war to destabilize the Dudayev regime was not going to work. Even after Dudayev's death in 1996, the Chechen war dragged on, piling up casualties and civilian destruction.

USED GOODS: OFFICIAL TELEVISION POLICY

What was also not going to work, though the Russian government deceived itself on this too, was the habitual control of information, and presumably of public opinion. The open conflict in Chechnya that began in mid-December 1994 had a striking unintended effect: it finally spelled the end of the Soviet media system. The war propelled forward an institutional change of considerable magnitude, because for the first time the private sector had deep enough roots to withstand, during a crisis, the winds of official displeasure. Chechnya *made* NTV, but only because NTV's leadership knew what to do. For the mass public, this combination of crisis and leadership legitimized the private news source, which also played a key role in setting the agenda for the political elites. With a hostile Russian government threatening to take away their license on virtually any pretext, and right-wing parliamentarians, including Vladimir Zhirinovsky, enraged by its "lack of patriotism," NTV got it right. It is an extraordinary tale of the gradual development of institutional autonomy in a new institutional environment, as well as of the guidance of unusual individuals.

There was no doubt that television was *the* medium for coverage of this war and that ordinary Russians were deeply attentive. In Moscow polls four-fifths of all people interviewed said that they were following the events in Chechnya.[2] When asked which sources of information they used, they named the three top television stations (Channel One, Two, and NTV) far ahead of the other media. Only half as many named the largest newspapers, and the most popular radio choice was given by two-thirds as many. Even in the provinces, people got their news about Chechnya from Moscow television first, then radio, and only then newspapers.[3]

The Russian government was stuck in a previous information age and the illusion of information control. Igor Malashenko, president of NTV, said, "'Our politicians thought this would be like Afghanistan . . . They didn't take the media into account.'"[4] In the Afghan war there was censorship of materials, and the state controlled television. Strict military censorship of the news was exercised and journalists from Moscow were both dependent on and sympathetic with their military companions in the field.[5]

In the Chechen war, the government once again produced its own information, but was slow to get moving and unprepared for the new competitive information market. Just as the combat operation appeared to have been launched in haste, so was the information campaign. A special information center was set up (late—one week into the operation) and its handouts were woefully thin and few. The paucity of information left even the most dedicated supporters of government policy, such as Gennady Shipitko, then news director of state television Channel One, helpless to perform their duties.[6] The government's behavior was familiar from decades past, but the structural basis for it had decisively changed. There was now an institutionalized television autonomy resting on the private sector and prepared to exploit open divisions within the elite for its newsgathering, including the highest ranks of the armed forces themselves.

Government handouts were now only part of the information universe ordinary Russians and Moscow elites could access. The most professional and successful news was produced by NTV. Well in advance of other news organs, it had made up several teams of reporters and cameramen and sent them to Chechnya when trouble was brewing before the official invasion was launched. When the war broke out, NTV was there reporting from the front and sending back pictures from neighboring regions.

The stage was now set for the news battle at home. All television stations covered the war at length as their top story.[7] Because they did not believe in counter-programming for the news, the big Moscow-based stations staggered their evening news programs. The public was clearly the winner in this, as they could watch NTV news at 7:00 P.M., *Vesti* (Channel Two) at 8:00 P.M., *Vremya* (Channel One) at 9:00 P.M., and the late NTV news again at 10:00 P.M. Russians could judge both whether the official reports matched the news from the front and whether the new phenomenon of private television deserved their trust in competition with the older, state-supported organizations. The extraordinary drama of deadly conflict and the graphic unfolding of the end of the myth of the Red Army marked a watershed.

The Yeltsin government's information policy made three costly mistakes: it relied on assertions that now could be disapproved from location; it brought pressure to bear on noncompliant stations, stiffening their resistance and inadvertently creating news stories; and it discriminated against independent-minded correspondents by keeping them out of territory controlled by the Russian army, and thus ceded the initiative to the Chechens.

The difference between Moscow's assertions and battlefield pictures was striking. On December 27, 1994, President Yeltsin (finally, after two weeks) addressed the nation and ordered an end to the bombing of Grozny. Shortly after, bombs hit the city again, for all to see on television, and on January 4, he issued a second order, which was ignored on January 5, when planes blasted the presidential palace in Grozny. Before the battle for Grozny levelled the city and cost so many lives, Russian Deputy Prime Minister Nikolai Yegorov, who had the Chechnya portfolio, told the media that "'Russian troops should take Grozny without fighting on January 5.'"[8] From January 1 on, official news agencies reported that Russian troops had "'full control' of Grozny."[9] Yet, on January 5, when the peaceful takeover of Grozny was to occur, bombing was ordered all over the city, and on television fighting was seen around the railroad station and elsewhere.

All the contradictions and official distortions were seen on television. When Sergei Kovalyov, the human rights activist, and other members of parliament visited Chechnya, they returned with horrifying stories for the media. The newspapers gave the prize to television: "The truth is being told either by Sergei Kovalyov and Deputy Kurochkin or by Valentin Sergeyev, director of the Russian Government's Interim Information Center. One of them is lying. Those people who saw the NTV pictures from Grozny have no doubts on that score."[10] An angered Defense Minister Pavel Grachev called Kovalyov an "enemy of the people" and parliamentary dissenter Sergei Yushenkov a "vile toad." In a news conference from a tent in the field, Grachev told viewers about the eighteen-year-old boys dying with a smile. But the pictures of the charred bodies of soldiers picked off in their clumsy tanks spoke to the public more effectively.

To bolster its standing with a skeptical public, the government attempted to discredit the media. In his December 27th address to the nation, Yeltsin said that several media were in the pay of Dudayev's side. No proof was ever brought to bear,[11] and the charge changed to opposition television's reaping commercial profits from the war. About television, Grachev snarled: "How can you consider yourself a Russian if you go all out to tear Russia apart? And what for? For that green buck, for that stinking dollar?"[12] There were also threats by First Deputy Prime Minister Oleg Soskovets to pull the license of NTV without legal basis.

NTV had to maneuver with great circumspection. Before the war in Chechnya, it had announced that it would run movies by Bernardo Bertolucci and other European directors late Friday and Saturday nights. However, the Duma had passed a vaguely worded prohibition on "propaganda of violence and obscenity," and Igor Malashenko, believing that since the start of the war, "any pretext will be used to shut down" NTV, canceled the films.[13] NTV also ordered its correspondents not to announce how many were killed in armed clashes or bombing, which would leave them open to charges of deliberate misinformation. Correspondents were told to say only what they saw on location and to show the evidence on film—the unrelenting succession of the agony of death.[14] NTV news director Oleg Dobrodeyev said, "in Grozny, we use *no* other sources than what they directly see."[15] While I was in the offices of NTV that January, word came that the president's security council was "considering the question of NTV." The pattern of leaks continued to flow, in Malashenko's view, to keep up the pressure and the threat of government shutdown.[16]

NTV's prominence and the influence of its graphic pictures established it as a counter-authority to the government, but the government had the power to coerce and intimidate, whether or not lawfully based. Sometimes behind-the-scenes political compromise could save the position of both. Evgeny Kiselyov recounted that a number of Duma deputies witnessed a Russian armored personnel carrier open fire on unarmed civilians on the road from Grozny. Returning to Moscow the next day, Ella Pamfilova, a prominent member of the legislative delegation, had a press conference and made bitter statements indicting the government and the military. Valentin Sergeyev, head of the government's press center, called Oleg Dobrodeyev at NTV and "pleaded" with him not to show the press conference, saying the anti-NTV sentiment was very strong in President Yeltsin's security council. If NTV broadcast the press conference, Sergeyev said, he did not know what would happen to the station. Kiselyov noted that the newspapers would be reporting the event and NTV would look ridiculous if they ignored it. Even foreign radio stations would pick it up.

NTV would not delay its coverage. Sergeyev brought that information to his superiors and in two hours told Kiselyov that he was still charged with stopping NTV's coverage of the press conference. Kiselyov's solution was a compromise in which NTV agreed to leave out the "most insulting statements, the emotional commentaries" but would leave in the facts and offered to work with Sergeyev on the government's statement. According to Kiselyov, Sergeyev, understanding his orders to be unworkable, agreed to take responsibility for the outcome and sat in Kiselyov's kitchen to work out the government's statement. Kiselyov agreed to broadcast the facts about the Russians opening fire on civilians, and the government version announced that the action was an error.[17]

The government's mistake in not producing information when competing sources were available was matched in the field by its policy of secrecy and obstructionism with journalists. By refusing to admit or cooperate with journalists, the Russian military left Dzhokhar Dudayev to welcome the media with almost courtly solicitude. This was not the Persian Gulf, where casual entry into the country was impossible and where the governments of Saudi Arabia and the United States and its United Nations allies almost completely controlled the movement of correspondents. This was Chechnya, part of Russia, accessible to the enterprising and home to the hospitable traditions of the Caucasus, buoyed by a very savvy information policy.

Russian officials made it difficult to get accreditation, telling one of the most intrepid journalists in Moscow, Elena Masyuk of NTV, that to get accreditation to go to the war zone she had to get to the military airport in Mozdok, and to get to the airport she had to have accreditation.[18] Two other correspondents for a private television production company brought parcels of food and cigarettes for Russian soldiers. The Russian commander and two officers ordered the journalists into their car, brushed aside their offer to show their accreditation, and kicked the parcel, spilling the food onto the ground. Requests for interviews were refused. In Chechnya, these journalists could speak with anyone if they showed their accreditation. They could go to any home or any administrative office. Transportation, always a problem in war zones, was not one here. A stranger picked up the journalists and asked for no money, because he knew they were journalists. The Chechen press center readily gave accreditation.[19]

Numerous Russian violations of journalists' rights were recorded by the Glasnost Defense Foundation. But the most blatant threat to the press was the apparent firing of Channel Two's founding head, Oleg Poptsov. This witty, sharp-tongued political scrapper had doggedly fought the Gorbachev administration for Boris Yeltsin's first television base, six hours on Channel Two. Poptsov had again helped Boris Yeltsin when he took over television broadcasting during the October 1993 revolt, keeping the lines open to the Russian people while the military temporized. But it was also Poptsov who had shown Boris Yeltsin waving his arms conducting a German band on a visit abroad, and covered Boris Yeltsin not greeting Irish officials at Shannon airport (his spokesman had said Yeltsin overslept).

On Chechnya, Poptsov became a fierce critic. On Friday, January 6, Sergei Kovalyov told reporters that President Yeltsin said he had signed the directive to fire Oleg Poptsov. No one saw the directive, but Kovalyov's testimony, coupled with the growing pressure on television and Poptsov's exposed position as head of a state-owned station, convinced the journalists, who moved to support Poptsov. NTV gave the story prominent coverage. Channel Two's staff met to voice support for their chief and to threaten a strike. Presidential directives and laws come into force only upon publication. The arrival of the Russian Orthodox Christmas delayed publication, and by the time newspapers resumed their work the order had been withdrawn.

A year later, as the presidential electoral campaign drew near, Poptsov was finally fired and Eduard Sagalayev returned to state television to take over Channel Two. Poptsov had been living on borrowed time as head of a state television channel and had toyed with making a run for parliament a few months before. That would have provided a safe haven and future employment, but in the early days of the campaign he pulled out of the weak, newly formed party led by Duma speaker Ivan Rybkin. When Boris Yeltsin summarily fired Poptsov, the cause of the dissatisfaction was all the "muck" (chernukha) Channel Two's news programs purveyed. The president was sick of the criticism and the corpses, constant reminders of the grim outcome of his Chechnya policy. An exhausted Poptsov accepted the president's decision and retreated to write occasional newspaper columns and the second volume of his memoirs. Unprotected, without buffers, vulnerable to executive power in constant crisis, state television was once again the political asset that could not be relinquished—not with a cataclysmic election coming up.

Here was the three-pronged problem for officials during the Chechnya war: their information organization was slow to get started and produced insufficient volume; the content of the government information handouts was the same old propagandistic pap thoroughly at variance with the events, only now reported from the scene with pictures by others; and the military viewed journalists as the enemy, thus shutting them out and, coincidentally, enhancing the position of the Chechens, only too eager to tell their side of the story. In turn, NTV and the other two channels were fully conscious that the Chechens were attempting to manipulate them, and the Russian government's inadequate understanding of the changed institutional rules was unwittingly abetting them.

THE WAR ON TELEVISION

NTV's flagship news analysis program was its Sunday show, *Itogi,* hosted by Yegeny Kiselyov. It was the most popular news program for viewers in NTV's range, and its coverage of Chechnya—including the story of the news from the front—was comprehensive. On December 18, before the storm of Grozny began, the disconnected governmental information policy was startlingly evident. From Chechnya came pictures of refugees and of maimed civilians, and from Mozdok's military hospital wounded Russian soldiers told of battles. In the studio, an advisor to President Yeltsin told the audience that the Russian military avoided massive confrontations with civilians; "they went to their positions practically on tiptoe." A representative of the Duma returning from Chechnya described "enormous losses." The confusion and contradiction raised the question of news accuracy, and Kiselyov presented a story on the differences between government information and NTV information, giving these examples:

> December 12: NTV told about the downing of a Russian helicopter and showed bodies of Russian soldiers. The government said nothing.
> December 14: NTV showed Russian prisoners taken in Grozny, young men standing in a line, looking vulnerable and defenseless. On the same day the government said there were no prisoners.

Kiselyov concluded that because the government provided so little information, NTV was forced to rely on the "Dudayev side," knowing the pitfalls of that position.

The next Sunday, December 25, *Itogi* quoted the Russian press center as saying that about one hundred fifty thousand civilians left Grozny. The terse official statement was transformed by NTV's pictures of horribly wounded people—a woman whose face was covered by a bloody wound, bodies littering the ground, desperate old people, bombed-out apartment houses, massively damaged ruins of buildings. Human rights activist Sergei Kovalyov spoke with contempt of the government's version that Dudayev himself was responsible for the destruction in order to "imitate" Russians and provoke his people to fight. Kiselyov editorialized, though without visible emotion, that if NTV had a person of the week it would be Kovalyov, who continued to risk his life by staying there and "transmitting by phone daily information that contradicted official sources of information." Another story from Chechnya gave the other view: civilians living under Dudayev's terror described how he rounded up the men of the village. These people welcomed the liberating Russians.

Kiselyov introduced the official side with the comment: "Now we want to show you without any commentary video material distributed by the press service of the Russian Federation." The first showed a Russian officer receiving weapons voluntarily turned in by Chechens. Long rows of guns, with Arabic script on some of them, were shown on a table. A second story showed humanitarian aid flown in, with a woman's voiceover sounding much like a travelogue. Cargo planes were shown landing; soldiers unload sacks and packages. The viewer was told that seventy-four tons of food were provided, three tons of medicine, and altogether over three hundred tons of humanitarian aid had been delivered to the region. After a studio conversation with a dissenting Yeltsin advisor (who complained that there was no political plan for this venture and no attempt to gain parliamentary or popular support), Kiselyov introduced a story on contemporary Afghanistan by saying that foreign observers call Chechnya a new Afghanistan.

Information politics was important news, and Kiselyov explained to viewers that his company had taken a position on the war: for the integrity of Russia and for ending the separatism of Chechnya and its export of "criminal influence." That said, he argued for press freedom and sought to convince the public to accept pluralism and NTV's loyalty in spite of its often critical coverage. He observed that "for the first time in history there is unanimity of position in the mass media." The components of this position were: first, there is no doubt that Chechnya belongs to the Russian Federation, but "we are also unanimous that the means and methods of solution which were chosen by the executive cannot but arouse many questions"; and second, the mass media have to bring people full information and our obligation is to "bring all points of view to the public, not just the official ones."

Although the war coverage of the three big television stations was distinctly different, reflecting institutional and leadership differences, it was largely a difference of sequence, priority, and emphasis, but not about *what* was happening. Looking at one day in the coverage of Chechnya tells three different stories, but they share the common core of the standard that NTV set in sending back the proof in the pictures.

January 7, 1995, was Russian Christmas, a state holiday in the Russian Federation. The nightly NTV news *Segodnya* was anchored by the sober, slightly melancholy Mikhail Osokin. The first story was Chechnya, and pictures showed fighting approaching the center of Grozny and the presidential palace, which still had not been taken. A government bulletin noted "new successes" for the military and the resistance. A mine killed internal troops' major general, Viktor Vorobyov. Then followed pictures from Grozny showing the presidential palace, its top floors on fire, but Dudayev's fighters still in control of the building. In another area, oil-soaked ground was on fire and refineries were burning. The Russian army, the report said, was using lasers and other "smart weapons," but there was danger from unexploded bombs. The next story asked how arms fell into Chechen hands, followed by a story on Russian policy in the Caucasus. From the capital of neighboring Dagestan, Elena Masyuk covered the Confederation of Peoples of the Caucasus calling for solidarity with "brother Chechens."

In the next story, television itself made the news once again. Anchor Osokin remarked that government officials blamed the media for "incorrectly" covering the Chechen story. How was one to understand what was correct? Poptsov appeared to have been fired. The rest of the program related foreign reaction to the Chechen conflict—some voiceover of Secretary of State Warren Christopher's criticism of Yeltsin's weak military advisors, and much longer footage about German opinion from a correspondent in Berlin.

Back in Moscow, the Cathedral of Christ the Savior, built by Alexander I to commemorate victory in the Napoleonic wars and blown up by Stalin, was once again to rise in the center of Moscow. There were pictures of the ground-breaking. In St. Petersburg a ball for Russian aristocrats, mostly from abroad, with dazzling jewelry and chauffeured limousines, struck a jarring note in wartime. Finally, a piece on Ukrainian domestic budgetary policies, on the ebola virus in Africa, and a brief statement at the end about a church in South Africa where there is an icon of Christ with AIDS.

Throughout, there was virtually no editorializing, and the opinion of the anchor was heard only in the Poptsov-firing story. The pace was rapid, the editing professional. The pictures from the front had an immediacy and "personality" only on-location crews can contribute.

Channel Two news, *Vesti,* was anchored by the popular Svetlana Sorokina. Sorokina's personality was as much a part of the news as the information she related. From its beginning in the spring of 1991, Russian Television was known for its combative and subjective, even provocative, approach to the news. It was what made it trusted in its battle with the Gorbachev administration's television. Sorokina's signature was her closing remark—"ironic and philosophical." Her news director approved of her approach; for her, each broadcast was "a finished product, unique," and each had its drama: "culmination, prologue, and epilogue."[20] Other Channel Two anchors followed suit. When the August 1991 coup plotters were amnestied, anchor Tatyana Khudobina told viewers she was outraged and concluded: "'We are at a loss to understand Russia.'"[21]

On *Vesti* on that Russian Orthodox Christmas in January 1995, the pace was, as always, slower than on NTV. The first pictures were from Grozny; a correspondent from Reuters was quoted in voiceover. A woman was shown saying that dogs were eating corpses. There were other interviews, and Agence France Presse and a Duma deputy (still photograph shown) were quoted. Then Sorokina said, "Here is an official communication from the press service." She read a text that was upbeat, describing factories being restored. *Vesti* then went to Dagestan for the same meeting that NTV covered, and then showed a story on General Vorobyov's death. This led into another story about the lack of information about the missing and killed and that it would be "more honest" to publish daily lists rather than make people rely on the "hotlines" of the ministries of Defense and Interior. From Chechnya, there was a collage of death: five different days' stories about the horrors of war, death, and destruction, filled with pictures of corpses. Day by day the civilians sob and the narration notes that officials have not said why they used recent draftees without adequate training.

Stories on how the Chechens acquired their arsenal of weapons and the Poptsov firing followed, and Sorokina then said that "a defining feature of our time" is the "information vacuum," not only for ordinary citizens, but also for officials, and she showed footage of Duma information committee chairman Mikhail Poltoranin saying that he learned of Poptsov's firing only from television. Sorokina added: "Who can say the mass media are useless?" Continuing the media story, there was an interview with Vsevolod Vilchek in which he stated that the ratings for Channel Two and NTV have soared.

Finally, the last piece was on the cathedral ground-breaking and a Moscow pageant commemorating the end of the Napoleonic wars in Russia. Sorokina closed by saying that Tsar Alexander I issued a directive on Christmas Day ending military activity on the territory of Russia. Let us hope that in our time, "this tradition is not only in words, but implemented."

Vesti was strongly opposed to the war in Chechnya. Oleg Poptsov told me that "from the first to the last day we were loyal to our position." If the war had been short, it would have a police action, and what was going on in Chechnya was a "criminal rebellion." But, he went on, the action was unplanned, it used the military, and "it killed civilians and our soldiers."[22]

In heavily loaded words, *Vesti* uncompromisingly criticized the conduct of the war, but without the resources to field as many journalists as did NTV it could not match the immediacy of the private station's new style of war coverage.

As always, Channel One's *Vremya* was expected to reflect the official governmental point of view. As the following account shows, it did so, but as it also shows, that point of view had to compete with others and with a disillusioned press corps.

At nine o'clock *Vremya* began its coverage of January 7. Its first story was a long one about Christmas and the rebuilding of the Moscow cathedral.

Anchor Sergei Medvedev, soon to be President Yeltsin's press secretary, began by saying that Christmas had come—it had been forbidden for many years, and sadly there was now war. The first story about the ground-breaking for the cathedral noted that it was a "symbol of unity, national identity, faith, and love." The story's point of view was that of a country with a single established religion, rather than a multi-ethnic, multi-religious federation of no official confessional identity. The program then shifted to Chechnya, with pictures of the presidential palace on fire and Chechen fighters still there. Chechen leaders were quoted as warning Russia that killing their civilians can have "unpredictable consequences" on the country at large, a warning that was to be fulfilled four months later in the southern Russian town of Budyonnovsk. The news program made the point that "not all Chechens" hold this view, and noted that many in Moscow offered to go to the republic to argue for peace. A correspondent in Grozny talked to Russian soldiers who had taken the airport.

Medvedev directly stated that "now it is clearly seen that the operation was senseless and the actions taken there were hasty." He noted that officers are refusing to fight and this would only increase losses on "our side." He asked how arms got to Chechnya, later to kill Russians, and then followed a long story on General Vorobyov—his last interview and his last address to the troops before a mine took his life.

The next story showed how many in Chechnya hoped the Russians would liberate them, saying that Dudayev's people took all their belongings and his snipers hid behind a shield of women to shoot down the Russian troops. Footage from the State Duma depicted increasing opposition to President Yeltsin, and deputy Boris Fyodorov was quoted as saying that, yes, it had to be done, but *how* is the question: seasoned troops should have been sent, not young boys.

Stories on the effects of civil strife in Dagestan, South Ossetia, and Abkhazia (the latter two in Georgia), and on the foreign position of Russia followed. A correspondent in Germany told viewers that all agreed that it was an internal matter, but there was concern for innocent civilians, a view echoed by President Clinton, Secretary of Defense Perry, and Secretary of State Christopher. Representative Tom Lantos bluntly criticized Russian violations of human rights. The anchor read a statement upholding press freedom in wartime by former President Jimmy Carter and Eduard Sagalayev, cochairs of the Commission on Radio and Television Policy, and the program returned to Christmas celebrations. Anchor Medvedev said that "by tradition our ancestors asked forgiveness for wrongs from people close to them and from enemies. They found in themselves the spiritual will to forget at least on the Christmas holiday the woe and the wrongs. God willing, may this happen for most of us."

Pictures followed of Moscow, of Christmas decorations, of an outdoor presentation of music and dance, sponsored, a sign said, by the Moscow city government in collaboration with the U.S. cigarette manufacturer Philip Morris. At a Christmas Eve service two Muslim men were shown in church, having come to "honor Christ" as an act of tolerance. In closing, the correspondent said that in a country where people are returning to spirituality, "there is a future," to which Medvedev added, "undoubtedly there is, of course." After a last piece on awards for excellence in the arts, Medvedev wished a happy Christmas to all who celebrated the Orthodox holiday, and "let it bring peace to every Russian home."

This, the third news program on this Christmas night in wartime, was the closest to the official view. Channel One was always the "president's channel," and its huge reach across all of the former Soviet Union and its legacy of authority from decades past also made it the least independent. It was far more nationalist and far more "Russian" than the other two. Gennady Shipitko, then news director of Channel One, said that the problem for a Russian, as opposed to a foreign, reporter was the integrity of Russia itself. Separatism could spell the destruction of Russia. Naturally, he said, stories about war, suffering, and bloodshed prompt condemnation of violence, but the reasons why it might be justified are lost in emotions.

Shipitko was not helped much by his government. The military would not allow correspondents at the front (like the U.S. Persian Gulf war policy, he said). Instead, they were stationed at the Russian forward base at Mozdok. There was no protection for journalists in the war zone; Grozny did not welcome his correspondents (being a voice of the government). The Ministry of Defense provided little information.

Shipitko eventually adopted the policy of juxtaposing various news sources, such as the statement by the government press center that Grozny was taken, and then the release by the independent press agency, Postfactum, indicating that the Russian troops had been repulsed. As Shipitko said, "We couldn't verify which was right and therefore did not say." His own sympathies were not in doubt. He said that Grozny knew NTV's position—that it "supported" Dudayev—and gave them carte blanche. Shipitko was opposed to this kind of coverage, and Channel One went with the troops and used military videos more than the other stations. Still, he could not defend the Chechen operation's botched military strategy and what he regarded as absurd official handouts.[23] Whatever Shipitko's personal proclivities and the political position of Channel One, *Vremya* could adjust the filter, but it could not blot out the facts—not in a new and competitive television system.

THE TELEVISION PUBLIC

The Russian public's interest in the Chechen war was intense, and Moscow-based television was the chief source of information for people all over the country. Television was showing pictures of Russian boys dying in ghastly ways, of desperately wounded and ill civilians, many of whom in this mixed-ethnic region, after all, were fellow Russians. "As always in Grozny," a report from the front a year later noted, "most of the victims have been civilians, largely ethnic Russians and elderly people with no place to go."[24] Television was also showing deep division among the people running Russia: within Yeltsin's own ruling circle, within the military, and in the parliament.[25] A Moscow poll the week of December 26, 1994, to January 1, 1995, showed that people were turning to the three main daily newscasts almost equally: Channel One, 55.7 percent; Channel Two, 58.5 percent; and NTV, 54 percent, and in this tense period watching more than one program daily. Bombarded by quite contradictory official and nonofficial messages, nearly two-thirds of the people interviewed were able to make judgments about news reliability. Asked which program provided the most "factual" information about the events in Chechnya, the answers were:

Vremya (Channel One)	12%
Vesti (Channel Two)	19%
Segodnya (NTV)	28%
Don't know/no answer	41%

When asked which program most "objectively commented on what was taking place and gave the most precise evaluations," the answers were:[26]

Vremya	10%
Vesti	17%
Segodnya	26%
Don't know/no answer	47%

Minister of Defense Pavel Grachev accused television of a signal lack of patriotism in his January 20 press conference. That month, a survey of Russians across the federation, urban and rural, asked: "What do you think? How should a real patriot of Russia regard the operation in Chechnya?"

A real patriot of Russia should support the military operation	19%
A real patriot of Russia should speak out against the operation	52%
Don't know/no answer	29%

As with all the other surveys about this war, women were the greater opponents.[27] The public also displayed sympathy with those who refused to fight in Chechnya, an open split in the military that television was covering. When asked if they thought it was right to "try servicemen for refusing to participate in military actions in Chechnya," the people interviewed overwhelmingly said it was not right (74 percent vs. 11 percent).[28]

In the battle for the television public, the Russian government had produced its version of the events. All of the major television channels broadcast these materials, in some cases with heavy-handed irony, but in all cases no matter which source occupied more airtime or editorial approval, the official story was forced to coexist with independently gathered information. Channel One, the station that most dutifully supported the official version, was the least credible for the Russian public, and, further, when Russians were asked: "governmental and nongovernmental sources of information covering the events in Chechnya often contradict each other. Which of them do you, personally, trust more?" the answers were:[29]

Governmental sources	14%
Nongovernmental sources	46%
Don't know/no answer	40%

Though many could not or did not want to answer, the fact remains that very few held the view that when different versions of an event were shown, it was the government's that gained their trust. In Soviet times, too, individual viewers did not have confidence in many government reports. They compared what they saw on the screen with their experiences and often accorded the latter greater weight. But the disagreements with officially televised news stories were, of necessity, private ones. During the Chechen war, the reactions of distrust could be communicated among people, were portrayed by television itself, and thus became public or social phenomena.

Even though people were watching more news overall during the conflict, the audience for Channel One did not increase, and its demographic base continued to reflect the obsolescence of its approach: the majority of its viewers were older and less well educated. In contrast, polls showed that the other two stations registered great increases in viewers. Channel Two's *Vesti* increased its audience by 30 to 40 percent, but NTV *doubled* its audience.[30] NTV's audience had usually been about two and one-half times smaller than Channel One's, and *Vesti's* was usually 40 percent lower.[31] At the peak of the Chechnya events, NTV's share of the market in Moscow was 48 percent, nearly half of all sets turned on at that time, and in a market with more choices than anywhere else in Russia.[32]

The Russian public was not asked its permission to go into Chechnya. Well before the Russian government began its effort to oust Dudayev, Russians were opposed. In August 1994, 67 percent said Russia should not send its troops there; 14 percent said yes, and 19 percent did not know.[33] During the conflict, polls both in Moscow and throughout Russia had pretty much the same numbers: from 58 to 63 percent opposed the war and many fewer supported it.[34]

The real question for the leaders of Russia—including its mass media influentials—was what effect, if any, public disapproval might have. Russian journalists, especially the ones who had uncovered deception and exposed failure, were keenly disappointed and embittered when their stories did not result in immediate changes in government behavior. It was not unusual to hear journalists say that the free press just yaps and power ignores it; freedom of speech isn't really worth much. The government kept up its bombing and the casualties kept climbing. If there was no immediate, decisive effect on governmental policy, there was a more subtle and indirect relationship, familiar in the West. Russian viewers now had a weapon; they connected disapproval of government actions in Chechnya to their future votes. In January 1995, Russians were asked: "In the course of future elections, when you vote, will you take into account the position of candidates with respect to the war in Chechnya?"[35] Russians declaring that they intended to vote for those who opposed the Chechen conflict did so irrespective of age, social status, or where they lived:

No, I won't	25%
Yes, I will vote for supporters of the military actions in Chechnya	8%
Yes, I will vote for the opponents of the military actions in Chechnya	42%
Don't know/no answer	25%

A week before the December 1995 parliamentary elections, Russians were asked if they will "take into account the position of parties and candidates on peaceful talks in Chechnya": will they be for supporters or opponents of a negotiated solution or indifferent to the candidate's stance? More than three-quarters of the likely voters said they would choose advocates of a peaceful resolution of the war; 5 percent said they would vote for opponents (Zhirinovsky primary among them); and 18 percent said they were unconcerned with the candidates' or parties' positions on the issue.[36]

When President Yeltsin decided to run for a second term, he announced that his re-election depended on an end to the Chechen war. He signed an armistice agreement just weeks before the June 1996 election and unexpectedly went to Chechnya, taking with him anti-war activist Boris Nemtsov, governor of Nizhny Novgorod. Just back from the trip, Nemtsov told Channel One viewers that their petitions for peace had an effect. No one was naive enough to believe that the way toward peace would be smooth or quick. There were many horrors to come, but the legitimacy of that war could no longer be argued convincingly.

It would be inaccurate to say that television "caused" Russians to turn away from the war in Chechnya. The process was much more complex, as it had been in the United States during the Vietnam war.[37] Russian society was strained by divisions: regional, religious, ethnic, economic, generational, in the population at large, and within its leadership, including the military leadership. New institutions were developing, but many people suffered from the changes in distributional benefits. Those who derived the greatest benefits from the new order were still in the minority and concentrated in the large cities; they were sometimes tainted by corruption and, increasingly, adopting "foreign" ways.

This was a bewildering time for most Russians. A poll of Muscovites showed their feelings and moods in January 1994 (after the October 1993 revolt and December elections), May 1994, and December 1994, just before the big assault on Chechnya and after the covert military operation had failed. Thirteen positive and thirteen negative feelings were presented. Only four positive feelings, but eleven negative ones, were named by at least 10 percent of those interviewed.[38]

Though stubborn belief in an unknown future still fed the springs of hope that enabled Russians to endure a sometimes bitter and difficult existence, the bloody events of the Chechen war had pushed their moods into greater disorientation. It did not take television, uniquely and solely, to make the case to ordinary Russians that things were not as they should be

	January 1994	May 1994	December 1994
Positive			
Hope	40%	41%	37%
Optimism	18	20	18
Calm	12	14	11
Confidence	12	13	10
Negative			
Alarm	49	48	57
Fatigue	37	37	39
Disappointment	26	27	34
Resentment	17	22	23
Falsehood	17	20	27
Poverty	14	18	27
Fear	12	16	21
Oppression	14	12	20
Depression	10	12	16
Demoralization	10	13	13
Indifference	10	12	11

and that the future held uncertainty to a degree that postwar generations had not imagined and about which they had enormous doubt. But the insistent drumbeat on television provided little letup from unwelcome news.

The public had also become aware of the shocking decline of the myth-bearing Russian Army. Stories of corruption followed its ill-planned evacuation from bases in Eastern Europe and the Baltics. Some who had command of resources and equipment (especially officers) sold them off for private gain. Supply for military bases at home was often interrupted and stories about sailors freezing in Murmansk and hungry in Sakhalin were on the evening news. General-turned-politician Alexander Lebed later pressed the country to alleviate these dire conditions or face revolt. Young men avoided call-up. Draftees were declining in large numbers and new "contract" enlisted men were drawn in wholesale without the requisite skills or preparation.[39] Two highly placed generals, Boris Gromov (the commander and last Russian soldier to leave Afghanistan) and Leonid Ivashov (secretary of the CIS Defense Ministers council) publicly decried the lack of preparation for the Chechen war. Gromov said that "'the operation was carried out without the relevant study and in a hurry . . . and the considerable forces that were mustered piecemeal across Russia were simply unable to collaborate without training.'"[40]

According to General Staff estimates, up to 60 percent of the tank and armored vehicle crews were formed on the way to the invasion point of Mozdok.[41] Ivashov argued that the Russian army was combat capable, but not for this kind of combat. "'The troops, the command, and the staffs were trained for classic combat operations, they were not taught to fight on their own territory against their own people.'"[42] Like American leaders pondering the use of the military in police actions, these Russian army officials recognized the inherent problems of such an operation, whether or not it was properly planned.[43] In Chechnya, the army was not the only force attempting a police action. The Ministry of Internal Affairs, which had jurisdiction over police militia forces, was also in the field, and that presented even greater problems of coordination. It was these militiamen whom Elena Masyuk described as shooting wildly into a welcoming crowd near Znamenskoye. She also recalled a group of forty-eight who parachuted into Chechnya. With them were no officers, food, heavy clothes, or documents. They gave themselves up and were taken prisoner. Dudayev offered to return them, but only to their mothers, a clever propaganda move.[44]

If the Russian military and police leadership expected a quick cleanup of Chechnya, instead of a war claiming large numbers of military and civilian casualties, it was mistaken. The example of Desert Storm, the lightninglike destruction of the Iraqi army in 1991, may have been a model for Chechnya, but the differences were substantial. Colonel Igor Alpatov described the Persian Gulf war as defined by high-precision weapons and minimal combat losses. Such an operation, he said, "needs a clever and strong headquarters, highly-educated military leaders and professionally trained troops. None of those 'victory components' are to be found in Russia now. Therefore, Pavel Grachev tried to compensate poor combat training with the quantity of troops, which led only to chaos and partial (in the conditions of the fighting) to full loss of control over military detachments, and as a result to great losses."[45] A Russian pilot echoed the view, saying that "'to work dexterously as the Americans did during Desert Storm one needs to fly two hundred hours a month. I flew thirty-two hours this year, which is even too much for the Russian air force today.'"[46]

The bombing was not "pinpoint"; it was often done during bad weather and poor visibility (to be expected from a campaign in the Caucasus initiated in December). It was all seen on television, but television did not create the conditions or determine the results of that fateful campaign. It was television that provided, for most people, the information they could not get in their everyday lives. It was television, with its startling pictures and angry, contentious disputes, that exposed the deep divisions in the government, the military, and other elites. It provided a series of messages for people not only to process as their own constructed information, but also on which to base judgments about the competence of their leaders.

The public opinion soundings confirmed that in the Chechen crisis it was television that commanded attention, and that it was Moscow-based television to which people turned. Most important of all, the entirely new look and content of the first private attempt to break the monopoly of news reporting gained the credibility and authority to secure its place in the new media environment. And by that very fact, NTV decisively changed the information environment for all the other players, including the government.

MASSACRE AT SAMASHKI, TERROR AT BUDYONNOVSK

Though belatedly, governmental information policy corrected its course. In the words of one observer, "Russian TV is literally overwhelmed" with material from "Military-TV, MVD [Ministry of the Interior]-TV and other ministerial departments."[47] Military leaders were also notably more willing to meet with journalists not only in military press centers, but even on the "enemy" territory of the Journalists Club.[48] Inevitably, the military and the government also learned to keep journalists out of territory it fully controlled. That is what they were able to do in that disputed, but highly probable, massacre in Samashki.

Samashki is a village eighteen miles west of Grozny; it was home to the Dudayev clan and controlled a railway connection to Grozny. It was also a rebel stronghold. When the Russian federal troops—it was the Ministry of

Internal Affairs' first independent military operation in its history[49]—approached Samashki in April 1995, they apparently believed the rebels were still there and presented a threat both in the village and in the surrounding tract of forest. It was the fanatic Chechen commander Shamil Basayev who had been active there, by no means a trivial adversary. The Russians gave the villagers an ultimatum to hand over their weapons and ordered Dudayev's men to leave. Accounts differed as to whether hostile forces remained in the village and posed a threat to the entering Russians (the Russian forces' story) or whether the rebels had left and there was no threat (as the villagers claimed). Accounts also differed as to what happened. Because the Russian army surrounded the village it imposed a cordon and denied entry to journalists, Duma deputies, and the Red Cross. For three days Samashki was the scene of violence, and when it was over there were reports of a massacre, people burned to death, whole streets of houses destroyed by grenades and flamethrowers, and civilians gunned down by machine gun fire. The MVD denied that unprovoked attacks had taken place and argued that rebels had stayed behind to fire on the advancing Russians.

When Russian and foreign journalists, representatives of the human rights group Memorial, Duma deputies, and medical personnel were let in, they interviewed the survivors and heard stories of atrocities.[50] Estimates of civilians killed ranged from 100 to 250. The military continued to say the fighting was confined mainly to the forested area and the villages in the region were untouched, and, moreover, on *Vremya* viewers could see the civilians returning to their homes.[51] Right-wing Duma deputy Stanislav Govorukhin flew to Grozny and reported that the Russian army did not do what the Memorial group charged, and that Samashki was not destroyed.[52]

Evgeny Kiselyov, the *Itogi* anchor, believed the massacre had taken place. He had been in Afghanistan as interpreter, he said, and he knew what could happen. He said that upon capturing an Afghan village after prolonged combat, solders killed everyone, just for revenge. Kiselyov remarked that the pattern of destruction in Samashki was limited to specific streets, and that if one flew above the village or did not see those streets one might call the reports exaggerated. Those who had seen the particular streets had no doubt.[53] He reiterated: there were no eyewitnesses; the military had successfully prevented the intrusion of observers.

After Samashki and after Vedeno, where Shamil Basayev's family was reported to have been killed, the Chechen commander set out for Moscow to perpetrate terrorist acts and bring the war to Russia, as he had so often threatened. He got as far as the southern town of Budyonnovsk, where he took two thousand hostages in a hospital. Some were rounded up on the streets, some were the staff and patients in the hospital. As before, NTV was first with solid information from the hostage site, and, as during the October 1993 revolt, Russian Television Channel Two kept its special faith with the Russian people, broadcasting a bulletin every hour even in the absence of breaking news.

Budyonnovsk was open to television. Both sides were eager to use it; all stations covered the prime minister's negotiations with the rebels. The victor was the burly prime minister Viktor Chernomyrdin. His square, distinctly old-fashioned image was exactly right for the task he undertook and the confidence he inspired in the viewers, while he negotiated the release of the hostages live on all the television channels. This was a civic spectacle in time of crisis. Chernomyrdin was a no-frills bureaucrat who could shoulder the task of freeing the hostages without obvious artifice or sophistication. His was a reassuring and familiar pretelegenic look, coupled with understated personal courage. In the words of a television critic, he was "the lone hero,"[54] and he pulled it off on television. It was a meaningful contrast to the president, off in Canada at a meeting of the world's economic powers. Throughout the standoff there was television inside the hospital and outside; the hostage-takers and the government were aware of and used the medium. Budyonnovsk coverage was a ratings peak when NTV's *Itogi* handily outdrew all the other programs.[55]

Like patterns of viewing everywhere, intense interest in television news and Chechnya did not last. After mid-January viewership for all the news programs fell off, but more so for *Vesti* and *Vremya*. NTV's daily news show *Segodnya* and its Sunday *Itogi* declined relatively less.[56]

There would be peaks and valleys in attention to television. There would be successful and not-so-successful strategies for launching political careers or gaining office with the help of television. There would be the usual attempts by the military to keep journalists out when security was believed to be threatened or just to prevent them from witnessing problems and failures. Military censorship has a long history, and in democracies it must be carefully situated along the thin line between preventing impediments to a military mission and mobilizing popular support.[57] The Afghan model of news reporting was no longer an option and a new game was in play for the future. In some cases, the military would successfully shield its actions, though not the testimony that would inevitably come out.

There was a victory in the Chechen war, one that was so powerful that it simply became part of the mental landscape. It was "normal"—and no longer remarked on as odd or outstanding. Pluralism had been achieved in the heat of crisis, but it was not predetermined—an inevitable outcome of modernization and economic development—or assured. A carefully-developed strategy, independence of mind, a notion of fairness, the resources to pay outstanding journalists, and the bravery of those journalists all contributed to the breakthrough that NTV made and the solid proof it offered.

Of course, these decisions were also the result of a calculation that included the likely profit-enhancing and political effect. Vladimir Gusinsky,

NTV's chief investor, at the time supported an opponent of the president. Yet there was evidently more in the decision than narrowly defined personal advantage. In talking to Elena Masyuk it was difficult to see a purely careerist motivation for a journalist who went to cover cholera in Dagestan and radiation in Chernobyl and who came back with a concussion from Grozny. When asked if she had been drawn to Chechnya by a desire to inform the public, she answered no. She could not, she said, sit in Moscow and listen to Reuters give reports; she had to find out for herself.[58] NTV's partners had strict rules for news coverage and engaged in less editorializing than did the other stations. The viewers noticed: the public "voted" for the new system, and in the process the old was jettisoned.

The autonomy that NTV fought so hard to acquire and withstood so many threats to maintain came under attack again in the June 1996 elections. This time the problem arose from a dilemma with no easy solution. Igor Malashenko voluntarily joined Yeltsin's team as press advisor to prevent a Communist victory and establishment of what he believed would be a hostile information policy. The election crisis foreshortened the time and constricted the space needed for "normally" operating, legally defended institutions of democratic government.

CHAPTER TWELVE

Changing Channels on the
Most Powerful Medium

Only four and-a-half years had passed between the 1990 May Day parade and the winter of the Chechen war. On May Day Mikhail Gorbachev was surprised by the public's hostility, and during Chechnya
Boris Yeltsin was surprised by the low impact of his information policy. In
both cases, the events taking place in a single, delimited space became nationally significant, in large part because of television. The old ways—on
the screen and in the polity—did not work any more, if, in fact, they had
ever worked as imagined. The battle for television reflects and explains
much in the demise of the Soviet Union and the transformation of Russia.
The enormous changes wrought there bear thinking about because of the
broader policy issues regarding the role of television in times that redefine
the meaning of a nation and its future.

For leaders, as for the public, television is often the focus of obsessive interest, but it may produce different meanings for leaders than for viewers.
In a democracy the two are inextricably intertwined because election to
office depends on interaction with the public, in whose hands lies the voting decision. In an authoritarian society such interdependence is not recognized because the public's own construction of messages and the generation of its own interests are of little moment to those in power. Viewers as
real people, not doctrinaire constructs, are unseen, but they are not absent.
During the process of democratization, Russia's effort to convert to high-
impact television tells us about the contradictions of control, the complexity of credibility, and the meaning of the nation that television did so much
to define.

Controlling television appears to be a mixed blessing. In their stewardship of television the Soviet government repeatedly sought total control

and made itself the principal target for dissatisfaction. When conflicts and tensions inevitably arose between ethnic groups or regions or social classes, the government invariably became the butt of charges of bias and prejudice on the part of at least one of the aggrieved parties. Framing news stories to display the power of the state (Soviet or Russian) and the grandeur of its leader, the leadership targeted itself for individual dissatisfactions, especially potent in the context and culture of Soviet-style socialism, which located the state as the source of individual welfare.

"Control" is, in any case, imprecise. How fully controlled is communication in a modern world freighted with messages carried by multiple channels? Apart from an only partially successful effort to eliminate intrusive foreign or other unapproved messages, Soviet leaders found it impossible to prevent multiple interpretations of the messages over which they thought they had full control. On their understanding of television messages, viewers brought to bear the baggage of their personal experiences and observations. They were less endowed in evaluating stories about foreign affairs and could only operate by analogy. When audiences deconstructed messages it was a private act, and Soviet authorities believed their television public to be a largely passive player, inert and malleable, because there was no public room for and no legitimation of unauthorized political views on the part of viewers. In only limited and informal ways could citizens know each others' views as worthy of consideration and possessing weight. Actually, the public/private tension went further. People could not merely slip into silence but had actively to show their agreement with official norms. "Were they all to stop talking, they would end up revealing their private preferences. . . . The term *spiral of prudence* is a superior alternative. . . . It accommodates the notion that in trying to escape the costs of truthfulness individuals can go beyond self-censorship."[1]

The ancient Greeks believed that at the founding of every political system is a coercive act that renders the grounding of legitimacy always problematic, even as the heroic founding myth is repeatedly reaffirmed through story and symbol. Without a constitution and without norms governing relationships of power among the elites, control of status-affirming institutions in the Soviet Union was vital both to assist the leaders' climb to the top and to ratify it. The symbolic politics so essential to a Soviet system that had to craft legitimacy from violent beginnings played out on television as on no other mass medium. For Soviet leaders this was the highest impact they could seek. When mass ownership of television sets came on the scene, the assets it provided were unprecedented: instantaneous saturation of the country with visuals to persuade the skeptics and the unliterary (or functionally illiterate).

The same understanding of television continued in post-Soviet Russia, where the stakes in the outcome of defining elections and referenda were very great. With a political system deeply divided about the legitimacy of democratization itself, the costs of granting television access to those who were not part of the consensus were considered infeasibly high. The state's attempt to monopolize television created a zero-sum environment in which those unable to exploit what was considered the chief political asset sought extra-legal measures of violent protest or seizure.

Credibility and objectivity are inseparable components of the canons of Western journalism. It was not always so and there is much debate about the meaning of objectivity. Dependence on government-generated news and highly placed sources tends to undercut the notion of objectivity, as does an understanding of facts that fragments them into receiver-constructed, multiple meanings until they disappear in a swirl of equal and opposed truths.

Objectivity in television news may be a different thing altogether for countries shedding an authoritarian past. Subjectively reported news was for many the first bold step toward accurate coverage and an alternative to the state-dominated message. The subjective was the credible and the tradition extended beyond the fall of the dictatorship. The ability of journalists to make themselves credible in the late Soviet period required them to present themselves as individuals separate from the institutions in which they worked. They told viewers their opinions; they reflected sarcastically or ironically on what they were told to say, what others said, and what they observed. They made of themselves stars and "personalities." Many did so for a political purpose: to provide viewers with a genuine alternative, to act as a counterweight to official pronouncements, and to educate the public. Many of the reporters during the 1996 presidential election believed strongly in their duty to educate viewers about the dangers of a Communist victory. How well suited this legacy was to the construction of an independent, credible, modern media system remained very much at issue. The Russian public continued its affectionate connection to the emoting, judging anchors as the conscience of the country. The place reserved for the poet-seer of nineteenth-century Russia had been filled by the anchor-prophet at the end of the twentieth.

In seeking to make television credible and more effective in Russia, visible censorship was removed and live programming expanded. New modes of discourse and more natural personal bearing replaced the alienating abstraction of officials skilled in the language of the organization but unaccustomed to seeking public approval. The wooden style of Communist Party bureaucrats did not compete effectively on television and, except for Mikhail Gorbachev, they were unprepared to communicate in the new accents of the television revolution. Later, Yegor Gaidar, though a risk-taking, pioneering economic reformer, had little understanding of the new requirements, nor did his party, nor did most of the candidates vying for public attention in the first multi-party competitive elections in post-Soviet Russian history.

The first political communicator on Russian television to address specifically identified, largely neglected parts of the public in their own language was Vladimir Zhirinovsky. His success, it is true, was a relative one; the competition was decidedly weak in its ability to make contact with the long ignored public. Zhirinovsky pioneered a new kind of electioneering and broke the mold. By the next elections, two years later, his "discoveries" had been appropriated by a wider field in the election races.

The removal of intrusive, identifiable, government censorship did much to enhance the credibility of Russian television. But the modern toolbox of methods for enhancing credibility is much richer than that and more problematic. The "technological" war of the Persian Gulf presented to American viewers a huge flow of information that was apparently comprehensive but controlled and light on reportage of civilian damage. Television docu-dramas, recreations of historical or current events, morphing, and computer-enhanced photographs all blur the line between news reporting and artifice. The diversions of celebrity and scandal can leave little room for more serious coverage and thus beg the issue of news credibility altogether. Who is, after all, interested in hard news? Soviet airbrushing was amateur in comparison.

If all politics is local, then is all truly effective television local? In Russia, the wrenching movement from the dictatorship of the past to the pluralism of the future went forward in the rhythms and packaging of the West. Whether or not the television principals preferred to convey a precisely Western appearance or content in their new wares, they had few alternatives with which to signal a radical, thoroughgoing change. Their distinctiveness had to be Western-looking, since that was what had been forbidden for decades, what so stunningly separated the controlled sameness of the past from a dynamic future, and what would be salient for a youthful generation opting out of the system. The Soviet government had short-sightedly adopted a dichotomous view of the world in which all that was not Soviet—political, cultural, or economic—was generated directly or indirectly by the United States. And so it appeared on television. Certainly, American models and collaboration, particularly news footage from CNN, and Ted Turner's personal interest and projects played an important role in the process of reform.

But the issue was more complex and could be seen as a four-layered dilemma. First was the layer of contemporary international trade. American companies, like others, were in search of global markets and particularly well positioned in the rapidly developing television programming market. Like most countries in the world, Russia was a consumer of American television programs and movies, and like them thought about the maintenance of local ways in a global market. That tension could be seen in many other countries, and as information markets developed was part of a worldwide process. The superimposition of the other three layers made the Russian case much more uncertain.

The second layer of the dilemma resulted from a severe contraction of the Russian economy. It had become very—usually prohibitively—costly for Russian firms to produce and air their own entertainment and news programs, even as Russia was attempting to define itself during great instability. The third layer of the dilemma was the rise of product advertising, domestic and foreign, to support what the state budget could no longer afford. To Russian viewers the glitzy, rock-scored images in those ads looked and sounded distinctly American, or at least seemed to be what Soviet propagandists of the past called American, though by then it had already been globalized.

Finally, the fourth layer regarded the notion of democracy. Democracy itself was associated with America, but in the minds of many in the public, the "American" principles of democracy and Americanized electioneering were not easily disengaged from the "American-looking" economic changes that had yet to produce wide benefits across social classes and regions. Of course, American democracy and the development of markets were not unconnected, but in Russia the arrival of both severe economic dislocation *and* drastic political change tended to displace, onto a construct called "America," the unwanted results of both. In a transitional period the effects were most pronounced. Searching for a stable definition of the country, some viewers escaped into the varnished past of Soviet films—a past that never was. Others moved into a competitive future in which individuals expected little from the state—not even legal protection—and acquired benefits, often by successfully converting state assets into personal ones.

If the nation was in flux even about its boundaries, if many of its cultural precepts had been delegitimized with great suddenness, if economic change had arrived with such force that many were disadvantaged, what kind of impact could television have for this "nation?" What was the public and what was in its interest? How could television function in the public interest as the state moved to reform its institutions, even if not along a straight path?

In some of the most serious crises in the fragile post-Soviet period, television connected people all across the country. At those times indigenous accents, points of view, and symbols had the greatest impact. The stolid square figure of Viktor Chernomyrdin negotiating in the broiling heat for thousands of lives in Budyonnovsk in June 1995 was exactly the right image. The public understood it. Russian Television's unrehearsed marathon of drop-ins to a modestly appointed reserve studio under fire in October

1993 was the common thread connecting a country that had yet to make up its mind about the two sides of a contested future. These were television events that brought together most of the people of the country, no matter where they lived and how much they earned. This was television in which viewers saw themselves as a collective and as connected.

Television portrays the nation to itself and defines the polity. Yet, dislocating change can make the definition of nation elusive. It was fundamentally at issue after the breakup of the Soviet Union, and Moscow-dominated television did little to grapple with the separate lives of regions and ethnicities. Differentiation in other respects was also increasing. The public was sharply divided by generation and by rapidly diverging economic interests and opportunities, ranging from the conspicuous consumption of the "new Russians" to the subsistence existence of pensioners.

In Soviet times, television officials played to a public imagined, in most important respects as homogenous. Viewers were not a uniform mass, but there were far fewer inequalities than later in Russia. The different demands and needs of the stratified public suggested that a wider range of messages and products was essential. Choice was developing briskly, ahead of an adaptable infrastructure and without fully guaranteed, lawful, competitive access. As elsewhere, both vectors—the integrative potential of national television and the fragmenting, customized, expensive new services—operated at the same time. In a resource-constrained environment, who would have access to information, culture, and entertainment on the most important medium? For most people the world of global interface had yet not arrived; the world of basic channel choice had *just* arrived.

But is access to channel choice enough? The development of market-based television pluralism—real choice among channels—was indeed a notable achievement in the new Russia. Opportunities for the expression of differing points of view were clearly enhanced, but did the market provide all the solutions? Some Western observers, familiar with their own huge array of channel choice that did not bring in its wake a correspondingly broad range of opinion alternatives, have argued that the market is a poor guarantor of the kind of diversity of speech and expression of minority opinions that democracy needs.

If we equate "free speech" with maximum diversity of views, then, strictly speaking, "free speech" involves not only the negative government function (that political views be protected from government sanctions) but also the positive one (that government be "held responsible for ensuring the expressibility of all views, including the misguided, the shocking, the hurtful, and the irreverent.")[2] Yet, even if it were possible or desirable, this expansive principle of government activism cannot guarantee that hostile public opinion will easily make room for views it regards with contempt. Given the often chilling effect of majority opinion on expressions of minority views and the failure of even a highly developed market to guarantee the widest possible expression of views, how interventionist should a government be to ensure diversity of views?

In the formative years of post-Soviet television policy, such an intrusive role for the state was not desirable. Market-based pluralism was a breakthrough; it brought alternative views on critically important issues to a mass public. The new commercial stations, not the state, served to broaden expressive choice. The range of choice was far from complete, perhaps, and the market was far from perfect in its operation and less buffered from grovernment than desirable. But bringing the state back in to rule on content was at this stage the much more pernicious alternative.

Under Mikhail Gorbachev, the impact of television was projected to be nothing less than undermining the stranglehold of the dead hand of bureaucracy. This it did with consummate effectiveness. Obstacles to change—though Gorbachev had an impossible kind of contained change in mind—were attacked and discredited, a striking event in the Soviet Union, where there was no sanctioned challenge to high officialdom before he came to power. Dethroning an oppressive system of colonial or authoritarian rule may unite disparate and contradictory elements on a provisional basis. But applying television to building new institutions is incomparably more difficult than setting about to dismantle the old order.

The dynamic of attack was difficult to harness for other outcomes. Soviet-style news and public affairs programming had always served up an overly positive version of reality. This set of tools was no longer available to a ruling group determined to dissociate itself from the past and to a public weary of exhorting dissonance. The polarized drama of exposé and the unleashing of criticism had an invigorating effect, but in vain Gorbachev and Yeltsin charged television with producing effective constructive programs. When television officials attempted to obey, as Vyacheslav Bragin did, the output was all too reminiscent of the past.

Elections are critical moments. In Russia, the power of television was considered to be so great that it was an exceptionally valuable prize for those in power to monopolize and those out of power to acquire—by the rules if possible and by force if not. In April 1993 state television was crudely biased, and in December 1993 and 1995 wanting in expert analysis or genuine debate.

In 1996, gravely threatened by a weak candidate, a strong Communist challenger, and the potential nullification of the reform project itself, the television networks framed the election as a referendum, just as they had done in April, three years before. Television—public and private—returned to open partisanship. Significantly, three factors made a difference: free time was given fairly to all candidates on the state stations; the candidates could buy additional advertising time; and a private station, NTV, provided considerable access to opposing candidates, even though it suspended analytic reporting critical of their candidate, the president. The weight of so many elections designed to solve so many systemic crises—nine in eight years—impaired the fragile autonomy.

TOWARD DEMOCRATIC TELEVISION

Russians use the word "normal" (*normalny*) very often. And when they do, to outsiders the term seems to describe not the quotidian but the exceptional. What isn't *normalny* for Russians is something sudden and extraordinary. Persisting conflict, bad news, problems, tragedy, all became *normalny.* The test for television—as for society—would be to establish democratic criteria for more truly normal times.

Political leaders, as well as television officials, would be well advised to draw a distinction between a tight grasp and a bully pulpit. As long as politicians—of whatever stripe—believe they have to keep television tightly in their grip, they likely forfeit the kind of impact they seek. Failure to communicate to the public effectively deprives political leaders of what Richard Neustadt called the American president's most powerful asset.[3] Used appropriately, television is indeed a bully pulpit, but leaders need to know how to use it. Technique is not really the issue. It is not merely a matter of adopting a professional on-screen presence and uniforms of tasteful suits and hair helmets. The most powerful impact of television on Russia in recent times came from an extemporizing unglamorous actress in a makeshift studio and a sweating bulky prime minister in a small provincial town. Television becomes a political asset to leaders who understand and connect with the viewers' values and concerns, since viewers are voters, in whom resides power. Effective leadership does more, and not only reflects but shapes those concerns.

The task of leadership is immeasurably more difficult when viewers are deeply divided along so many fault lines, and in the early days of a new country it is especially difficult to forge coalitions. Coalitions and compromise are necessary modes of behavior in the political arena, but also on the nation's greatest educational medium, television. A zero-sum approach is ill-suited to a media market in which the private sector provides a multiplicity of news and public affairs options. Television could do much to legitimate a game in which there are payoffs for many and more than one side wins, but it should do so as a result of professional judgment, without government intrusion over content.

For generations the Russian public was basically a cipher for the people who ran the country and television. Still, those leaders should have understood that even with few choices, viewers were telling their political leaders where their interests lay by switching to each new more challenging option as soon as it arrived. They did it in Soviet times with *12th Floor, Vzglyad,* and with *Vesti,* the Yeltsin-partisan news program, and they did it in post-Soviet times with NTV's coverage of the Chechen war.

I am referring to the large, mass public as well as a small circle of elites in Moscow. That the public also enthusiastically opted for game shows and soap operas should not obscure the fact that it could mix escapism with discerning judgments about information. Vladimir Zhirinovsky's success was by no means the unique result of his televised ranting, but was also a reaction of his voters' insecurities and a negative evaluation of the competence of his rivals, most particularly incumbents. Alexander Lebed was popular because he acted decisively and talked little, and he single-handedly arrested the war in Chechnya. Gennady Zyuganov's formidable challenge was turned back primarily because most people did not believe in the future the Communists promised and did not want to change course, however harsh the journey. Many now had a stake in the future and, retrospectively (always less suspenseful than prospectively), it is entirely possible that they did not have to be battered by partisan television to make their choices. Perhaps post-Soviet political executives—and those from television—should learn to appreciate the complexity of the public and be less dismissive of the mass they like to term "lumpen."

New television stations sprang up with amazing rapidity in Russia. Practically everybody had television sets; many households had more than one, and some had a wide range of channels from which to choose. For most people, choice—especially in news and public affairs—was still limited and few stations reached very large audiences. Because of these limitations, the public-interest responsibility of leading national channels may be unusually great, which means that television officials have a particularly critical duty to understand the needs of the public. Ratings numbers tell them only who watches in the contest of a limited array of contenders for a given time slot, obviously critical to an advertising-driven bottom line—and survival. Yet reputation and prestige are also part of the more intangible profit picture. Taking only the soap-opera-loving side of the numbers obscures both the public's other interests and the differences among various segments of the public, not to mention the role television might play in a "national conversation."

As they move into the twenty-first century, some of the old combative habits the stations adopted to achieve credibility and assist democratic reform in a hostile environment may have to give way to a lower temperature, a more "normal" way of operating. What to throw overboard and what to retain of the homegrown ways will not be an easy decision.

Television officials and legislators pondering their role in helping to forge a newly rediscovered nation are often tempted to substitute protectionism for creativity. Under conditions of diminished domestic program production the danger of foreign saturation appears enormous. Applying quotas to imports raises all sorts of problems: What, exactly does "foreign" mean? Are the states of the former Soviet Union, to which Russia wants to build ties and in which reside large numbers of coethnics, as foreign as those across the Atlantic? Does delivery of programs by direct broadcast satellite leapfrog rules? Does foreign investment, with locally formed consortia? And isn't there another, more fundamental question: competing for one's own domestic public is not only a matter of rich production values and internationally recognized stars; it is much more about crafting programs that connect to the public with integrity, veracity, and artistry. Viewers do not need to be forced to recognize achievements of this rank; they do not need to have other choices eliminated.

To address the public in ways that matter, television must be able to tackle problems of great moment, and it cannot do so as long as vaguely worded, intermittently enforced laws prohibit much speech relating to war, religion, social class, ethnic differences, and other profoundly important questions. The prohibitions do not forbid people from talking about these issues in their private lives. They do not restrain the extremists in their bid to unleash popular frustration.

The prohibitions *do* restrain television from introducing responsible discourse and developing a way of illuminating issues in a fashion that does not seek to annihilate the opponent or arouse bigotry. It is not just a matter of talking-head panels and television used as radio. Such television cannot possibly reach the emotions and minds of the national public. It takes the pictures and sounds of compassion and discerning understanding to do this. Perhaps in no other country in the world is there a greater opportunity and greater role for television than in rapidly changing, transitional Russia.

Afterword

Boris Yeltsin's ride to victory in the summer of 1996 had taken him from the thin edge of popular contempt and physical frailty to the apparently firm ground of guarantor of a democratically reforming Russia. The election, framed as either forward or back to the Communist past, had given the president a second term, in spite of his absence from the second round of the vote. The Communist Party electorate, aging and penurious, was solid but fixed, and, as the Russians said, *besperspektivny:* it had no future. The national television networks had agreed on a strategy of support for the president, had advised him, and had coordinated their programming, even deciding which movies to put on and at what times. In the exultant victory celebrations, one of the networks, NTV, Russia's strongest commercial television station, worried how to rebuild its credibility and how to fend off a government that had become accustomed to cooperation.

Confidence was in the air in Moscow. By the end of 1996, the president had come through a serious heart operation and there was supposed to be a respite of three years before another parliamentary election and four before the presidential election in 2000. Media properties were hot; business was booming. The advertising market was growing so fast that for the first time local stations became attractive and the race was on to expand the Moscow-based networks into owned-and-operated properties in the provinces. Commercial television stations mushroomed, popping up everywhere from the frozen east all across to the densely populated European regions. There were now over a thousand stations in the country. The Russian market had cable, direct broadcast satellite, and broadcast. Television, mainly broadcast, was still by far the primary source of news and entertainment for this vast country of eleven time zones.

But nothing had been done about the flaws in this picture. Boris Yeltsin had pulled through a multiple heart-bypass operation but was still prone to incapacitating bouts of pneumonia, influenza, and a bleeding ulcer. By 1998 he was barely present in the Kremlin. His old habit of capricious personnel changes was undiminished but the consequences were increasingly dangerous for the fragile society. Constitutional power was overwhelmingly lodged in the presidency and presidential decrees could almost dispense with the parliament. Almost, but not quite. The elected deputies of the Duma, smarting from presidential disdain and Yeltsin's high-handed exclusion of them from what little constitutional power they did have, struck back as the president's power declined along with his health.

Then, too, nothing had been accomplished in reining in the out-of-control corruption in the entertainment and advertising industries or the concentration of media ownership discussed in Chapter 10. Concentration was justified using the argument that television's expenses dwarfed those of radio and newspapers, which can be produced and distributed at a fraction of the price of television. It takes big money and heavy investments to get the signal out to viewers and to provide programs they will watch. To construct a counterweight to the existing infrastructure and resources of the state—to provide a national-scale information alternative—would require an impressively large amount of private money. In post-Soviet Russia, such money was not well dispersed.

Ensuring access to significant numbers of potential entrants into the information market is a cornerstone of democratic pluralism. Open discussion among competing points of view serves both to enlighten the public and to curb official power. That first step toward achieving ownership diversity requires the existence and enforcement of structural regulation: transparent and fair rules for acquiring frequencies, attracting investment, and curbing excessive concentration. Those institutions had not come into being during the wild ride from Soviet state monopoly to frantic privatization. After the crash of 1998, it was not clear which television companies would survive. Regional channels were most vulnerable; the big Moscow-based networks had the best prospects.

CONCENTRATION OF OWNERSHIP
AND THE CRASH OF 1998

True, concentration of ownership in the media was a growing worldwide phenomenon. In the United States, 80 percent of the nation received television programs from six cable companies. Seven companies controlled 70 percent of the programming on cable. In the music industry, five international companies controlled over 60 percent of the world market in music sales. In the European Union, the top ten European publishing conglomerates controlled 50 to 70 percent of the market. The new East European media markets were mainly foreign dominated. In the Czech Republic, Hungary, and Poland, the print market was dominated by German capital. The Central European Media Enterprises Group, founded by

U.S. investor Ronald Lauder and later acquired by SBS Broadcasting, created TV Nova in the Czech Republic. By the mid-1990s it had captured over two-thirds of that market and then set its sights on Romania, Slovakia, and Hungary.

In Russia, the owners were overwhelmingly domestic and few in number; they included the huge natural resources and banking industries, often with direct national and local government investment and control. One of Russia's richest men, Boris Berezovsky, was the largest private stockholder (or rather his company was) in the hybrid state/private partnership of Channel One (ORT—Russian Public Television), the biggest television network in Russia. Not only did he call the shots in the decisions of that station, he was also an investor in the commercial station, TV-6, and controlled newspapers (for example, *New Izvestia* and *Independent Newspaper*) and a large-circulation magazine, *Ogonyok*. Berezovsky had political ambitions and after the 1996 election he was appointed secretary of the National Defense Council, from which he was removed at the end of the next year and shifted to a position with the Commonwealth of Independent States apparatus. In 1999 when Berezovsky was in Azerbaijan on official CIS business, he was summarily dismissed by the president. Berezovsky had locked horns with Evgeny Primakov, the prime minister whom Yeltsin installed in the aftermath of the '98 crash. Primakov, a former foreign minister and head of intelligence, launched a campaign to reduce Berezovsky's influence. He sent teams of corruption investigators to raid the offices of Berezovsky's companies and he complained about Berezovsky's use of Channel One to attack the government. Berezovsky, in turn, ratcheted up his media war on the government, using his properties to charge cabinet ministers with corruption and criticize a do-nothing economic policy. Channel One had a peculiarly divided ownership structure (51 percent belonged to the state); the government had an acute shortage of money (and relied on "oligarch" Berezovsky, a minority stockholder, for investment); and that stockholder had a close relationship with the Yeltsin family, especially the president's daughter and adviser, Tatyana. The standoff was protracted and nasty.

The Uneximbank empire, run by Vladimir Potanin, included such media properties as the papers *Izvestia, Komsomol Pravda,* the Prime news agency, *Expert* magazine, and the Europe Plus radio station. The natural gas industry, the huge Gazprom with which former prime minister Viktor Chernomyrdin had been associated, had its own media properties, investing in the daily newspapers *Trud* (Labor) and *Workers' Tribune,* the magazine *Profil,* and the private NTV's DBS operation. NTV's principal owner, Vladimir Gusinsky, was the closest thing to a specialized media baron. Starting out with his MOST bank, he went over in the winter of 1997 to head his MOST media group, an amalgam of the big commercial network NTV and all its spin-offs, such as NTV+ (the DBS service) and TNT (called THT outside Russia—the network made up of regional stations). In addition, Gusinsky controlled the newspaper *Segodnya,* the radio station Moscow Echo, the magazine *Itogi,* and the program guide, *7 Days.* In the fall of 1998, NTV launched its own U.S.-built satellite providing substantial digital television transmission capacity. This event marked the first time that satellite signal dissemination capability was in private hands and did not depend on Russian governmental facilities.

Though there were a few other big business players in the media market, the most notable and energetic rising media property buyer was the politically ambitious mayor of Moscow, Yury Luzhkov, who had plenty of municipal funds to invest. Until the crash, Moscow was the center of vigorously growing foreign investment and business, and the canny, powerful mayor had no hesitation in commandeering as much as he could to enhance his city. He produced showy projects, like the multimillion-dollar underground mall across from the Kremlin or the colossal, hideously ugly statue of Peter the Great overwhelming the newly rebuilt Cathedral of Christ the Savior. At the same time, pieces of downtown structures collapsed, as termite-ridden wooden supports crumbled, reducing parts of the street and apartment buildings to rubble. While the main streets were showpieces and new, gated, luxury housing sprang up on the periphery, the alleys and side streets of the city got older; the subway was living on borrowed time; the infrastructure needed investment badly.

Luzhkov, as all the other leaders and contenders for power, understood the value of media properties to a political life. He converted the local television station into a new channel, TV-Center; he invested in the struggling commercial station REN-TV; and he could influence all the other media properties the city had a piece of: the Moscow radio station and a newspaper group that included *Evening Moscow.* He had some shares of TV-6, and he went looking for alliances with politically compatible regional television stations outside Moscow. The crash of '98 reined in the exuberance of expansion, but not the ambitions. With media properties in hand, Luzhkov considered his run for the presidency significantly strengthened. What he and all the other owners failed to consider was, of course, the viewer. As long as expensive Western serials and movies filled the airtime, ratings went up. But making TV a boring political vehicle for talking heads was quite a different matter as long as viewers had a choice.

The Russian government was also a big player, directly controlling a number of electronic communications properties, including 51 percent of Channel One; Channel Two (Russian Television and Radio—the second largest of the Soviet-era channels); big radio stations, such as Radio Russia and Mayak; two big news agencies; and over a hundred state-owned radio and television properties in the provinces. In the fall of 1997, the Yeltsin government converted the St. Petersburg Channel (broadcasting through-out European Russia with very low ratings and inferior programming) to the Culture Channel, urged on by the great cellist Mstislav Rostropovich, who became one of its directors. This channel was to bring back to view-ers programs on high culture and serious public affairs. Unfortunately, its budget from the state was woefully inadequate. Forgoing the intrusive, jan-gling advertising the intelligentsia particularly despised, the new channel also renounced the race for ratings, understanding that providing a public service might mean reaching smaller demographic groups neglected by the mass market. As the economic vise tightened after the crash, the channel increasingly relied on old films and programs from the archives. Television analyst Vsevolod Vilchek thought the channel was a "still birth," not because its public-interest mandate was not important, but because Russia could not afford the BBC model. "Every democracy," he said, "looks out for and protects the rights of minorities, and cultural minorities ought to be served by the state budget."[1]

Did it matter that such media concentration existed and that political and economic agendas could be transmitted from these media empires? Media owners did indeed use their properties to advance their agendas, most obviously in television through the weekend opinion programs. One such opinion "star," anchor Sergei Dorenko, put it bluntly: "Yes, I never criticized a single stockholder of ORT, including Berezovsky. . . . I have not yet touched a single commercial structure belonging to stockholders."[2] Though the field of owners was far narrower in Russia, the adverse conse-quences of concentration worried American observers about their own media system. In the United States, Ben Bagdikian warned that "if execu-tives of dominant media corporations are personally silent about dangers of concentrated ownership, it is not surprising: the process benefits them in terms of both money and power. But the media they control are also silent."[3] How to cover parent companies with huge nets of interest was vexing for *Slate* editor Michael Kinsley when his owner Microsoft was taken to court, and also, apparently, for ABC, when Disney exposés were contemplated.

One could always be saved by the pluralist rationale. As the openly parti-san Dorenko opined, his weekend program was just one of three on televi-sion and "together with my colleagues on the various channels, we present viewers with the entire spectrum of the political rainbow."[4] This is the ar-gument of external diversity. No single channel, the argument goes, need ensure representation of all salient points of view if overall, across the chan-nels, there is reasonable diversity. It requires viewers to sample broadly, which is a significant commitment of scarce time resources.[5] This imposes a heavy responsibility on the public, for whom time is limited, and trade-offs must be calculated between acquiring information (and choosing among the varying utilities of different kinds of information) and relaxing with entertainment. Perhaps paradoxically, as I explain below, this operation of information collection and sorting has been streamlined by the habits of the still-recent Soviet past, for Russian viewers are uncommonly skilled in devising mental shortcuts to order and evaluate television news.

The worrying degree of cross-ownership and media concentration in post-Soviet Russia certainly resulted in using properties as mouthpieces. On the whole, though, it is not a simple matter to trace the precise effect of ownership on news content. The exact interests of the owners and the clear imposition of those interests on the news are easier to assume than prove. It is rare that documents such as transcripts of the alleged Berezovsky tapes surface. These secretly recorded telephone conversations, the authenticity of which Berezovsky disputed, revealed the tycoon ordering Channel One news anchor Dorenko to play up the weaknesses of companies competing for ownership of Russian oil shares with Berezovsky and his allies. In the United States where concern about the effects of economic interests on the news has been growing, the most rigorous studies relate quality and volume of news coverage (or lack thereof) to a specific case—for example, the expected economic benefits stemming from the Telecommunications Act of 1996. In this case, some media owners plainly stood to gain or lose from the bill and, in addition, there was substantial public lobbying by media interest groups.[6] In Russia, to the extent there was disclosure, the owners were players in several industries, with a variety of policy preferences, and some wanted political offices as well. A complex and confusing picture emerged as alliances and mergers were crafted and fell apart as the policy environment and the economy shifted.

Before the crash, both Russian and Western critics sometimes too easily connected content with interests they imputed to the owners. Reasoning backward from news content to owners' known or assumed preferences was the favored strategy. It appeared to work best when applied to the limited universe of the three big networks' highly personalized weekend news-review/opinion programs. On these three shows battles were most likely to erupt along the lines favored by their owners, and there were some notable ones. For example, in the summer of 1997 the results of a telecommunications auction disadvantaged two of the biggest media moguls, Vladimir Gusinsky of NTV and Boris Berezovsky of Channel One, and the weekend opinion programs on these two stations criticized insider favoritism (Sergei Dorenko on Channel One was downright ferocious). Most cases were not so clear-cut. Making the job of analysis more difficult, the weekend opinion programs tended to be quite different in format, tone, and range of stories from the much greater volume of daily evening news shows. For example, clear editorial bias (generated by either the selection of materials or the broadcaster's opinionated speech) in national network coverage of presidential hopeful

General Alexander Lebed's 1998 gubernatorial campaign in Krasnoyarsk varied from 20 percent of the daily news stories on Channel One, 63 percent on Channel Two, and none on NTV, to 100 percent of the weekend programs on Channels One and Two and none on NTV.

The big news stories were often investigations of corruption and malfeasance. For some of these stories, journalists paid with their lives; especially, but not only, in the provinces, these were very risky forays. *Kompromat,* information compromising the reputations of public figures, was rife in Russia; security police and justice officials had plenty of secretly recorded, confidential tapes to sell. In some stunning cases, journalists succeeded in pushing onto the public agenda issues of corruption. In the summer of 1997, for example, the Russian minister of justice was immediately relieved of his post after television aired footage of him cavorting in the baths with women linked to organized crime. *Kompromat* also revealed cash "advances" (nearly $100,000 each) privatization chief Anatoly Chubais and his associates had received for a phantom book. Revealingly, the payoffs came from the beneficiaries of the same telecommunications privatization auction Berezovsky and Gusinsky had criticized through their TV stations. Without legal protections and established professional canons governing conflicts of interest, the line separating news coverage from the economic interests of journalists or their employers could blur, as Chapter 10 details. And to the extent that the blurring produced misinformation, the public was ill served, and "democracy" became synonymous with wholesale appropriation of state property and deception. On the other hand, when the press uncovered corruption to check governmental malfeasance, it acted as a surrogate for a public that did not have direct influence over its elected officials, and the risks for journalists were very serious. Under such conditions it was understandable that reporters were often incensed when their revelations did not provoke instant change and that the increasingly crowded news terrain of governmental irregularities diminished the effect of each new disclosure. Even this had become *normalny.*

Before the crash, the television market was a growth industry. Television advertising revenues were expected to double from 1997 to 1998, the year of the crash. In the spring of 1998, warning signs were already discernible, and stations began reversing their growth estimates, predicting a downturn of 25 to 30 percent. But then the ad market collapsed. The few big agencies that controlled the market registered a whopping 70 to 80 percent drop in business. The president of the association of advertising agencies said that before the collapse, up to $200 million was in circulation monthly, but afterward the figure had fallen to $40 million.[7] Because the television industry, including state television, was heavily dependent on advertising, the fallout was devastating. State-owned broadcast stations, numbering 113 nationwide, faced a tough crunch. They were victims of reduced ad expenditures and anemic government subsidies. The government's empty pockets were hardly a surprise—it had been breaking its promises to the stations for a long time. Before the bottom fell out of the economy, Channel Two complained of receiving only 12 percent of its scheduled support; it had not been more than 20 percent for several years. Mikhail Shvydkoi, head of Channel Two in 1998, said the state had given him only 7 percent of the promised budget for programming before the crash and nothing at all after. That meant, among other things, more vigorous downsizing of still bloated staffs. Less responsive to market forces, the state-owned channel employed four thousand people, while about one and one-half thousand worked at Channel One, and a little over a thousand at NTV. Even at leaner NTV, 8 to 10 percent of the workforce were immediately let go and pay cuts were ordered for the remaining employees. If all else failed, the broadcast day would have to be cut back.

The Russian economic disaster made foreign imports more expensive. Advertising prices were discounted to attract buyers. There had always been a sliding scale of discounts for volume advertisers, but now on average the discounts became deeper, as much as 80 percent off the published price list. Even these inducements were not enough to attract many foreign products, now priced out of reach. Movies typically drove ratings on all the national television networks; now they would be fewer, older, and frequently repeated. High-quality domestic entertainment program production was even more expensive and the equipment had to be imported. All this disadvantaged local stations much more than the big Moscow-based companies and a real shakeout seemed likely to occur. Talk shows, both entertainment and public affairs, were least expensive of all, and viewers saw much more of them. More made-in-Russia programs were in the offing, a consolation for some.[8]

As wrenching economic problems and political discord grew, local governments introduced their own desperate measures. Some ordered taxes to be paid to local authorities and not to Moscow; some instituted price controls; some ordered embargoes on food and other critical goods. These local improvisations could not function effectively, embedded as they were in the larger whole, but they were symptoms of a continuing erosion of central power and authority. Under these circumstances, the role of national media gained in visibility and political importance. Because national newspapers, as Chapter 10 discussed, had long since ceased to be truly national in circulation, the remaining national medium was, of course, television.

EROSION OF GOVERNMENTAL CONTROL

Even before the crash of August '98, the Russian Federation government had ceased to control the messages sent by the Moscow-based television networks: the unity of the '96 election campaign was gone. The president's "story," together with its desired spin, could be assured of carriage only on the national channel his government controlled directly: RTR (Channel Two). This was an increasingly unattractive forum, since the ratings showed RTR losing viewers. Ratings did differ, depending on which company provided the service. Gallup used people meters in European Russia; the Russian Research company relied on diaries. But however the ratings were generated, NTV was moving up fast, and viewers were tuning in to news and public affairs in unprecedented numbers. The August 1998 crash resulted in a huge spike in viewership. NTV doubled its numbers to get the highest ratings in its history, and ORT's ratings increased substantially. ORT still enjoyed a considerable technological advantage; its programs could be received by virtually the entire country, while NTV reached about 60 percent of the population. Still, in Moscow and other cities across Russia, NTV was expanding and gaining fast.

With its typical lurching response to dilemmas, the Yeltsin government issued a decree on May 8, 1998, designed to prop up the state television sector's influence. Under the terms of the decree, all local state stations and government-owned technical facilities (such as transmitters) were placed under the sole authority of state-owned Channel Two. Before this order, the huge Ostankino transmitters on which Moscow-based state and commercial broadcasters relied were controlled by a ministry-like federal organization. Now they were to be concentrated in the hands of only one competitor in the television market. Clearly the creation of this new Holding Company, as it was called, could provide the government a political advantage as the elections of 2000 approached, either by charging preferential rates or imposing punitive measures on different users of the resource. The handwriting was on the wall: In the future, technological independence would be no less important than the rules regarding censorship.

The government's frustration that it could not control television news content boiled over in May 1998. Russia's coal miners had gone on strike. They had done so often, since the days of Gorbachev's perestroika, but this time the action was unprecedented. The miners succeeded in halting trains by occupying the railroad tracks running from east to west. Railroad transport was vital to the movement of goods and people in this direction. From north to south, air and truck freight was affordable, but over the vast distances across the country, there was no real alternative to rail traffic. At the height of the strike, thousands of trains (whole trains, not cars) were stranded; nuclear power plants lacked critical operating materials; medicine, food, and fuel were held up. The miners sat on the tracks, huddled over fires.

NTV's coverage showed a map of Russia, with little points illuminated at each strike site. The viewer could see the spread of the movement, as new glowing dots appeared in the south of Russia, then in the north and the west. Coverage was objective and avoided editorializing, allowing newsmakers to speak in their own words—both protesters and government officials—and providing extensive reporting from the various new scenes. As Oleg Dobrodeyev said—he had risen from head of news to president of the network—how could it not be covered? The country had been "cut in half by the strike."[9] Dobrodeyev spoke defensively, for the Yeltsin government had come down hard on the station for what it regarded as provocative coverage.

During those days, journalists from around the world had congregated in Moscow for the annual Congress of the International Press Institute. Together with the rest of the participants, I went to the Kremlin to hear Boris Yeltsin complain about the role of television in bringing bad news and inflaming tensions. He began his comments in the Kremlin that May by decrying censorship and governmental pressure on the press but quickly identified as a problem of no less severity the "dependence of the mass media on private owners" and complained that "unfortunately, far from all Russian journalists have learned to use their freedom sensibly."[10] The next day, Oleg Dobrodeyev told the international meeting that he found Yeltsin's words "insulting." Just two days later, Yeltsin summoned the heads of all the Moscow-based national channels to reassure them about the plan to award the transmitters to Channel Two, and he remarked that strike coverage had improved. He requested the NTV and ORT news chiefs to transmit governmental policy through television, but he neither threatened nor commanded them. That weekend Yeltsin's radio address was conciliatory. He promised to engage the media in a dialogue, and he admitted they were not at fault for the bad news they transmitted. He did ask for responsible reporting and for more positive and fewer negative stories, but the tone had changed markedly from the earlier bellicose challenge.

The government did not and could not control the way television news programs framed the strike. That framing was substantially different across the three channels, and the severity of the economic problem could be appreciated most fully on NTV. Neither a unified oligarchy nor a single government line determined the news of that event, nor of other nationally important news such as the election of the governor of Krasnoyarsk province, the make-or-break contest for presidential hopeful General Alexander Lebed, discussed below. These were tactical defeats. The government had not abandoned its strategic interest in shaping the news on stations it controlled.

PRESSURE FROM THE PAST

Throughout, this book chronicles the fight for the prize that control over television represented. It was a zero-sum game in which those who were excluded became determined to gain power over this near-magical political asset. The Communist Party, leading the opposition-dominated Duma, was not reconciled to the hand dealt it by the 1996 presidential election. As the government's economic woes deepened, the Duma's budgetary authority grew more salient. Capricious and ill-planned governmental personnel changes turned into a dysfunctional game of musical chairs, while the Duma's power over the confirmation of the prime minister gave it the upper hand. The president could have called for new elections but they were unlikely to improve his position. The nascent middle class was the first to be hit hard, but soon the effects spread, and many Russians were deprived of essentials they could not afford, such as foreign medicines and an adequate diet. Fuel and food supplies were uncertain in the frozen north, the distant east, and the isolated outpost of Kaliningrad. Calling early elections offered only hazards to the cause of the increasingly remote and weakened president.

When the Communist Party sensed it had gained important political leverage, it pursued the same asset it had always coveted: power over television. It reestablished its television forum, *Parliamentary Hour*. This, the show's second birth after premiering in the bitterly divisive spring of 1993, was another attempt to gain coverage that was not mediated by the Yeltsin government or by hostile journalists. With this show the Duma's leadership would have control over at least some airtime on a national channel. After the August '98 crash, Prime Minister Evgeny Primakov formed a compromise government, combining indigestible portions of leftover liberal reformers and their opponents, mainly Communist Party former government officials. Gennady Zyuganov went after television with renewed purpose. In the fall of 1998, he laid down his conditions for support of an austerity budget and the ratification of the START II arms control treaty. Control over television was high on his agenda, and he called for a supervisory council to monitor coverage. Defenders of press freedom hoped the council would be large, unwieldy, overly diverse in composition, and unsuited to do more than give diffuse advice to a television head who could choose to ignore it.

In a concession to the Duma's leadership, Channel Two agreed to the creation of a council; it met for the first time in October 1998. The council's membership was large; nominations came from each parliamentary chamber, from the president's office, from the cabinet, and from various professional and social organizations. Channel Two hoped to protect its autonomy by giving in to the watchdogs. It would be a balancing act: seeking the assistance of the new overseers to deal with the budget disaster, while nullifying unwanted interference by ignoring advice that came with no sanctions and no power. In fact, just such a council had been operating at Channel One, since the end of 1997. It rarely met, attendance was spotty, it took no decisions, and made no recommendations.[11] What the stations did not have and had never had was institutionalized autonomy, guaranteed by buffers defending them from both presidential and parliamentary interference. Throughout the dramatic course of the battle over television in post-Soviet Russia, when the demands of those who would take over the medium were sufficiently diffuse, television, even state television, had room to maneuver. But this freedom came from institutional incapacity and, in the case of NTV, the independence afforded by the market. A more consistent and dependable insulation could come only from legal institutions and a legal culture.

The Communist Party's quest for control was gaining momentum. Zyuganov proposed investigating the process by which Channel One had been privatized and annulling the outcome. Then he moved on to the question of individual television officials. First he set out to change the head of Channel Two. His candidate, Leonid Kravchenko, the last head of Soviet-era state television, had already made a comeback as head of the media effort of the upper house of parliament. Ominously, the Party declared it would mark the November 1998 celebration of the 1917 Revolution by preparing accusations against the leading television news anchors. At the same time, the Communists began another, more sweeping campaign of anti-Semitism. As Chapter 9 discussed, during the Soviet era the prohibition of stirring up hatred among ethnic groups (of which the Jews were considered one) put public expressions of anti-Semitism off limits, though anti-Zionism (seen as interference by a foreign state, Israel) was official policy. In fact, they were indistinguishable in practice, and quotas, purges, and daily discrimination were very much in force. In post-Soviet Russia the official prohibition of public statements that stirred up ethnic or racial hatred prevented law-abiding citizens from adequately responding to those who called for pogroms. Russia lacked the institutions to safeguard promptly, consistently, and visibly the rights of those who were victimized by intolerance. Nor did it have institutions for teaching—in the broadest sense—the values of tolerance.

Vladimir Zhirinovsky, as this book showed, ranted with impunity. In the fall of 1998, he was eclipsed by another: the rabble-rousing former general, Albert Makashov, one of the leaders of the violent takeover of the television center in 1993. When Makashov publicly insulted and threatened Jews, Yeltsin and other public figures spoke out in condemnation, but Duma deputies refused to strip their colleague of immunity or even to censure him. A mild slap on the wrist was all that could be mustered. A fellow Communist deputy spoke of a connection between Jews in Yeltsin's entourage and his "genocidal" oppression of the Russian people. It was still a crime to stir up ethnic hatred, and the Kremlin talked of prosecution but, as before, indecisively. The campaign of anti-Semitism singled out those in the reform government who had some Jewish ancestry, such as privatization head Anatoly Chubais, economic adviser Alexander Livshits, and prime ministers Evgeny Primakov and Sergei Kirienko. But as always, a central target of anti-Semitism was television. NTV was owned by Vladimir Gusinsky, a practicing Jew, who publicly championed Jewish causes; ORT (Channel One) was controlled by its chief private stockholder, Boris Berezovsky, a recent Russian Orthodox convert of Jewish ancestry. Jews were prominent among on-air experts, hosts, and reporters, after many years of Soviet rule when they were not allowed to be shown on air. This was not the first campaign against Jews in television, but it was the most publicly virulent. From the Communist/nationalist alliance, the calls came again to return Russian airtime to "real" Russians.

Institutions to deal fairly and expeditiously with hate speech in the media were not in place. There was the Judicial Chamber for Information Disputes, an organ appointed by the Russian president and accountable to him. Chapter 9 discussed this body and its quandary in dealing with the obviously illegal hate speech of Vladimir Zhirinovsky. It was no match for the even more incendiary General Makashov. As Frances Foster notes, the chamber viewed the state and its institutions as ineffective in enforcing what minimal law there was and that, perforce, the chamber must act in its stead, but it lacked power.[12] From my discussions with the chamber's head and others, it seemed that the chamber believed its opinions were most important in the symbolic court of public opinion—certainly a weak alternative. It did turn cases over to government prosecutors, but the legal system was too slow and too often unable to resolve conflicts.

The world of television enjoyed a high profile and Russians believed it had nearly magical power to influence elections. Beyond that, it conferred legitimacy and status; appearing on that medium made one a part of the national conversation. Thus, television was the target bigots went after and their threat was strengthened by the inability of the courts of law and other institutions (professional ethics codes, civic and voluntary institutions, and more generally, patterns of social interaction) to function in ways to marginalize extremists.

THE SMART PUBLIC: HOW RUSSIAN VIEWERS "READ" THE NEWS

The intensity of the political elite's struggle for power over television rested on assumptions about how the public processed televised information. Little was known about the way people actually watched the news—what their thoughts and emotions were and whether they were interested enough to spend time and energy engaging the issues. In the West, economic models of information acquisition show that the likelihood citizens will access and digest large amounts of political information is quite low. Some information, according to Anthony Downs, is sought as an end in itself, as a kind of entertainment—say, for news junkies. But mostly, information seeking falls into three categories: what people need to guide their consumption decisions, what they need to guide their production or business decisions, and information they need as citizens—political information.

We know that in the United States, most people are characterized as poorly informed. For example, they flunk pollsters' tests that question whether they know who their representatives in Congress are, the level of U.S. foreign aid, even the geography of the world. They make up for their lack of information about issues or events that matter to them by taking mental shortcuts that rely on both emotion and reason, the heuristics discussed below.[13] There is a significant gap between people who have the cognitive capacity to process large amounts of information and those who do not, but this ability cannot be reduced to the level of formal education. Other kinds of learning—from varieties of experiences—also expand the individual's ability to process information.[14] So, asking about current events or specific recall of news may not reveal how people filter and process the news and thereby make sense of their world.

In analyzing the Russian viewer, I use a constructionist approach, one in which, in Ann Crigler's words, "all participants in the communications process—media, officials, and the public—are viewed as actively engaging in constructing messages and meanings."[15] The most dramatic finding of the research that follows is the Russian viewer's extraordinary sophistication. This might come as something of a surprise, given the dismissive or even contemptuous view of the public voiced by some Russian television officials, journalists, and politicians. But we should not really be surprised: for decades of Soviet rule, outsiders remarked on the ingenious ways ordinary people could wring out of the sparse news a trove of information. Those habits survived, in part from a high degree of interest in acquiring information to survive. Russian viewers scanned the news for hints of planned official actions, looming threats, or widening corridors of the permissible. These habits developed, too, as a reaction to the extremely limited amount of information provided overall by the system. Information poverty, not overload, was the problem, and interpreting the news involved taking apart each frame to see what unintended cues had crept in. Soviet television viewers were deconstructionists from long ago. The impressive media literacy of post-Soviet Russian viewers will not likely survive after today's adults but for the present, their skills are enviable.

Focus groups offer a way to explore a dynamic model of opinion formation and television viewing, albeit with well-known disadvantages. Bringing a small number of people to a special room, no matter how comfortably arranged, is not the same as eavesdropping on discussions at home or at work. The results are also not as representative as mass public opinion surveys that capture the views of large numbers of respondents selected as representative of larger populations. However, focus groups do enable the researcher to look at how social interaction affects opinions. The group setting and largely undirected flow of conversation permits unanticipated views to surface. It offers "a compromise between the generalizability of large-scale quantitative analysis and the depth of qualitative analysis."[16]

Four focus groups were convened toward the end of May 1998 in Moscow at the Public Opinion Foundation, one of the two or three leading public opinion firms in the country. Their professional facilitator initiated the discussion and, in a limited way, occasionally directed it. But for the most part, the conversation was only among the participants. The first two were groups of college-educated men and women; the third, high school–educated men; and last, high school–educated men and women. The relaxed evening sessions with eight to ten participants were held in a pleasant, small room around a table, with tea and sweets provided. The participants tended to be interested in the issues and eager to talk.[17]

As I have written in this book and elsewhere, Moscow is not Russia. It is a more cosmopolitan, prosperous, and lively center than any other Russian city.[18] However, even if Muscovites have more choice and more access to the media, and even if they are more consciously and obviously citizens of the capital of a vast country, they and their fellow citizens elsewhere in Russia developed similar strategies to overcome the information deficit during Soviet times. The way they watch the news today shows the effects of those years.

Life in the capital may not have particularly helped Muscovites to invent better strategies than their cousins in smaller cities, because it was risky to voice nonconforming views everywhere. Thus, the "conversation" between the viewer and television news had to be internalized and private, whether one lived in the capital or the provinces. In some ways, life in the shadow of the Kremlin was under special scrutiny. The evening news for the Moscow edition was subjected to controls that far-away Pacific Rim viewers never. had. Moscow viewers are on average more highly educated and have access to more newspapers and television stations than Russians in smaller cities and rural settlements. But these facts do not turn out to be the main issue. The "Soviet-era heuristic," as I call it, is not a test of the supply of knowledge or volume of facts that viewers bring to news watching; it is, rather, the *process* by which they make sense of the news in their own way, with their own resources. Experience of the Soviet past is a large part of the creation of individual strategies, and it is a shared past that goes well beyond Moscow.

The focus groups were convened at an interesting time, right after the concluding round of the Krasnoyarsk election. Presidential hopeful Alexander Lebed was running for governor of the province, a huge region accounting for nearly 30 percent of Russia's raw materials. If he lost, he was unlikely to attract support for a run for the Russian presidency in 2000. This Krasnoyarsk race attracted intense national interest and for the focus groups, it was a perfect experiment. The big television networks regarded the regional contest as nationally significant and gave it prominent coverage on the daily news programs and the weekend opinion programs. On the Lebed candidacy, the owners of channels One and Two disagreed. Boris Berezovsky (Channel One) backed Lebed and helped to finance his campaign. The Yeltsin government (Channel Two) opposed Lebed. An outsider, coming into the Siberian race with clear intentions to move on in two years, Lebed still won convincingly. His opponent, mild-mannered incumbent Valery Zubov, had to run on a record of unfulfilled promises in a declining economy and the wan hope of better things to come.

VIEWERS' STRATEGIES: THE SOVIET-ERA HEURISTIC

The foundation of the Soviet-era heuristic is skepticism. For decades, television news was rationed, centrally controlled, and confined to a single authoritative source. Viewers questioned the credibility of the source, even as they attentively watched, and that skepticism, together with high interest, created the basis for today's exceptionally media-literate Russian viewer. That said, I do not mean to imply that Russians reject everything they see on the news as meaningless rubbish. They do not. Their strategies enable them to tease out what is important for them and to correct for methods that trouble them. It is a continuous process of discovering and refining. These are subtleties and dynamics that the mass public opinion survey can rarely capture.

Our focus groups talked about television in general—what they liked and disliked about it—and then looked at excerpts of Lebed election coverage on the three daily network news shows and the three weekend opinion shows. They were not told from which network the excerpts were taken. After each, there was discussion of the content and the source. During the two-hour sessions, the participants' conversation ranged widely over the influence of television, the way it was run, and their reactions to what they saw. The sessions were lively and informal, and the discussion was frequently emotional, even passionate. From these sessions four basic dimensions of the Soviet-era heuristic emerged: suspicion of overly positive messages, attention to the structure of news programs, the search for sources and who benefits from the news story, and detection of internal inconsistencies on the news. On the basis of these evaluative methods, the viewers then engage in different types of responses.

Viewers are keenly aware of overly positive messages. Because Soviet news programs were intended to inspire and lead the public to a desired policy goal, stories were frequently about hoped-for rather than realized progress. Small gains were exaggerated into large-scale achievements on the theory that the future was tending in that direction in any case. As a result, post-Soviet viewers deflate stories of excessive optimism. One man put it this way: when "the lying begins, when somebody is asked something concrete and he answers sweetly, well, that it's good for everybody, I know that it's all lies. And it's completely uninteresting for me and I think that more of the same is coming and I switch to the next [program]." Another man: "It's not hard for us—living twenty years under Soviet rule—to hear when they are trying to manipulate opinion. Probably no one has forgotten this yet." In all the groups, the participants spoke specifically about their recent history and the lessons that remained in their consciousness—even participants in their twenties.

Viewers are attentive to the way news stories are sequenced in the program. The 9:00 evening news during the Soviet era was broadcast simultaneously on all channels and was the single most authoritative program in the country. A strict order governed the course of the broadcast. One focus group member said that although he liked the commercial station, NTV, he objected that the sequence of stories still followed the Soviet mode, with first domestic news, then international, then culture, sports, and weather. He maintained that the most important news should be first, "no matter where it occurs." Habits acquired during Soviet times also affected the viewers' behavior. One woman said that she watched the nine o'clock news "because it's genetically implanted in me. My grandmother used to leave off gardening and at 9:00 run to watch television, like a bedtime story." Another woman noted that "basically old people watch this channel. They used to watch the program *Vremya,* and now they watch this program and nothing else. Young people watch more NTV."

Considering who might benefit from a news story is part of the critical apparatus ordinary Russians bring to their consumption of the news. During the Soviet era, the public was instructed to look for hidden agendas behind messages from bourgeois or anti-Soviet sources. Viewers applied those lessons to domestic sources as well. Because struggles for political power during the Soviet era were concealed by proclaimed unanimity of purpose, they were submerged, but signs of hidden conflicts could sometimes be decoded. A woman in a focus group concluded: "As they taught us: it's in someone's interests." A man, reflecting on the lessons of the Soviet era, said, "I think that in the many years of *perestroika* and the subsequent events in our country, we've acquired an immunity to our being deceived: something is not expressed; or they try to show [something] from the point of view that's needed by someone." College-educated Sasha laughingly pointed out to the others that candidate Zubov was shown wearing a cap and "that," he said, "is a hint: Luzhkov [known for sporting the same kind of cap] supported Zubov."

Viewers in Russia are sensitive to inconsistencies on the news. Here is how one man described his reaction to hearing a news anchor he respected present a stupid script. Sometimes, he said, "our commentary doesn't always fit, and because of this commentary, the anchor who prepares this material doesn't always seem intelligent. And then you understand that he didn't prepare it. And right away there's a negative attitude toward this channel."

Searching for Correctives

Citizens employ a system of correctives, in part drawn from their own, real-world experience and that of others whose opinions they know to be close to their own. Here is an example of a college-educated woman who told the group that when she was watching news about Latvia she called her relatives there to check it out. As a result, she had "a very insulted feeling that they're showing something that doesn't correspond to reality." A man with high school education reported that he had been in Turkmenistan, where the official line boasts of no crime and great prosperity. This man compared what he saw there with news stories on NTV and told the group that NTV was correct. He himself had evidence of the dictatorship there: "I can say that there was a Lenin street, a party headquarters. . . . You go and you see only one face [the leader's]. I counted forty-six [pictures of the leader] on the main street. In the shops there is nothing." A woman with relatives in the north of Russia objected to news stories about pension arrears, because her family had in fact received theirs. But another woman in the group said that her relatives near Moscow had called her because they had not received their pensions. Down's theory suggests that in order to save time and other resources, people find others whose values they share and, as a shortcut, turn to them to seek interpretation and information. As one of the college-educated women remarked, "if it's a serious issue, and there is somebody to ask, then I ask specific people with whom I have ties."

Focus group participants displayed both active and passive responses to biased news and both were found in all the groups. College-educated viewers have more strategies and can articulate the reasons for their choices in more detail, but the basic strategies were common to all groups. The active strategy is to change channels or turn off the set; the more common passive strategy is to continue watching, but with a changed attitude. This passive option of staying with an unsatisfactory news program often involves comparisons among news sources. Remember, in Russia, prime-time news programs are staggered, with NTV's *Segodnya* coming on at 7:00 P.M., RTR's *Vesti* at 8:00 P.M., ORT's *Vremya* at 9:00 P.M., and then NTV's late edition at 10:00 P.M. Viewers dissatisfied with biased news coverage on one program will not immediately find another one to turn to. They can compare coverage, though, as they did during the war in Chechnya.

There is no question that viewers do not like obviously manipulative messages. How they handle this varies. Sometimes they become angry and irritable; sometimes that anger spills over into family relations. Take, for example, the experience related by college-educated Masha, who deliberately conceals her aversion to television news bias in order to preserve domestic peace. In her words:

> I have a complicated situation at home. My brother-in-law lives with us and he's very interested in politics and when something of this sort [of obvious bias or spin] begins, it's better for me to leave and close the door. Because when obvious manipulation goes on, he says, "All of you keep quiet and this is going on here; we have to do something. . . . We have to go out on the street, and you just sit here and keep quiet. That's why the wrong people are in power. We don't have the right television, precisely because we behave this way." That's why it's better to keep quiet; you notice [manipulation] and keep quiet.

All of the participants who described the passive strategy of staying with the news program when bias was detected, believed they could withstand the intended persuasive effects. Naturally. Who would admit to being so malleable and weak as to be prey to manipulation? But the anger displayed at obvious attempts to bias viewers was impressive. Focus group members were emotional about the station's intent to deceive as well as their own capacity to resist. Among the high school–educated, one said that he often noticed bias and attempted manipulation and when he sees it, "I curse and keep my opinion." Another said that "I believe my own intuition. I don't switch." Another: "Each person has his sympathies and antipathies. Each decides." Still another: "Each has his own opinion. And he keeps it. It's in him." Another: "If the news is interesting, the story interesting, then I can watch it and draw my own conclusions." The better educated were equally confident of their ability to withstand the effects of persuasive messages. One woman said that she continues to watch the news even when "there is obvious manipulation, I know my point of view. I'm me; it's difficult to manipulate me." Another woman said that "I watch. I don't switch, but I filter, of course." Some of the well educated said they continued to watch obviously biased news out of a perverse desire to see just how the lies will be couched. As college-educated Evgeny put it: "I do not switch. If there's a theme that interests me . . . I'm interested in how they do it. . . . Do they lie well or skillfully; will they lie dazzlingly; will they lie disgustingly, vilely?" Katya observed that it is useful to monitor even these messages: "Even if you don't like something, you have to know your enemies; that is, you have to know how the other side is presented. That's why it pays to see it and stay abreast of things."

In some cases, attempted persuasion leads to backlash. One college-educated woman said that a negative portrayal of Lebed would lead her to vote for him. "When the commentator tries to talk, talk, talk to me and I want to say all right, but over there [in Krasnoyarsk] they are voting against what you are saying, and I am against it." A college-educated man talked of loss of credibility for the news source because of obvious intent to persuade: "You simply change your attitude toward the one who's not objective. If he pours filth on one of the candidates, you simply change your attitude toward him [the news reader or anchor]." How and in what circumstances viewers spot bias—if they can—is explored below.

Multiple-Source Comparisons and Objectivity

As might be expected from surveys of media consumption patterns, the college educated are also the information rich. They have more time and means to seek additional news sources. Being in Moscow is another bonus: there are more sources, including foreign ones. One man liked to compare CNN's news reporting norms to those of domestic stations and was particularly interested in that during the Persian Gulf War. The college educated use multiple sourcing routinely. Consider Olga: she reads the lively, popular newspaper *Moscow Komsomol* and when "I feel that it's some kind of slander or simply some gossip, I can hear this news on radio or on television. In this case, of course, I listen to the end, and even if I feel that it is attempting to manipulate me, I hear this news to the end and then try to listen to it on other channels and choose the point of view that's closer to mine." Sasha answers: "Yes, that's the way to do it. I watch NTV; sometimes I compare it with TV Center." Irina remarked that her husband reads the newspaper cover to cover and then, when he watches the evening news on television, points out each instance of disagreement. Another college-educated man has the following media-consumption patterns: two newspapers (one of which is devoted to sports), television news, and radio news, which he listens to when driving. In general, the college educated typically consume television, radio, and newspapers.

High school–educated focus group participants used fewer sources with which to draw comparisons. They tended to mention radio and, especially, other television channels. In comparing television news programs, they understood that the framing of the event could be quite different on the three national newscasts and not necessarily invalidate the coverage. Rather, it was up to the viewer to look for the common properties of differently framed stories. Then, a determination could be made of at least the minimum shared aspects of a news story, and in this the viewer could have confidence. About the rest, viewers might simply suspend judgment. They believed that objectivity in the news was elusive and so they searched for ways to assure some minimal level of truth. Not all succeeded, as the following exchange suggests. Here, even seeing might not be believing, if camera angles are part of the spin. This is a conversation between high school–educated Denis, Ivan, Yura, and Anton:

> Denis: I'm a partisan of facts. If they say the wall is white, but if you look, and the shadow falls on the corner, then the result is a shadow and it's not completely white. For me, that one fact is enough, that the wall is white. Beyond that I can see the angle for myself. I'll look for the shading.
>
> Ivan: But there can be such shading.
>
> Yura: Five people got together for a demonstration. You can write that a demonstration took place. At the same time, one hundred people gathered; that's also a demonstration. There are facts. You believe facts. And not only the facts which can be plainly spoken, but the facts you see.
>
> Denis: If on all the channels there's one and the same news: a demonstration of five people took place. And on all the channels they say five people. That means five. But if one says five thousand, another fifteen, and the third that it didn't happen, then you take the fact that there was a demonstration. Such inconsistencies happen.
>
> Anton: That also depends on the photographer. He can choose five people. He showed one part, one compartment. But another [photographer shows it] from above and the whole thing. There's your one fact. It was dictated. The one who orders the music paid for it.

Do Viewers Care about Media Owners?

This afterword began with a look at media concentration in Russia and problems of ownership diversity and pluralism. Do Russian viewers know or care? Do they know that the news is part of a media market? That owners may have agendas? About market imperatives, high school–educated Ivan said: "It's natural. That's the way it is all over the world. They serve us 'fried facts' [very hot material] which can increase interest in the program and raise ratings." "Showing a lot of negative [news]," said college-educated Evgeny, "attracts viewers. Naturally." Comments about NTV, the only commercial station among the big three national networks, were more likely to invoke market imperatives as determining the style of news delivery, and the college educated were particularly likely to link its output with market goals. Sasha observed that "they [NTV] were a little provocative, that is, they show both candidates [in the Krasnoyarsk electoral campaign] in an unflattering light, to somehow interest the opposing viewers." Maxim said Gusinsky "is purely a businessman," and that news decisions were based on business considerations. Another college-educated man said that NTV shows a good deal of negative news, because "it's interesting; it attracts viewers." Sasha pushed the idea of commercial imperatives onto the plane of political strategy. In his view, NTV "is the most commercial channel," and that meant that coverage could not be overly partisan because of the need to protect the business from possibly vindictive winners. Sasha believed that NTV tries not to offend anyone, because "if this one wins, we will work with him. They see a utility only in things being good for them."

Our focus groups were asked to imagine the room at Channel One headquarters (and then Channel Two and NTV) where decisions about what to put on the news were being made. Who, they were asked, is in that room?[19] All four groups began with on-the-spot television news people: they talked about "journalists," "commentators," "news readers," "news directors," "editors," and "correspondents." But very soon, in every conversation, talk turned to the people behind the scenes. Sometimes, believing that the Soviet period was not really over, they brought up a Soviet-era position: two groups (high school–educated and college educated) thought that "censors" (not necessarily from the government) played a role. One college-educated group member referred to the "commissar" as being present. All four groups quoted the proverb, "he who pays the piper calls the tune," and launched into a discussion of who really decides what is news.

The high school–educated groups were familiar with Boris Berezovsky's name and regarded him as the single most important media-owner figure. Since the owners were frequently shown on the news, we showed the groups their pictures. Only Berezovsky was identified by most. But the less well educated groups could not be sure which channel Berezovsky controlled, and although some in the group also referred to Vladimir Gusinsky, they could not identify his television station and they did not recognize his picture. Some thought the rival media magnates were not competitors but co-executives of the same properties. Several invoked the government and "officials," but they were unsure of the connection, except in the case of the government-run Channel Two. They felt on much firmer ground talking about advertiser power over the stations, even though they agreed that the nexus would never be revealed. Ivan asked why the channels "were so shy about revealing who orders the music." Yura immediately responded with heavy irony, "If you call up NTV and ask, 'are you bought?' They'll answer, 'no.' And you'll say, 'I don't believe it.'" As these viewers discussed the piper and his tune, they thought more about the behind-the-scenes power of the advertising agencies and sponsors. Denis noted the illogic of this kind of conspiracy theory. He observed that the same products were advertised on all three network news programs. "If you take the view," he said, "that advertisers dictate the program, then on absolutely all stations they advertise exactly the same products. That means our television is run by the three Ps: Pampers, dandruff [perkhot], and sanitary napkins [prokladky]. And Snickers."

The college educated had a good deal more political information. They could name which influential person was behind each of the networks, citing Berezovsky for Channel One, Anatoly Chubais (Boris Yeltsin's former overseer for television) for Channel Two, and Gusinsky for NTV. When they spoke of Berezovsky, they spoke of a very powerful man, who was not himself in the room they imagined, but who was certain to dominate it.

> Sergei: Berezovsky hardly sits and watches what they intend to broadcast. He simply says, "I need this slice of time for this piece of the program" and that's all. The rest is basic news.
> Misha: Of course, Berezovsky doesn't sit there. In his place there's a person who understands what Berezovsky needs and who, if suddenly he begins not to understand, is replaced by another one.
> Sasha: No doubt about it. [The owner's representative] must be there. That's the traditional post-Soviet practice and it was so in Soviet times.

The majority of the members of all the focus groups saw a strong element of continuity with the past. Even so, in each of the college-educated focus groups some opinions ran counter to the trend. In one of them, a man said: "I am not interested in who's in charge of Channel One or Two. I am interested only in the program."

Spotting Bias on the News: The Experiments

Many in our focus groups thought they had pretty good bias-detecting and repelling mechanisms. To find out more about their ability to spot bias, the groups were shown excerpts from stories on three network evening news programs. The identifying logo was covered, to lessen the temptation to fit their reactions to what was known about the station's position. The clips were short and all were taken from the last day of coverage before voting in the first round of the Krasnoyarsk election.

First shown was NTV's nightly news program, *Segodnya*. It began with a visit by General Gromov, the man who oversaw the Soviet retreat from Afghanistan. He had come to Krasnoyarsk to support the incumbent, Valery Zubov. Gromov talked to reporters, praising his candidate and criticizing Lebed as unprepared for the job and unpredictable in his actions. Gromov told viewers that if he lived in Krasnoyarsk, he would vote for Zubov. Then Alexander Lebed and his wife were shown arriving at a campaign stop and greeting supporters. He invited reporters to a lunch buffet to thank them for their coverage of the campaign. He then spoke about the many people he had met—at least 100,000—and how he looked them in the eye and told them that they might have a negative image of him that television produced, but "I have two sides, right?" His wife commented on the beauty of the region and her pleasure in contemplating living there if her husband won. They were joined by French film star Alain Delon, who had flown in to show support for his fellow paratrooper. Then, back to Zubov, who said that a former movie star comes to Krasnoyarsk as if to some provincial place, and "we're supposed to sigh, 'Alain Delon came.' Maybe if he'd come thirty years ago, that would have been an event." The reporter's voice-over ended the story by saying that if elected Zubov said he will look into campaign violations, but will not pursue his opponents. Both candidates had their sound bites and neither was the subject of editorial comment by the station.

Channel Two's news, *Vesti,* was shown next. It, too, began with Zubov and Gromov at the campaign stop. Then Zubov, in a close-up, said that he hoped the campaign would proceed in a principled manner and that the people of Krasnoyarsk would be able to make their own decision, as is their right. He hoped there wouldn't be boorishness, but if there was, "it will get a well-deserved rebuff." The story went next to the arrival of Lebed and his wife at a reception and the reporter spoke of Lebed greeting Alain Delon. Then Lebed spoke, saying that "I am so bad, malicious, and wicked. Public opinion [i.e., the media] is prepared to remove me. I think that nothing will come of this." In a voice-over, the reporter says that Lebed announced that he is now getting ready for the second round; he does not intend to lose. Turnout is expected to be high because there has never been such a high-profile election in the region. Again, both have their sound bites, and the visuals are the usual shots of the city, people on the streets, and the candidates in close-up.

The third excerpt was from Channel One's *Vremya.* After the usual introduction and shots of candidate posters, Lebed is said to have firmly rejected any role in printing materials and posters insulting other candidates and any connection to the group of homeless brought out to campaign for him. The candidate called for an investigation. The reporter talks of other campaign violations (without naming individual candidates), and then the local prosecutor speaks, saying that he will be looking into irregularities. The reporter then says that Krasnoyarsk has not encountered such passion before, and an unidentified woman is shown saying that "I don't like it that this electoral campaign—that they try to insult one another, dig out things, something that wasn't known, some unclear facts." Another woman says, "I like how the candidates behave. . . . I think that's how it can be and should be. That's how it is in the West, and let it happen here, too. Maybe even . . . people get to thinking more deeply." Zubov is mentioned but not shown, except on posters in the street shots. Neither candidate has a sound bite.

The groups of high school–educated participants could not agree on possible bias. One group thought the first story was for Lebed ("they said so much about him"); against Lebed ("Gromov spoke against Lebed"); or neutral ("the people who did this story are generally not for anyone"). This group saw more advantage for Lebed in the second story but still with much disagreement. In the final story, the group was divided: a woman thought Lebed was featured more than the opponent, but a man said that "it could be ten times, but it tended to be on the bad side." Others saw neutrality, with each candidate accusing the other. Summing up, a man in this group said "when the three stories were shot, they were simply shot, objectively. Everything there was. They didn't want you to favor anyone."

In the other high school–educated group, there was the same division about the NTV story, with most seeing neutrality, the remaining seeing both pro-Lebed and pro-Zubov elements. The same was true for their viewing of the Channel Two story: mostly neutral votes, with one pro-Lebed and one pro-Zubov vote. The last story, on Channel One, was said to be mainly neutral. The lively and engaging Ivan presented to the group his rather sophisticated understanding of the notion of bias in television news by pronouncing the first story to be "pseudo-neutral," yet actually anti-Lebed. "I said 'pseudo.' They try to show both candidates seemingly objectively. They appear to let Lebed speak on his side. They appear to let people supporting his opponent Zubov speak on their side—as though they show you all points of view, the entire possible range. In fact, [that range] is a lot wider and it's up to you to make the decision." Ivan knew that the definition of objectivity that shows a limited number of sides of a question always ends up privileging a relatively narrow set of views.

These three stories were for the most part neutral as compared to the weekend pieces, discussed below. And unlike the discussion of the very partisan weekend pieces, there emerged no collective judgment about bias. It is entirely understandable that viewers were thoroughly divided about who was favored and thus, to a significant degree, found the stories neutral.

Did the two college-educated groups differ from the less well educated groups? They, too, did not agree on whose advantage, if anyone's, was promoted. For example, in the third story homeless people were carrying posters supporting Lebed, and the discussion went as follows: a woman said that the homeless are shown voting for Lebed. A man responded that showing homeless for Lebed "precisely pours water on the mill of the opponents." A woman answered, "yes, it says 'look who's voting with you for Lebed.'" A man joined the conversation by calling the homeless the pejorative "lumpen," and another man said that "these homeless weren't done by Lebed but by someone trying to show him badly." No, argued the woman, it shows that the homeless are for Lebed, and the same man responded, "but Lebed doesn't need them." Some argued that the first story was to Zubov's advantage, others, to Lebed's and some saw it, as one said, "absolutely even in coverage; people will decide it." Several spoke of the neutrality and balance of the coverage. In another group, a woman said she thought the second story favored Lebed. A man responded that he did not think so, to which the woman answered, "When a person stands and speaks to the television reporter that 'I am so bad,' then it's clear to everyone that he is saying, 'I am so good.'" In this group, too, there was no consensus and a good many said it was more or less neutral.

Excerpts from each of the weekend analytic/opinion programs were shown next. In my view the pieces on channels One and Two were grossly partisan, favoring, respectively, Lebed and Zubov, while the NTV piece was relatively balanced. The focus groups were first shown the excerpt from Channel One's program. It begins with a street scene and then the correspondent's voice-over says that "one part of the Krasnoyarsk electorate is for him [Zubov]—they are middle-aged women. They are enraptured when the governor sings Russian romances." Then follows an extended scene of Zubov singing about love. His baritonal sentimentality fills the screen. In all the focus groups, Zubov's syrupy singing caused giggles of embarrassment to erupt.

In sharp contrast, Alexander Lebed is seen arriving with a small staff, and the correspondent says, "General Alexander Lebed is Zubov's principal opponent in the election and he doesn't sing." The rest is on Lebed, who is shown as businesslike, direct, competent. The correspondent says that "in the five preceding years Governor Zubov showed that he makes too easy a compromise with the federal center and with banking structures, which are now stealing from the region. On the contrary, Alexander Lebed has already shown his independence many times. This will, more than anything else, attract Krasnoyarsk voters to him."

Both groups of the college educated securely identified the pro-Lebed, anti-Zubov bias (only one in each group thought it might be neutral). One man noted that Lebed was photographed from below, enhancing his authority. Several said that the program was carrying out orders from the owners. When a woman said that might be so, but the anchor "effectively gave it his own touch," a man responded, "It's enough to give Zubov an opportunity to sing to the end, and it won't be necessary to say anything against him." Nearly all the members of the high school–educated groups agreed that there was a pro-Lebed bias. One of the few who disagreed with the general view was a woman who appreciated Zubov's performance, saying it showed a "human side" and that Lebed appealed to "nostalgia for a strong hand."

The second excerpt was from Channel Two's weekend *Zerkalo* [*Mirror*] program. It begins with a graph of poll results showing Zubov's increasing and Lebed's decreasing numbers. After showing some street scenes, Zubov appears in a dark gray coat coming down the stairs and getting into a car. The voice-over says "Valery Zubov wants to do what is not done in life—to come to power and in his electoral campaign refuse absolutely to cheaply toy with people or allow his allies to collect compromising material about his opponents." This is counterposed to Lebed's "image makers" and supporters—for example, a middle-aged woman who says, "Yes, I believe Stalin is needed by our people because our people have let themselves go. We need Stalin, I think. We need a firm leader who can impose order on the region." Then we see General Lebed speaking to a crowded hall. A man stands up to ask Lebed a question. He has a lined face, mustache, and tousled hair receding at the temples. A wired, intense figure, he angrily berates Lebed, pointing at him and stabbing the air with each charge. He takes Lebed to task for signing a truce agreement in Chechnya. In so doing, he says, Lebed betrayed the people of three Russian districts, now given over to the Chechens. "I am a live witness," he says, and he questions why there has been no information in the media about the 50,000 Russians left without any protection from the Chechens, who "beat, cut throats, and kill," or about the "1,000 prisoners of war still there. . . . You could have gotten an agreement for the security of the Russian population, for the Cossacks. But you did this!" Lebed, stung by the accusation and unaccustomed to the free play of open forums, is quick to respond. He yells into the microphone above the rising voices of the crowd and punctuates his points with a hammering hand. He calls the questioner a "hard-boiled type" and tells him, "Now you listen to me!" The general grows loud and angry. He speaks with contempt of the poor performance of the Russian troops, saying that they left their weapons behind and were rounded up like dumb cattle by the Chechens. At one point in this tirade, Lebed orders his questioner to, "Listen up, here!" The story ends with ordinary people telling why they support Zubov.

In all four focus groups, "Listen up, here!" became a slogan for Lebed's authoritarianism. It was the image that stood for the candidate, just as was Zubov's treacly singing on the other program. All four groups were in general agreement about bias, that it was pro-Zubov and anti-Lebed. High school–educated Ivan, who had noticed "pseudo-neutrality" in the news stories, said this was "openly and stupidly pro-Zubov." Another man in his group said that the story was against Lebed, but "nobody forced Lebed to shout 'Listen up, here!'" College-educated Evgeny said, "It shows Lebed unable to answer a simple soldier who says, 'you're zero, absolutely zero, there's nothing behind your bass voice, just betrayal.'"

The last test was an excerpt from the Sunday *Itogi* [*Wrap-up*] program on NTV. It shows the two candidates campaigning and a hotel in Krasnoyarsk where Moscow-based political consultants engaged by both campaigns are lodged. It speaks of the campaign literature each has and notes that Lebed has more of it. Lebed says that his supporters are ordinary people who are fed up and that they came to campaign headquarters bringing brochures, posters, and other material they contributed. The story notes that Lebed is often criticized for not being a local Siberian; his answer is that we are all Russians. Lebed, the voice-over continues, assures his supporters that he is a specialist in crisis situations and knows how to make the region flourish.

A supporter (old man, fur hat, plaid shirt, teeth missing) rues having voted for Yeltsin because nothing good has come of it and says that Lebed will have discipline and maybe put things right. Zubov is shown campaigning, and viewers are told that he is rather indifferent to his image, that his campaign emphasizes he is an economic manager, practical and not interested in political games. Zubov calls for common sense in choosing the region's governor and tells viewers not to wait for miracles but to strengthen what is positive and depend on themselves.

Neither of the college-educated groups could agree on bias. Several said there was none. Anna remarked that in this story, they were shown lots of facts, and Olga said she agreed: "Here there are only facts, and no one is shown better or worse than the other. More or less equally. A little for Zubov, a little for Lebed, about their work. . . . And you decide for yourself." In both college-educated groups, some thought it slightly pro-Lebed, but far weaker than the first weekend program sample, and more thought it neutral. The high school–educated groups arrived at no consensus about bias; some thought it was pro-Zubov, some thought pro-Lebed, but more thought it was "neutral," "objective," or "truthful." Because the station had no clear or powerfully presented bias in this story, the focus group members were divided as to the partisanship displayed, if any. Like the three daily news stories, but unlike the first two weekend stories, no collective judgment of bias emerged.

Two of these weekend programs were heavily partisan and most of the members of the focus groups identified that partisanship and objected to it. At the same time, they were aware that the candidates were responsible for their behavior, even if coverage was biased against them. Though they objected to the obvious pro-Lebed treatment by Channel One, they recognized that Zubov's lightweight performance was his own responsibility. Similarly, though they thought the balance unfair, they believed that Lebed was at fault for his autocratic harshness shown on Channel Two. They tended to reject both the program and the candidates as a result.[20] The daily news shows and the weekend NTV program were much more balanced, and the focus groups found them neutral or, because of their habit of skepticism, possibly biased. But opinions about the direction and strength of the bias were scattered, with no tendency to agreement.

GOOD NEWS AND BAD NEWS: WHAT RUSSIANS WANT FROM THE NEWS

Conversation about television always fixed on the balance of good and bad news on television. The old Soviet way of presenting the news was to stress the positive to gain support for central directives and to mobilize participation in public acts and work obligations. Bad news was reserved for accounts of natural disasters and political failings in capitalist countries. The new post-Soviet news had a decidedly different mix of good and bad news, reflecting post-Soviet Russia's descent into economic crisis, disintegration of order, and unending conflicts. Some, especially men with a high school education, spoke of a preference for crime and disaster news, among other subjects. Most, in all the groups and both men and women, were dissatisfied with what they saw on the small screen. As one college-educated woman said about television news in general, "You can't be raised only on accidents and misfortunes, although it's necessary to talk about them." And a man in that group objected to the emphasis on muckraking. Another college-educated man applauded NTV's anti-drug spots, and proposed "social advertising" so that "it's not all chewing gum and those things." Another woman spoke with disgust of the "horrible killings, the corpses all the time," and the "beggar children." A man with high school education wanted more "positive facts" in the news—there were so many negative ones, and it was not good to weigh down the mind so much. "I'm an optimist," he said, and "there's no need to have all these difficulties fill my head. It will all pass."

In the college-educated, as in the high school–educated, groups this objection to negative news was altered as a result of the group conversation. At some point in the crescendo of dissatisfaction, a grave and peculiarly post-Soviet response surfaced—a response rejecting the normative model of the Soviet news. High school–educated Ivan, who rejected "pseudo-neutrality," said in response to the "optimist" quoted above: "I don't agree that they should feed me sugar-coated kasha." Boris agreed, "It's not necessary to dress up [the news]," and Ivan went further, saying that "dressing it up—for the news, that's death." The concluding touch came from Andrei, who said: "It's necessary to show what goes on. Even bad things."

The college-educated participants' debate on these issues was more complex because many of them had specialized knowledge and raised what they believed to be empirically proven effects of bad news. Vera had a specific case in mind. In 1987, she said, the government addressed the problem of drug abuse by choosing certain school districts to read a newspaper article about drug taking and drug abuse. She said that the result was "a huge increase in narcotics use in those experimental schools. When I say news should educate, I mean that the information on the news has that effect." And bad news, she concluded, has a predictably bad effect. Tatyana chimed in that violence on television inured children to the notion of crime as commonplace and cost-free. "For them killing a person doesn't cost anything . . . and life is so valueless, thanks again to the news." Evgeny added, "so, unconsciously, news educates." But, responded Tatyana, "not at all the way we want." This is a conversation not very different from the discussions one hears in the United States whenever adults gather to talk about the

state of television, violence, alienation, and the generation gap. But ordinary Russians have powerful counterarguments. In this group Vladimir
said, "It's better to see it on the screen than . . . how it was before. [Before,]
rumor could inflate some insignificant thing practically into civil war." And
quiet, thoughtful Anatoly said that yes, it is necessary to educate, but "at the
same time, all of you here know the danger of this approach. We lived for a
long time in conditions where all this was used for education." He went on
to recount the list of censored subjects. The rest of the group agreed, just as
the rest of the high school–educated group, when confronted with the objection to "sugar-coated kasha," agreed. In both groups, the participants
wished that the news was not all bad, and they hoped for a few bright spots
in the dreary rubble. As college-educated Irina said, all she asks for is "a little light in this dark kingdom."

As the focus groups drew to a close, the conversation turned to the influence of television on ordinary people like themselves. In the focus group
of high school–educated men and women the conversation went from received opinions and abstract formulations to modifications based on personal experience and multiple-sourcing correctives. Here is the exchange
between Oleg and Vadim:

> Oleg: [Television] can move public opinion to any side.
> Vadim: It [television] can make robots of people. Before, there was [only]
> one television channel. [Party] congress, Always Prepared [slogan of the
> Young], Pioneers, whatever.
> Chorus of voices: That's how it was.
> Oleg: But how can you make robots of people if they say one thing on
> television and you go out and there's a different life? And you see something
> else on television?
> Vadim: And before, there was one channel . . . and the same thing was
> said. [That's how it was] under Leonid Ilych [Brezhnev]. And now there is at
> least some diversity in the press. And you can draw your own conclusions.
> Oleg: They say what they say. OK, they said it. You go out on the street
> and on the street there's another life.

Neither ends up agreeing with his own initial, off-the-top-of-the-head
position—the position that station owners and politicians seem to favor—
that television makes robots of us all.

I ended the earlier edition of this book by saying that a great change had
been made since the days of the restrictive Soviet information policy but
that the coming times of turbulent change and deprivation—racing ahead
of benefits from reform—would demand much more of the television system. After the crash of 1998, Russians again and in greater numbers turned
to television to help them understand their difficult lives. Viewers there
bring to their television watching a deeply ingrained skepticism. They also

bring the willingness and habits to engage actively with the news. They may not change the channel and affect the ratings, but behind that apparently passive strategy is a very active challenge to the news. It is a challenge to politicians, owners, and anchors alike that viewers do not appreciate stories in which the deck is stacked and the public is held in contempt. The viewers' ability to make sense of the news and their lives depends on a process of comparison and correction, consistent with their values. The experience of daily life is one such corrective. A broader field of comparison comes from juxtaposing media sources. The college-educated use numerous sources; the high school–educated widen their perspectives by comparing television and radio and one television network with another. The crash of '98 was bound to reduce their choice, with newspapers failing first and then smaller television stations. At the same time, the pressure of elections may again, as so often before, deform fragile, nascent, unstable institutions.

The information environment of ordinary people and elites has changed powerfully since the days of Soviet rule and now affords them a genuine, if limited choice. Even in shambles the market has been the main prop of news diversity. Keeping that choice alive is the most important public service television can perform, as Russians try to guide themselves through daily misfortunes and rebuild their society.

NOTES

CHAPTER ONE

1. Interview with Vladimir Pozner, March 1996.
2. S. Bogatko and Iu. Kazmin, "Solidarnost lyudei truda," *Pravda,* May 2, 1990, 1.
3. Interview with Yegor Ligachev, 1993.
4. Interview with Oleg Dobrodeyev, May 1992.
5. Quoted in RE/RFL, *Report on the USSR,* May 18, 1990, 7.
6. "V Verkhovnom Sovete SSSR," *Izvestia,* May 23, 1990, 4.
In post-Soviet Russia, a law forbidding the media to insult the head of state was also on the books. In 1995 this provision of the criminal code was used by the attorney general to initiate action on behalf of President Yeltsin against NTV for its program of political satire, *Puppets.* The suit was dropped, and the prosecutor was dismissed. (He had also brought criminal charges against NTV's Chechen war reporter Elena Masyuk for interviewing a terrorist.) When Mikhail Gorbachev was asked his view of the alleged insult to President Boris Yeltsin, he answered, "I like all kinds of parodies in general very much, and specifically about myself. If, of course, it is not insulting." Mark Deich, "Mikhail Gorbachev: master varit kashu," 7 *Dnei,* no. 34 (August 21–27, 1995), 38.
7. Simon Midgley, "Around the World," *Independent,* June 26, 1990, 12.
8. This and the following three incidents from covering the Chechen war are drawn from an interview with Elena Masyuk, March 1995.
9. The first quotation was cited by Harrison Salisbury, in "Gorbachev's Dilemma," *New York Times Magazine,* July 27, 1986, 33. The second quotation is from Steven Erlanger, "Up from Propaganda," *New York Times,* November 13, 1994, 16.
10. Mikhail Gorbachev, *Erinnerungen* (Berlin: Siedler Verlag, 1995), 306.
11. Interview with Alexander Yakovlev, May 1992.
12. Interview with Mikhail Gorbachev, June 1995.
13. Mikhail Gorbachev, *Erinnerungen,* 266.
14. The term, from Nietzsche, was introduced into Russian letters at the beginning of the twentieth century. I am indebted to Denis Mickiewicz for this information.
15. Kayaton Ghazi, "The Revolution Erodes in Rural Iran," *New York Times,* February 18, 1995, 4.
16. Steven Erlanger, "Singapore Leader Blames Television for Tiananmen Deaths," *New York Times,* October 16, 1990, A9.
17. Ved Mehta, "Letter from New Delhi," *The New Yorker,* August 19, 1991, 66–77.
18. Michael J. O'Neill, *The Roar of the Crowd: How Television and People Power are Changing the World* (New York: Times Books, 1993).
19. Thomas E. Skidmore, ed., *Television, Politics, and the Transition to Democracy in Latin*

America (Washington, D.C.: Woodrow Wilson Center Press and Johns Hopkins University Press, 1993).

"As the World Turns, It's News with a Spin," *New York Times,* June 24, 1990, sec. 2, 1, 28.

20. Nicholas D. Kristoff, "TV Personalities Defeat Politicians in Tokyo and Osaka Governor Elections," *New York Times,* April 10, 1995, A7.

21. Richard A. Brody, *Assessing the President: The Media, Elite Opinion, and Public Support* (Stanford, Calif.: Stanford University Press, 1991), 4.

22. Jean Baudrillard suggests that the public, barraged and penetrated by media messages and charted obsessively by public opinion surveys, resists absorption by withholding choice and confounds the political elites dependent on their opinions, by a volatility of responses. *Selected Writings* (Stanford, Calif.: Stanford University Press, 1988).

23. W. Russell Neuman, Marion Just, and Ann N. Crigler, *Common Knowledge: News and the Construction of Political Meaning* (Chicago: University of Chicago Press, 1992).

24. John Zaller, "The Myth of Massive Media Effects Revived: New Support for a Discredited Idea," *Political Persuasion and Attitude Change,* ed. Diana C. Mutz, Paul M. Sniderman, and Richard Brody (Ann Arbor: University of Michigan Press, 1996).

John Zaller and Mark Hunt, "The Rise and Fall of Candidate Perot," parts 1 and 2, *Political Communication,* vol. 11, no. 4, 357–391, and vol. 12, no. 1, 97–123.

25. Michael McFaul, "Party Formation after Revolutionary Transitions," and response by Philippe Schmitter, *Political Parties in Russia,* ed. Alex Dallin (Berkeley, Calif.: University of California Press, 1993).

26. Ellen Mickiewicz, *Split Signals: Television and Politics in the Soviet Union* (New York: Oxford University Press, 1988).

27. Data for December 1992.

Postfactum News Agency, *Mass Media Audience,* (Moscow–St. Petersburg: Postfactum News Agency, 1993).

28. Quoted by Sergei Muratov in "Television and Democracy: Who Will Prevail," *Moscow News,* no. 14 (August 7–14, 1991), 10.

29. Quoted by Samuel H. Barnes, *Politics and Culture* (Ann Arbor, Michigan: University of Michigan, Center for Political Studies, Institute for Social Research, 1988), 8.

30. Interview with Mikhail Gorbachev, June 1995.

31. Mikhail Gorbachev, *Erinnerungen.*

32. This is a point made by Rasma Karklins, "Explaining Regime Change in the Soviet Union," *Europe-Asia Studies,* vol. 46, no. 1, (1994), 29–45.

33. Robert Putnam, *Making Democracy Work* (Princeton, N.J.: Princeton University Press, 1993).

34. Conversely, it is television that, by its principle of inclusion or exclusion, defines the national entity for the public. One Russian comment on this was provided by Vladimir Shumeiko, Russian First Deputy Prime Minister, who said, "There will be no single political entity without a single information entity of Russia, as you call it." Channel One, "TV Today and Tomorrow," August 12, 1993. Translated in FBIS-SOV-93-155, August 13, 1993, 18.

35. Joshua Meyrowitz, *No Sense of Place: The Impact of Electronic Media on Social Behavior* (New York: Oxford University Press, 1985).

36. In the United States the way that television news frames events may create a climate of opinion in which responsibility for public policy is diverted away from the political actors and administrations who, according to the way democracies work, ought to have been held accountable. Shanto Iyengar, *Is Anyone Responsible?* (Chicago: University of Chicago Press, 1991).

This finding depends on the way the political culture understands the "government" and the "individual," and the responsibility each has for different domains, ranging from foreign policy, crime, welfare, economic status, and other social policies.

An extremely interesting comparison of Finnish and U.S. television news cultures relates the collectivist approach of Finnish news and culture and contrasts it with the individualistic American style. Ritva Levo-Henriksson, *Eyes Upon Wings* (Helsinki: Hakapaino Oy, 1994).

37. Philip Roeder, *Red Sunset* (Princeton, N.J.: Princeton University Press, 1993).

Russell Bova, "Political Dynamics of Post-Communist Transition," *World Politics,* vol. 43, no. 3 (1991), 113–38.

38. The breakdown in consensus along a soft-line/hard-line axis produced the sorts of cleavages within the authoritarian regime that generally become important in transitions from authoritarian rule. Guillermo O'Donnell and Philippe Schmitter, *Transitions from Authoritarian Rule: Tentative Conclusions About Uncertain Democracies* (Baltimore: Johns Hopkins University Press, 1986).

39. Elinor Ostrom gives three reasons why the effects of institutional change of even much smaller magnitude are difficult to predict: first, the changes in rules are apt to be longer lasting than the changes in the individual interests of the participants; second, human beings devise inventive new ways to respond to rule changes; and third, rules frequently operate in a "configural," or systemic, manner, so that "how a change in one rule will affect incentives and behavior over time depends on the particular configuration of other rules that are involved." Elinor Ostrom, "New Horizons in Institutional Analysis," *American Political Science Review,* vol 89, no. 1 (March 1995), 176.

40. Timur Kuran, *Private Truths, Public Lies: The Social Consequences of Preference Falsification* (Cambridge, Mass.: Harvard University Press, 1995), 255.

41. M. Steven Fish summarizes and develops this literature on transitions with respect to the growth of opposition political parties. *Democracy from Scratch* (Princeton, N.J.: Princeton University Press, 1995).

42. The development of the political party system in the post-Soviet world was related to the way the parties evolved and the overall degree of shared values in the political system. In democratic systems, parties are structured by the usual kinds of cleavages (political ideology, class, religion). To the extent that these features shape new party systems in the former Communist world in an accommodating fashion, the system tends toward equilibrium. However, where disagreements, including those about the very definition of the country, evoke increasingly absolutist competition with little agreement on basic rules, the party system veers to disequilibrium.

See Herbert Kitschelt, "The Formation of Party Systems in East Central Europe," *Politics and Society,* vol. 20, 7–50; and Thomas F. Remington, "Conclusion," *Parliaments in Transition: The New Legislative Politics in the Former USSR and Eastern Europe* (Boulder, Col.: Westview Press, 1994), 217–32.

43. William A. Gamson, *The Strategy of Social Protest* (Homewood, Ill.: Dorsey Press, 1975), 142.

44. Gaye Tuchman, *Making News: A Study in the Construction of Reality* (New York: Free Press, 1978).

See also the study done of experts appearing on the *MacNeil/Lehrer Newshour,* a public broadcasting program and, therefore, presumably less dependent on the kinds of choice dictated by market considerations. William Hoynes and David Croteau, *All the Usual Suspects* (New York: Fairness and Accuracy in Reporting, 1990).

45. A.Petrenko, "Pakazushny sindrom," *Argumenty i Fakty,* no. 8 (February 25–March 3, 1989), 3.

46. Vladimir Shlapentokh, *Public and Private Life of the Soviet People: Changing Values in Post-Stalin Russia* (New York: Oxford University Press, 1989).

47. Arthur Koestler, in *Darkness at Noon* (New York: New American Library, 1961) based the logic of Stalin's purges on generalized acceptance of the notion of long-lasting crisis.

48. Ellen Mickiewicz, *Split Signals: Television and Politics in the Soviet Union.*

49. David Swanson and Paolo Mancini, *Politics, Media, and Modern Democracy* (Westport, Conn.: Praeger, 1996).

50. Irina Petrovskaya, "Nam vsem dali poshchechinu," *Nezvisimaya Gazeta,* November 28, 1992, 5.

CHAPTER TWO

1. Interview with chief newsreader Igor Kirillov, summer 1988.

2. Irina Petrovskaya, "Svobodnye vybory nevozmozhny," *Nezavisimaya Gazeta,* October 10, 1993, 5.

3. A survey of fifty-six Soviet emigrés with media experience was conducted by the RAND Corporation between 1978 and 1980. It found that "manipulation of the media by individual leaders in defense of some minority position would be a very unusual event. The notion that such interventions could be an accepted feature of Soviet politics was incredible to them." Lilita Dzirkals, Thane Gustafson, and A. Ross Johnson, *The Media and Intra-Elite Communication in the USSR* (Santa Monica, Calif.: RAND, 1982), 80.

4. Interview with Vadim Medvedev, May 1992, and Alexander Terekhov, "Zalozhnik," *Ogonyok,* November, 1991, 10–12.

5. TASS, "On the Pulse of Restructuring; Sixth USSR Journalists' Union Congress," *Pravda,* March 15, 1987, 3; FBIS, USSR National Affairs, March 20, 1987, R11.

6. R. Eugene Parta, John C. Klensin, and Ithiel DeSola Pool, "The Shortwave Audience in the USSR: Methods for Improving the Estimates," *Communication Research,* vol. 9, no. 4 (October 1982), 581–86.

7. In general, the Soviet system may have "create[d] expectations about wider citizen influence that conventional organizations cannot satisfy." Donna Bahry, "Politics, Generations, and Change in the USSR," *Politics, Work, and Daily Life in the USSR,* ed. James R. Millar (Cambridge, England: Cambridge University Press, 1987), 89.

The Soviet Union—and Soviet-type states patterned on its model—were among the world's most vigorous developers of communications relative to their political development. Phillips Cutright, "National Political Development: Measurement and Analysis," *American Sociological Review,* vol. 28 (April 1963), 253–64.

See also James L. Gibson, Raymond M. Duch, and Kent L. Tedin, "Democratic Values and the Transformation of the Soviet Union," *Journal of Politics,* vol. 54, no. 2, (May 1992), 329–71.

8. Shanto Iyengar, *Is Anyone Responsible? How Television Frames Political Issues* (Chicago: University of Chicago Press, 1991).

9. Ellen Mickiewicz, *Media and the Russian Public* (New York: Praeger, 1981).

10. Scott Shane writes of the KGB as providing a kind of feedback in *Dismantling Utopia: How Information Ended the Soviet Union* (Chicago: Ivan R. Dee, 1994), 104.

11. V. E. Shlapentokh, *Problemy sotsiologii pechati,* vols. 1 and 2 (Novosibirsk, 1970); David Wedgwood Benn, *Persuasion and Soviet Politics* (Oxford: Basil Blackwell, 1989).

12. B. Z. Kogan and Iu. I. Skvortsov, "Stroky, temy, zhanry," *Problemy sotsiologii pechati,* vol. 2, ed. V. E. Shlapentokh, 43–49; V. E. Shlapentokh, *Problemy sotsiologii pechati.*

13. For a good summary of this model in Western literature, see Elihu Katz, "On Con-

ceptualizing Media Effects," *Studies in Communication,* vol. 1, ed. Thelma McCormack (1980), 119–41.

14. Ellen Mickiewicz, *Media and the Russian Public.*

15. Brian Silver, "Political Beliefs of the Soviet Citizen: Sources of Support for Regime Norms," *Politics, Work, and Daily Life,* ed. James R. Millar, 132.

16. See, for example, Seweryn Bialer, *The Soviet Paradox* (New York: Knopf, 1986).

Jerry Hough, *Russia and the West: Gorbachev and the Politics of Reform* (New York: Simon and Schuster, 1988).

These were inter-generational changes, not merely life-cycle effects that would disappear or attenuate as people grew older.

17. T. I. Zaslavakaya, "Perestroika kak sotsialnaya revolyutsia," *Sotsiologia Perestroiki,* ed. V. A. Yadov (Moscow: Nauka, 1990).

18. Philip Roeder, *Red Sunset* (Princeton, N.J.: Princeton University Press, 1993).

19. Ellen Mickiewicz, "Feedback, Surveys, and Soviet Communication Theory," *Journal of Communication,* vol. 33, no. 2 (spring 1983), 97–110.

20. Yegor Ligachev, *Inside Gorbachev's Kremlin* (New York: Pantheon, 1993), 87.

21. Ellen Mickiewicz, *Split Signals: Television and Politics in the Soviet Union.*

22. Philip Roeder, *Red Sunset.*

Moshe Lewin, *The Gorbachev Phenomenon: A Historical Interpretation* (London: Radius, 1988).

William Eastery and Stanley Fischer, "Living on Borrowed Time: Lessons of the Soviet Economy's Collapse," *Transition* (published by the World Bank), vol. 5, no. 4 (April 1994), 1–3.

23. Mikhail Gorbachev, *Erinnerungen,* 375.

24. For a summary of this period, see Sarah E. Mendelson, "Internal Battles and External Wars: Politics, Learning, and the Soviet Withdrawal from Afghanistan," *World Politics,* vol. 45 (April 1993), 327–60.

Western analysts differ as to when, if at all, Gorbachev achieved a working majority of policy allies. Anders Aslund, *Gorbachev's Struggle for Economic Reform,* 2nd ed. (Ithaca, N.Y.: Cornell University Press, 1991), for example, puts it at March 1990.

Jerry Hough detailed Gorbachev's personnel changes in the Communist Party and found his power "greatly strengthened" by the spring of 1989. "The Politics of Successful Economic Reform," *Milestones in Glasnost and Perestroyka: Politics and People,* ed. Ed A. Hewett and Victor H. Winston (Washington, D.C.: Brookings, 1991), 246–86.

Mikhail Gorbachev, approaching the 1988 party conference, said he could name as firm allies only five Politburo members and maybe two others, but counted on the power of the General Secretary to win the day. Mikhail Gorbachev, *Erinnerungen.*

25. Yegor Ligachev, *Inside Gorbachev's Kremlin,* 11.

The differences between ruling politicians who favored rescuing the status quo and those with more radical agendas were also at issue at the time in many of the defections from authoritarianism across southern Europe and Latin America. (See, for example, Giuseppe Di-Palma, *To Craft Democracies: An Essay on Democratic Transitions* (Berkeley, Calif.: University of California Press, 1990).

26. Interview with Mikhail Gorbachev, June 1995.

One of the chief objects of his charge were the authors of *Inogo ne dano,* a group of sharply reformist critics of Gorbachev.

27. For an excellent overview of the Gorbachev policies, see: Archie Brown, "The Gorbachev Era, 1985–91," *The Cambridge Encyclopedia of Russia and the Former Soviet Union* (Cambridge, England: Cambridge University Press, 1994), 127–43.

28. Anders Aslund, *Gorbachev's Struggle for Economic Reform,* 225–30.

Archie Brown, to the contrary, believed privatization was a deep interest of Gorbachev and that he was proceeding slowly only because of constraining circumstances. "Gorbachev's Leadership: Another View," *Milestones of Glasnost and Perestroyka: Politics and People,* ed. Ed A. Hewett and Victor H. Winston (Washington, D.C.: Brookings, 1991), 446–59.

29. As Donna Bahry and Brian Silver note, popular accountability shifted the center of balance. Donna Bahry and Brian Silver, "Public Perceptions and the Dilemmas of Party Reform in the USSR," *Cracks in the Monolith: Party Power in the Brezhnev Era,* ed. James R. Millar (Armonk, N.Y.: M. E.Sharpe, 1992), 141–77.

30. Thomas F. Remington observes that Gorbachev's strategy of maintaining both a centralized party and popularly elected legislatures failed because it "upset the balance between central controls and local autonomy that maintained the union of republics." "Introduction: Parliamentary Elections and the Transition from Communism," *Parliaments in Transition* (Boulder, Col.: Westview Press, 1994), 2.

Mary Buckley notes that Gorbachev hoped the Nineteenth Party Conference would place him at an advantage over his Party associates who resisted reform, but the demands from the Baltic states soon outdistanced the "officially sanctioned goals of perestroika." *Redefining Russian Society and Polity* (Boulder, Col.: Westview Press, 1993), 46.

31. Mary Buckley writes that "genuine pluralism required supporting institutional structures and facilitating mechanisms that an authoritarian one-party state lacked" (p. 153). She also argues that although he was ambiguous on the subject and may have concealed his intentions from his Party opponents, Gorbachev was fundamentally opposed to a multi-party system in 1989, even before his determined turn away from reform. Mary Buckley, *Redefining Russian Society and Polity,* 151.

32. Interview with Mikhail Gorbachev, June 1995.

33. Mikhail Gorbachev, *Erinnerungen,* 374.

34. Interview with Mikhail Gorbachev, June 1995.

35. Zhores Medvedev, *Gorbachev* (New York: Norton, 1986).

An emigré film-maker recounted that Suslov was in charge of the screening of a (then) daring film for General Secretary Leonid Brezhnev and Prime Minister Kosygin, and threateningly asked the film's director, "Why is it that you have such a dislike for us?" *The Soviet Censorship,* ed. Martin Dewhirst and Robert Farrell (Metuchen, N.J.: Scarecrow Press, 1973), 114.

36. Vitaly Korotich, "Kogda budet nevmogotu . . ." *Ogonyok,* no. 28 (July 28, 1991), 12–15.

37. Ronald J. Hill and Alexander Rahr, "The General Secretary, the Central Party Secretariat and the Apparat," *Elites and Political Power in the USSR,* ed. David Lane (Hants, England: Edward Elgar Publishing, 1988), 62.

38. Yitzhak Brudny, "The Heralds of Opposition to Perestroyka," *Milestones in Glasnost and Perestroyka: Politics and People,* ed. Ed A. Hewett and Victor H. Winston (Washington, D.C.: Brookings, 1991), 153–89.

39. Scott Shane, *Dismantling Utopia: How Information Ended the Soviet Union* (Chicago: Ivan R. Dee, 1994), 162.

40. Philip Schlesinger, "From Production to Propaganda?" *Culture and Power,* ed. Paddy Scannell, Philip Schlesinger, and Colin Sparks (London: Sage, 1992), 293–316.

Gaye Tuchman, *Making News: A Study in the Construction of Reality* (New York: Free Press, 1978).

Pamela Shoemaker, *Gatekeeping* (Newbury Park, Calif.: Sage, 1991).

Edward Jay Epstein, *News from Nowhere* (New York: Random House, 1973).

41. Daniel Hallin, *The "Uncensored" War: The Media and Vietnam* (Berkeley, Calif.: University of California Press, 1986). Though disunity among political elites was fundamentally

important, it was not, of course, the only factor relating to the changing shape of television coverage: as time went on, lack of consensus in society and the growing problem of morale among the troops made television coverage more critical.

42. Mikhail Gorbachev, *Perestroika: New Thinking for Our Country and Our World* (New York: Harper and Row, 1987), 76–77.

43. Mikhail Gorbachev, *Erinnerungen,* 317.

44. Ibid., 330.

45. Interview with Alexander Yakovlev, May 1992.

46. Yegor Ligachev, *Inside Gorbachev's Kremlin,* 106.

47. It was a system in which, in the view of Vadim Bakatin, the reform-minded head of the KGB under Gorbachev, "the selection was rather strict and the mistakes were few . . . there is no doubt that they [the cadres and organization departments of the Central Committee] thoroughly trained people capable of occupying high state offices and implemented a strict selection." In addition, this system was a "multi-year system of training of individual, professional qualities of people, selection, study, practice of interns and much else."
Mikhail Nenashev, *Posledneye pravitelsvto SSSR: lichnosti, svidetelstva, dialogi* (Moscow: A. O. Krom, 1993), 69.

48. For a discussion of this point, see: Ada W. Finifter and Ellen Mickiewicz, "Redefining the Political System of the USSR: Mass Support for Political Change," *American Political Science Review,* vol. 86, no. 4 (December 1992), 857–74.

49. Yegor Ligachev, *Inside Gorbachev's Kremlin.*

50. Mikhail Gorbachev, *Erinnerungen,* 339.

51. Ibid., 416.

52. Interview with Leonid Kravchenko, May 1992.

53. Mikhail Gorbachev, *Erinnerungen,* 391.

54. Bill Keller, "Gorbachev, in Finland, Disavows Any Right of Regional Intervention," *New York Times,* October 26, 1989, A1, 7.

55. "Vyklyuchenie iz kadra," D. Biryukov, *Ogonyok,* no. 21 (1990), 3.

56. "Zapreshchayetsya zalyvat dalshe vsekh," *Zhurnalist,* no. 8 (August 1988), 29.

57. For discussions of Soviet television coverage, see:
Ellen Mickiewicz, *Split Signals: Television and Politics in the Soviet Union.*
Erik P. Hoffmann, "Nuclear Deception: Soviet Information Policy," *Bulletin of the Atomic Scientists,* August/September 1986, 32–37. Hoffmann refers to observations by dissident Roy Medvedev about probable divisions in the Politburo on the Chernobyl question.
Hans Olnik, "Galina Khavrayeva, 'Posle Chernobylya ya bolshe ne mogla terpet nespravedlivosti . . .' osledstvia opasnogo reportazha," *Efir,* no. 7 (1992), 14–15.

58. For an excellent overview of this issue within the context of ecological and nuclear issues, see: Vladimir Shlapentokh, "Ecology and Nuclear Danger in Soviet Ideology and Public Opinion," *Television and Nuclear Power: Making the Public Mind,* ed. J. Mallory Wober (Norwood, N.J.: Ablex, 1992).

59. Felicity Barringer, "Kremlin, Offering No New Data, Assails West on Nuclear Disaster," *New York Times,* May 3, 1986, 1, 4.

60. Serge Schmemann, "The Lag in the Ukraine," *New York Times,* May 9, 1986, A1, 6.

61. Philip Taubman, "Chernobyl Reconsidered," *New York Times,* April 26, 1996, A14.

62. Mikhail Gorbachev, *Erinnerungen,* 290. Archie Brown, in his study of Gorbachev, remarks that the Soviet leader regarded Chernobyl as a turning point in the development of openness. *The Gorbachev Factor* (New York: Oxford University Press, 1996).

63. Interview with Alexander Yakovlev, May 1992.

64. V. A. Legasov, published in *Pravda,* June 2, 1986; reprinted as "It Is My Duty to Tell About This," *Chemtech,* August 1989, 461–65.

65. Interview with Alexander Yakovlev, May 1992.

66. Grigory Medvedev, *The Truth About Chernobyl* (New York: Basic Books, 1991).

67. David M. Rubin, "How the News Media Reported on Three Mile Island and Chernobyl," *Journal of Communication,* summer 1987, 42–57.

68. Interview with Yegor Ligachev, October 1993.

69. Gorbachev was also shrewd in his understanding of timing. Arriving at the April 1989 summit in Washington, he had his plane delayed for about an hour so his arrival would be covered on the Sunday evening newscasts. Bill Carter, "Anchors Are Drawn Into Gorbachev Orbit," *New York Times,* April 5, 1989, A22.

70. Boris Yeltsin, *The Struggle for Russia* (New York: Random House, 1994), 75.

71. For example, Gorbachev routinely accented the wrong syllable in words he often used, such as "thinking" (he called his program "new thinking"), the verb "to begin," and the republic of Azerbaidzhan. For a discussion of leaders' problems with words, see David Filipov, "The Gorbachev Guide to Poor Verbal Skills," *Moscow Times,* September 13, 1994, 9.

72. Fedor Burlatsky, "Brezhnev i krusheniye ottepeli," *Literaturnaya Gazeta,* September 14, 1988, 13–14; quote is on page 14.

73. Ellen Mickiewicz, *Split Signals: Television and Politics in the Soviet Union.*

74. Yegor Ligachev, *Inside Gorbachev's Kremlin,* 67.

75. Mikhail Gorbachev, *Erinnerungen.*

76. Leonid Parfyonov, "Television Camera Zooms In," *Otchestven front,* June 23, 1989, 6. Translated in FBIS-SOV-89-131, July 11, 1989, 82.

77. Raisa Gorbachev, *I Hope* (New York: HarperCollins, 1991).

A particularly vindictive account of life with Mrs. Gorbachev was provided by bodyguard Vladimir Medvedev. Taking orders from an assertive woman was clearly irritating to him. About television, though, his account squares with that of others concerning her ambitions to appear on the medium as often as possible. He said that after visits abroad she requested videotapes and that she always "rushed to make the program *Vremya* to see herself." Vladimir Medvedev, *Chelovek za spinoi* (Moscow: Russlit, 1994), 239.

78. Mikhail Gorbachev, *Erinnerungen.*

79. Interview with Yegor Ligachev, October 1993.

80. Irina Petrovskaya, "Lebedinoye ozero predumal ne ya . . .", *Nezavisimaya Gazeta,* September 26, 1992, 5.

81. Interview with Mikhail Nenashev, October 1993.

82. Each time Gorbachev selected a television boss, he signaled a particular policy direction to shape not only television, but the country at large. A thoughtful and perceptive observer of television in the Soviet Union and post-Soviet Russia remarked that "television periods coincide amazingly with defined epochs in the life of the country. Change of chairman was a sign of change of policy." Irina Petrovskaya, "Nam vsem dali poshchechinu," *Nezavisimaya Gazeta,* November 28, 1992, 5.

83. Mikhail Nenashev, *Zalozhnik vremeni* (Moscow: Progress Publishing, Kultura, 1993), 244.

84. Mikhail Nenashev, *Zalozhnik vremeni.*

85. Interview with Vadim Medvedev, May 1992.

86. Gennady Zhavoronkov, "Nenashev's Example and/or Lesson," *Moscow News,* no. 14 (1992), 16.

87. Mikhail Nenashev, *Zalozhnik vremeni,* 260.

88. Interview with Eduard Sagalayev, January 1995.

89. Mikhail Nenashev, *Zalozhnik vremeni,* 270.

90. Interview with Mikhail Nenashev, October 1993.

91. Ibid.

92. Brian McNair, *Glasnost, Perestroika, and the Soviet Media* (London: Routledge, 1991); Thomas Remington, "Parliamentary Government in the USSR," *Perestroika-era Politics,* ed. Robert T. Huber and Donald R. Kelley (Armonk, N.Y.: M. E. Sharpe, 1991). The monopolist TASS was also challenged by the independent wire services Postfactum (registered in 1989), Interfax (begun by state television people in 1989 to supply news mainly to foreigners and registered as an independent agency in 1990), and others. Terhi Rantanen and Elena Vartanova, "News Agencies in Post-Communist Russia: From State Monopoly to Competition," *European Journal of Communication,* vol. 10, no. 2, 207–20.

93. For a review and translation of this decree, see Michael J. Bazyler and Eugene Sadovoy, "Television and the Law in the Soviet Union," *Loyola Entertainment Law Journal,* vol. 11, no. 2, (1991), 293–351.

94. "USSR President's Decree on Democratization and Development of Television and Radio Broadcasting in the USSR," *Izvestia,* July 16, 1990, 1. Translated in FBIS-SOV-90-136, 56–57; all quotes from page 56.

95. Mikhail Nenashev, *Zalozhnik vremeni.*

96. Interview with Mikhail Gorbachev, June 1995.

97. Interview with Eduard Sagalayev, January 1995.

98. "Ukaz Prezidenta Soiuza Sovetskikh Sotsialisticheskikh Respublic O sozdanii Vsesoyuznoi gosudarstvennoi teleradioveshchatelnoi kompanii," *Izvestia,* February 9, 1991, 1.

99. V. Arsenev, "Vsesoiuznaya teleradiokompania: novoe nazvaniye ili novaya zhizn?" *Izvestia,* February 12, 1991, 8.

100. Interview with Leonid Kravchenko, May 1992.

CHAPTER THREE

1. "Velikomu synu Indii," *Sovetskaya Kultura,* July 9, 1988, 1; "Velikomu synu Indii," *Moskovskaya Pravda,* July 9, 1988, 1.

2. I am grateful to Laura Roselle Helvey for her added memories of this event.

3. Interview with Pyotr Reshetov, May 1992.

4. Interview with Leonid Kravchenko, May 1992.

5. Survey of the Soviet Union, December 1989. For a description of the methods, see Ada W. Finifter and Ellen Mickiewicz, "Redefining the Political System of the USSR: Mass Support for Political Change."

6. Sarah E. Mendelson, "Internal Battles and External Wars: Politics, Learning, and the Soviet Withdrawal from Afghanistan," *World Politics,* vol. 45 (April 1993), 327–60.

7. Interview with Alexander Yakovlev, May 1992.

8. Laura Roselle Helvey, "Legitimizing Policy Shifts: Leadership Television Strategies in the Cases of American Withdrawal from Vietnam and Soviet Withdrawal from Afghanistan," unpublished Ph.D. dissertation, Stanford University, 1993.

9. "Concerning Coverage by the Central Press of the Life and Activity of the Armed Forces," *Krasnaya Zvezda,* July 6, 1989, 2. Reprinted in FBIS-SOV-89-138, July 20, 1989, 85.

10. Interview with Boris Nepomnyashchy, May 1992.

11. Interview with Yegor Ligachev, October 1993.

12. Interview with Mikhail Poltoranin, May 1990.

13. In April 1990, a letter signed by the top military brass, including Marshals Kulikov and Ogarkov, castigated the opening of the movie *Shtrafniki* (Penalty Battalion Soldiers). The letter said that "It is no accident that the film's release was timed to coincide with the 45th anniversary of our Victory in the Great Patriotic War." The reason for the film and its carefully timed release date was, according to the military, to call into question the very basis

of the patriotic values and sacrifices the country experienced in the collective memory—or at least that memory so assiduously fostered by a unified media system until that point.

"Concerning the Film *Disciplinary Battalion,*" *Literaturnaya Gazeta,* March 7, 1990, 8. Translated in *Current Digest of the Soviet Press,* vol. 42, no. 12 (April 25, 1990), 20.

14. "The Spring Call-Up—General of the Army D. Yazov, USSR Minister of Defense, Answers Questions from an Izvestiya correspondent," *Izvestia,* March 12, 1990, 3. Reprinted in *Current Digest of the Soviet Press,* vol. 42, no. 10, (April 11, 1990), 10.

15. V. Medvedev, "V zhizni i . . . na ekrane," *Komsomolskaya Pravda,* January 29, 1991, 1.

16. Kononykhin's appointment to head film programming on television was justified by the fact that he had graduated from the Communist Party Central Committee's Academy of Social Sciences (not to be confused with the scholarly Academy of Sciences) and had written a thesis on the history of art.

17. Eldar Ryazanov, "Pochemu v epokhu glasnosti ya ushel s televidenia?" *Ogonyok,* no. 14 (April 2–9, 1988), 26–27.

18. In an article opposing Ryazanov's complaints, the newspaper *Sovetskaya Kultura* said that cuts (or edits) can improve a product, as Ryazanov himself said that "with their help [of scissors] one can avoid unwanted, unsuccessful, imprecise mistaken expressions." "O Chem umolchal Eldar Ryazanov," *Sovetskaya Kultura,* June 16, 1988, 4. I am indebted to Martin Dewhirst for providing me with this article.

19. Mikhail Gorbachev, *Erinnerungen,* 374.

20. "O chem umolchalo Gosteleradio," *Ogonyok,* no. 26 (1988), 26.

21. In a study of local Communist Party organizations in the Brezhnev era based, in part, on the testimony of emigrés, Donna Bahry indicates that Party scrutiny of newspapers was somewhat more serious than that of television because a "mistake" aired on radio or television was quickly forgotten, while a political error in the newspaper remained on the page to be read by all. Donna Bahry, with Mark Rykoff, "Ambiguous Mandate: The Impact of Party Controls at the Soviet Grassroots," *Cracks in the Monolith: Party Power in the Brezhnev Era,* ed. James R. Millar (Armonk, N.Y.: M. E. Sharpe, 1992), 179–212.

This pattern is substantially different from the Gorbachev years, when the (relatively) small scale of newspaper readership made of that medium a kind of safety valve, while television attracted huge audiences and was subjected to more careful scrutiny. It is also possible that even under Brezhnev, monitoring print journalism at the local level was more important for the Party than was television, since local television was then relatively weak compared to national television.

22. "Do i posle Vremeni," *Ogonyok,* no. 5, February 1992), 9.

CHAPTER FOUR

1. Mikhail Gorbachev, "Politichesky doklad tsentralnogo komiteta KPSS XXVII sezda kommunisticheskoi partii sovetskogo soyuza. Doklad generalnogo sekretarya TsK KPSS tovarishcha Gorbacheva," *Pravda,* February 26, 1986, 10.

2. O. Kushnereva, "Televidenie v sisteme kontropropagandy," *Auditoria,* State Committee of USSR for Television and Radio Broadcasting, no. 1 (1987), 38.

3. O. Kushnereva, "Televidenie v sisteme kontropropagandy," 39.

4. Irina Petrovskaya, "Eduard Sagalayev: 'Ya iz dela ushel,'" *Nezavisimaya Gazeta,* June 27, 1992, 5.

5. Interview with Vladimir Pozner, March 1996.

For a study of the "spacebridge" process by a pioneer in the development of this form of interactive television, see Helene Keyssar, "Spacebridge Planning: A Case History," *Television and US-Soviet Dialogue,* ed. Michael Brainerd (Lanham, Md.: Citizen Exchange Council, 1989), 59–71.

6. Interview with Eduard Sagalayev, January 1995.

7. Channel One, *12th Floor,* February and May 1986.

8. Irina Petrovskaya, "Ya normalny chelovek i ne khochu, chtoby iz menya delali idiota,"*Nezavisimaya Gazeta,* October 23, 1993, 5.

9. Iury Zerchaninov, "Kto est kto vo 'Vzglyade,'" *Yunost,* no. 1 (1989), 17–18.

10. Vladimir Pozner, *Parting with Illusions* (New York: Atlantic Monthly Books, 1990), 202.

11. Irina Petrovskaya, "Vzglyad na 'Pole chudes,'" *Ogonyok,* no. 4 (Janaury 1992), 28–29.

12. Mikhail Nenashev, *Zalozhnik vremeni,* 289.

13. Interview with Eduard Sagalayev, January 1995.

14. Interview with Alexander Lyubimov, May 1992.

15. For a description of this survey, see chapter 9.

16. Viktor Yasmann, "Zigzags of Glasnost and Soviet Television," *RFE/RL Report on the USSR,* March 31, 1989, 12–17.

17. Moscow Television Service, March 18, 1989. Translated in FBIS-SOV-89-052, March 20, 1989, 64.

18. *Vzglyad,* April 21, 1989. Translated in FBIS-SOV-89-082, 57.

19. "Vystuplenie tovarishcha Aksyonova, A.N.," *Pravda,* April 27, 1989, 6.

20. Anastasia Nitochkina, "Vzglyad iznutri," *Ogonyok,* no. 1 (January 1991), 11.

21. Ellen Mickiewicz, "Soviet TV Viewers Want Public Affairs," *New York Times,* letter to the editor, April 4, 1991, A14.

22. Anastasia Nitochkina, "Vzglyad iznutri," 10–13.

23. *VID,* December 7, 1990. Translation in FBIS-SOV-90-237, December 10, 1990, 51.

24. Shevardnadze later noted that he felt guilty that the young producers of *Vzglyad* were punished for a program about his team. He said he had heard that Channel One had forbidden even mention of his name. *The Future Belongs to Freedom* (New York: Free Press, 1991).

25. TASS, February 26, 1991. Translated in FBIS-SOV-91-041, 32.

26. D. Bykov, "Do We Need a Different Outlook?" *Sobesednik,* no. 3 (1991), 7. Translated in *Soviet Press Digest,* January 18, 1991.

27. "Pryamoi razgovor," April 9, 1991; hosted by Lomakin.

28. Interview with Vadim Medvedev, May 1992.

29. Interview with Eduard Sagalayev, January 1995.

30. Interview with Oleg Dobrodeyev, May 1992.

31. Interview with Yegor Ligachev, October 1993.

32. Mikhail Gorbachev, *Erinnerungen.*

33. Interview with Alexander Tikhomirov, October 1993.

34. Interview with Alexander Yakovlev, May 1992.

35. Interview with Yegor Ligachev, October 1993.

36. D. Biryukov, "Vyklyuchenie iz kadra," *Ogonyok,* no. 21 (May 19–26, 1990), 1–3.

37. Interview with Alexander Tikhomirov, October 1993.

38. D. Biryukov, "Vyklyuchenie iz kadra."

39. Stephen White, *Gorbachev and After-*(Cambridge, England: Cambridge University Press, 1991), 160–61.

40. D. Biryukov, "Vyklyuchenie iz kadra."

41. Alexander Tikhomirov, "Seven Days," January 28, 1990. Reprinted in FBIS-SOV-90-019, January 29, 1990, 42.

42. Interview with Alexander Tikhomirov, October 1993.

43. Interview with Eduard Sagalayev, January 1995.

44. Interview with Mikhail Gorbachev, June 1995.

45. Interview with Mikhail Nenashev, October 1993.

46. D. Biryukov, "Vyklyuchenie iz kadra."

CHAPTER FIVE

1. T. H. Friedgut, *Political Participation in the USSR* (Princeton, N.J.: Princeton University Press, 1979).

Thomas Remington, *The Truth of Authority* (Pittsburgh, University of Pittsburgh Press, 1988).

2. Yegor Ligachev, *Inside Gorbachev's Kremlin,* 90.

3. M. Steven Fish, *Democracy from Scratch* (Princeton, N.J.: Princeton University Press, 1995), 73. Emphasis in the original.

4. Ada W. Finifter and Ellen Mickiewicz, "Redefining the Political System of the USSR: Mass Support for Political Change."

5. Yegor Ligachev, *Inside Gorbachev's Kremlin,* 90.

6. Ibid., 92.

7. Ibid., 91.

8. Article 125 of the Soviet Constitution stipulated that all citizens ware guaranteed the "right of unimpeded agitation for a registered candidate at meetings, in the press and other means . . ." M. Krutogolov, *Vybory u nas i u nikh* (Izdatelstvo instituta mezhdunarodnykh otnoshenii, 1962), 28.

Interestingly, this provision was also used to attack television censorship. A program investigating land and water use violations was canceled days before the elections when ministerial bureaucrats intervened. The program producer's appeal referred to violation of the law on elections, which established the rights of candidates to present their programs on television. Among the panelists on the shelved program had been a parliamentary candidate. "Ban on Criticism," *Moscow News,* no. 10, (1989), 14.

9. V. Dolganov, "Elections of USSR People's Deputies," *Izvestia,* February 5, 1989, 2. Translated in FBIS-SOV-89-206, February 9, 1989, 49.

10. The first opposition party, Democratic Union, was illegally formed in 1988, to challenge the rule of the Communist Party. The Party attempted to campaign in 1989, but its "outrageously radical concepts" for ending the cult of Lenin and the monopoly of the Communist Party met with official resistance. Without a parade permit, its supporters' demonstration in front of Leningrad's Kazan Cathedral was broken up. An angry *Leningrad Pravda* accused the activists of "acting outside the framework of socialist pluralism . . . [they] are concerned with utterly different aims." Moreover, "they had absolutely no intention of discussing the candidate deputies' election platforms." I. Losev, et al., "Conflict Situation: What Happened Outside Kazan Cathedral," *Leningrad Pravda,* March 12, 1989, 3. Translated in FBIS-SOV-89-057, 76. What they really sought was prominent coverage by foreign media. The tactic of planned symbolic actions to gain foreign media coverage was used extensively in the East German revolution of 1989. Patricia J. Smith, "Political Communication in the East German Revolution of 1989: Assessing the Role of Political Groups," paper prepared for the American Political Science Association, 1994.

11. Boris Yeltsin, *Against the Grain,* (New York: Simon and Schuster, 1990). 174.

12. Yegor Yakovlev took this view about the new importance of television in an interview in *La Repubblica,* March 26, 1989, 2. Translated in FBIS-SOV-89-063, April 4, 1989, 41.

13. He was ultimately successful in his campaign for election to the Russian republic parliament.

14. Interview with Alexander Tikhomirov, October 1993.

15. Tatyana Svetlova, "'Television Must Be Conservative'—Believes Bella Kurkova, Chairman of the St. Petersburg Radio-Television Company," *Trud,* August 10, 1994, 7. Reprinted in FBIS-USR-94-089, August 16, 1994, 41–43.

16. TASS, "People's Deputies Congress: Another Perestroika Landmark," May 24, 1989.

17. Francis X. Clines, "New Candor Transfixes a Soviet Factory Town," *New York Times,* June 8, 1989, A5.

18. Vl. Arsenev, "The Television Dimension of the Congress," *Izvestia,* June 17, 1989, 7. Translated in FBIS-SOV-89-122, June 27, 1989, 44.

19. David Remnick, "The USSR's 'Talking Revolution'; New Congress is Place to Let Off Steam, Not Shake Foundations," *Washington Post,* June 11, 1989, A29.

20. Quoted in Vladimir Solovyov and Elena Klepikova, *Boris Yeltsin: A Political Biography* (New York: Putnam, 1992), 162–63.

21. TASS, "Voters Want All Power to People's Deputies Congress," May 24, 1989.

22. Francis X. Clines, "New Candor Transfixes a Soviet Factory Town."

23. Elena Chekalova, "Reportery v parlamente," *Sovetskaya Kultura,* December 16, 1989, 2.

24. Interview with Leonid Kravchenko, summer 1988.

Irina Petrovskaya, "Lebedinoye ozero pridumal ne ya . . .," *Nezavisimaya Gazeta,* September 26, 1992, 5.

25. David Lane and Cameron Ross, "The Political Elite of the Supreme Soviet of the USSR: The Terminal Stage, 1984–1991," *Europe-Asia Studies,* vol. 46, no. 3 (May 1994), 437–64.

26. Elena Chekalova, "Reportery v parlamente."

27. Nenashev, Mikhail, *Zalozhnik vremeni.*

28. For the biographies of fifty-eight journalist-deputies, see "Zhurnalisty—narodnye deputaty SSSR," *Zhurnalist,* March 21, 1989, 3–9.

29. "Lyudyam sneobychnymi familiami vsegda vezyot na klichki, kak ego tolko nezvali: Politura, Politok, Politburo," *TV Revyu,* no. 3 (1993), 7.

30. "Trudnaya shkola demokratii," *Argumenty i Fakty,* no. 25 (June 24–30, 1989), 8.

31. Bill Keller, "Kremlin Deputies Bask in New Role," *New York Times,* August 6, 1989, 5.

32. Nikolai P. Popov, "Political Views of the Russian People," *International Journal of Public Opinion Research,* vol. 4, no. 4 (winter 1992), 321–25.

33. In discussing institutional change, Jack Knight identifies changes in the relative bargaining power of the actors as consequential. *Institutions and Social Conflict* (Cambridge, England: Cambridge University Press, 1992).

34. The Yeltsin news blockade was enforced beyond Russia. When Yeltsin went to Kiev in the fall of 1990 as chairman of the Supreme Soviet of the Russian republic to address the Ukrainian parliament, that republic's television refused to cover the story. The address and discussion that followed it were neither broadcast nor taped. The parliamentary opposition wing called it an "information boycott." The head of state television in Ukraine would not "officially confirm" that there had been a ban, and Leonid Kravchuk, later elected president in a post-Soviet Ukraine, indicated that it was not necessary to show Yeltsin. The rebellious *TSN* team told viewers of Channel One that "you will not see a report on this [Yeltsin signing a treaty with the Ukraine] because Orlovsky, republican television's news editor in chief, banned Kiev journalists . . . from putting together reportage."

"Reportage on Russia-Ukraine Treaty 'Banned,'" Moscow Television Service in Russian, November 19, 1990. Translated in FBIS-SOV-90-225, November 21, 1990, 84.

35. John Morrison, *Boris Yeltsin: From Bolshevik to Democrat* (New York: Dutton, 1991), 102–6.

36. Mikhail Nenashev, *Zalozhnik vremeni.*

37. Alexander Terekhov, "Zalozhnik," *Ogonyok,* November 1991, 10–12.

38. David Remnick, "Yeltsin's Playback Performance," *Washington Post,* October 2, 1989, D1.

39. In an interview with journalist Andrei Karaulov, published in *Teatralnaya Zhizn,* Yeltsin said that he had a letter from "specialists at Central Television" that indicated that the sound on the tape was not synchronized with the picture. "Today's technology is such that they can elongate sounds and whole words—and this is what was done with the tape [when Ostankino sent it out for doctoring]." "Popytka obyasnitsya?" no. 1 (1990), 30–31. This citation is what Vladimir Solovyov and Elena Klepikova use in their partisan biography of Yeltsin, writing that "a source from Ostankino TV would reveal that the tape had been tampered with by 'experts.'" They also say that "Incidentally, Yeltsin did stumble a few times." *Boris Yeltsin: A Political Biography* (New York: Putnam, 1992), 177.

John Morrison's earlier biography describes the allegation of drunkenness but draws no conclusion as to its veracity.

Mikhail Nenashev said that on the tape there are other people, other voices, in the background, and it would be impossible to produce a seamless montage.

Oleg Dobrodeyev's remarks, from a January 1995 interview.

40. Ellen Mickiewicz, *Media and the Russian Public* (New York: Praeger, 1981).

41. Mikhail Nenashev, *Zalozhnik vremeni,* 279–80.

42. Interview with Mikhail Nenashev, October 1993.

43. Boris Yeltsin, *The Struggle for Russia* (New York: Random House, 1994), 21.

44. Viktor Yasmann, "Soviet Television After Glasnost," *RFE/RL Report on the USSR,* November 9, 1990, 10.

45. Interview with Oleg Poptsov, June 1995. Emphasis was in the interview.

46. Interview with Mikhail Nenashev, October 1993.

47. Interview with Sergei Lomakin, November 1993.

48. N. Loginova, "Censors Have It Out with the People," *Moscow News,* no. 6 (February 1991), 4. Translated in FBIS-SOV-91-040, February 28, 1991, 36.

49. Ksenia Rozhdestvenskaya, "Budte ostorozhny s budushchemi prezidentami," *Izvestia,* September 9, 1994, 10.

50. Interview with Leonid Kravchenko, May 1992.

According to Boris Yeltsin, it took "at least four forceful conversations" with Gorbachev to get permission to begin the channel. Kravchenko maintains that Gorbachev swore to him that he had never promised Yeltsin the second channel. Silaev, Poptsov, and Poltoranin were certain that Gorbachev did promise it. "To this day, I don't know who was telling the truth," Yeltsin noted. According to Poptsov, in January 1991, when Kravchenko rejected the claims of Russian television, he said: "But where are the papers, where is it written down, all this about the second channel? It isn't, so there you have it. In other words, no." Poptsov's response was that "the president told you one thing, and he told me something else."

Russian Television, January 19, 1991. Translated in FBIS-SOV-91-017, January 25, 1991, 82.

51. Interview with Oleg Poptsov, June 1995.

52. Interview with Mikhail Gorbachev, June 1995.

53. "'Data' nachinaet i vyigryvaet," *Informatsionnoe agenstvo data predstavlyaet,* no. 2 (June 1991).

CHAPTER SIX

1. See controversy about New World Information Order in Johan Galtung and Richard Vincent, *Global Glasnost* (Cresskill, N.J.: Hampton Press, 1992).

2. Philip Taubman, "In the Soviet Baltic, Openness Yields Unsought Nationalism," *New York Times,* February 10, 1988, A1, 8.

3. Esther B. Fein, "Latvians Extending a Hand to Outsiders in Their Midst," *New York Times,* October 11, 1988, A6.

4. Lembit Annus, "The USSR is Our Common Home: Pluralism Inside Out," *Pravda,* December 3, 1988, 6. *Current Digest of the Soviet Press,* vol. 40, no. 47 (December 31, 1988), 6, 8–9.

5. Bill Keller, "Lithuania Nationalists: A Fine and Fragile Line," *New York Times,* March 14, 1989, A5.

6. Lt. Col. N. Medvedev, "Pickets Outside the Military Commissariat—Who Is Inciting Young Men to Boycott the Autumn Call-Up in the Baltic Republics?" *Sovetskaya Rossia,* November 16, 1989, 4. Reprinted in *Current Digest of the Soviet Press,* vol. 41, no. 46 (December 13, 1989), 4.

7. *Eesti TV,* January 23–29, 1989.

8. "Alternativnoe TV. Da? ili nyet?" *Literaturnaya Gazeta,* May 30, 1990, 2.

9. Newspapers, even quite large ones with national circulation, like *Komsomol Pravda,* defied the official line and strongly condemned the occupation of the Baltics. *Izvestia,* more prudent, disapproved of contravening constitutional procedures. Wild card *Moscow News,* with its mainly foreign audience and limited Russian-language circulation, pulled no punches and denounced the takeovers. Editor Yegor Yakovlev publicly left the Party. Actually, the effect of *Moscow News* was far greater than its relatively small numbers of readers would imply, for the weekly had become the scout of *glasnost*—riding ahead, challenging, experimenting, and taking the blows. For the communications policy elite, this was the living experiment to watch. *Moscow News* ran a front-page story under the headline "Bloody Sunday," recalling the tsar's response to a peaceful march led by a priest in 1902.

10. S. Belyayev, "No Volunteers Found," *Komsomolskaya Pravda,* February 2, 1991, 1. Translated in FBIS-SOV-91-025, February 6, 1991, 76.

11. Mikhail Gorbachev, *Erinnerungen.*
Vitaly Ignatenko believed that Gorbachev was not involved in the decision to apply force in Vilnius, but he faulted the Soviet leader for not acting decisively afterward and not punishing those responsible. Reported in Archie Brown, *The Gorbachev Factor.*

12. Stephen Foye, "Gorbachev Denies Responsibility for Crackdown," *RFE/RL Research Institute Report on the USSR,* vol. 3, no. 4 (1991), 1–3.

13. Tatyana Putrenko, "600 sekund s Aleksandrom Nevzorovym," *Literaturnaya Gazeta,* October 11, 1989, 8.

14. George Stein, "A Portrait of Aleksandr Nevzorov," *RFE/RL Report on the USSR,* March 8, 1991, 8–9.

15. Yury Zubtsov and Vladimir Martynov, "Aleksandr Nevzorov, drug kommunistov," *Argumenty i Fakty,* no. 8 (February 1995), 3.

16. Moscow Central Television, first program, January 16, 1991. Translated in FBIS-SOV-91-012, January 17, 1991, 66.

17. Yury Zubtsov and Vladimir Martynov, "Aleksandr Nevzorov, drug kommunistov."

18. *TSN,* January 13, 1993.

19. A. Binev, "V Litve—tanki, na ekranakh—tantsy," *Agrumenti i Fakty,* no. 8 (1991).

20. Natalya Davydova, "Tatyana Mitkova's Choice," *Moscow News,* no. 3 (1991), 7.

21. "Zapret na fakt," *Ogonyok,* January 26–February 2, 1991, 4.

22. Bill Keller, "Gorbachev Tries to Oust Editor Over a Poll," *New York Times,* October 18, 1989, A1, 6. The editor, Vladislav Starkov, did not resign and his staff threatened a walk-out if he was removed. Archie Brown's study of Gorbachev stresses that the Soviet leader did not suspend the law and broke with past practice in acceding to parliament's will. *The Gorbachev Factor* (New York: Oxford University Press, 1996).

23. Moscow Radio, January 16, 1991. Translated in FBIS-SOV-91-012, January 17, 1991, 18.

24. "'Data' nachinaet i vygryvaet," *Informatsionnoe agentstvo data predstavlyaet.*

Note that as criticism of television fare increases, so does the number of people saying they don't know or don't have an opinion. That suggests an increase in both real perplexity but also a likely increase in dissenting voices unwilling to answer.

25. Evgeny Zhirnov, "'Sobiraya griby,' reshali sudbu Khrushcheva," *Argumenty i Fakty,* no. 43 (1995), 9.

26. Boris Yeltsin, *The Struggle for Russia* (New York: Random House, 1994), 56.

27. Leonid Kravchenko, "I tried not to ask too many questions," recorded by I. Kadulin, *Komsomol Pravda,* September 20, 1991, 2. Translated in *Current Digest of the Soviet Press,* October 23, 1991, vol. 43, no. 38, 28.

28. "Getting the News on '*Vremia.*'" Interview with Sergei Medvedev in *Russia at the Barricades,* ed. Victoria Bonnell, Ann Cooper, and Gregory Freidin (Armonk, N.Y.: M. E. Sharpe, 1994), 301–7.

29. Interview with Sergei Lomakin, November 1993.

30. "Getting the News on '*Vremia.*'" Interview with Sergei Medvedev in *Russia at the Barricades.*

31. Boris Yeltsin, *The Struggle for Russia* (New York: Random House, 1994), 81.

32. Vladimir Pozner noted that Alexander Dzasokhov, Politburo ideology chief, had responsibility for the media during the coup. *Parting with Illusions.* Dzasokhov was later elected to parliament in post-Soviet Russia.

33. In St. Petersburg, the city council chairman opposed the coup and requested of Boris Petrov, director of St. Petersburg radio and television, that he be allowed to broadcast an emergency meeting of the council. Petrov refused. When mayor Anatoly Sobchak headed for television later that Monday night to make an appeal against the coup, he was preceded by sixty specially armed OMON (riot police) militiamen. Petrov later told the newspaper *Smena* that he called Viktor Samsonov, commander of the Leningrad military district. General Samsonov approved the Sobchak request. As it turns out, that was the first time that the general had dissented from the emergency committee, which had ordered him to make sure that no contrary view be broadcast. That night, Sobchak came on the air with a counter-coup message for which Petrov had arranged satellite transmission facilities.

"Breakthrough: The Coup in St. Petersburg." Interview with Anatoly Sobchak in *Russia at the Barricades,* 218–25.

34. Nursultan Nazarbayev, *Neither Rightists or Leftists* (Alma-Ata: Noy Publications, 1992), 151.

CHAPTER SEVEN

1. Interview with Yegor Yakovlev, June 1995.
2. A number of those present used this word to refer to the leather-coated Tikhomirov.
3. Interview with Yegor Yakovlev, June 1995.
4. Ibid.

5. Ellen Mickiewicz, "The Functions of Communications Officials in the USSR: A Biographical Study," *Slavic Review,* vol. 43, no. 4 (winter 1984), 641–56.

6. "Times Publishes Names of British KGB Informers," *Moscow News,* no. 8 (February 24–March 2, 1995), 11.

7. Oleg Kalugin, *The First Directorate: My 32 Years in Intelligence and Espionage Against the West* (New York: St. Martin's Press, 1994).

8. Interview with Oleg Dobrodeyev, October 1993.

9. Amy W. Knight, *The KGB: Police and Politics in the Soviet Union* (Boston: Allen and Unwin, 1988).

10. "From the CPSU Central Committee," *Moscow News,* no. 28 (1992), 7.

11. Amy W. Knight, *The KGB: Police and Politics in the Soviet Union.*

12. Victor Yasmann, "Where Has the KGB Gone?" *RFE/RL Research Report,* vol. 2, no. 2 (January 8, 1993), 17–20.

13. Iulia Mikhailevskaya, "Vospominanie o proshedshem 'vremeni,'" *Izvestia,* June 3, 1994, 10.

14. Ibid.

15. David Remnick, "The Tycoon and the Kremlin," *The New Yorker,* February 20, 1995, 133.

16. Interview with Yegor Yakovlev, June 1995.

17. Interview with Oleg Dobrodeyev, May 1992.

18. Central TV, Program One, "The Prize is Air Time," October 7, 1991. Translated in Summary of World Broadcasts, October 17, 1991, SU/1205B/1.

19. Interview with Yegor Yakovlev, June 1995.

20. Interview with Boris Nepomnyashchy, fall 1992.

21. Elena Chekalova, "My bolshe ne budem stroit TV v otdelno vzyatoi strane," *Moskovskie Novosti,* no. 39, September 29, 1994, 15.

22. ITAR-TASS, June 28, 1992. Translated in FBIS-SOV-92-125, June 29, 1992, 31.

23. Channel One, "Itogi," June 21, 1992. Translated in FBIS-SOV-91-120, June 22, 1992, 43.

24. Oleg Poptsov, *Khronika vremyon "Tsarya Borisa": Rossia, Kreml. 1991–195* (Moscow: Edition Q Verlags-GmbH, 1995), 114.

25. Irina Petrovskaya, "Informatsia—garant gosudarstvennoi stabilnosti," *Nezavisimaya Gazeta,* March 27, 1993, 5.

26. Vladimir Tsvetov, "Vremya i portret," *Nezavisimaya Gazeta,* March 14, 1992, 5.

27. This notion was put forward by Yegor Yakovlev, who asserted that the role of opponent was played by Mikhail Poltoranin. Yu. Solomonov, "Yegor Yakovlev: Posttotalitarian Society is Living According to the Laws of the Herd," *Literaturnaya Gazeta,* March 24, 1993, 11. Translated in FBIS-SOV-93-052, April 25, 1993, 8.

Irina Petrovskaya, "Rezonans za kremlyovskoi stenoi," *Nezavisimaya Gazeta,* April 3, 1993, 5.

28. "Chto by ni predprinyal prezident, ya ostavlyayu za soboi pravo dumat, kak mne byt dalshe—skazal Yegor Yakovlev," *Moskovsky Komsomolets,* November 25, 1992, 1.

29. For a discussion of this provision, see chapter 9.

30. Interfax, November 24, 1992. Translated in FBIS-SOV-92-228, November 25, 1992, 48.

31. Sergei Snopkov, "Galazov Did Not Demand Resignation," *Moscow News,* no. 49 (December 6, 1992), 25.

32. Galina Starovoitova, a well-known Yeltsin partisan and specialist on ethnic relations, learned from the media she was fired.

33. Yegor Yakovlev, "To President Boris Yeltsin of the Russian Federation," *Moscow News,* no. 49 (December 6, 1992), 3.

34. Irina Petrovskaya, "Nam vsesm dali poshchechinu," *Nezavisimaya Gazeta,* November 28, 1992, 5.

35. Interview with Yegor Yakovlev, June 1995.

36. Ibid.

37. Olga Kuchkina,"'Ya ukhozhu v otstavku . . .,'" *Komsomolskaya Pravda,* February 23, 1993, 6.

38. Tamara Zamyatina, ITAR-TASS, February 22, 1993. Translated in FBIS-SOV-93-034, February 23, 1993, 7.

39. I. E. Malashenko, "Otkrytoye pismo predsedateliu rossiiskoi gosudarstvennoi teleradiokompanii 'Ostankino'V. I. Braginu," *Nezavisimaya Gazeta,* February 23, 1993, 1.

40. For an analysis of the context of cleavages in the parliament and the development of the anti-Yeltsin majority, see: Thomas F. Remington et al., "Transitional Institutions and Parliamentary Alignments in Russia, 1990–1993," 159–80; and Alexander Sobyanin, "Political Cleavages Among Russian Deputies," 181–215, both in *Parliaments in Transition: the New Legislative Politics in the Former USSR and Eastern Europe,* ed. Thomas F. Remington (Boulder, Col.: Westview Press, 1994).

41. Interview with Sergei Yushenkov, October 1993.

42. Oleg Poptsov, head of Channel Two, said the decree had been in preparation for over three months and had gone through several instances of bureaucratic approval. Tatyana Akkuratova, "Television—Olive Branch or Bone of Contention?" *Rossiskie Vesti,* January 27, 1993, 2. Translated in FBIS-SOV-93-018, 25.

43. Aleksandra Lugovskaya, "Sword of Damocles of Censorship Still Hangs over Television," *Izvestia,* April 21, 1993, 2. Translated in FBIS-SOV-93-079, April 27, 1993, 44.

44. "Protecting the Freedom of the Mass Information Media," TASS-SCRIPT, April 1, 1993, 1–29. Translated in FBIS-SOV-93-052, April 25, 1993, 31.

45. Aleksandra Lugovskaya, "Sword of Damocles of Censorship Still Hangs over Television."

46. Russian Television, "Vesti," September 7, 1993. Translated in FBIS-SOV-93-172, 54.

47. "Protecting the Freedom of the Mass Information Media," TASS-SCRIPT, April 1, 1993, 1–29. Translated in FBIS-SOV-93-052, April 25, 1993, 23.

48. Radio Rossii, June 8, 1993. Translated in FBIS-SOV-93-109, June 9, 1993, 42–43.

49. Interview with Oleg Poptsov, October 1993.

50. RTV, "Parliamentary Hour," July 12, 1993. Translated in FBIS-SOV-93-132, 53.

51. "Pero priravnyali k shtyku," *Komsomolskaya Pravda,* September 27, 1993, 1.

52. Tamara Zamyatina, ITAR-TASS, July 3, 1993. Translated in FBIS-SOV-93-127, July 6, 1993, 24.

53. Irina Petrovskaya, "Podaite byvshemu sovetskomu televideniu!" *Nezavisimaya Gazeta,* August 14, 1993, 1.

On the other hand, Yury Marchenkov, head of the parliamentary press service and creator of the "TV-Parliament" company saw the elimination of *Santa Barbara* as a most satisfactory outcome, calling the soap opera "real ideological and political subversion against the Russian people. An evil, low-quality, production." Olga Bychkova,"'Bely dom''v plane kultury i nravstvennosti,'" *Moskovskie Novosti,* no. 35 (August 30–September 5, 1993).

54. "Vesti," August 13, 1993. Reprinted in FBIS-SOV-93-156, August 16, 1993, 15.

55. Elena Chekalova, "Vyacheslav Bragin: 'Psikhika u menya ustoichivaya,'" *Moskovskie Novosti,* no. 11 (March 14, 1993), 12.

56. Interview with Vyacheslav Bragin, October 1993.

57. T. Tsiba, "TV: 'Aqua Vitae' Urgently Needed," *Argumenty i Fakty*, no. 8 (February 1993), 6. Translated in FBIS-SOV-93-025, March 5, 1993, 34.

58. Elena Chekalova, "Vyacheslav Bragin: 'Psikhika u menya ustoichivaya.'"

59. Irina Petrovskaya, "Dva kapitana," *Nezavisimaya Gazeta*, September 25, 1993, 5.

60. T. Tsiba, "TV: 'Aqua Vitae' Urgently Needed."

61. "V 'Ostankino' opechatyvayut kabinety," *Nezavisimaya Gazeta*, March 19, 1993, 1.

62. Irina Petrovskaya, "Vremya trebuyet peremen," *Nezavisimaya Gazeta*, May 8, 1993, 5.

63. Interview with V. V. Lazutkin, June 1995.

64. Irina Petrovskaya, "Dva kapitana."

65. Interview with Oleg Dobrodeyev, October 1993.

66. Irina Petrovskaya, "'Na gosudarstvennom TV segodnya rabotat neprilichno,'" *Nezavisimaya Gazeta*, September 14, 1993, 5.

67. Interview with Sergei Yushenkov, October 1993.

68. Interview with Vyacheslav Bragin, June 1995.

69. Sergei Muratov, "Konets epokhi mitingovogo tv," *Nezavisimaya Gazeta*, October 31, 1992, 5.

70. Irina Petrovskaya, "Vspyat," *Nezavisimaya Gazeta*, September 25, 1993, 5.

71. Alexander Gordeyev, "Uprising's Death Toll Finalized at 143," *Moscow Times*, October 23, 1993, 3.

72. Boris Yeltsin, *The Struggle for Russia* (New York: Random House, 1994), 275.

73. Irina Petrovskaya, "'Ostankino' otklyuchilo samo sebya," *Nezavisimaya Gazeta*, October 9, 1993, 5.

Though television was turned off, radio still functioned, but as television specialist Marianna Orlinkova wrote, "Of course, radio remained, but without the familiar faces and pictures on the screen the situation seemed hopeless." "Eto pochti potryasenie: russkoe TV tozhe mozhet rabotat v ekstremalnhykh usloviakh," *Obshchaya Gazeta*, October 8–14, 1993, 13.

74. Igor Andreev, "Oborona teletsentra: vzglyad iznutri," *Izvestia*, October 12, 1993, 2.

75. Irina Petrovskaya, "'Ostankino' otklyuchilos samo sebya," *Nezavisimaya Gazeta*, October 9, 1993, 5.

76. Boris Yeltsin, in his memoirs, describes the difficulties he had in persuading the military leadership to join his cause and enter the fray from which they had so notably and visibly abstained. Boris Yeltsin, *The Struggle for Russia*, 275.

77. Ibid.

78. The following material is drawn from an interview with Vyacheslav Bragin in June 1995:

Valery Vyzhutovich, "Reshenie prekratit veshchanie po kanalam 'Ostankino' vecherom 3 oktyabrya prinyal Chernomyrdin," *Izvestia*, October 13, 1993, 8.

Irina Petrovskaya, "'Bud ya na meste Chernomyrdina, ya by tozhe velel otklyuchit pervy kanal, no . . . ,'" *Nezavisimaya Gazeta*, October 16, 1993, 1, 5.

79. Oleg Poptsov, *Khronika vremyon "Tsarya Borisa": Rossia, Kreml. 1991–1995*, 378.

80. Interview with Valentin Lazutkin, June 1995.

81. The following is based on interviews with Oleg Poptsov in October 1993 and June 1995, Valentin Lazutkin in June 1995, and Vyacheslav Bragin in June 1995:

Irina Petrovskaya, "'Ostankino' otklyuchilos samo sebya."

"Kogda 'pribyli vrazhdebnye nam BTRy'. . . ," *7 Dnei*, October 18–24, 1993, 2.

82. Boris Yeltsin, *The Struggle for Russia*, 275.

83. "Rossiskaya drama glazami ee uchastnikov," *Argumenty i Fakty*, no. 41 (October 1993), 2.

84. Andrey Titov, "Vid Members Turn to Prosecutor's Office for Protection. 'Ostankino' Chairman Accused of Breaking Law," *Kommersant-Daily,* December 7, 1993, 14. Reprinted in FBIS-SOV-93-234, December 8, 1993, 35.

Media policy boss Mikhail Poltoranin said that when Lyubimov and Politkovsky were called to come to the makeshift studio, he expected that, like "normal people," the pair would speak in support of democracy but that they brought "shame" to Ostankino and to journalists, which could have been predicted. After all, for a long time, "they had been making money by using state [television] airtime." "Rossiyskaya drama glazami ee uchastnikov."

85. "Journalists Fired over Television Appeal During Crisis," United Press, October 13, 1993.

86. Interview with Sergei Lomakin, October 1993.

87. Interview with Sergei Yushenkov, October 1993.

88. Oleg Poptsov, *Khronika vremyon "Tsarya Borisa": Rossia, Kreml. 1991–1995,* 391.

89. Interview with Alexander Tikhomirov, October 1993.

CHAPTER EIGHT

1. Olga Kuchkina, "'Ya ukhozhu v otstavku . . . ,'" *Komsomolskaya Pravda,* February 23, 1993, 6.

2. Boris Yeltsin, *The Struggle for Russia* (New York: Random House, 1994), 212. However, in a June 1995 interview, Gennady Burbulis said it was "collective creativity."

3. Eduard Klyamko, "Komu prinadlezhit TV, tomu prinadlezhit strana," *Rossiiskaya Gazeta,* April 21, 1993, 4.

4. Elena Chekalova, "'Ostankino': vozrashchenie v Vid?" *Moskovskie Novosti,* no. 2 (February 14, 1993), 10.

5. ITAR-TASS, April 23, 1993. Translated in FBIS-SOV-93-072, April 23, 1993, 23.

Working Russia and the Russian Communist Party spoke of organizing public demonstrations to protest their exclusion from television and to advocate live coverage of their assembly. *Novosti,* Channel One, April 11, 1993; translated in FBIS-SOV-93-068, April 12, 1993, 26.

6. When he was interviewed by Moscow city television, the other high-profile Yeltsin opponent, parliament speaker Ruslan Khasbulatov, took the opportunity to spray accusations of corruption, including the rather bizarre one of dipping into church coffers to buy votes. Wendy Slater, "No Victors in the Russian Referendum," *RFE/RL Research Report,* vol. 2, no. 21 (May 21, 1993), 10–19.

7. The analysis included all such messages daily, from 6:00 P.M. to midnight, and on Sunday from 3:00 P.M. to midnight. It is drawn from a collaborative project of Vsevolod Vilchek and Ellen Mickiewicz, and directed by Vilchek.

8. These figures represent averages of the percentages in each category combining Channel One and Channel Two.

9. For example, *Novosti,* April 23, 1993.

10. *Novosti,* April 24, 1993.

11. Russian Television, *Vesti,* April 20, 1993. Translated in FBIS-SOV-93-074, April 20, 1993, 14.

12. Russian Television, *Vesti,* March 31, 1993. Translated in FBIS-SOV-93-060, March 31, 1993, 31.

13. Leaflet of the "Democratic Association" "Free Russia," and the Front of National Salvation of the October District of Moscow, 1993. I am indebted to Andrei Richter for providing me with this source.

14. Russian Television, *Vesti,* March 31, 1993. Translated in FBIS-SOV-93-060, March 31, 1993, 31.

15. In their subsequent publicity about the program, the REN TV company states that "according to the western experts' data it helped the President to collect about one-third votes more." Alexander von Hahn, general manager, promotion leaflet.

Though this program was well received and was indeed a pioneering piece of political advertising, it would be difficult to connect this increase in votes uniquely to this factor.

16. Boris Yeltsin, *The Struggle for Russia,* 212.

17. I. M. Klyamkin, "Politicheskaya sotsiologia perekhodnogo obshchestva," *Polis,* no. 4 (1993), 41–64.

18. Michael Urban notes that in general the discourse on Russian national identity during the transition from Soviet rule "tends to magnify rather than diminish the divisions" in the political arena. Michael Urban, "The Politics of Identity in Russia's Postcommunist Transition: The Nation Against Itself," *Slavic Review,* vol. 53, no. 3, (fall 1994), 748.

19. Thomas F. Remington uses this term in a paper presented to the Soviet Nationalities Workshop, Center on East-West Trade, Investment, and Communications, at Duke University, May 1990.

20. An event purposefully crafted mainly to attract media attention is a pseudo-event, from Daniel J. Boorstin, "From News-gathering to News-making: A Flood of Pseudo-events," *The Process and Effects of Mass Communication,* ed. Wilbur Schramm and D. R. Roberts (Urbana, Ill.: University of Illinois Press, 1971), 116–50.

E. Guretskaya, correspondent on *Vesti,* Russian Television, April 15, 1993. Translated in FBIS-SOV-93-072, April 16, 1993, 19–20.

21. Russian Television, *Vesti,* April 23, 1993. Translated in FBIS-SOV-93-078, April 26, 1993, 16.

22. "MN express poll," *Moscow News,* no. 46 (November 12, 1993), 1.

23. Goddard, who had worked on ballot issues and political campaigns, later developed the "Harry and Louise" ads opposing President and Mrs. Clinton's health care reforms. In this, and later campaigns, he pioneered what was referred to as "astroturf" campaigns: creating an umbrella grass-roots organization to diffuse the narrow economic interests of the major sponsor. See Elizabeth Kolbert, "When a Grass-Roots Drive Actually Isn't," *New York Times,* March 26, 1995, 1, 12.

A later article in the Russian press examining the creators of paid advertising for the Yeltsin side in the April referendum noted that "political scientists and specialists of the [Russian] Institute of the United States and Canada, experts in the field of psychology of advertising, and foreign sociologists were enlisted as consultants." No specific mention was made of the role Goddard and his assistants assumed nor of the financial basis on which the foreign consultants were engaged. Dmitry Dmitriadi, "Who Helped Yeltsin Win the April Referendum: The First Test of Paid Large-Scale Advertising in Russia," *Nezavisimaya Gazeta,* October 13, 1993, 6. Translated in FBIS-USR-93-151, December 1, 1993, 48.

24. Mark Schone, "Russian Dressing: American Political Agency Goddard+Claussen/First Tuesday Is Out to Make Yeltsin's Allies Look Good in Upcoming Elections," *Adweek,* November 29, 1993, 23.

The Times of London indicated at the time that Yeltsin had engaged the advertising firm of Saatchi and Saatchi to help mobilize turnout. Anne McElvoy, "Capitalist's Triumph Cheers Yeltsin," *The Times,* April 13, 1993.

25. Lecture by Ben Goddard at Duke University, November 29, 1994.

26. This and following observations were made by Ben Goddard in a telephone interview on March 23, 1994.

A Russian observer wrote that although it "wasn't advertised, and even hidden," it was Burbulis who pulled the levers in the government's April referendum campaign, and the center of activity was at Burbulis's think tank, Strategy. Viktor Gushchin, "Gennady Burbulis vedet svoiu igru," *Nezavisimaya Gazeta,* November 30, 1993, 5.

27. Oleg Poptsov, *Khronika vremyon "Tsarya Borisa": Rossia, Kreml. 1991–1995.*

28. Interview with Gennady Burbulis, June 1995.

29. Interview with Ben Goddard, March 1994.

30. Interview with Gennady Burbulis, June 1995.

31. Thomas E. Skidmore, ed., *Television, Politics, and the Transition to Democracy in Latin America* (Washington, D.C.: Woodrow Wilson Center Press and Johns Hopkins University Press, 1993).

32. Boris Yeltsin, *The Struggle for Russia,* 212.

33. "The Referendum: False Interpretations and Reality," *Rossiskaya Gazeta,* April 30, 1993, 3–4. Translated in FBIS-SOV-93-083, May 3, 1993, 27–28.

34. "The Referendum: False Interpretations and Reality." Translated in FBIS-SOV-93-083, 28, 30.

35. Interview with Valentin Lazutkin, June 1995.

36. Interview with Vyacheslav Bragin, June 1995.

37. Telephone interview with Mark Malloch Brown, July 1995.

38. Interview with Gennady Burbulis, June 1995.

39. Telephone interview with Ben Goddard, June 1995.

40. Erik Komarov, "Post-Referendum: The Arithmetics Wrangle, or What the Referendum Results Imply," *New Times International,* no. 29 (July 1993), 13–15. Translated in FBIS-SOV-93-107, August 18, 1993, 1–3.

41. K. Chertkov, "Index of Growing Boycott," *Sovetskaya Rossiya,* June 10, 1993, 3. Translated in FBIS-SOV-93-083, July 6, 1993, 5–13.

42. Erik Komarov, "Post-Referendum."

43. Public Opinion Foundation, *V pole zrenia,* no. 9 (February 1993).

44. "Ekranny obraz pretendenta na Rossiisky prestol," *Zhurnalist,* no. 12 (1991), 32–33. I thank Irina Petrovskaya for this source.

45. Howard Kurtz, *Hot Air: All Talk All the Time* (New York: Random House, 1996).

46. Matthew Wyman et al., "The Russian Elections of December 1993," *Electoral Studies,* vol. 13, no. 3 (1994), 254–71.

47. Herbert Kitschelt, "The Formation of Party Cleavages in Post-Communist Democracies: Theoretical Propositions," paper presented at Workshop on Public Opinion and Party Formation in Post-Communist and Post-Authoritarian Democracies, Duke University, March 24–25, 1995.

48. Richard S. Flickinger and Donley T. Studlar, "The Disappearing Voters? Exploring Declining Turnout in Western European Elections," *West European Politics,* vol. 15, no. 2 (April 1992), 1–16.

49. Yuri Levada, "Posle referenduma: varianti deistvii," *Izvestia,* May 6, 1993, 4.

50. Amy Corning, "Public Opinion and the Russian Parliamentary Elections," *RFE/RL Research Report,* vol. 2, no. 48 (December 3, 1993), 16–23.

51. Richard Rose, "Mobilizing Demobilized Voters in Post-Communist Societies," *Studies in Public Policy* (Glasgow: University of Strathclyde, Centre for the Study of Public Policy, 1995), 3. Emphasis in the original.

52. *Mir mnenii i mnenia o mire,* vol. 3, no. 87 (November 1993), Moscow, Vox Populi Service.

53. In the United States, voters, as compared to nonvoters, are more likely to see differences between parties and individual candidates. John R. Petrocik and Daron Shaw, "Non-

voting in America: Attitudes in Context," *Political Participation and American Democracy,* ed. William Crotty (New York: Greenwood, 1991), 67–88.

See also: "Sotsoprosy," *Argumenty i Fakty,* no. 23 (June 1994), 2.

54. Aleksandra Lugovskaya, "Televizionny 'Chas izbiratelya' provet 22 noyabra," *Izvestia,* November 19, 1993, 4.

55. Even so, the BBC keeps a stopwatch account of the time devoted to each party.

56. November 1 to December 10, 1993. Time Allotted to Each Party in News Coverage.

	Channel One	Channel Two
Russia's Choice*	1 hour 30 min. 45 sec.	43 min.
Pres*	25 min. 55 sec.	10 min. 5 sec.
Movement for Democratic Reforms*	12 min. 20 sec.	5 min. 5 sec.
Yabloko***	12 min. 45 sec.	5 min.
Communist Party**	4 min.	6 min. 25 sec.
Agrarian Party**	3 min. 50 sec.	1 min. 20 sec.
Liberal Democratic Party**	1 min. 50 sec.	3 min. 55 sec.
Democratic Party***	6 min. 40 sec.	4 min. 40 sec.

*party generally supporting presidential reform platform
**party opposing presidential reform platform
***centrist party

This table is based on data collected by Vsevolod Vilcheck.

57. *RFE/RL News Briefs,* November 8–10, 1993, 1.

58. Article 15 of the Regulations on Information Guarantees in the Election Campaign of October 29, 1993. For the full text, see *Post-Soviet Media Law and Policy,* vol. 1, no. 2 (November 17, 1993) 8–11.

59. *Voter's Hour,* 1993.

60. Interview with Valentin Lazutkin, June 1995.

61. Ibid.

62. Interview with Vyacheslav Bragin, June 1995.

63. ITAR-TASS, December 17, 1993. Translated in FBIS-SOV-03-242, December 20, 1993, 5.

64. Interview with Anatoly Vengerov, June 1995.

65. V. Kostousov, *TV Today and Tomorrow,* Channel One, August 12, 1993. Translated in FBIS-SOV-93-155, August 13, 1993, 17.

66. Interview with Vyacheslav Bragin, June 1995.

67. Channel One, *Voters' Choice,* December 1994.

68. Vladimir Gusinsky and his MOST Bank group contributed to the campaigns of Grigory Yavlinsky, Gavriil Popov, Anatoly Sobchak, Sergei Shakhray and Yegor Gaidar. Interview with Oleg Moroz, "Give Us Two–Three Years," *Literaturnaya Gazeta,* November 10, 1993, 10. Translated in FBIS-USR-93-141, December 1, 1993, 50–55.

69. Before the elections, an analysis listed a large number of banks and industrial conglomerates that contributed to several of the democratically oriented parties, among them, some probusiness parties that never made it past the 5 percent cutoff. Leonid Volodin and Vadim Malakhitov, "Businessmen Have Politicians in Their Pocket," *Novaya Yezhednevnaya Gazeta,* November 3, 1993, 3. Translated in FBIS-SOV-91-151, December 1, 1993, 43–45.

Michael Urban wrote that the Liberal Democratic Party appeared to have received millions of dollars donated clandestinely from European right-wing and fascist organizations and by former East European Communist parties and secret police. Michael Urban, "December

1993 as a Replication of Late-Soviet Electoral Practices," *Post-Soviet Affairs*, vol. 10, no. 2 (1994), 127–58. He cites an unnamed State Department source and Eric Geiger, "Communists, Nazis Finance Zhirinovsky," *San Francisco Chronicle*, June 10, 1994, A10. Geiger, in this article, refers to "analysts," "experts," and "Western spy agencies" as his sources for his conclusion that on a postelection visit to Austria, Zhirinovsky held discussions about continuing to tap "a vast amount of funds stashed away by European Communist parties before communism's collapse at the end of the 1980s." There is no further identification of sources, although he adds that Mikhail Gorbachev "hinted" at it and Anatoly Sobchak also "advanced" this view. Other guesses were made by the newspaper *Argumenty i Fakty*, which published what it identified as "rumors" of such sources of contributions as Muamar Quaddafi (Libya), Radovan Karadjcic (Bosnia), Slobodan Milosevic (Serbia), Sadaam Hussein (Iraq), and Kim Song Il (North Korea) in "Vodka budet nesvezhei," *Argumenty i Fakty*, no. 21 (May 1995), 2. A noted Russian television critic said that no documentation had surfaced and she had seen no proof of these allegations. Interview with Irina Petrovskaya, May 1995.

70. Ivan Rodin, "Dengi na vybory: komu i za chto," *Nezavisimaya Gazeta*, November 11, 1993, 6.

71. Darrell M. West, *Air Wars: Television Advertising in Election Campaigns, 1952–1992* (Washington, D.C.: Congressional Quarterly, 1993).

Thomas E. Patterson and Robert D. McClure, *The Unseeing Eye: The Myth of Television Power in National Elections* (New York: Putnam, 1976).

72. For an analysis of this issue and options involved, see Ellen Mickiewicz and Charles Firestone, *Television and Elections* (Washington, D.C.: The Aspen Institute and Atlanta: The Carter Center, 1992).

73. Advertising Time: Television Buys of Selected Parties, December 1993.

	Channel One	Channel Two
Civic Union (Volsky)	88 min. 30 sec.	34 min.
Unity and Accord (Shakhray)	88 min.	89 min. 15 sec.
Russia's Choice (Gaidar)	87 min. 20 sec.	156 min. 50 sec.
LDPR (Zhirinovsky)	84 min.	90 min.

Treteisky Informatsionny Sud i Pervye Svobodnye Vybory (Moscow: Iuridicheskaya Literatura, 1994).

74. Wendy Sloane, "Roll the Cameras—Russia's Politicians Are on the Air," *Christian Science Monitor*, December 2, 1993, 6.

75. Telephone interview with Ben Goddard, March 1994.

76. Al Kamen, "A Government of the Eastern Elite, Still," *Washington Post*, September 3, 1993, A23.

77. Andrew Stanford and Michael A. Hiltzik, "Russia may have used U.S. aid for political purposes; funding ads that were supposed to promote privatization are pulled after partisan overtones were added to them," *Los Angeles Times*, November 24, 1993, A4.

78. Igor Karpenko, "Goskomimushchestva otritsaet zloi umysel, no priznaet nedosmotr," *Izvestia*, November 30, 1993, 2.

The difficulty of transposing symbols from one culture to another was a fairly constant problem in the foreign assistance program. Ukraine's privatization public relations program featured a television ad with the clearly foreign images of an elderly Ukrainian woman sitting in a rocking chair alone in a bare room. The Western consultants obviously thought of the symbols of loneliness and fear an American audience would perceive, but in Ukraine, where rocking chairs are unknown and rooms are small and full of bric-a-brac, the ad was wasted. Jane Perlez, "Ukraine Sells Its Companies, but Buyers Are Few," *New York Times,* November 2, 1995, 1, 7.

79. Mr. Yevstavyev refused on multiple occasions to be interviewed for this book.

80. Telephone Interview with Mark Malloch Brown, July 1995.

81. Telephone interview with Kirby Jones, executive vice president and managing director of privatization for Burson Marsteller, May 1995.

82. Stanford and Hilzik.

83. "Russian Security Ministry and Russia's Choice Reject Charges," *Kommersant-Daily,* December 2, 1993, 14. Translated in FBIS-SOV-93-231, 28.

The hard-line military newspaper *Krasnaya Zvezda* noted without comment the report circulated by the U.S. Embassy in Moscow that the U.S. government had no knowledge of the insertion of the text about Russia's Choice in the AID-funded public service announcement and that the ad was pulled after protest by Americans. Mikhail Pogorely, "Americans Are Not Advertising 'Russia's Choice,'" *Krasnaya Zvezda,* December 3, 1993, 3. Translated in FBIS-SOV-93-232, December 6, 1993, 31.

84. The founding convention of Russia's Choice was uncertainly organized and more fractious than intended. Thomas de Waal and Natalya Koposova, "Gaidar Launches Campaign for Duma," *Moscow Times,* October 19, 1993, 1–2.

85. Interview with Gennady Burbulis, June 1995.

86. "Kolichestvo telereklamy vosrastaet, interes zritelei—padaet," *Izvestia,* May 27, 1994, 9.

87. Yury Bogolomov, "TV Advertising scrutinized by a sociologist," *Moscow News,* no. 25 (June 18, 1993), 12.

Vsevolod Vilchek, "'Ostankino' sredi drugikh," *Izvestia,* February 4, 1994, 9.

88. "Kolichestvo telereklamy vosrastaet, interes zritelei—padaet," *Izvestia,* May 27, 1994, 9.

89. Public Opinion Foundation, *Spravochnik 'Media-Quest'* (Moscow: Public Opinion Foundation, 1994), 1–28.

90. Margarita Kvasnetskaya, "Nastoyashchaya America," *Rossiiskaya Gazeta,* May 14, 1993, 2.

91. Irina Petrovskaya, "Kokos na postnom masle," *Nezavisimaya Gazeta,* September 11, 1993, 5.

92. *Nakanune vyborov: mnenia rossian,* vol. 3, November 8, 1993, Fond "Obshchestvennoe Mnenie." Survey conducted October 30, 1993.

93. In an insightful analysis of Dmitry Dibrov's self-centered and irresponsible performances as a talk-show host, critic Lidia Polskaya develops the notion of "marginal journalism," which is seductive, empty, and focused on the most trivial emotions and habits of the host. See "Televidenie na obochine," *Izvestia,* July 8, 1994, 10.

94. Interview with Gennady Burbulis, June 1995.

95. For a discussion of this, see Herbert Marcuse, *Soviet Marxism* (New York: Columbia University Press, 1958). Marcuse argues that the Soviet regime attempted to refashion the consciousness or psychology of individuals by taking the private into the public domain and thus making individuals accountable for the recesses of their minds and also subject to the government's intrusive attempts to transform those minds. Thus, the profound dilemma of conflicts between private morality and the political order could not, theoretically, take place. There was no justification for Antigone in this doctrine.

Another formulation is that of Richard Rose, who notes that "Communist rule transformed public opinion into private opinion. Individuals held different views about government, politics, and Moscow's domination, but there were no institutional means to aggregate or express such ideas." Richard Rose, "Postcommunism and the Problem of Trust," *Journal of Democracy,* vol. 5, no. 3 (July 1994), 18–30; quote is on page 22.

96. "Spektr"/"Viewpoint," no. 3 (January 1993), 6 (unpaginated).

Looking back on the Soviet period, a newspaper article recalled that when the sober newsreader Igor Kirillov appeared in a sweater instead of the usual dark suit, viewers expected a consequent shift away from "dry and official" discourse, but "nothing changed." Iury Zubtsov, "Fenomen Dibrova," *Argumenty i Fakty,* no. 22 (June 1994), 22.

97. Andrei Bystritsky, "Ostorozhno: vybory!" *Sem Dnei,* no. 44 (1995), 38.

98. A month after the elections, Gaidar told an interviewer that in the past (as opposed to the postelection present) he never watched himself on television to look for his mistakes. "In ninety-two, I did not watch at all; there wasn't time. Perhaps that is why I made so many mistakes." "Zritel budushchei nedeli," *Izvestia,* January 14, 1994, 6.

99. Interview with Valentin Lazutkin, June 1995.

100. Channel One, *Chto, gde, kogda,* November 12, 1993.

101. Interview with Valentin Lazutkin, June 1995.

102. Russia's Choice ads also featured pop singers appealing to "those who are suffering and those driving a Mercedes" and praying for "the new generation that chose Pepsi." Steven Gutterman, "Russians Tune into First Television Campaign," *Los Angeles Times,* November 30, 1993, 5.

103. Ellen Mickiewicz and Andrei Richter, "Television, Campaigning, and Elections in the Soviet Union and Post-Soviet Russia," *Politics, Media, and Modern Democracy,* ed. David Swanson and Paolo Mancini (Westport, Conn.: Praeger, 1996).

104. Interview with Valentin Lazutkin, June 1995.

105. Interfax, December 25, 1993. Translated in FBIS-SOV-93-246, December 27, 1993, 1.

106. "Decree Issued by the Russian Federation Central Electoral Commission," *Rossiiskaya Gazeta,* December 25, 1993, 1. Translated in FBIS-SOV-93-246, 2.

107. Vera Tolz and Julia Wishnevsky, "Election Queries Make Russians Doubt Democratic Processes," *RFE/RL Research Reports,* vol. 3, no. 13 (April 1, 1994), 1–6.

108. St. Petersburg Channel, *Itogi,* November 28, 1993.

109. Matthew Wyman et al., "The Russian Elections of December 1993," *Electoral Studies,* vol. 13, no. 3 (1994), 254–71.

110. Vladimir Shokarev, "Kto golosoval za LDPR," *Izvestia,* December 30, 1993, 4.

111. Alexander Oslon and Elena Petrenko, "Faktory electoralnogo povedenia: ot oprosov k modelyam," *Voprosy sotsiologii,* vol. 5 no. (1994), 3–26.

It is also possible that selective perception may be at work, so that viewers may be predisposed to follow a particular candidate or campaign. If the undecided had covertly chosen Zhirinovsky and therefore followed his campaign more closely, that would, of course, affect the results. However, it should also be borne in mind that Zhirinovsky's heaviest advertising buys came in this period.

In scoring the "effectiveness" of ads, the researchers used not only recall measures, but also a scale of voting intentions, with higher grades for recalling ads of a party for which the respondent was *not* intending to vote. Oslon and Petrenko, *Parlamentskie vybory i oprosy obshchestvennogo mnenia v Rossii vo vtoroi polovine 1993 goda.*

112. Oslon and Petrenko, *Parlamentskie vybory i oprosy obshchestvennogo mnenia v Rossii vo vtoroi polovine 1993 goda.*

113. Interfax, December 16, 1993. Translated in FBIS-SOV-93-241, December 17, 1993, 52.

114. Lidia Lukyanova, "It is no good blaming the messengers . . . Vyacheslav Bragin's last

interview in his capacity as chairman of the Ostankino TV and Radio Company," *Kuranty,* December 17, 1993, 4. Translated in FBIS-SOV-93-241, December 17, 1993, 53.

115. "Monitoring Osveshchenia SMI Parlamentskikh Vyborov 1995 goda v Rossii," *Sreda,* no. 2 (1996), 9–10.

116. Sarah Oates, "Vying for Votes on a Crowded Campaign Trail," *Transition,* vol. 2, no. 4 (February 23, 1996), 29.

117. Stephen White, Richard Rose, and Ian McAllister, *How Russia Votes* (Chatham, N.J.: Chatham House, 1996), 227.

118. "Obshchie problemy i metodologia," *Ekonomicheskie i sotsialnye peremeny: Monitoring obshchestvennogo mnenia* (Economic and Social Change: Monitoring Public Opinion), no. 3 (July), Intertsentr (Interdisciplinary Academic Centre for Social Sciences) and VTsIOM (Russian Center for Public Opinion Research), 5–12.

119. The uncertainty was exacerbated by quite varying practices adopted by the media in reporting poll results. Surveys were often reported without indicating the dates of the interviews; others were reported citing only the month of the interview; sampling procedures were rarely made clear, and at times it was implied that the entire population of a region had been polled. A. Oslon and E. Petrenko, *Parlamentskie vybory i oprosy obshchestvennogo mnenia v Rossii vo vtoroi polovine 1993 goda* (Moscow: Fond "Obshchestvennoe Mnenie," 1994).

120. Interviews with Vsevolod Vilchek, October 1993 and January 1994.

121. Celestine Bohlen, "Russia Parties Subdued by Early Vote Return," *New York Times,* December 13, 1993, 6.

122. Interview with Gennady Burbulis, June 1995.

123. Boris Yeltsin, *The Struggle for Russia,* 152, 159.

124. Interview with Gennady Burbulis, November 1991.

125. Interview with Gennady Burbulis, June 1995.

126. FOM-INFO, Fond "Obshchestvennoe Mnenie" Moscow, no. 40 (80), October 13, 1995, 3–4. Survey fielded in September 1995; 1,581 respondents nationwide.

127. Sarah Oates, "Vying for Votes on a Crowded Campaign Trail."

128. N. V. Krivelskaya, "Informatsionnaya Bezopasnost Naselenia," Parliamentary Hearing, June 4, 1996. I am indebted to Vsevolod Vilchek for this source.

129. "Za Kogo golosuyet NTV?" *Argumenty i Fakty,* no. 23 (June 1996), 3.

130. Channel One was criticized for pulling a Zyuganov spot. The station claimed that his campaign had not paid for the time needed for the spot; the campaign denied it.

131. Among campaign newspapers, one of the most talked about was a harshly anti-Communist publication, *Ne Dai Bog* [God forbid], paid for by banking and commercial firms as a contribution to the Yeltsin campaign, which had a print run of ten million copies and was distributed free during the campaign. It sought to evoke old memories and warn of new offenses. For example, one article entitled "Zyug khailov" (zyug-heil [Hitler]-ov), compared quotations from Hitler's *Mein Kampf* to Zyuganov's speeches. There were indeed similarities, but quite superficial ones, considering the apocalyptic tone of the piece. Hitler was quoted decrying German poverty, saying Germany had enormous opportunities and that the domestic market had to be protected from foreigners. Zyuganov said that Russia had many resources and was losing its markets, even the domestic one, which they should protect from foreigners.

132. Interview with Vladimir Pozner, March 1996.

133. Interview with Igor Malashenko, May 1996.

134. Michael Kramer, "Rescuing Boris," *Time,* July 15, 1996, 28–37.

Alessandra Stanley, "The Americans Who Saved Yeltsin (Or Did They?), *New York Times,* July 9, 1996, A3. Interview with Alexander Oslon, July 1996.

135. Telephone interview with Richard Dresner, September 1996.
136. Telephone interview with Igor Malachenko, October 1996.
137. Telephone interview with Richard Dresner, September 1996.
138. *Odin na odin,* Channel One, June 6, 1996.
139. Survey of 495 residents of Khabarovsk, April 18–19, 1996, "Rezultaty sotsiologich-eskikh issledovanii," Fond "Obshchestvennoe Mnenie," April 21, 1996, 2.
140. Antonina Belyayeva, "'Reflection': 'According to "the Laws of a Balloon'": "With What My Needs Are, I Don't Have To Be a Millionaire," Eduard Sagalayev Says,'" *Nezavisimaya Gazeta,* April 20, 1996, 4. Translated in FBIS-SOV-96-093-S, May 13, 1996, 43.
141. Yury Zubtsov, "Alexander Nekhoroshev: 'Mozhete pobit menya kamnyami,'" *Argumenty i Fakty,* no. 21 (May 1996), 3.
142. Interview with Alexander Oslon, May 1996.
143. For a discussion of television and the changing nature of political parties and campaign coverage in the United States, see, for example, Gladys Engel Lang and Kurt Lang, *Politics and Television Re-Viewed* (Beverly Hills, Calif.: Sage, 1984).

See also: Ben Wattenberg, *The Rise of Candidate-Centered Politics* (Cambridge, Mass.: Harvard University Press, 1991).

A reconceptualization of the development of political parties in the United States may be found in John Aldrich, *Why Parties?* (Chicago: University of Chicago Press, 1995).

A comparison of the impact of television on elections in a number of countries may be found in David Swanson and Paolo Mancini, eds., *Politics, Media, and Modern Democracy.*

144. Michael McFaul, "Explaining the Vote," *Journal of Democracy,* vol 5, no. 2 (April 1994), 3–9.
145. A good deal of research is directed at understanding the relationship between attitudes toward the economy and attitudes toward democracy in post-Soviet Russia. Whitefield and Evans maintain that there is a connection, a kind of learning experience in which utopian expectations are lowered and a reorienting of political culture takes place. Stephen Whitefield and Geoffrey Evans, "The Russian Election of 1993: Public Opinion and the Transition Experience," *Post-Soviet Affairs,* vol. 10 (1994), 38–60.

For other studies, see James Gibson and Raymond Duch, "Emerging Democratic Values in Soviet Political Culture," *Public Opinion and Regime Change: The New Politics in Post-Soviet Societies,* ed. Miller, Reisinger, and Hesli (Boulder, Col.: Westview Press, 1993).

Ada W. Finifter and Ellen Mickiewicz, "Redefining the Political System of the USSR: Mass Support for Political Change."

CHAPTER NINE

1. For an analysis of this issue in the United States, see Cass R. Sunstein, *Democracy and the Problem of Free Speech* (New York: The Free Press, 1993).
2. Peffley and Sigelman argue for the relevance of Samuel Stouffer's classic study of the McCarthy period precisely because of the widespread agreement on the object of intolerance. Mark Peffley and Lee Sigelman, "Intolerance of Communists During the McCarthy Era: A General Model," *Western Political Quarterly,* vol. 43, no. 1 (March 1990), 93–111.
3. The questions in 1989, 1992, and April 1993 asked respondents to answer with respect to the printed press, television, and institutions of higher education. In December 1993 and 1995, the question included only television. The question read: "Is it permissible to express on television the view that the main responsibility for the creation of an inhumane political system in the country lies not only with Stalin but also with Lenin?" The percentage of no answer/no opinion was:

Soviet Union survey 1989	6.8%
Russian survey 1992	13.9%
Moscow survey postreferendum, May 1993	30%
Russian survey preelection, December 1993	27.6%
Russian survey postelection, December 1993	25%
Russian survey preelection, December 1995	33%
Russian survey postelection, December 1995	31%

"Is it permissible to disseminate views according to which the Communist Party should be the single political power running the country?" Percentage of no answer/no opinion:

Russian survey 1992	18%
Moscow survey postreferendum, May 1993	20%
Russian survey preelection, December 1993	21.2%
Russian survey postelection, December 1993	18.4%
Russian survey preelection, December 1995	21%
Russian survey postelection, December 1995	17%

"Is it permissible to advocate the official legalization of prostitution?" Percentage of no answer/no opinion:

Soviet Union survey 1989	5.4%
Russian survey 1992	10.1%
Moscow survey postreferendum, May 1993	21%
Russian survey preelection, December 1993	10.5%
Russian survey postelection, December 1993	8.5%
Russian survey preelection, December 1995	9%
Russian survey postelection, December 1995	12%

"Is it permissible to express views that different ethnic groups are inherently unequal? That some are superior to others?" Percentage of no answer/no opinion:

Soviet Union survey 1989	5.7%
Russian survey 1992	8.9%
Moscow survey postreferendum, May 1993	22%
Russian survey preelection, December 1993	9.2%
Russian survey postelection, December 1993	8.2%
Russian survey preelection, December 1995	11%
Russian survey postelection, December 1995	12%

4. A quite different approach asks people what groups they like least and whether that group should be permitted to disseminate its views publicly. Thus, the researcher does not determine which groups are salient for which people, but rather lets the people interviewed make that decision. On the other hand, there may not be adequate consistency of degree of dislike or threat across people's responses. See, for example, James L. Gibson, "Alternative Measures of Political Tolerance: Must Tolerance Be 'Least-Liked?'" *American Journal of Political Science*, vol. 36, no. 2 (May 1992), 560–77.

In the United States, even studies conducted at a single point in time find little consensus on the most disliked group. According to Sullivan, Piereson, and Marcus, such diffuse intolerance bodes well for the future, since a kind of pluralism of dislike reduces the threat to any one group. John L. Sullivan, James E. Piereson, and George E. Marcus, "An Alternative Conceptualization of Political Tolerance: Illusory Increases 1950s–1970s," *American Political Science Review*, vol. 73 (1979).

On the other hand, rather than this pluralistic intolerance in which dislike is spread around and unfocused, there is evidence that fascists as a group, do stimulate some consensus. See

James L. Gibson, Raymond M. Duch, and Kent L. Tedin, "Democratic Values and the Transformation of the Soviet Union," *Journal of Politics*, vol. 54, no. 2 (May 1992), 329–71.

The exact meaning of *fascist* is quite unclear, however, and in Russia lawsuits by those who claim damage by being termed fascist in the press are often protracted affairs in which the definition of *fascist* and how the accused might or might not be one plays a part.

Our task is somewhat different: to see what range of particular, well-known opinions can be accommodated by society. In the Soviet Union and its successor states, very few groups persist over time, from city to countryside and across the expanses of territory and ethnic groups. Groups spring up, combine, fracture. Few observers can keep up with the alphabet soup generated by new movements, parties, groups, and parliamentary factions. In the volatile post-Soviet world, groups rarely link consistent and predictable stances; more often, fairly contradictory positions coexist within the group, and that, of course, adds to the instability of the associations.

It should not matter which groups are identified by the respondents as most disliked, since only the relationship between measures of tolerance and the named group is of interest. However, in the conflict-ridden post-Soviet nations, people polled in surveys may consider their least-liked group genuinely threatening and violent. Other people may not have either considered these groups in their personal inventories or may not have included a group that they believe targets them personally. When people are asked in polls whether their least-liked group should be allowed speech and participation rights, perception of threat may differ across the range of those interviewed.

For television stations in the Soviet period, the issue was less over allowing a group to gain airtime (pluralism was very limited and organized groups even rarer) than a particular point of view that television could or could not broadcast. No one in charge of television predicted that a theater director named Mark Zakharov would stun the Party leadership and viewers with his televised opinions about Lenin.

5. All of the surveys reported here were conducted in the local language by local interviewers. All were the product of face-to-face interviews.

The first survey was jointly designed by the author and Ada W. Finifter, George Gerbner, Boris Grushin, and Nikolai Popov. At the time, Grushin was director of research of the All-Union Center for Public Opinion Research and later formed his own survey organization, Vox Populi. The sample, designed to represent the fifteen republics of the Soviet Union, was clustered in seven republics in which 88 percent of the Soviet population was located. The weighted sample size was 2,006; the data were collected in late November and early December, 1989. For a more detailed explanation of the methods, see Ada W. Finifter and Ellen Mickiewicz, "Redefining the Political System of the USSR: Mass Support for Political Change." The data for Russia, used in this study, are taken from this survey. To achieve representativeness, the Moscow polling organization oversampled the Russian republic, with data drawn separately from five major economic-political regions (East Siberia, West Siberia, the Northwest, Volga, and Moscow) and both urban and rural sites. The graphs are based on the Russian sample; the personal testimony of some individual respondents is drawn from the larger Soviet sample.

The second survey of 1,982 citizens in thirty-five locations in the Russian Federation between January 31 and February 26, 1992, was conducted by the public opinion organization Vox Populi, directed by Boris Grushin.

The third survey was a poll of 1,822 citizens of Moscow, conducted from May 24 to 30, 1993. It was carried out by the staff of the sociological department of Ostankino Television, then headed by Vsevolod Vilchek.

The fourth and fifth surveys were carried out by the Public Opinion Foundation, a private polling facility under the direction of Alexander Oslon. The project director was Leila

Vasilieva. The preelection survey was fielded on December 4, 1993, and had a sample size of 1,629 citizens of Russia; the postelection survey, fielded December 18, 1993, had a sample size of 1,593 Russian citizens. The surveys were conducted in large, medium, and small cities and in rural areas in ten regions of Russia.

The sixth and seventh surveys were also carried out by the Public Opinion Foundation using the same methods as the December 1993 surveys. The preelection survey in 1995 was fielded from December 9 to 10, with 1,364 respondents. The postelection survey was done on December 23, 1995, with 1,352 respondents.

6. In a 1990 study, Gibson, Duch, and Tedin found that responses to questions on political tolerance differed from those to questions on abstract democratic norms because of the concrete, applied dimensions of the former and not the latter. James L. Gibson, Raymond M. Duch, and Kent L. Tedin, "Democratic Values and the Transformation of the Soviet Union."

7. Serge Schmemann, "Yeltsin Extols 1921 Rebellion, Denouncing Its Repression by Lenin," *New York Times,* January 11, 1994, A3.

8. Roy Medvedev's dissident book *On Socialist Democracy* (New York: Knopf, 1975) advocated multiple parties but was circulated only in *samizdat.*

For a summary of the *Neva* article, see: Bill Keller, "Another Soviet Taboo Is Broken: Paper Attacks Communist Party," *New York Times,* February 9, 1989, A1, 5.

9. Even though the Communist Party of the Soviet Union was not registered it had a secret membership list, according to a 1994 interview with Dmitry Pushkar, one of its legal directors. Sergei Skvortsov, "Posledny romantik," *Moskovskie Novosti,* no. 8 (February 20–27, 1994), 6.

10. Yevgeny Yanayev, "Yeltsin Departization Edict," *Kommersant-Daily,* April 29, 1993, 10. Translated in FBIS-SOV-93-082, April 30, 1993, 30.

11. Aleksandr Sargin, "Budet li okhota na vedm?" *Argumenty i Fakty,* August 1995, 2.

12. Iu. G. Karpukhin and Iu. G. Torbin, "Prostitutsia: zakon i realnost," *Sotsiologicheskie Issledovania,* no. 5 (1992), 111–17.

13. S. I. Golod, "Prostitutsia v kontekste izmenenia polovoi morali," *Sotsiologicheskie Issledovania,* no. 2 (1988), 65–70.

A. S. Meliksetyan, "Prostitutsia v 20-e gody," *Sotsiologicheskie Issledovania,* no. 3 (1989), 71–74.

14. Ostankino TV, January 2, 1994.

15. *The Constitution of the Russian Federation,* eds. Vladimir V. Belyakov and Walter J. Raymond (Brunswick Publishing Corp. and Novosti Agency, 1994), 25.

16. In their study of anti-Semitic attitudes in the Moscow region, Gibson and Duch found that a large number of respondents said they were "uncertain" (i.e., refused to answer) about their personal prejudices against Jews. As many as 45 percent refused to answer a question asking them to agree or disagree with the statement "When it comes to choosing between people and money, Jews will choose money." Forty-one percent refused to respond to a question about the acceptability of a Jew with similar economic status marrying into the respondent's family. At the time, these results appeared to the authors to be a concealed response of prejudice. James L. Gibson and Raymond M. Duch, "Anti-Semitic Attitudes of the Mass Public: Estimates and Explanations Based on a Survey of the Moscow Oblast," *Public Opinion Quarterly,* vol. 56 (spring 1992), 1–28.

In a later article James Gibson explores the problem of "don't know" responses at greater length and finds the results less worrying since, in his view, a good many in this category actually do not know, have not formed an opinion, and respond similarly that they do not know about other political, social, and economic questions. James L. Gibson, "Understandings of Anti-Semitism in Russia: An Analysis of the Politics of Anti-Jewish Attitudes," *Slavic Review,* vol. 53, no. 3 (fall 1994), 796–806.

However, it should be borne in mind that the normative or rhetorical (and unobserved in practice) strictures of the law have been unvarying over many years, and the more blatant questions eliciting evidence of anti-Semitism in responses may call forth caution from the respondent. The gap between official rhetoric deploring anti-Semitism (but engaging in anti-Zionism) and criminalizing ethnic insults (while practicing discrimination based on ethnicity) is at the heart of the controversy between Gibson, Hesli, Miller, Reisinger, and Morgan on the one hand and Brym on the other in *Slavic Review,* vol. 53, no. 3 (fall 1994) over how Russians understand survey questions on the topic. Brym believes that the context of these legal prohibitions and minatory public rhetoric makes respondents cautious and likely to avoid intolerant answers.

17. Timur Kuran, *Private Truths, Public Lies: The Social Consequences of Preference Falsification* (Cambridge, Mass.: Harvard University Press, 1995), 86.

18. Vladimir Pribylovsky, "A Survey of Radical Right-Wing Groups in Russia," *RFE/RL Research Report,* vol. 3, no. 16 (April 22, 1994 , 28–37.

19. "We Must Energetically Carry Out Perestroika," *Moscow News* (supplement), no. 47 (1987), 3.

20. Andrei Petrov assembled letters to and responses from Nina Andreyeva, "Nas gorazdo bolshe, chem vy dumaete," *Smena,* February 9, 1990, 2.

Prosecution of the anti-Semitic Pamyat organization did take place and one of its leaders, Konstantin Smirnov-Ostashvili, later committed suicide in jail. In the fall of 1992, the organization claimed responsibility for raiding the offices of the liberal Moscow newspaper *Moscow Komsomolets* and, according to mayor Luzhkov, threatened writers who failed to uphold the greatness of the Russian people. Nikolai Detkov was put on trial in Moscow in March 1993. Pamyat leader Dmitry Vasiliev charged that the judges were out to destroy the organization. *Moscow News,* no. 13 (March 26, 1993), 14.

By 1994 the organization had declined, but the torch had been passed to a myriad of other extremist political fringe organizations. Vladimir Pribylovsky, "A Survey of Radical Right-Wing Groups in Russia."

Most people, two Russian social scientists concluded, did not calculate the consequences of the intolerant positions because of the Soviet legacy. In public opinion surveys asking Russians about commitment to principles of tolerance, those who agreed with the broad statements of tolerance probably had in mind tolerance on the part of the state in relation to themselves. Lacking the experience of a society in which different interests and points of view contended, these respondents probably did not think through all the consequences of the tolerant position—that it makes possible the expression of others' interests sharply at odds with one's own. Tolerance is not just reining in the state. G. Kapustin and I. M. Klyamkin, "Liberalnye tsennosti v soznanii rossiyan," *Sotsiologicheskie issledovania Fonda "Obshchestvennoe Mnenie"* (Moscow, 1994), 70–71.

21. For example, at television, according to Vladimir Pozner, anti-Semitism was rife at Gosteleradio, where the hiring of Jews was discouraged. *Parting with Illusions.* Interviews with emigrés who had worked at Gosteleradio in the Brezhnev era confirm this, as well as Gostel's concern that Jewish-sounding names be kept off the screen.

For an overview of the problem, see William Korey, *The Soviet Cage: Anti-Semitism in Russia* (New York: Viking, 1973).

22. Keith Bush, "Zhirinovsky to Be Investigated," *RFE/RL Daily Report,* December 17, 1993.

Prosecution of Zhirinovsky required revocation of his parliamentary immunity, not a likely prospect. See Vera Tolz, "Duma Rejects Lifting Zhirinovsky's Immunity," *RFE/RL Daily Report,* June 27, 1994.

23. Sergei Kozlov, "V Alma-ate poyavilis dissidenty," *Nezavisimaya Gazeta,* May 28, 1993, 3.

24. Mikhail Berger, "Anti-Semitism Infects Debate on Television," *Moscow Times,* June 14, 1995, 8.

25. Irina Petrovskaya, "ORT: i poslednie stanut pervymi?" *Obshchaya Gazeta,* September 7–13, 1995, 13.

26. Fred Kaplan, "Moscow Cracks Down—on Outsiders," *Boston Globe,* October 14, 1993, 2.

27. "Kogo by vy ne khoteli videt svoim zyatem?" *Mir Mnenii i Mnenia o Mire,* no. 5 (July 1991), 5.

This Soviet-wide poll found that the majority (54 percent) of respondents said that they were indifferent to ethnicity; 13 percent named the Caucasians, 6 percent named "any non-Russian," 4 percent named Central Asians, and 3 percent, each, named Jews and blacks. The rest were scattered among Eastern ethnicities and Muslims, foreigners, Tatars, and others. Eleven percent did not answer the question.

28. Natalya Gevorkyan, "Racism in a 'Weak Form,'" *Moscow News,* no. 18 (May 6–12, 1994), 13.

29. Framing these kinds of issues makes a great difference. See, for example, the works of Shanto Iyengar and others, referred to in chapter 2. An example drawn from the tolerance literature: in studying support of or opposition to race-targeted policies in the United States, Bobo and Kluegel found that framing these policies as "opportunity-enhancing," rather than race-related entitlement or specifically equalizing outcomes, significantly increased levels of public support. Lawrence Bobo and James R. Kluegel, "Opposition to Race-Targeting: Self-Interest, Stratification Ideology, or Racial Attitudes?" *American Sociological Review,* vol. 58 (August, 1993), 443–64.

By framing the news stories as Russian military blunders killing and maiming young Russian men, television tended to undercut the Chechen threat scenario advanced by the Yeltsin government.

30. Samuel Stouffer's, *Communism, Conformity, and Civil Liberties* (New York: Doubleday, 1955) is the classic formulation of the direct and powerful effects of education. See also Herbert McCloskey and Alida Brill, *Dimensions of Tolerance* (New York: Russell Sage Foundation, 1983). But specification of these effects has provoked considerable controversy in the literature, with some confirming Stouffer but others finding that education has weaker effects than he claimed. For example, Sullivan, Piereson, and Marcus find that although education has a stronger association with tolerance than other status variables, it is weaker than the Stouffer-based measures. They conclude that status (including education) is not so much a structural variable as a cognitive factor. John L. Sullivan, James E. Piereson, and George E. Markus, *Political Tolerance and American Democracy* (Chicago: University of Chicago Press, 1982).

31. Raymond M. Duch and James L. Gibson, "'Putting Up with' Fascists in Western Europe: A Comparative, Cross-Level Analysis of Political Tolerance," *Western Political Quarterly,* vol. 45, no. 1 (March 1992), 237–73.

32. James L. Gibson, "The Political Consequences of Intolerance: Cultural Conformity and Political Freedom," *American Political Science Review,* vol. 86, no 2 (June 1992), 338–56.

James L. Gibson, "Understandings of Justice: Institutional Legitimacy, Procedural Justice, and Political Intolerance," *Law and Society Review,* vol. 23, no. 3 (1989), 469–96.

33. James L. Gibson, "The Resilience of Mass Support for Democratic Institutions and Processes in the Nascent Russian and Ukrainian Democracies," unpublished manuscript. Cited with permission.

James L. Gibson, "A Mile Wide but an Inch Deep(?): The Structure of Democratic Commitments in the Former USSR," *American Journal of Political Science,* vol. 30, no. 2 (May 1996), 396–420.

This finding can be seen as an issue of rational calculus: it has been found that, on the issue of language rights in Canada, "a minority has a stronger incentive to grant to a majority a right the minority itself wishes to enjoy, as compared to the incentive a majority has to grant to a minority a right the majority wishes to exercise," in Paul M. Sniderman et al., "Political Culture and the Problems of Double Standards: Mass and Elite Attitudes Toward Language Rights in the Canadian Charter of Rights and Freedoms," *Canadian Journal of Political Science/Revue canadienne de science politique,* vol. 22, no. 2 (June 1989), 282.

34. Timur Kuran, *Private Truths, Public Lies,* 102.

35. "Appear" is a play on words: appear is literally give the appearance or look, which is "vid" in Russian. VID is also the name of the production company issuing from the *Vzglyad* program. VID stands for "*Vzglyad* and others." Red Square (Krasny kvadrat) was a political talk show in which Alexander Lyubimov moderated discussions between opposing political figures.

36. Andrei Aronov, "Volteryantsy? Net, Sbitenshchiki," *Moskovsky komsomolets,* October 13, 1993.

37. Donald Philip Green and Lisa Michele Waxman, "Direct Threat and Political Tolerance: An Experimental Analysis of the Tolerance of Blacks Toward Racists," *Public Opinion Quarterly,* vol. 51, no. 2 (summer 1987), 149–65.

In addition, respondents may have a quite different view of "nonconformist viewpoints" expressed by groups with a potential for and record of violence, and others with whom one does not agree. This difference, in turn, may skew the relationship of education and other explanatory factors in variation of political tolerance. See: Lawrence Bobo and Frederick C. Licari, "Education and Political Tolerance: Testing the Effects of Cognitive Sophistication and Target Group Affect," *Public Opinion Quarterly,* vol. 53, no. 3 (fall 1989), 285–308.

38. John Mueller, "Trends in Political Tolerance," *Public Opinion Quarterly,* vol. 52, 1–25.

The relationship between threat and intolerance may be indirect, rather than immediate and direct.

James L. Gibson, "Political Intolerance in the Fledgling Russian Democracy," paper prepared for delivery at the 1996 Midwest Political Science Association meeting, Chicago Ill., April 18–20, 1996.

John L. Sullivan et al., *Political Tolerance in Context: Support for Unpopular Minorities in Israel, New Zealand, and the United States* (Boulder, Col: Westview Press, 1965).

Mark Peffley and Lee Sigelman, "Intolerance of Communists During the McCarthy Era: A General Model," *Western Political Quarterly,* vol. 43, no. 1 (March 1990), 93–111.

Robert LeVine and Donald Campbell, *Ethnocentrism: Theories of Conflict, Ethnic Attitudes and Group Behavior* (New York: Wiley, 1972).

39. James L. Gibson and Raymond M. Duch, "Anti-Semitic Attitudes of the Mass Public: Estimates and Explanations Based on a Survey of the Moscow Oblast."

40. Leonard A. Cole, "Blacks and Ethnic Political Tolerance," *Polity,* vol. 9, no. 3 (spring 1977), 302–20.

41. Walter Goodman, "The Roots of Terrorism in the Power of Speech," *New York Times,* May 9, 1995, C16.

42. Quoted in Kieth Schneider, "Hate Groups Use Tools of the Electronic Trade," *New York Times,* March 13, 1995, A8.

In the United States, the networks have internal guidelines rejecting, as ABC's do, programs that attack "an individual or group on the basis of age, color, national origin, race, religion, or sex." Capital Cities/ABC Inc., "Program Standards," Department of Broadcast Standards and Practices, May 15, 1989, 18.

There are no written rules about the news. The news producer is expected to present a fair balance of viewpoints, (telephone interview with Lisa Heiden, conducted by Edith Dulacki, March 1995), but the representation of ethnic and racial minorities on television news and entertainment programming in general has continued to elicit complaints and dissatisfaction with the nature of the networks' solutions. Jannette L. Dates and William Barlow, eds., *Split Image: African Americans in the Mass Media* (Washington, D.C.: Howard University Press, 1990).

See also: the famous Kerner Report detailing the role and impact of skewed reporting of race issues as a factor in civil disorders. "The News and Civil Disorders," *Report of the National Advisory Commission on Civil Disorders,* Otto Kerner, chairman (New York: Bantam Books, 1968).

See also the two follow-up reports: U.S. Commission on Civil Rights, "Window Dressing on the Set: Women and Minorities in Television" (Washington, D.C.: GPO, 1977).

U.S. Commission on Civil Rights, "Window Dressing on the Set: An Update" (Washington, D.C.: GPO, 1979).

Sally Steenland, *Unequal Picture: Black, Hispanic, Asian, and Native American Characters on Television* (Washington, D.C.: National Commission on Working Women for Wider Opportunities for Women, 1989).

There are many other scholarly studies of message content; one very interesting study of effects is: George Comstock and Robin E. Cobbey, "Television and the Children of Ethnic Minorities," *Journal of Communication,* vol. 29, no. 1 (winter 1979), 104–15.

For a comparative study of ethnic and race group representation in television news in the Soviet period, see Ellen Mickiewicz and Dawn Plumb Jamison, "Ethnicity and Soviet Television News," *Journal of Communication,* vol. 41, no. 2 (spring, 1991), 150–61.

43. Mikhail Gorbachev, *Erinnerungen.*

44. Only 48 percent in Moscow would allow the Party position to be aired; 66 percent in the rural areas and (highest of all) 69 percent in small cities would do so.

45. Matthew Wyman et al., "The Russian Elections of December 1993."

46. Jerry Hough also makes this point when writing about the December 1993 parliamentary elections. "The Russian Election of 1993: Attitudes Toward Economic Reform and Democratization," *Post-Soviet Affairs,* vol. 10, no. 1 (1994), 1–37.

47. A wholesale return to the past was not generally appealing, as the following 1994 poll of 3,535 Russians suggests. Question: "Our current political system is not the only possible one. Some people say that another would be better for us. What do you think? Here are some statements; please tell me to what extent you agree with each of them."

"It would be better to restore the former Communist system."

	18–29	30–59	60+	Total (%)
Completely agree	5	8	18	9
Generally agree	8	14	19	14
Generally disagree	30	29	23	28
Completely disagree	41	36	22	34
Difficult to answer	16	13	19	15

Richard Rose and Christian Haerpfer, "New Russia Barometer III: The Results," *Studies in Public Policy,* no. 228, (Glasgow: University of Strathclyde, 1994), 29.

48. The relationships are significant at less than .01 unless otherwise indicated, and all control for the indicated demographic variables.

49. In the regression equation, I have used the responses to the four marker positions and demographic variables. There is no intent to model voting preferences as such, but only to see, as regards these marker views, if there is a relationship to voting preferences independent of age, education, sex, and rural or urban residence.

50. The former, adherence to the full presidential formula, is comprised of 643 respondents (67.8 percent); the second, voting yes on confidence in the president, comprised 853 voters (80 percent).

51. James Gibson, too, found little agreement on democratic norms among Yeltsin voters and argues that Yeltsin supporters (defined as voting yes on the question of trust in the president) exhibited views that were not "entirely democratic," and that the Yeltsin vote represented support for economic reform rather than democratization. James L. Gibson, "Political Reform in the Fledgling Russian Democracy: The Mass Politics of the April 1993 Referendum," unpublished manuscript. Cited with permission.

52. Preference falsification and its operation under different conditions and in a number of cases is explored by Timur Kuran, *Private Truths, Public Lies: The Social Consequences of Preference Falsification* (Cambridge, Mass.: Harvard University Press, 1995).

53. The views of people saying they intend to vote and have voted, rather than likely and reported nonvoters, should provide a better understanding of processes associated with election outcomes. See, for example, Alexander Oslon and Elena Petrenko, "Faktory electoralnogo povedenia ot oprosov k modelyam," *Voprosy Sotsiologii,* vol. no. 5 (1994), 3–26.

54. Ellen Mickiewicz, *Media and the Russian Public.*

55. $R^2 = .31$, as opposed to the R^2 for Our Home is Russia (.01), Yabloko (.02), and the Liberal Democratic Party (.07). Variables included are the four marker positions only, with party vote as dependent variable.

56. Igor Klyamkin, "What Do Russians Think?" *Moscow News,* no. 37 (September 16–22, 1994), 3.

57. Matthew Wyman et al., "The Russian Elections of December 1993," 263.

58. Darrell Slider, Vladimir Gimpelson, and Sergei Chugrov, "Political Tendencies in Russia's Regions: Evidence from the 1993 Parliamentary Elections," *Slavic Review,* vol. 53, no. 3 (fall 1994), 711–32.

59. In the 1991 presidential election, Zhirinovsky ran well in the Pskov oblast, bordering Estonia, and in thirteen other areas where ethnic tension ran high. N. Petrov and Ye. Safronov, "Areas of Risk," *Rossiskie Vesti,* April 24, 1993, 2. Translated in FBIS-SOV-93-063, 9–11.

60. Nonvoters were significantly younger and less well educated than voters.

61. Young people are typically less likely to vote than older people. In the 1988 American presidential elections, only 36 percent of Americans aged eighteen to twenty-four voted, as compared to more than 65 percent over twenty-five. *The Age of Indifference: A Study of Young Americans and How They View the News,* June 28, 1990, Times Mirror Center for The People and The Press, Washington. The study also found a considerable "news and information gap" dividing the young from their elders.

62. William Crotty, "Political Participation," in *Political Participation and American Democracy,* ed. William Crotty (New York: Greenwood, 1991), 22.

63. Matthew Wyman et al., "The Russian Elections of December 1993"; quote is on page 259.

64. Richard L. Berke, "Nonvoters Are No More Alienated Than Voters, Survey Shows," *New York Times,* May 30, 1996, A11.

65. William Crotty, "Political Participation." Emphasis in the original.

66. Vladimir Shokarev, "Kto golosoval za LDPR," *Izvestia,* December 30, 1993, 4.

67. In the Soviet period, Communist Party members were distinguished by their higher consumption of media and by the particular way in which they read the media. Ellen Mickiewicz, *Media and the Russian Public.*

CHAPTER TEN

1. Andrei Bystritsky, "Skazki Venskogo lesa," *Izvestia,* March 11, 1994, 9.
2. Andrei Bystritsky, "Skromnoe ocharovanie radio," *Izvestia,* April 15, 1994, 9.
3. "Circulation of Major Newspapers," *Post-Soviet Media Law and Policy Newsletter,* November 17, 1993, 7.
V. Shelikhov, "The Main Trends in Subscription Development in the Russian Federation in 1993," *Rasprostraneniye Pechati,* no. 4 (July 1993), 2–3. Translated in FBIS-USR-93-114, November 10, 1993, 73–75.
V. Shelikhov, "Subscription-94 Results Summarized," *Rossiyskaya Gazeta,* December 31, 1993, 1. Translated in FBIS-SOV-94-001, January 3, 1994, 37.
4. Postfactum News Agency, *Mass Media Audience* (Moscow-St.Petersburg: Postfactum News Agency, 1993), 101.
5. Interview with Alexander Oslon, June 1995.
6. Vera Nikitina and Elena Petrenko, "Sredstva massovoi informatsii: portrety auditorii," *SMI: Portrety auditorii,* vol. 1, Fond "Obshchestvennoe Mnenie," Moscow, 1992.
7. Celestine Bohlen, "Few Russian Papers Thriving with the New Press Freedom," *New York Times,* January 26, 1993, 1, 4.
8. Interview with Sergei Yushenkov, October 1993.
9. Marianna Orlinkova, "Kabelnoe televidenie kamennogo veka," *Izvestia,* June 24, 1994, 9.
10. Vsevolod Vilchek, "Televidenie Rossii: politika i dengi," unpublished paper prepared for the Aspen Institute, The Carter Center, and Duke University for the Working Group of the Commission on Radio and Television Policy, May 1995.
11. "7 raz otmer," *Sem Dnei,* April 17–23, 1995, 3.
12. Interview with Vladimir Shmakov, May 1992.
13. Marina Denisova, "Nostalgia," *Izvestia,* April 8, 1994, 10.
14. Alexander Petrov, "'24-i kanal,'" *Sem Dnei,* no. 13, (1993), 3.
15. Elena Karaeva, "Litsenzia—ne pokhvalnaya gramota," *Nezavisimaya Gazeta,* October 10, 1992, 5.
16. Ibid.
17. Marina Denisova, "'TV 6-Moskva' stanovitsya obshcherossiiskim kanalom," *Izvestia,* April 8, 1955, 9.
18. "Printsipy rasprostranenia, tekhnicheskie sredstva i potentsialnaya auditoria telekanala 'TV-6 Moskva,'" information distributed by TV-6. I thank Elena Zlotnikova, director for regional relations, for this material.
19. Interview with Igor Malashenko, October 1993.
20. Alexei Simonov, head of the Glasnost Defense Foundation in Moscow and a member of various regulatory commissions, argued that NTV was awarded its frequency "without competition and practically without serious discussion of the concept of broadcasting." "Open letter 'to A. N. Yakovlev and V. V. Lazutkin, heads of the Russian Federal Television and Radio Broadcasting Service' from Aleksey Simonov, former co-chairman of the former licensing commission," *Rossiya,* no. 9, March 2–8, 1994, 3. Translated in FBIS-USR-94-029, March 24, 1994, 63–65.

21. "Ostankino"Television Channel One, "The Price of Publicity Time from January 1, 1993, till June 30, 1993." Price list by hour by day distributed by Ostankino Television to prospective buyers.

22. Galina Chermenskaya, "Nezavisimoe televidenie brosaet vyzov," *Izvestia,* October 16, 1993, 12.

23. I thank Marianna Orlinkova for this information.

24. Interview with Oleg Dobrodeyev, October 1993.

25. Tom Birchenough, "Russian TV cuts free from state," *Variety,* February 13, 1994, 36.

26. Interview with Igor Malashenko, October 1993.

27. Interview with Oleg Dobrodeyev, January 1995.

28. Interview with Igor Malashenko, January 1995.

29. David Remnick, "The Tycoon and the Kremlin," *The New Yorker,* February 20, 1995, 118–39.

30. Interview with Evgeny Kiselyov, June 1995.

31. Lidia Polskaya, "Novosti est. Odnako 'Novestei' ne vidno," *Izvestia,* March 25, 1994, 9.

32. "Zerkalo dlya TV," *Argumenty i Fakty,* no. 28 (1994), 12.

33. "The Plan for Merging Two State Companies Has Influential Backers," *Obshchaya Gazeta,* September 9–15, 1994, 13. Reprinted in FBIS-SOV-94-175, September 9, 1994, 23–24.

Report of the Commission on Radio and Television Policy (Atlanta: The Carter Center, 1995).

34. Sergei Klimov, "Vershiteli televizionnykh sudeb," *Izvestia,* March 17, 1995, 13.

35. "Shakeup at Russian Federal Press Committee, Mironov Dismissed for Nationalist Boasts," *Post-Soviet Media Law & Policy Newsletter,* no. 10 (September 10, 1994), 1.

36. "Mayak" radio, October 14, 1994. Translated in FBIS-SOV-94-200, October 17, 1994, 25.

37. Interview with Valentin Lazutkin, June 1995.

38. Peter Krug, "Will Russian Defamation Law Acquire a Constitutional Dimension?" *Post-Soviet Media Law & Policy Newsletter,* no. 10 (September 10, 1994), 6–7.

39. Irina Petrovskaya and Alexander Trushin, "Osobo vazhnoe zadanie Olega Vakulovs-kogo," *Obshchaya Gazeta,* March 2–8, 1995, 13.

40. The program menus for these directly broadcast programs were in some cases drawn from the American firm's inventory, but in some cases, like Disney, adapted for local languages and traditions. Richard W. Stevenson, "Lights! Camera! Europe!" *New York Times,* section 3, February 6, 1994, 1, 6.

41. "Asian Regimes Confront 2-Edged Nature of Internet," *New York Times,* May 29, 1995, A1, 22.

China's policies and rhetoric also reflected a technological reality at odds with changing political emphases.

42. Thabo Mbeki, quoted in Nathaniel C. Nash, "Group of 7 Defines Policies About Telecommunications," *New York Times,* February 27, 1995, C1, 3.

As Monroe Price writes, in Singapore, Malaysia, and much of the Islamic world, the influence of Western television is thought to be subversive beyond what is specifically outlawed, such as pornography, or the coverage of news and public affairs challenging the officially decreed construction of events. "A ruling party may see the images of advertising and the narratives of foreign programmes as a threat both to the culture and, perhaps more centrally, to its continued power." *Television, The Public Sphere, and National Identity* (Oxford: Oxford University Press, 1995), 72.

43. Jill Hills with Stylianos Papathanassopoulos, *The Democracy Gap: The Politics of Information and Communication Technologies in the United States and Europe* (New York: Greenwood, 1991).

44. Andrei Fomin, "Chita Power Engineers Switch Off Transmitters," ITAR-TASS, June 25, 1993.

45. Sergei Suntsov, *Novosti,* Channel One, July 6, 1993. Translated in FBIS-SOV-93-128, July 7, 1993, 23–24.

Vadim Glusker, NTV, September 15, 1994. Translated in FBIS-SOV-94-180, September 16, 1994, 24–25.

46. Natalya Gorodetskaya and Andrei Nikolaev, "Communications Workers Intend to Stop TV Broadcasts," *Segodnya,* February 10, 1994, 1. Translated in *Russian Press Digest,* February 10, 1994.

47. Data drawn from a survey conducted in 1991 by the Penta survey organization under the direction of Leila Vasilieva, currently project director of the Public Opinion Foundation, Moscow. I thank Ms. Vasilieva for providing this information.

48. Anna Petrova, "Mir Reklamy: orientatsii potrebitelei," *Problemy Reklamy,* no. 1 (1992).

49. Anatoly Verbin, "Soviet TV Chief Declares New Era, But Future Vague," Reuters, September 13, 1991, and "Broadcasts Blacked Out All Over Russia," February 10, 1994, Agence France-Presse.

50. Interview with Gennady Shipitko, January 1995.

51. "ORT: Revolyutsia ili kompromiss," *Izvestia,* December 2, 1994, 9.

52. Natalya Arkhangelskaya, "The 'Big Eight' Does Not Need Elections," *Kommersant-Daily,* March 14, 1995, 3. Translated in FBIS-SOV-95-064-S, April 4, 1995, 25–28.

53. Nikolai Zyatkov, "Current Interview: First—in the First," *Argumenty i Fakty,* no. 16 (April 1996). Translated in FBIS-SOV-96-093-S, May 13, 1996, 45–47.

54. Vsevolod Vilchek, "'Ostankino' sredi drugikh," *Izvestia,* February 4, 1994, 9. Adtime for October 1993 was fifty-nine minutes for week-days and seventy-three minutes for weekends, averaging sixty-six minutes daily. Adtime for February 1993 was thirty-six minutes daily. This does not include ads for late-night, low-viewership programs. It also excludes sponsorships of programs.

55. Irina Petrovskaya, "Igra bez pravil," *Obshchaya Gazeta,* March 30, 1995, 13.

56. Interview with Valentin Lazutkin, June 1995.

57. Interview with Vsevolod Vilchek, January 1995.

58. One angry response to the creation of ORT and the removal of guaranteed airtime from Ostankino complained of "falsified ratings" driving programming decisions arrived at dishonestly. "Pismo iz 'Ostankino,'" *Sovetskaya Rossia,* April 8, 1995, 2.

59. "Ofitsialnaya Informatsia," *Vestnik televizionnoi informatsii,* no. 23 (May 22), 1996.

60. Irina Petrovskaya, "TV dlya vsekh i peredachi dlya nemnogikh," *Nezavisimaya Gazeta,* September 12, 1992, 5.

61. Lidia Polskaya, "Esli rezat, to po zhivomu i bez narkoza," *Izvestia,* February 19, 1994,16. These figures are based on surveys taken of the population at large and do not represent the percentage of those who are watching television at the time. They are not *shares,* but closer to *ratings,* in American terminology.

62. "Do Moskvy daleko," *Izvestia,* April 1, 1994, 9.

63. Yury Levada, "Critical Balance of 'Extraordinary' Year," *Moscow News,* no. 1 (January 5, 1993), 3.

64. Ellen Mickiewicz, *Split Signals: Television and Politics in the Soviet Union.*

65. Fond "Obshchestvennoe Mnenie," *V pole zrenia,* no. 10 (March 1993).

66. Irina Petrovskaya, "TV dlya vsekh i peredachi dlya nemnogikh," *Nezavisimaya Gazeta,* September 12, 1992, 5. The quote is by Sergei Muratov.

67. Grigory Shevelyov, "Dividendy ne ozhidaiutsya," *Izvestia,* June 22, 1994, 9.

68. "Pismo iz 'Ostankino.'"

69. "Gennady Zyuganov:'S grustiu smotriu na ekran,'" *Moskovsky Komsomolets,* April 11, 1996, 8.

70. Interview with Sergei Blagovolin, June 1995.

71. Michael R. Gordon, "Communist Platform Looks to Soviet Era," *New York Times,* April 5, 1996, A1, 8.

72. "Pismo iz 'Ostankino.'"

73. Interview with Vyacheslav Bragin, June 1995.

74. "Gennady Zyuganov:'S grustiu smotriu na ekran,'" *Moskovsky Komsomolets,* April 11, 1996, 8.

75. "Starye filmy ottesnyaiut amerikanskie boeviki," *Izvestia,* March 25, 1995, 13.

76. Poll conducted by Vsevolod Vilchek, October 24–30, 1995.

77. "Televidenie na proshloi nedele—96/13-07," *FOM-INFO,* no. 13 (105) (1996), 6–7. "Khronika," *Vestnik televizionnoi informatsii,* no. 24 (May 29, 1996).

78. "Trekhgroshovy: kak mechtaem," *TV Revyu,* no. 23 (1993), 9.

79. Janet Johnson, "Portrayal of Women in post-Soviet Television Advertising," paper for course at Duke University, unpublished. Ms. Johnson analyzed the content of all commercials (N = 164) on November 17, 1994, from 7 to 11 P.M., and Saturday, November 19, from 7:30 A.M. to 11 P.M. Cited with permission.

80. Marina Denisova, "Dmitry Kiselyov prorubil 'okno v evropu,'" *Izvestia,* May 20, 1994, 9.

81. Irina Petrovskaya, "Kiselyov—da ne tot," *Obshchaya Gazeta,* June 6–12, 1995, 13.

82. Ellen Mickiewicz and Andrei Richter, "Television, Campaigning and Elections in the Soviet Union and Post-Soviet Russia."

83. Andrei Bystritsky and Andrei Filatov, "Uteshitelnoe sladkoe," *Izvestia,* November 18, 1994, 10.

84. Patricia Kranz, "In Moscow, the Attack of the Killer Brands," *Business Week,* January 10, 1994, 40. I thank Danielle Lemon for this information.

85. "Reklama i TV," *Reputatsia,* no. 1 (August 1993), 12.

Snickers and Mars also appeared, though to a much slighter degree, in the most disliked column among eight- to seventeen-year-olds, apparently because of the inability of some young people to buy something they found very desirable.

86. "Na TV emotsii perevodyatsya v tsifry," *Ivestia,* June 17, 1994, 9.

Mikhail Berger, economics editor for *Izvestia,* called MMM "Russia's chief advertiser"; quoted by Frances Foster, "The MMM Case: Implications for the Russian Media," *Post-Soviet Media Law and Policy Newsletter,* no. 10, (September 10, 1994), 2.

87. Advertisement in *Argumenty i Fakty,* no. 29 (1994), 10.

88. For a concise overview of the MMM case, see Frances Foster, "The MMM Case: Implications for the Russian Media."

89. Mavrodi gained the immunity that came with this election to parliament but was later stripped of the mandate and immunity.

In campaigning for the Duma seat, Mavrodi promised to spend ten million dollars to provide every family with a telephone and turn his district in a town north of Moscow into a "'little Switzerland.'" Reported by Steven Erlanger, "Russian Tied to Stock Scheme is Elected to Parliament," *New York Times,* November 1, 1994, A14.

90. Irina Petrovskaya, "Igra bez pravil."

91. Irina Petrovskaya interview with Vsevolod Vilchek, "'Gosudarstvennye telekompanii Rossii segodnya yavlyaiutsya mafioznymi strukturami,'" *Nezavisimaya Gazeta,* July 31, 1993, 1.

92. "Kontrolery podschitali kto proslezitsya," *Izvestia,* April 1, 1994, 9.

93. Interview with Alexander Tikhomirov, October 1993.

94. Andrew Solomon, "Young Russia's Defiant Decadence," *New York Times Magazine,* July 18, 1993, 21; article is from pages 16–23, 37–39, 41–42, 51.

95. T. Tsyba, "'Cherny yashchik' TV, ili chto mozhno uvidet za dengi," *Argumenty i Fakty,* no. 4 (January 1993), 6.

96. Interview with Eduard Sagalayev, October 1993.

97. Interview with Sergei Yushenkov, October 1993.

98. Interview with Gennady Shipitko, January 1995.

99. Interview with Oleg Dobrodeyev, January 1995.

100. Vsevolod Vilchek, "Ya pokidaiu 'Ostankino's tyazhelym serdtsem," *Izvestia,* January 6, 1995, 6.

"Variant efirnoi setki, predlozhenny Vladom Listevym khranilsya v taine," *Izvestia,* March 17, 1995, 13.

The numbers vary: for example, that Reklama-Holding was retaining 8,800 of every 10,000 dollars per minute of airtime sold. Some of the difference between airtime rates and receipts by Ostankino might have gone into other costs associated with programming, but the fact remains that Ostankino's most significant revenue source was to a great extent denied it.

CHAPTER ELEVEN

1. Interfax, December 15, 1993. Translated in FBIS-SOV-93-240, December 16, 1993, 15.

2. See, for example, material supplied by Vsevolod Vilchek for December 19–25, 1994, for Moscow, 2,073 respondents:

Did you follow the events in Chechnya?
yes 80.4%   no 11.8% (rest are no answer)
December 26, 1994 to January 1, 1995; for Moscow, 2,073 respondents:
Did you follow in the past days and weeks the events in Chechnya?
yes 80.1%   no 16.7% (rest are no answer)
Responses to different sources of information reported here.

3. Nikolai Petrov, "The Regions Are Not Silent: The Closer to the Central Power Structures, the More Approval," *Nezavisimaya Gazeta,* January 20, 1995, 3. Translated in FBIS-SOV-95-017, January 26, 1995, 48–50.

4. "Russia's TV War" *Newsweek,* February 8, 1995, 30.

5. In analyzing the relationship between media information and support of foreign policy in the United States, Benjamin I. Page and Robert Y. Shapiro note that the government may be "tempted to suppress the truth or to disseminate misleading information or falsehoods, albeit it in the name of national security and national interests," when it is difficult for the public and the press to access information independently. But when there is alternative information and disagreements among elite factions, the effect on public opinion is quite different. *The Rational Public: Fifty Years of Trends in American Policy Preferences* (Chicago: University of Chicago Press, 1992), 283–84.

The differences between relatively open and closed scenarios are discussed by W. Lance Bennett, "The News About Foreign Policy," *Taken by Storm: The Media, Public Opinion, and U.S. Foreign Policy in the Gulf War,* eds. W. Lance Bennett and David L. Paletz (Chicago: University of Chicago Press, 1994), 12–40.

6. Interview with Gennady Shipitko, January 1995. There was no doubt that Shipitko's personal and professional sympathies lay with official Russian policy on Chechnya, but he was frustrated by the government's failure to provide him with what he needed.

7. For a breakdown of time devoted to the Chechnya story on television channels in Moscow, see P. Klebnikov and A. G. Richter, eds., *Zhurnalistika i voina* (Moscow: Russian-American Press Center, 1995).

8. ITAR-TASS, January 4, 1995. Translated in FBIS-SOV-95-003, January 5, 1995, 13.

9. Genine Babakian, "Propaganda Struggles to Survive Onslaught," *Moscow Times,* January 5, 1995, 3.

10. Valery Simonov, "No Powder, No Truth, No President," *Komsomoskalya Pravda,* January 5, 1995, 1. Translated in FBIS-SOV-95-003, January 5, 1995, 16.

11. The editor of *Moskovsky Komsomolets* said later that some months before the war in Chechnya, "people sent by Dudayev were in Moscow with money. They went around to the editorial offices." He said that as far as he knew no one took the money and that it might have been a provocation to discredit the press, but it could not be known on whose part. P. Klebnikov and A. G. Richter, eds., *Zhurnalistika i voina,* 9.

12. *Vremya,* January 20, 1995.

A more virulent version of this position was taken by the powerful Mikhail Poltoranin, who said "'If I see NTV or *Segodnya* [the newspaper] speak vehemently against it [some issue], I draw a conclusion: This is something that annoys the MOST Bank group. This darned financial dependency of journalists!'" Quoted in Andrei Uglanov, "'Does One Have to Turn Into a Wolf in Order Not to Be Mauled to Death by Wolves?'" *Argumenty i Fakty,* nos. 1–2 (January 1995), 6. Translated in FBIS-SOV-95-017-S, January 26, 1995, 29.

13. Interview with Igor Malashenko, January 1995.

14. In their graphic depiction of the horrors of this war, Russian private and state television presented to the viewers an image of war wholly different from the "technological" remote war in the Persian Gulf that television conveyed to Americans. For a discussion of the latter, see Daniel C. Hallin and Todd Gitlin, "The Gulf War as Popular Culture and Television Drama," *Taken by Storm: The Media, Public Opinion, and U.S. Foreign Policy in the Gulf War,* 149–63.

15. Interview with Oleg Dobrodeyev, January 1995.

16. Oleg Malashenko, interviewed on *Chelovek Nedeli,* Channel One, January 20, 1995.

17. Interview with Evgeny Kiselyov, June 1995.

18. Interview with Elena Masyuk, March 1995.

19. Konstantin Kudryavtsev, "Televidenie na voine," *Izvestia,* December 30, 1994, 9.

20. P. Dmitriev, "Sergei Vozianov: My skazali o Chechne vse, chto khoteli skazat," *Literaturnaya Gazeta,* April 5, 1995, 14.

21. Irina Petrovskaya, "Novosti-Minus," *Obshchaya Gazeta,* March 4–11, 1993, 13. Translated in FBIS-USR-94-029, March 24, 1994, 63.

On this story NTV had sent two camera crews to await the release of the plotters from prison, and precisely and professionally covered the events. While Channel One's coverage was disorganized and based on "informed, unnamed sources," NTV presented its analysts to the public.

22. Interview with Oleg Poptsov, June 1995.

23. Interview with Gennady Shipitko, January 1995.

24. Michael Specter, "Belying Yeltsin Statement, Chechens Press Attack in Grozny," *New York Times,* March 8, 1996, 3.

25. Much of the Moscow-based press was also highly critical and published pictures condemning the war. In the provinces, however, where the local newspapers were becoming increasingly influential, the press was "silent altogether," because it was so largely "under the control of local administrations." Thus, the news disseminated by Moscow television, "despite all the efforts of the authorities, fortunately, make up for the forced passivity of the locals."

Nikolai Petrov, "The Regions Are Not Silent: The Closer to the Central Power Structures, the More Approval." Translated in FBIS-SOV-95-017, 49.

26. Poll by Vsevolod Vilchek, December 26, 1994–January 1, 1995, of 2,073 people. In the first survey, 3 percent of the questionnaires were not returned or missing, and in the second, 5 percent. In February 1996 ten leading television critics ranked NTV first among all Moscow-based broadcasters, ahead by a particularly wide margin on "authoritativeness," "professionalism," "intellect," "respect for viewers," and "quality of information." Valery Kichin, "Vstrechi u kanalov: po mneniu kritikov, lidiruyet NTV," *Obshchaya Gazeta*, February 1–7, 1996, 13.

27. *FOM-INFO*, Fond "Obshchestvennoe Mnenie" Moscow, weekly bulletin no. 5 (45), February 10, 1995, 2; 1,367 respondents, January 1995.

28. *FOM-INFO*, Fond "Obshchestvennoe Mnenie" Moscow, weekly bulletin no. 3 (43), January 27, 1995, 3. Survey from January 20, 1995, 1,353 respondents. The rest found it difficult to answer.

29. *FOM-INFO*, Fond "Obshchestvennoe Mnenie" Moscow, weekly bulletin no. 1 (41), January 13, 1995, 5. Survey of 1,341 respondents in cities and the countryside, January 1995.

30. Vsevolod Vilchek: "Vsevolod Vilchek: Ya pokidaiu 'Ostankino's tyazhelym serdtsem," *Izvestia*, January 6, 1995, 6.

31. Interview with Vsevolod Vilchek, January 1995.

32. Interview with Yevgeny Kiselyov, June 1995.

33. *FOM-INFO*, Fond "Obshchestvennoe Mnenie" Moscow, weekly bulletin no. 37, December 9, 1994, 4. Survey fielded in August 1994 of 1,184 respondents nationwide.

34. There was also general agreement among the polling agencies and fairly stable expressions of support of or opposition to the war. However, charting the fluctuations over time proved more elusive and the margin of error in the polls was such that the changes could not reliably be asserted. (Support decreased after a poorly planned and executed attempt to take Grozny on New Year's Day but had increased before, possibly because negotiations no longer appeared to be a viable option.) P. Klebnikov and A. G. Richter, eds., *Zhurnalistika i voina*.

35. *FOM-INFO*, Fond "Obshchestvennoe Mnenie" Moscow, weekly bulletin no. 4 (44), February 3, 1995, 3. Survey fielded in January 1995; 1,353 respondents nationwide.

36. For a description of the survey, see chapter 9; 13 percent did not answer the question.

37. Daniel Hallin, *The "Uncensored" War: The Media and Vietnam* (Berkeley, Calif.: University of California Press, 1986).

38. Surveys from Vsevolod Vilchek ending with December 19–25, 1994; 2,074 respondents.

39. For a good, concise overview of the problems, see Stephen Foye, "Warning Signs: Anticipating Russia's Debacle," *Transition*, April 14, 1995, 2–5.

40. Livia Klingl, "'Idiots Are Responsible for the Organization,'" *Kurier*, January 5, 1995, 5. Translated in in FBIS-SOV-95-003, January 5, 1995, 10.

41. Alexander Zhilin, "One Hundred Days of War in Chechnya," *Moscow News*, no. 10 (March 17–23, 1995), 2. Translated in FBIS-SOV-95-076-S, April 29, 1995, 42.

42. Livia Klingl, "'Idiots Are Responsible for the Organization.'"

43. Former Secretary of Defense Les Aspin, in a lecture at Duke University in March 1995, spoke about the reluctance of the military to engage in police actions and the prospect of increasing numbers of requests that the United States engage in them.

44. Interview with Elena Masyuk, March 1995.

45. Colonel Igor Alpatov, "Russian Army Revealed Its Inconsistency," *Moscow News*, no. 1 (January 6–12, 1995), 3.

46. Alexander Zhilin, "I Fear I'll Go Mad," *Moscow News*, no. 52 (December 30, 1994–January 5, 1995), 3.

47. Alexander Zhilin, "Hatred Coming Full Circle, *Moscow News*, no. 5 (February 3–9, 1995), 2.

48. Leonid Nikitinsky, "Frustrated Generals Take Aim at Journalists," *Moscow News*, no 5 (February 3–9, 1995), 12.

49. According to MVD commander in Chechnya, Lieutenant General Anatoly Antonov. Pavel Felgengauer, "The Taking of Samashki is MVD Troops' First Independent Operation. Dudayev's Last Fortified Point Should Be Taken This Week," *Segodnya*, April 12, 1995, 2. Translated in FBIS-SOV-95-070, April 12, 1995, 28–29.

50. See, for example, Michael Specter, "Killing of 100 in Chechnya Stirs Outrage," *New York Times*, May 8, 1995, 1, A4.

51. "There Were No Missile or Bomb Strikes," statement by Russian Federation Ministry of Defense Information and Press Directorate," *Red Star*, April 12, 1995, 1. Translated in FBIS-SOV-95-070, April 12, 1995, 28.

52. NTV on April 19, 1995. Translated in FBIS-SOV-95-076, April 20, 1995, 40.

53. Interview with Evgeny Kiselyov, June 1995.

54. Galina Chermenskaya, "Premyer—geroi, a prezident—khozyain?" *Obshchaya Gazeta*, June 22–28, 1995, 13.

55. Information from Masha Shakhova, head of press and public relations for NTV. I am grateful to Ms. Shakhova for making this material available to me. *Segodnya* (the nightly news on NTV except on Sundays) trailed the pack, but it had steadily picked up viewers, so that it had 15.3 percent the week of May 29 to June 4; 18 percent from June 12 to June 18, and 23.8 percent from June 19 to June 25, when it had pulled ahead of *Vesti* but still was substantially behind *Vremya* at 39.2 percent.

In January 1995, Vsevolod Vilchek said that NTV was usually two and one-half times lower in ratings than Channel One.

56. P. Klebnikov and A. G. Richter, eds., *Zhurnalistika i voina*.

57. In Desert Storm, the military controlled access in a situation where that was more than normally possible. It also provided a barrage of video material and briefings, such that the public believed it had received a comprehensive amount of news about the war. In general, the public, unlike the media organizations, were unaware of what was missing. See Everette E. Dennis, *The Media at War: The Press and the Persian Gulf Conflict* (New York: Gannett Foundation, 1991).

58. Interview with Elena Masyuk, March 1995.

CHAPTER TWELVE

1. Timur Kuran, *Private Truths, Public Lies: The Social Consequences of Preference Falsification* (Cambridge, Mass.: Harvard University Press, 1995), 113. Kuran counterposes this active collaboration to the "spiral of silence" of Elisabeth Noelle-Neumann.

2. Ibid., 85.

3. Richart Neustadt, *Presidential Power* (New York: John Wiley, 1960).

AFTERWORD

1. "Interviu s rukovoditelem sluzhby sotsiologicheskogo analiza 'NTV-Kholdinga' Vsevolodom Vilchekom," *Teleskop*, no. 133, November 4, 1998.

2. Sergei Varshavchik, "Drakulu zakazyvali?" *Obshchaya gazeta*, no. 50, December 18–24, 1997, 13.

3. Ben Bagdikian, *The Media Monopoly* (Boston: Beacon Press, 1962), 6.

4. Varshavchik, "Drakulu zakazyvali?"

5. For the theory of information costs on which this is based, see Anthony Downs, *An Economic Theory of Democracy* (New York: HarperCollins, 1957).

6. James H. Snider and Benjamin I. Page, "Does Media Ownership Affect Media Stands? The Case of the Telecommunications Act of 1996," paper prepared for delivery at the 1997 annual meeting of the Midwest Political Science Association, April 1997; J. H. Snider and Benjamin I. Page, "The Political Power of TV Broadcasters: Covert Bias and Anticipated Reactions," paper prepared for delivery at the 1997 annual meeting of the American Political Science Association, August 1997; Darrell West, *The Sound of Money* (New York: Norton, 1998).

7. Olga Likhina, "So skidkoi po zhizni," *Kommersant*, November 6, 1998, 5.

8. The candy market was another indicator. The foreign share of the chocolate market dropped precipitously from 80 percent right after the break-up of the Soviet Union to about 33 percent in 1998. According to one report, "worried about negative connotations," the makers of Snickers were eager to point to their use of domestic ingredients. Christian Caryl, "We Will Bury You . . . with a Snickers Bar," *U.S. News and World Report*, January 26, 1998, 50–52.

9. Interview with Oleg Dobrodeyev, May 1998.

10. Boris Yeltsin, "Speech to the Congress of the International Press Institute." Official Russian-language copy of remarks given to Congress participants.

11. Natalya Pachegina, "Vladislav Surkov: 'Gosudarstvo—eto kto?'" *Profil*, no. 44, 24–25.

12. Frances Foster, "Parental Law, Harmful Speech, and the Development of Legal Culture: Russian Judicial Chamber Discourse and Narrative," *Washington and Lee Law Review*, vol. 54, no. 3 (summer 1997), 923–92.

13. Paul Sniderman, Richard A. Brody, and Philip E. Tetlock, *Reasoning and Choice: Explorations in Political Psychology* (Cambridge: Cambridge University Press, 1991).

14. See, for example, Doris Graber, *Processing the News: How People Tame the Information Tide*, 2d ed. (New York: University Press of America, 1994). On the differences in education and information-rich/information-poor differences, see, for example, Shanto Iyengar and Donald Kinder, *News that Matters: Television and American Opinion* (Chicago: Chicago University Press, 1987), and works by John Zaller, cited in Chapter 1.

15. Ann N. Crigler, "Introduction: Making Sense of Politics; Constructing Political Messages and Meanings," in *The Psychology of Political Communication,* ed. Ann N. Crigler (Ann Arbor: University of Michigan Press, 1996), 1.

16. William A. Gamson, "Media Discourse as a Framing Resource," in Crigler, ibid., 152.

17. Group One had ten participants aged 25–36, with an average age of 31.2. Group Two had ten participants aged 39–59, with an average age of 47.5; Group Three had nine participants, aged 38–52, with an average age of 48; and Group Four had eight participants, aged 32–46, with an average age of 38. I have not used their real names. All participant quotes in the afterword came from this focus group study. As a foreigner, my presence would have altered the setting, and I was not in the room. I would like to thank Leila Vasilieva and Olga Oslon for their superb professional assistance.

18. See, for example, the survey data reported in Chapter 9.

19. I thank Cyril Mickiewicz for contributing this question.

20. In some ways, these responses are similar to those found in the United States in studies of the effects of negative advertising. See, for example, Stephen Ansolabehere and Shanto Iyengar, *Going Negative: How Political Advertisements Shrink and Polarize the Electorate* (New York: Free Press, 1995).

CHRONOLOGY

SELECTED EVENTS AT THE END OF THE SOVIET ERA

November 1982	Death of Leonid Brezhnev; Yury Andropov becomes leader
February 1984	Death of Yury Andropov; Konstantin Chernenko becomes leader
March 1985	Death of Konstantin Chernenko; Mikhail Gorbachev becomes leader
July 1985	Eduard Shevardnadze named Foreign Minister
July 1985	Alexander Yakovlev heads Central Committee Propaganda Department
July 1985	Yegor Ligachev becomes "second secretary"
November 1985	Gorbachev/Reagan summit in Geneva
December 1985	Boris Yeltsin becomes 1st secretary of Moscow City Party
March 1986	Alexander Yakovlev becomes Central Committee Secretary in charge of ideology
April 1986	Chernobyl explodes
October 1986	Reagan/Gorbachev summit in Reykjavik
December 1986	Riots in Alma-Ata, Kazakhstan over appointment of ethnic Russian Party leader
December 1986	Andrei Sakharov informed by Mikhail Gorbachev that he is free to return to Moscow from exile in Gorky
January 1987	Alexander Yakovlev becomes candidate member of Politburo
May 1987	Jamming of Voice of America ends
June 1987	Alexander Yakovlev becomes voting member of Politburo
August 1987	Demonstrations in Baltic republics mark anniversary of Hitler–von Ribbentrop Pact
October 1987	Boris Yeltsin attacks Yegor Ligachev at Party Central Committee meeting
November 1987	Boris Yeltsin ousted from Moscow Party leadership
December 1987	Gorbachev/Reagan summit in Washington, D.C.
February 1988	Boris Yeltsin removed from Politburo
February 1988	Ethnic rioting and anti-Armenian pogrom in Sumgait, Azerbaijan
June 1988	19th Party Conference
September 1988	Vadim Medvedev takes over ideology and propaganda

October 1988	By vote of Supreme Soviet, Mikhail Gorbachev becomes President of USSR
	Anatoly Lukyanov named Vice President
December 1988	Earthquake in Armenia
February 1989	Last Soviet troops leave Afghanistan
March 1989	First multicandidate competitive parliamentary elections
April 1989	Violence in capital of Georgia kills unarmed demonstrators
May 1989	Lithuania and Estonia declare sovereignty
July 1989	Miners strike in Kuznetsk Basin and Donets Basin
July 1989	Latvia declares sovereignty
September 1989	Yeltsin visits United States
December 1989	Bush/Gorbachev summit off the coast of Malta
December 1989	Death of Andrei Sakharov
January 1990	Anti-Armenian pogroms in Azerbaijan; Soviet troops in Baku
March 1990	Russian Republic parliamentary elections
March 1990	Communist Party monopoly mandated by Article Six of Constitution repealed
March 1990	Mikhail Gorbachev elected by new legislature to new presidency of USSR
May 1990	Boris Yeltsin elected chairman of Russian Republic Parliament
May–June 1990	Gorbachev/Bush summit in Washington, D.C.
July 1990	28th Congress of the Communist Party of the Soviet Union
	Yegor Ligachev and Alexander Yakovlev lose positions on Central Committee and in Secretariat of Party
December 1990	Eduard Shevardnadze resigns post of Foreign Minister, warning of coming dictatorship
January 1991	TV tower in capital of Lithuania attacked by Soviet Interior Ministry troops
March 1991	National referendum on preservation of Soviet Union
May 1991	At Novo-Ogaryovo, Gorbachev and heads of most republics agree on federation form for Union Treaty
June 1991	Yeltsin wins Russian presidential election
June 1991	Leningrad renamed St. Petersburg
August 1991	Attempted coup; Gorbachev held in Crimea. "Emergency Committee" arrested and Gorbachev restored to presidency, but power resides with Yeltsin
December 1991	Dissolution of Soviet Union

SELECTED EVENTS IN THE RUSSIAN FEDERATION

January 1992	Economic reform program frees most consumer prices
March 1992	Russian Federation Treaty signed by 18 of 21 autonomous republics, leaders of Russian administrative regions, and mayors of Moscow and St. Petersburg

June 1992	Yegor Gaidar appointed Acting Prime Minister
October 1992	Privatization program using vouchers begins
December 1992	Congress of People's Deputies rejects Gaidar nomination
March 1993	Congress of People's Deputies reduces Yeltsin's powers of presidential decree
March 1993	Yeltsin impeachment narrowly defeated in Congress of People's Deputies
April 1993	Referendum on presidential/parliamentary standoff
July 1993	Draft constitution approved by Constitutional Convention
July 1993	Old rubles withdrawn from circulation to control inflation
September 1993	Vice President Alexander Rutskoy suspended from duties
September 1993	Yeltsin appoints Yegor Gaidar First Deputy Prime Minister
September 1993	Yeltsin suspends parliament (Congress of People's Deputies)
October 1993	Congress of People's Deputies instructs Rutskoy to form cabinet
October 1993	Demonstrators storm office of Moscow mayor and Ostankino; army fires on White House; Khasbulatov and Rutskoy surrender
October 1993	Censorship decreed temporarily for media; some political parties of "red/brown" views suspended or outlawed
October 1993	Yeltsin presents draft constitution
December 1993	Russian parliamentary elections and referendum on new constitution
February 1994	State Duma grants amnesty to perpetrators of August 1991 coup attempt
June 1994	Formation of reform-oriented political party, Russia's Democratic Choice, led by Yegor Gaidar
June 1994	Yeltsin crime decree increases police investigative powers
July 1994	Soviet-era dissident Alexander Solzhenitsyn returns to Russia from exile in Vermont
August 1994	Last Russian troops withdrawn from the Baltic states
September 1994	Chechnya's separatist president Dzhokar Dudayev imposes martial law in region due to fighting between forces loyal to him and forces supported by Russia
October 1994	Ruble drops over 20 percent in a single day, causing a financial panic; Central Bank chairman resigns
December 1994	Russian troops invade Chechen Republic in Russian Federation
January 1995	Russian Federation troops take Grozny, capital of Chechen Republic
March 1995	Duma dismisses Human Rights Commissioner Sergei Kovalyov for his criticism of the war in Chechnya
April 1995	Civilians killed in Samashki, Chechnya
May 1995	Earthquake near Sakhalin island in Far East kills nearly 2000
May 1995	President Clinton visits Russia to celebrate 50th anniversary of the allied victory in Europe
May 1995	Creation of centrist political movement Russia is Our Home with Prime Minister Chernomyrdin as its chair

June 1995	Chechen commander Shamil Basayev holds hostages in Budyonnovsk Prime Minister Viktor Chernomyrdin negotiates their release; covered live by television
December 1995	Yeltsin returns to work after October heart problems
December 1995	Hundreds killed in Chechnya in election-related violence
December 1995	Parliamentary elections; Communists win one-third of Duma seats
January 1996	Foreign Minister Andrei Kozyrev replaced by Yevgeny Primakov, the head of Russia's intelligence service
January 1996	Chechen guerillas seize hostages in Dagestan
January 1996	Anatoly Chubais, Deputy Premier in charge of privatization, resigns
January 1996	Council of Europe votes to accept Russia as member
February 1996	Boris Yeltsin declares his candidacy for president
February 1996	Gennady Zyuganov nominated as Communist Party presidential candidate
March 1996	State Duma votes to annul 1991 treaty formally disbanding Soviet Union
April 1996	Yeltsin and Belarusian president Alexander Lukashenka sign treaty joining their countries, but stopping short of full merger
April 1996	Yeltsin visits China
April 1996	Chechen leader Dzhokhar Dudayev slain
May 1996	Russian Prime Minister Viktor Chernomyrdin and Chechen Zelimkhan Yandarbiyev negotiate a cease fire agreement
June 1996	Anatoly Sobchak defeated in reelection bid for mayor of St. Petersburg by Vladimir Yakovlev
June 1996	First round of presidential election won by Boris Yeltsin and Gennady Zyuganov
June 1996	Boris Yeltsin appoints General Alexander Lebed (third-place finisher in June election) to top security post. Yeltsin fires presidential security chief, Alexander Korzhakov, internal security chief, Mikhail Barsukov, and Deputy Prime Minister Oleg Soskovets; Yeltsin also fires Minister of Defense Pavel Grachev
June 1996	Yeltsin fires seven top generals associated with Grachev
July 1996	Second round of presidential election won by Yeltsin, whose serious illness after first round was not disclosed
August 1996	Alexander Lebed and Chechen rebels agree on peace accord and postpone decision on status of Chechnya
September 1996	Lebed warns of revolt if military do not receive delayed salaries
October 1996	From sanitorium where he is resting before heart surgery, Boris Yeltsin fires Alexander Lebed

INDEX

Postfactum, 313n92
Pozdnyak, Elena, 105, 109–10
Pozner, Vladimir, 5, 23, 66, 67, 173, 320n32, 336n21
Pravda (newspaper), 78, 92, 98, 103, 132, 219
PRES Party. *See* Unity and Accord Party
president: Channel One as channel of, 50, 51, 254; election of, 87; insulting the, 7–8, 31, 32, 305n6; legitimacy of, 89; parliament names Rutskoy acting, 126; parliament removes Yeltsin as, 126. *See also* Gorbachev, Mikhail; Yeltsin, Boris
press conferences, 125
Press Law for Russia (1992), 102, 117, 133, 218, 226–27
Price, Monroe, 342n42
print media: and Brezhnev era, 314n21; and censorship, 314n21; impact of, 64; and insulting the president, 304n6; and intellectuals, 48, 64, 109; and legal issues, 48; local, 314n21; Nenashev's views about, 48; and political icons, 63–64; and printing presses and paper supply, 219; privatization of, 48, 49, 218–20; and property rights, 48; television compared with, 64
printing presses, 219
private media/television: and Chechnya coverage, 244, 245; credibility of, 240; and elections of 1993 (December), 149; funding of, 221, 228; legitimacy of, 244; local, 221; news programming on, 82; and radio, 218; and state television, 18, 20, 220–25; and transmitters and satellites, 226. *See also* NTV; privatization
privatization, 48, 49, 116, 121, 145, 155–57, 161, 218–25, 310n28, 328n77
product advertising. *See* advertising
production companies, 49, 123–24, 238, 239–40
programming: decision-making about, 80, 124, 204–6; and ratings system, 233–34; and top ten programs, 234. *See also type of programs*
Prokhanov, Alexander, 114, 169
Prokofyev, Yury, 196
propaganda: advertising as, 234–36; and Communist Party hierarchy, 34–35; and elections of 1993 (April referendum), 137–38; Gorbachev reform as means of counteracting Western, 65–66; and ideology, 34–35; media as mechanism of, 27–28; and prohibited speech, 227; television as apparatus for, 136; television as means to counter, 66; *12th Floor* as counter to Western, 66–69; *Vzglyad* as counter to Western, 70
Propaganda Department (Central Committee), 46

property rights, 48
prostitution: legalization of, 191–92, 194–95, 201, 202, 203, 204, 206, 209, 214, 333n3; public opinion about, 201, 202, 203, 204; television policymakers' views about, 206; viewers' attitudes about, 209; and voter preferences, 214
Prozhektor Perestroiki [Spotlight of Perestroika] (Channel One), 76–78, 82
public: alienation of, 30, 38; complexity of, 269, 272; and Gorbachev reforms, 38, 40; ignorance about Desert Storm of, 348n57; ignorance about political parties of, 148; and live programs, 40. *See also* viewers
public affairs programs, 137–39, 225, 234, 270
public interest: definition of, 18; and television reform, 268–69
public opinion, 308n7, 320n24; about Chechnya, 254–60, 347n34; about controversial views on television, 190–216; about ethnicity, 337n27; about military, 258–60; about NTV, 347n26; about pluralism, 191–92, 201–4; and private opinion, 330n95; in U.S., 345n5. *See also* viewers
Public Opinion Foundation, 174, 178, 334–35n5
Pugachova, Alla, 183
Pugo, Boris, 100
Puppets (NTV program), 305n6
Pushkar, Dmitry, 335n9

radio: and armed revolt (October 1993), 323n73; audience for, 218; Chechnya coverage on, 247; early development and expansion of, 25–26, 218; and elections, 149; foreign, 27, 247; hate, 200; importance of, 27, 93, 122, 218; private, 218; as target for unrest, 114; in U.S., 200; and Yeltsin-parliament relationship, 121; and Yeltsin's access to media, 93, 94–95. *See also specific station*
Radio Liberty, 26
Radio Moscow, 70
Radio Rossia, 94–95
Rahr, Alexander, 34
Ramayana (Hindu program), 12
RAND Corporation, 318n3
ratings system, 232–34, 252, 262, 272, 343n58, 348n55
Reagan (Ronald) administration, 30
Reklama-Holding agency, 239–40, 345n100
Red Square (*Krasny kvadrat*) talk show, 338n35
regional television, 26, 66, 121, 152
regulation: of advertising, 232, 237–38; and cultural programming, 227–28; and journalists, 229; overlapping bodies for, 229; and politics, 225–29; of television, 225–29. *See also* licensing

Ellen Mickiewicz is James R. Shepley Professor of Public Policy Studies and Director of the DeWitt Wallace Center for Communications and Journalism at Duke University. Her many books include the award-winning *Split Signals: Television and Politics in the Soviet Union* (1988); and *Media and the Russian Public* (1981). She was the first American to be honored by the Journalists Union of Russia for her contribution to democratic media in the region, and she is the recipient of the American Political Science Association's Murray Edelman Award for distinguished scholarship in political communication.

Library of Congress Cataloging-in-Publication Data

Mickiewicz, Ellen Propper.
    Changing channels : television and the struggle for power in
Russia / Ellen Mickiewicz. — Rev. and expanded ed.
      p. cm.
    Originally published: New York : Oxford University Press, 1997.
    Includes index.
    ISBN 0-8223-2463-6 (pbk. : alk. paper)
    1. Television and politics—Russia (Federation) 2. Television and
politics—Soviet Union. 3. Television broadcasting—Russia
(Federation) 4. Television broadcasting—Soviet Union. I. Title.
PN1992.6.M48   1999
302.23'45'0947—dc21   99-28624
                                              CIP